Cary L. Cooper is Head of the Psychology Group in the Department of Management Sciences at the University of Manchester Institute of Science and Technology. He is European Associate Editor of the international quarterly psychology journal *Interpersonal Development* and the author of several books *T-Groups: A Survey of Research* (1971), *Group Training for Individual and Organisational Development* (1973), and *Experiential Group Methods for Management Education* (1975). In 1975 Cary Cooper was appointed Professor of Educational Methods at UMIST, a Chair supported by the Foundation of Management Education.

He is currently director of a research project, sponsored by the U.K. Training Services Agency assessing the psychological effects of small group training in industry, and is also leading a team of researchers examining 'mental stress at work'.

Theories
of
Group Processes

WILEY SERIES ON
INDIVIDUALS, GROUPS AND ORGANIZATIONS

Series Editor
Cary Cooper,
Department of Management Sciences,
University of Manchester Institute
  of Science & Technology,
Manchester

Associate Editor
Eric J. Miller,
Centre for Applied Social Research,
Tavistock Institute of
  Human Relations,
London

Theories of Group Processes
Edited by Cary Cooper,
University of Manchester Institute of Science & Technology

Task and Organization
Edited by Eric J. Miller,
The Tavistock Institute of Human Relations
(In Press)

Theories
of
Group Processes

Edited by

Cary L. Cooper
Professor of Educational Methods
University of Manchester
Institute of Science and Technology

JOHN WILEY & SONS

London · New York · Sydney · Toronto

Library of Congress Cataloging in Publication Data:
Cooper, Cary L.
  Theories of group processes.

  1. Group relations training—Addresses, essays,
lectures. I. Title.
HM134.C66   301.18′5   74-28089

ISBN 0 471 17117 4

Photosetting by Thomson Press (India) Limited, New Delhi
and printed in Great Britain by The Pitman Press, Bath, Avon.

Contributors

CARY L. COOPER
Editor

Head of Psychology, Department of Management Sciences, University of Manchester Institute of Science and Technology, Manchester, England.

CHRIS ARGYRIS

James Bryant Conant Professor of Education and Organization Behaviour, Graduate School of Education, Harvard University, Cambridge, Massachusetts.

G. T. BARRETT-LENNARD

Professor of Human Relations, Department of Human Relations and Counselling Studies, University of Waterloo, Waterloo, Canada.

ROBERT R. BLAKE

Scientific Methods, Inc., Austin, Texas.

PHILIP R. COSTANZO

Associate Professor of Psychology, Department of Psychology, Duke University, Durham, North Carolina.

SAMUEL A. CULBERT

Associate Professor of Human Development Systems, Graduate School of Management, University of California, Los Angeles, California.

RONALD FRY

Alfred P. Sloan School of Management, Massachusetts Institute of Technology, Cambridge, Massachusetts.

ROBERT T. GOLEMBIEWSKI

Research Professor, Department of Political Science, University of Georgia, Athens, Georgia.

DAVID A. KOLB

Associate Professor of Organization Psychology and Management, Alfred P. Sloan School of Management, Massachusetts Institute of Technology, Cambridge, Massachusetts.

MARTIN LAKIN

Professor of Psychology, Department of Psychology, Duke University, Durham, North Carolina.

RICHARD D. MANN

Professor of Psychology, Department of Psychology, University of Michigan, Ann Arbor, Michigan.

MARK McCONKIE

Department of Political Science, University of Georgia, Athens, Georgia.

JANE S. MOUTON

Scientific Methods, Inc., Austin, Texas.

W. BRENDAN REDDY

Program Director and Associate Professor of Psychology, Community Psychology Institute, University of Cincinnati, Cincinnati, Ohio.

Editorial Foreword to the Series

Over the last decade, there has been an enormous growth of interest in the social and psychological aspects of institutional and organizational life. This has been reflected in a substantial upsurge in research and training in the field of organizational behaviour particularly in Institutes of Higher Education and Research throughout the Western World. Attention in this development has focused on the interrelationship between the individual, the variety of groups to which he belongs and the organizational environment within which he and his group operate.

The purpose of this series is to examine the social and psychological processes of these interrelationships, that is the nexus of individual/personal development, group processes and organizational behaviour and change. Within this context, a wide range of topics will be covered. These will include: the individual, his role and the organization; multiple roles and role conflict; the impact of group processes on personal and organizational development; strategies for 'humanizing' the organizational environment to meet individual and group needs; and the influence of technical and economic factors on organizational life.

The series will attempt to draw together the main schools of organizational behaviour including, for example, the American behavioural science tradition as reflected by Harvard, UCLA and National Training Laboratories, and the British socio-technical and open systems approaches of the Tavistock Institute of Human Relations. It is hoped that this will add significantly to understanding the distinctive characteristics of the various approaches and also provide a link between them through which individual, group and organizational behaviour can be seen in fuller perspective.

CARY COOPER
ERIC MILLER

Preface

A great deal of experimental work has been carried out in group behaviour over the last decade but there has not been a concomitant development in *theory*. There is an increasing need to encourage people interested in group processes to begin to build sound theoretical schemas in this field. It is the intention of this book to provide a platform for the development of these models. This volume therefore will focus on theory-building in the understanding of small and large groups, with particular reference to experiential group processes. It includes *original* contributions from some of the most distinguished scholars of group processes. It was the intention of the editor to select contributors who would not only reflect a range of expertise but also would emphasize different aspects of group process (i.e. leader behaviour, group composition, individual learning strategies, etc.) and how these variables might be linked with one another to provide us with a fuller picture of group dynamics.

In 1964 Lee Bradford, Jack Gibb and Kenneth Benne started their book *T-Group Theory and the Laboratory Method* (New York, Wiley) by saying 'this book is the story of an innovation in education—the T (Training) Group'. Since then this particular educational technology has not only grown (in use and application) at a geometric rate but has also given birth to what is currently termed 'the human potential movement'. Experiential groups of one sort or another are now used in numerous settings: in helping married couples; in training social workers; as part of organization development programmes in industry; in group team-building as in a hotel/restaurant or football club, etc. Although they have undergone critical shifts in emphasis, design and scope, these group approaches still retain and provide their participants/students with some degree of influence in the learning process, which is, after all, their unique educational contribution. In addition, these groups have become the focal point for an enormous amount of research activity over the years, more than any other educational/learning technique of the century. It is with this growth and development that we are forced to consider the conceptual or theoretical substance of the processes of these groups. And more importantly, in order to enhance our understanding of group behaviour *generally*, it is essential that we build on the voluminous data generated by experiential groups over the last two decades. One of my early mentors and close friends, Fred Massarik of UCLA, once suggested that the enormous potential contribution to understanding individual and group behaviour, from the experiential group movement, would one day be at risk, since many of its devotees and advocates were 'academic cowboys', not settling for long on any particular patch of group terrain. While, on balance this is true, particularly of the large number of people who have done 'one-off' research into group processes, the over-whelming body of literature in this field still provides for those who are interested and committed to understanding group phenomena the opportunity to build a more coherent conceptual framework of social interaction and relationships. It is with this in mind that the contributors in this book discuss their ideas with you, the reader. I hope you feel we are successful, at the very least that we are moving in the right direction.

I should like to thank all the contributors for their interest in the project, also John Beck of the University of Manchester for his comments on earlier drafts of various chapters, Helen Betts and Ena Glover for their help in typing and indexing the book, and all the participants of all the experiential groups that have contributed to the ideas, thoughts and ruminations that follow.

Contents

Chapter 1

Armchair Speculation, Data Collection and Theory Building about Group Processes

Cary L. Cooper

University of Manchester Institute of Science and Technology

Historical roots

The development of the understanding of group processes seems rooted in two historical traditions—the existential and the scientific (Durkin, 1964). The former sprang from the industrial revolution of the nineteenth century and the accompanying poverty which followed its economic upheaval. Man's social and psychological life was in the process of change and the institutions upon which the foundations of his security and sense of belonging were based were shifting. As a result, more and more people became estranged from themselves and others and the security of the individual more disrupted and fragmented. Furthermore, the scientism of the time provided little comfort to the human problems of loneliness, alienation and uncertainty. Kierkegaard (1954), the Danish philosopher, sensing man's despair and primary loneliness, reflected 'despair is a sickness in spirit, in the self, and so it may assume a triple form; in despair at not being conscious of having a self; in despair at not willing to be oneself; in despair at willing to be oneself.' Thus, the seeds of a phenomeno-logical movement were planted with the emphasis on the exploration of the 'being' or meaning of the person. Heidegger (1929) encouraged the analyst's participation, emphatically, in the existence of the other. Applied to later methods of self-exploration (i.e. psychotherapy, counselling, sensitivity train-ing, etc.) this way of experiencing the person implied a new egalitarian relation-ship between educator and student. Whereas Heidegger emphasized individual existence, Buber (1937) stressed the communion 'between man and man' and carried it into the nature of group relations. For Buber the heightening of self-awareness was impossible without genuine interaction with 'the other'. His interest in the 'essential we' (man's needs to meet others in genuine en-counter) as distinct from the 'primitive we' (enforced group consensus with a low degree of individuation) makes his work particularly relevant to our understanding of the development of experiential group processes.

Psychotherapists were the first to utilize existential philosophy in treating and investigating mental disorders. The 'Daseins' analysts, Rogerian counsellors and existential analysts (like Binswanger) have adapted the phenomeno-logical conceptualization into methods for psychotherapeutic purposes. As Kahler (1957) suggested 'the steady development of self-reflection and intro-spection through psychotherapy together with the underlying historical reaction to rationalism and the search for inner understanding have contributed pro-foundly to the emergence of T-group training.' Experiential group training has not only emerged in his phenomenological tradition but reflects, with its stress on the emotional process of immediate group experience in self-under-standing, the techniques implicit in Heidegger's notion of EINFÜLUNG (emphathy) and Buber's 'Essential We'

As Durkin (1964) has suggested, the scientific basis of group processes owes its beginnings to the nineteenth- and twentieth-century sociologists. Durkheim, for instance, emphasized the idea that the group was a 'collective representation', that is, it had an identity and existence of its own. Simmel, in the early twentieth century, stressed the importance of interaction and belongingness in the group, which later provided a basis for a typological theory of group conflict. As the scientism of the twentieth century grew, these concepts and many others were formulated more rigorously, and empirically tested. Triplett (1897) and Moede (1920) did the first early group studies by comparing the difference between individual and group performance and the effects of the group on the individual. Reflecting the scientific revolution and emergent interest in groups, sociologists and psychologists performed in the late 1930s an enormous amount of empirical work on group behaviour. Sherif (1936) carried out a systematic analysis of the 'social norm' under controlled laboratory conditions. Newcomb (1943) investigated students at Bennington College to see what effect the university culture had on individual attitude change. Lippitt and White (1939) studied the effect of different types of leadership patterns on the social climate of the group and individual behaviour. In this atmosphere Kurt Lewin emerged as the main representative of group research, which he coined as 'group dynamics'. He developed a 'field theoretical' method of examining group behaviour that provided the foundations for dealing with psychological data. He conducted numerous experiments into group decision making, communication patterns in groups, and so on.

In the tradition of Lewin's action research a number of group psychologists came together (headed by Lewin himself) in Connecticut in 1947 to run the first human relations training group—the forerunner to the National Training Laboratory, currently the central focus of group training in North America. They applied their own experience and research knowledge of the dynamics of the group process to the problems of American society.

Development of the science of group processes

Our knowledge of group dynamics has also undergone a process of scientific development which is common to all fields of academic study, that is, the movement progressively through the stages of armchair speculation, data collection, to theory building (Cartwright and Zander, 1960). In this respect there have probably been two parallel developments in the group field, one in the area of *experimental* group psychology and the other in the field of *experiential* group psychology. Although these two approaches have different sources of influence they do share a number of common theoretical denominators, which would indicate that they are not entirely mutually exclusive developments. In experimental group behaviour, as Cartwright and Zander suggest, much of the early speculation and stimulus for theory building stemmed from the work of Lewin's field theory, Bales' interaction theory, system theories (i.e. Newcomb), Moreno's notion of sociometric relationships, etc. Many of these 'theories' were indeed nothing more than insightful observations of group behaviour, speculations about the phenomenon of group interaction, most of which were not easily testable or had enough empirical support. As in all sciences, there are those who become dissatisfied with hypothesis formation and speculation and begin to objectively evaluate the phenomena. So in the 1950s to the present day we have had a dearth of group empiricism (Berkowitz, 1954; Barnlund, 1959; Gamson, 1961; Wyer, 1966; Stoner, 1968). Much of this work has concentrated on limited, highly identifiable areas of research which have helped to heighten the development of experimental methodology and replication but have blatantly ignored theory, deifying the maxim 'research for its own sake'. Presently, we are in the position of possessing mountains of empirical work in experimental group psychology, much of which has not been incorporated in the development of building viable and useful theories. Some limited movement has been made in this direction, however, primarily from people (Bales, 1970; Fiedler, 1967) who have built on their own empirical work over the years and who have entered what Cartwright and Zander suggest is the advanced stage of scientific enterprise, which consists of 'developing hypotheses and theories from observations, checking these theoretical formulations by new observations and experiments, revising the hypotheses, checking these new hypotheses in new investigations and so on...'.

If we explore experiential group psychology we find a similar development. Much of the original speculation stemmed from Argyris, Bion, Bennis and Shepard, Tannenbaum, *et al.*, and from them the ideas, thoughts, personal observations of the phenomena of group and organizational behaviour were nurtured. Since much of the work in experience-based groups was done in applied settings such as within industrial organizations or as part of organizational development (OD) programmes, there was a cry by the participants' sponsoring organizations for *evaluation*, particularly in view of the person-centred approach of these experiences which raised the spectre of personal disturbance and possible psychiatric breakdown in the minds of many personnel officers, training managers, etc. Coincidential to this development, social and organizational psychologists were looking for opportunities of applying their research skills to the problems of industry, the social services, hospitals, and away from the artificial group experiments with undergraduate students in psychology laboratories. As a result of these two forces an enormous amount of research was carried out in the 1960s into experiential group methods such as T-groups, encounter groups, gestalt groups, OD-type groups (Campbell, 1971; Campbell and Dunnette, 1968; Cooper and Mangham, 1971; House, 1967). Again, however the research became more and more removed from the early seminal thoughts and speculations and the restricted research orientations gained a status of their own. This is not to say that there was no theoretical development during this phase (Mann, 1967; Argyris, 1962; Golembiewski, 1972; Cooper, 1969), but rather that it was less global or in a form that would encourage further refinements in the scientific process. It is at this stage that we find ourselves today, a wealth of empirical data with little theoretical framework to store it in. It is my view that we are now ready for the third stage of the scientific process in which, to paraphrase Cartwright and Zander 'theorizing and data collection can mutually contribute to our understanding by a process of approximation.' This will require some movement in the direction of theory-building and one way to stimulate this development is to encourage people who are actively involved in research to stop and explore the theoretical implications of their own and their colleagues empiricism. This is the intention of this volume.

The dichotomy described between experimental and experiential group processes presents us with a difficult decision. Do we attempt here the mammoth task of encouraging theoretical developments in both areas and then attempting to integrate or bridge the gap between them or do we concentrate on one at a time. It was decided to do the latter, for it was felt that until each of the areas had developed sound theoretical foundations within the confines of their own disciplines, the task of integration would be Herculean. This conclusion was reached after extensive discussion with colleagues working in both fields of group processes. This volume therefore will focus on theory-building in the area of experiential group and organizational processes. It will include original contributions from some of the most distinguished scholars of group processes, some of whom have been in the field for many years and have done a great deal of research and theoretical work, and others who are at the brink of Cartwright and Zander's third stage of scientific development. It was the purpose of the editor to select contributors who would not only reflect a range of different orientations but also would be concerned about different aspects of group processes (i.e. leader behaviour, group composition, learning strategies, etc.). The intention was not to restrict the contributors to a set topic but to issue them with a licence to build theoretical schemas in those areas of group process of their own choosing. Although the editor leaves himself open to some overlap or dulpication of ideas or to the criticism of lack of continuity among the various chapters, it was felt that the potential gain of allowing the contributors freedom of theoretical development would be greater.

The contributions in this volume represent a unique attempt to develop theoretical links between some of the more important aspects of group and organizational processes. It might be useful at this stage to provide a simple

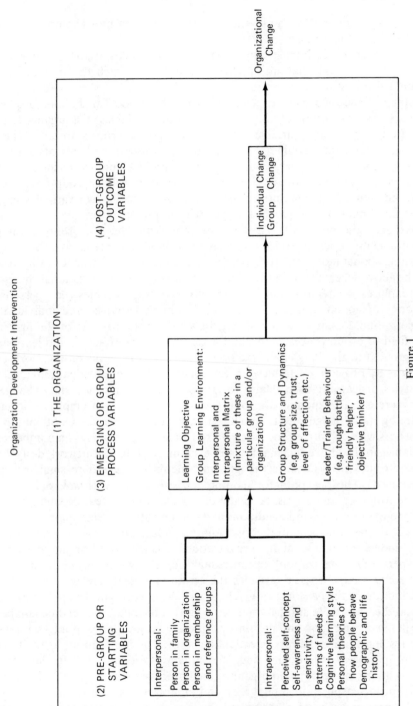

Organization Development Intervention

(1) THE ORGANIZATION

(2) PRE-GROUP OR STARTING VARIABLES

(3) EMERGING OR GROUP PROCESS VARIABLES

(4) POST-GROUP OUTCOME VARIABLES

Interpersonal:

Person in family
Person in organization
Person in membership and reference groups

Intrapersonal:

Perceived self-concept
Self-awareness and sensitivity
Patterns of needs
Cognitive learning style
Personal theories of how people behave
Demographic and life history

Learning Objective

Group Learning Environment:

Interpersonal and Intrapersonal Matrix (mixture of these in a particular group and/or organization)

Group Structure and Dynamics (e.g. group size, trust, level of affection etc.)

Leader/Trainer Behaviour (e.g. tough battler, friendly helper, objective thinker)

Individual Change
Group   Change

Organizational Change

Figure 1

schema as a guide to some of the theoretical relationships explored by the contributors (Figure 1).

This rather crude, simplistic model will, it is hoped, allow us to focus in on the kinds of issues and relationships between variables which the authors have examined in the book.

Many of the theoretical expositions in this book look at the interface between pairs or a combination of the four central variables; the organization, pre-group or starting variables, emerging or group process variables, and post-group outcome variables. Five of the contributions provide global theories, that is, either involve a large number of the variables outlined in the schema or explore concepts at the level of organizational as well as group processes. The remaining four concentrate their focus on basically two variables (e.g. trust and change). The global theories will be presented first.

We start the book with Argyris's theory of the effective group learning environment, which provides the basis for a more comprehensive theory of learning about (and from) group processes. His ideas span the range of variables in the above schema from starting or pre-group ones to organizational change. He explores the relationship between intrapersonal variables (i.e. 'personal theories of action'), group learning environment variables and individual/ organizational change variables. Argyris's contribution is one of the first in the field of group processes to build a general theory of action and learning (in groups) in the Parsonian tradition. Kolb and Fry build on the work of Argyris by providing a framework for conceptualizing individual differences in styles of learning as it relates to group processes and individual change. They present an experiential group learning model, which emphasizes that 'learning and change result from the integration of concrete emotional experiences with cognitive processes'. Barrett-Lennard also surveys a number of variables in the above schema, he presents a more global framework designed to contribute to systematic thought and enquiry in regard to small group phenomena. The focal point for his approach is concerned with ways of looking at the *within-group* process. A model of change is presented, beginning with pre-group experience and conditions and ending with indirect long-range outcomes. In the same general theory tradition, Culbert attempts to build a five-stage model for individual and organizational change, based on interpersonal (i.e. person in organization), intrapersonal (i.e. self-awareness and sensitivity) and some group process variables (i.e. group support). He focuses on the relationship of the *person* vis-a-vis the *system* he operates in. In the last of the global theories Blake and Mouton carry on this theme of the relationship between the organization and person by exploring various types of interventions and resultant individual/organizational change. The implications at the level of group process are obvious since they attempt to identify five fundamental interventions into group and organizational processes which could serve as the basis for increasing individual, group and organizational effectiveness.

The next category of contribution focuses in on the relationship between pairs of group variables in sections 2, 3 or 4 in Figure 1. Golembiewski and

McConkie do an exhaustive survey of research on the relevance of *trust* and individual/group change. From this they build some hypothetical linkages of trust with learning outcomes, which should provide a solid foundation for further theoretical and empirical work on this important learning environment variable. Reddy focuses in on *group composition* (interpersonal and intra-personal matrix) and individual change. He reviews the research literature and then attempts to build a theory of optimal group composition and learning. Lakin extends the simple relationship between some of the learning environment variables and change, to explore the interrelationship between *group dynamics* and *leader behaviour* in increasing personal effectiveness in relationships. Mann, on the other hand, is interested in the effect of the *development* of group relationships/issues on individual change, particularly in respect to win–lose strategies within groups. He asks 'what does it mean that so many group members experience a painful kind of losing, while others experience a painful kind of winning, and still other find that the whole win–lose modality blocks their involvement in the group and offers them an either/or in which neither winning nor losing holds much appeal?' How does the development of this important dynamic affect individual and group growth?

If we look at each of the contributions in this book it can be seen that they cover a wide range of connections between the variables outlined in the schema. More conceptual and theoretical work is needed to complete the myriad of possible interconnections between various aspects of group processes. We have attempted here a beginning of this exploration.

References

Argyris, C. (1962) *Interpersonal Competence and Organizational Effectiveness*. London: Tavistock.

Bales, R. F. (1970) *Personality and Interpersonal Behaviour*. New York: Holt, Reinhart, and Winston.

Barnlund, D. C. (1959) 'A comparative study of individual, majority and group judgement.' *Journal of Abnormal and Social Psychology*, **58**, 55–60.

Berkowitz, L. (1954) Group standards, cohesiveness, and productivity.' *Human Relations*, **7**, 509–519.

Buber, M. (1937) *I and Thou*. Edinburgh: R. Clark.

Campbell, J. P. (1971) 'Personnel training and development.' *Annual Review of Psychology*, **22**, 565–602.

Campbell, J. P. and M. D. Dunnette (1968) 'Effectiveness of T-group experiences in managerial training and development.' *Psychological Bulletin*, **70**, 73–104.

Cartwright, D. and A. Zander (1960) *Group Dynamics*. Evanston, Illinois: Row, Peterson.

Cooper, C. L. (1969) 'The influence of the T-group trainer on participant change.' *Human Relations*, **22**, 515–530.

Cooper, C. L. and I. L. Mangham (1971) *T-Groups: A Survey of Research*. New York and London: John Wiley and Sons.

Durkin, H. E. (1964) *Group in Depth*. New York: International University Press.

Fiedler, F. E. (1967) *A Theory of Leadership Effectiveness*. New York: McGraw Hill.

Gamson, W. A. (1961) 'An experimental test of a theory of coalition formation.' *American Sociological Review*, **26**, 565–573.

Golembiewski, R. T. (1972) *Renewing Organizations*. New York: Peacock.

8

Heidegger, M. (1929) *What Is Metaphysics.* Frankfurt: Klostermann.

House, R. (1967) 'T-group education and leadership effectiveness.' *Personnel Psychology,* **20,** 1–32.

Kahler, E. (1957) *The Tower and the Abyss.* New York: Braziller.

Kierkegaard, S. (1954) *Fear and Trembling, and Sickness Unto Death.* New York: Doubleday.

Lippitt, R. and R. K. White (1939) 'Patterns of aggression in behaviour in experimentally created climates.' *Journal of Social Psychology,* **10,** 271–299.

Mann, R. D. (1967) *Interpersonal Styles and Group Development.* New York: Wiley.

Moede, W. (1920) *Experimentelle massenpsychologie.* Leipzig: S. Hirzel.

Newcomb, T. M. (1943) *Personality and Social Change.* New York: Dryden.

Sherif, M. (1936) *The Psychology of Social Norms.* New York: Harper.

Stoner, J. A. F. (1968) 'Risky and cautious shifts in group decisions.' *Journal of Experimental Social Psychology,* **4,** 442–459.

Triplett, N. (1897) 'The dynamogenic factors in pacemaking and competition.' *American Journal of Psychology,* **9,** 507–533.

Wyer, R. S. (1966) 'Effects of incentive to perform well, group attraction and group acceptance on conformity in a judgemental task.' *Journal of Personality and Social Psychology,* **4,** 21–26.

Chapter 2

Learning Environment
for Increased Effectiveness*

Chris Argyris

Harvard University

Effectiveness learning

In this chapter I should like to describe some recent thinking and experimentation with new directions in experiential learning. The motivation for these studies was partially caused by the apparent difficulties people, who had attended various types of laboratories, had in utilizing their newly acquired knowledge and skills.

A second source of motivation for these studies was the trend, in much experiential learning, to exclude the cognitive and task dimensions to the point where an anti-intellectual bias developed, where task achievement was de-emphasized, evaluation activities were resisted, if not abhored, and interpersonal closeness and warmth became more valued than effective task accomplishment (Back, 1973). Learning processes that excluded cognitive dimensions, de-emphasized task achievement and effectiveness, while emphasizing warmth and interpersonal closeness, left themselves open to serious questions of whether they could achieve their purpose of educating the whole person.

I. *The relationship of thought to effective action*

The approach to be described is based partly upon my work on effective intervention (Argyris, 1970) and more importantly upon the work by Donald Schon and myself. We have recently proposed a theory of action and practice, in a book entitled *Theory in Practice* (1974) that may provide some useful guidepoints toward a new thrust for experiential learning.

It is not possible to describe all our findings nor to present the complete theoretical framework. However, an outline of the points relevant to this chapter are presented below.

(1) Effectiveness, consistency, congruence and competence are central to life. I should like therefore to call the learning to be discussed, *effectiveness learning* or *education*. Associated with behaving effectively are such factors as the need for behaving competently, the compellingness of real tasks, the involving

*I should like to express my appreciation to William Torbert for his thoughtful comments.

quality of problem-solving, and the exhilarating, exhausting quality of membership in hard-working groups that accomplish difficult but reachable goals.

(2) Individuals use explicit and tacit knowledge in problem-solving. Both kinds of knowledge have emotional and intellectual components that are so interwoven that the only sensible meaning of human rationality is the inclusion of feelings and intellect.

(3) Individuals strive to have explicit or tacit reasons to explain their behaviour to themselves and to others. Human action without reasons does not, apparently, make sense to them. This view is so prevalent that it can be proposed as their criterion for human sanity. Although most respondents want to reserve some psychological space of free movement for behaviour that does not have reasons connected with it (such as personal moments of spontaneity and love) they seem to insist that the rest of life should make sense so that it can be manageable.

Some illustrative reasons are:

'That's easy, I did that to A because I know him and the way to move him is . . . .'

'The best way to deal with subordinates is. . . .'

'I'm not clear why I did that, but if you give me a few minutes, I'm sure that I can tell you.'

'Come to think of it, what I'm saying is not completely true. What I really felt was . . . .'

(4) With enough discussion and thought, the reasons people give to explain their behaviour can be translated into propositions: 'Under these conditions, do such and such, in order to accomplish the following and expect the following consequences.' These propositions may be viewed as propositions in their *theories of action*. They are like other propositions in any theory in that they purport to predict what will happen under given conditions and they stipulate the probable consequences.

Human behaviour therefore may be informed by micro-theories of action. The purpose of the micro-theories of action is to help people behave effectively; to have some criteria by which to monitor the effectiveness of their behaviour; and to help make their behaviour intellegible to others.

Individuals assume and act as if others also construct and hold personal theories of action which, if understood, would help everyone behave more effectively. In other words, in the world of infinite information possibilities, the self and relationships with others become manageable with the assumption that behaviour is informed by 'reasons' formulated into personal micro-theories of action.

(5) The theories of action that people give us to explain their behaviour (either before or after the fact) may be called their *espoused theories*.

The empirical research we conducted suggested that the predictive validity of these espoused theories varied widely, but for most of the cases, and with a few rare exceptions, was unexpectedly low. Examples of the rare cases were a few highly authoritarian administrators who were aware and accepting of parts of their theories-in-use. For example, they were aware of their authoritarianism, that they espoused highly controlling micro-theories and that they behaved congruently with these theories. However, these respondents were unable to specify accurately the probable consequences of their behaviour upon others. Indeed, their blindness about the consequences of their behaviour upon others helped to make it possible for them to continue their behaviour. Moreover, they were unaware of other aspects of their theory-in-use (e.g. suppression of feelings, discomfort with hostility and open indications by subordinates of dependence and submission).

The large majority of the respondents, however, tended to behave incongruently with their espoused theories, *and* they were blind to this fact. The blindness was largely limited to their being unaware of their own behaviour and the lack of congruity with their espoused theories. The same individuals were significantly less blind in seeing the incongruity 'in' others.

(6) Why should people hold espoused theories that do not seem to inform much of their behaviour? Why are micro-theories with such low predictive validity held with such high intensity? Why does there appear to be a massive condition of blindness, on the part of the actors, regarding the incongruity between espoused theory and their behaviour? Why is it that when actors become observers of others they can report accurately the incongruities and inconsistencies 'in' others?

II. *Theories-in-use: their underlying logic and structure*

In order to begin to answer these questions, several steps were taken. First, specimens of human behaviour were obtained in as directly observable form as possible (e.g. audio or video tape; scenarios written by the actors; nonparticipant observation). Next, we constructed a theory that would explain the behaviour of each individual as sampled from these tapes. This theory represented the respected individual's *theory-in-use*.

The theories-in-use collected were then translated into a model called Model I. The model now 'accounts' for 396 cases out of 400 respondents. (Why a model might account for such an unusually high degree of the cases will be discussed below.)

Model I had a structure of five categories. First, there was the *directly observable behaviour* that was collected from which the theories in use were inferred.* Second, was the meanings that could be inferred that the behaviour had for the actors and the others. We called these meanings the *behavioural strategies* the individuals were manifesting.

Since the concern was on effectiveness, we then inferred the consequences the behaviour would have upon (a) the *world in which the individuals were immersed*, (b) the *nature and quality of learning*, and (c) the *degree of effectiveness* of the behaviour.

*I do not wish to become involved in the issues of what is 'directly' observable data in this paper. The interested reader may wish to refer to our book, especially the first five chapters.

The criteria for effectiveness were:

(a) The degree to which the individual (group or whatever the size of unity in question) was aware of the variables relevant to the problem being solved.

(b) The degree to which the problem remained solved.

(c) The degree to which (a) and (b) were accomplished without deteriorating the present level of problem-solving effectiveness (Argyris, 1970).

Finally, the model proposed that human beings made their behaviour manageable to themselves and to others by governing the meanings of their behaviour and that these meanings were informed by certain key values which we have called the *governing variables*.

III. *A model of theory-in-use*: *Model I*

In Figure 1, a summary is presented of Model I. In examining the model, it should be kept in mind that all models are abstractions and therefore we cannot include all the variance and detail of the data collected. Most of the theories-in-use that we have collected were composed of the following:

(1) *Governing variables* or values that emphasized achieving the purpose as the actor defined it, maximizing winning and minimizing losing, minimizing the eliciting of negative feelings, and maximizing rationality.

(2) *Action strategies* where the environment was designed and managed so

I	II	III	IV	V
Governing variables for action	Action strategies for actor and toward environment	Consequences on actor and behavioural	Consequences on learning	Effectiveness
(1) Achieve the purposes as I perceive them	(1) Design and manage environment so that actor is in control over factors relevant to me	(1) Actor seen as defensive		
(2) Maximize winning and minimize losing		(2) Defensive interpersonal and group relationships	(1) Self-sealing	
(3) Minimize eliciting negative feelings	(2) Own and control task	(3) Defensive norms	(2) Single loop learning	Decreased effectiveness
(4) Be rational and minimize emotionality	(3) Unilaterally protect self	(4) Low freedom of choice, internal commitment, and risk-taking	(3) Little testing of theories publicly	
	(4) Unilaterally protect others from being hurt			

Figure 1. Model 1

that the actor was in control of the task, the activities of protecting self and others, and other relevant factors.

(3) *Consequences on the actor and the behavioural world* that lead the actors to be experienced by others as defensive; the creation of defensive interpersonal and group relationships and norms, and low degrees of free choice, internal commitment and risk-taking.

(4) *Consequences on learning* that were primarily self-sealing, focused on remaining within predefined parameters (single-loop learning), and little public testing of micro-theories.

(5) Finally, the above lead to *decreased effectiveness of the actor.* The decreased effectiveness, coupled with the single-loop, self-sealing type of learning, made it more probable that the actors' blindness to their effectiveness was reinforced and to react to reinforcing, for themselves, the potency of the governing variables of Model I (make sure they win, not lose; focus on rationality, not feelings; etc.).

We may now return to the question of why people tend to hold espoused theories that do not inform much of their behaviour. One reason is that others, being programmed with Model I, are careful not to inform the actors of their actual impact upon others and upon the situation. They were careful to 'satisfice' on the Model I governing variables, as 'Minimize the expression of negative feelings', 'Win, don't lose', and consequently follow such behavioural strategies as 'Withhold information from the actors (when they are behaving incongruently with their espoused theories or when they are behaving ineffectively) in order to save their face'.

If individuals know they are deceiving the actors, they may eventually wonder if others are not deceiving them. Since according to Model I that type of question would rarely be discussed and would rarely be subjected to public testing, the actors may eventually come to live with the continual thought that others are deceiving them (as they are deceiving others). Given the governing variables of Model I, the testing of these views will tend to be private. This results in what social psychologists call attribution of motives to others and what the layman may call 'two-bit psychoanalysis'.

The world sanctions beliefs and norms, and the individuals in it come to believe them, to the effect that personal effectiveness requires deception; an 'optimal' degree of blindness, and an effective network and layers of social norms and defences all supporting behaviour variously called 'diplomatic', 'civilized' or 'realistic'.

To those of us interested in developing new options for behaviour, these norms and social defences become a very difficult barrier to overcome. They act to support individuals' views that other types of behaviour, even if presumably desirable, are romantic, unrealistic, and would ultimately lead to a new set of causes for personal ineffectiveness. Moreover, they tend to make learning environments designed to explore new models personally threatening and socially deviant. Finally, they tend to make learning of new models seem hopeless because the people from whom one might learn are also programmed according to Model I.

IV. *Model II*

To the extent individuals are programmed with Model I, one can make three predictions. First, they will experience the increasing ineffectiveness in themselves, in others, as well as in groups and institutions populated by people programmed with Model I. Second, the resulting feelings of frustration and feelings of incompetence (personal and institutional) will lead eventually to a need for change in their or others' behaviour. Third, individuals may be able to design the consequences that they wish in life (e.g. increased effectiveness) and infer some of the conditions necessary to achieve these consequences (less defensiveness, more trust, more free choice, etc.) but they will not tend to be able to manifest theories-in-use that will lead to these consequences. Human beings may be the best source for evidence that they and their society are not very effective, but they will not tend to be the source for micro-theories of action that will help them to alter the situation.

Individuals (and eventually groups and institutions) can become a source for genuine change if they are offered new models of theories-in-use and if they are helped to learn these models in such a way that they can use them under real-time conditions and without returning to Model I when stress is moderate (under extreme personal stress Model I may be functional because it is defensive).

One such model is Model II. It purports to be a framework for increasing human effectiveness. It may also be used to enhance institutional effectiveness partially by re-educating participants to new behaviours and partially by using the model as a basis of designing new organizational structures, management information systems, leadership behaviour and organizational norms.

Briefly, Model II (see Figure 2) is composed of the following:

(1) *Governing variables* that value valid information, free and informed choice, and internal commitment to the choice.

(2) *Action strategies* where the environment and the task are jointly influenced by the actors. Included in the concept of jointly sharing is the criterion of legitimately sharing. Individuals would be given power according to their competence and their ability to use their competence to fulfil the objectives defined by the participants.

The unilateral creation of constructs, and programmes for behaviour, which as we have seen are necessary for human effectiveness, are basically Model I acts. Their degree of Model-I-ness may be decreased by supplying the directly observable data from which they were informed, as well as making the processes of inferences public, and finally making all three (constructs, data and inference processes) genuinely and publicly confrontable.

Moreover, conditions of psychological success, confirmation and essentiality

I	II	III	IV	V
Governing variables for action	Action strategies for actor and toward environment	Consequences on behavioural world	Consequences on learning	Effectiveness
(1) Valid information (2) Free and informed choice (3) Internal commitment to the choice and constant monitoring of the implementation	(1) Design situations or encounters where participants can be origins and experience high personal causation (2) Task is controlled jointly (3) Protection of self is a joint enterprise and oriented toward growth (4) Bilateral protection of others	(1) Actor experienced as minimally defensive (2) Minimally defensive interpersonal relations and group dynamics (3) Learning-oriented norms (4) High freedom of choice, internal commitment, and risk-taking	(1) Disconfirmable processes (2) Double loop learning (3) Frequent testing of theories publicly	Increased effectiveness

Figure 2. Model II

would be used to design and manage the environment. Under these conditions saving face (self or other) would become ineffective behaviour because it inhibits critical learning.

(3) The consequences of the action strategies above on the behavioural world will tend to be (a) the actors will tend to be experienced as minimally defensive, (b) the interpersonal and group dynamics will also tend to be minimally defensive and (c) the norms will be learning-oriented.

(4) As a result of increasing psychological success, the frequency of free and informed choice will tend to increase. The effectiveness of problem-solving and decision making, especially for the difficult problems, will also tend to be enhanced.

(5) Individuals will tend to strive to state their important views in ways that they can be explicit, clear *and* publicly testable and disconfirmable. Advocacy, under Model II, encourages advocacy coupled with confrontation by self and others of whatever one is advocating.

Instead of learning remaining within the constraints of the existing system (single-loop learning) double-loop learning will be encouraged where the basic values and ideas are continually challenged.

(6) Finally, this should lead to a world where individuals (or whatever the

unity under consideration) should (a) be more aware of the variables relevant to the problems, (b) the problems will tend to be solved in ways that they remain solved and (c) the present level of problem-solving effectiveness will be maintained, or, more probably, increased.

This is the model that acts both as a programme for the design of the new learning environments as well as the basis for criteria regarding the degree to which the learning environments are effective.

One final word about Model I and Model II. To the extent that they inform human behaviour they are coercive and can be self-sealing. The difference between the two on this issue is that Model II openly acknowledges this possibility and builds in behaviour (e.g. encouraging confrontation, double-loop learning) that helps to cope with the inherent difficulties. Most importantly, Model II behaviour is based on values of valid information, free choice and internal commitment which, if followed, would discourage self-sealing single-loop learning.

To summarize: the model of the theories-in-use purports to map the variables that individuals, in our society, tend to use to select the meanings that are appropriate in settings of action.

Models of theories-in-use do not predict simply to actual future behaviour. They purport to be more powerful. They predict the meanings of the behaviour that actors will select and the consequences of these behaviours. For example, the Model I theory-in-use may predict that Mr A will behave in ways to control Mr B, and that such behaviour will have certain kinds of consequences. The model will not predict the specific behaviour that Mr A will use to control Mr B.

There is an important practical relevance of this view of theories-in-use. Theories-in-use would not be very useful for human beings if they were limited to predicting actual behaviour. This would mean that individuals would have to store and retrieve unwieldly numbers of theories-in-use. The number would probably be so large that they could not be stored unless they were highly abstracted. They would soon become abstract espoused theories. The number of these theories would be so large that, given human beings' information-processing capacities, they could not retrieve them under real-time conditions (Simon, 1969).

The decision of what behaviour to select and to express in a given situation is not simply under the control of the actor. The environment, in the form of other actors, groups, institutions, societal norms, plays an active role; one that may not be completely predictable ahead of time.

The requirements for effective action, under these conditions, are for the individuals to programme themselves with theories-in-use that lead to behaviour that fits their values; that encourages real-time learning and reflection; that facilitates action and advocacy; and that sets the stage for a re-examination of the situation in order to generate as much learning as possible regarding the effectiveness of their respective theories-in-use and the appropriateness of the socio-politico-economic matrix in which they are immersed.

V. *An espoused theory of transition from Model I to Model II*

What kinds of learning experiences may be helpful for learning Model II and for learning to behave according to its requirements? The underlying assumption for designing learning environments that help individuals move toward Model II is that these environments should mirror the properties of Model II. The educational means toward Model II are defined by the ends. Since in learning there is no end, the means also define the ends.

It is possible to derive from Model II an espoused theory of transition (Figure 3).

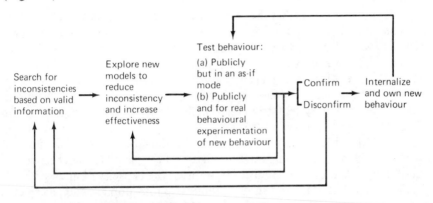

Figure 3. The transition from Model I to Model II

The transition processes begin with the search for inconsistencies and dilemmas. Next, new models are generated that may help to reduce the inconsistencies. The next phase has two aspects. First, the individuals experiment privately and publicly with new behaviour in an as-if manner. It is a dry-run attempt. The second phase is public, overt and a wet-run. The individuals actually try to design new behavioural strategies and to behave according to them. Next is the phase of inviting and receiving valid and usable feedback to correct the behaviour. Finally there is the phase of owning and internalizing the new behaviour.

The reader, who is familiar with the literature of experiential learning, will find the model similar to the ones espoused by T-group theory. The similarity exists at the level of *espoused* theory. The theories-in-use that inform T-groups and effectiveness groups tend to differ in several important respects.

The theory-in-use of the transition from Model I to Model II is more complex than the model presented above. One key reason for the complexity is related to the peculiarity of going from a model that is self-sealing, self-protected and closed to confrontation (Model I) toward Model II which represents openness to confrontation and double-loop learning.

Moving toward Model II requires that the individual internalizes behaviours that are significantly different from those required by Model I. For example, the individual will strive to confront self and others, to publicly test attributions and to generate double-loop learning. All these behaviours are suppressed by Model I theories of action. As suggested above, Model I tends to be the predominate theory of action in our world. Therefore, if one moves toward Model II, one is required to learn and use behaviour that presently violates the norms of a Model I society. This, in turn, means that individuals will have to go through a high degree of unfreezing of old behaviour. Moreover, whereas Model I assumes that human autonomy and effectiveness are accomplished by withdrawal, which means minimizing interdependence among human beings, Model II assumes that autonomy and effectiveness are best achieved through enhancing interdependence.

Model I also assumes that the individual should be able to correct and alter his behaviour subject to the constraint of remaining within Model I requirements. Model II encourages continual challenge to its constraints. Finally, given the difficulties above, the amount of individual discomfort while learning Model II will tend to be significantly higher than learning related to Model I. All these difficulties may be shown to hold if we consider moving organizations, or any other human system, from their predominant Model I make-up toward Model II (Argyris and Schon, 1974).

Thus Model II learning represents several orders jump in the magnitude of difficulty from most learning. First, it requires the capacity to be reflective and questioning about one's present theory-in-use. The capacity to question one's personal and societal theories-in-use requires double-loop learning, a capacity not acquired by people programmed with Model I theories of action. Second, if progress is to occur individuals need to develop the capacities to overcome their presently learned behaviour that leads to private testing and self-sealing processes. The ability and skill to test publicly one's ideas and feelings and do so in a way that is disconfirmable are also not learned by those programmed with Model I theories of action. Finally, effective learning requires that the individual learn to involve others and to live with ambiguity and frustration. Again these are states of affairs not valued by persons programmed with Model I.

Thus the transition from Model I to Model II is full of paradoxes. It would appear that the individual is expected to have the skills of Model II when, in fact, he is in the learning situation to learn these skills. Also it would appear that the group in the learning environment should manifest Model II group dynamics when, in fact, this is not possible because it is composed of individuals programmed with Model I theories of action.

To compound the problem, the person choosing to learn Model II behaviour will enter a world full of dilemmas. The first set of dilemmas is related to discovering the inconsistencies within one's espoused theory and theory-in-use respectively. The second set of dilemmas is related to discovering the incongruity between one's espoused theory and one's theory-in-use. The third set of dilemmas is related to discovering the ineffectiveness of the interpersonal skills and competence with which most of us have been acculturated. The fourth set of dilemmas is related to learning with others who may wish to be of help but who, like the actor, are also programmed according to Model I. Finally, there is a set of dilemmas related to the fact that people who are programmed with Model I theories-in-use will also tend to create group processes of the same kind, thereby creating, within the learning environment, group dynamics that are congruent with Model I.

VI. *A theory-in-use of the transition from Model I toward Model II*

A. Surfacing inconsistencies or dilemmas. The first step in the transition process is to identify and to surface dilemmas that (1) are produced genuinely by the participants, (2) that the participants cannot attribute to techniques used by the faculty in generating the learning processes (i.e. the learners must be able to accept ownership of the dilemmas that they produce), (3) that are created in such a way that the differentiation between the here and now and the there and then is minimized (i.e. the dilemmas are valid in the back-home world as well as the learning environment), (4) that are stated in the form of directly observable data (people cannot understand their theories-in-use from examining their espoused theories—theories-in-use can only be inferred from directly observable data) and (5) that are related, as much as possible, to central issues of the individual's sense of competence and effectiveness. (When people, by their own actions, question their sense of competence and effectiveness energy will be generated to learn in order to resolve the dilemma.)

In order to obtain the data needed several methods have been used. Tape recording of individuals in their home setting, of actual problem-solving meetings have been obtained. Tapes were sent to the faculty ahead of time who selected portions of them to be transcribed, mimeographed and used as case studies during the learning seminar.

Another technique has been to ask individuals to write a case of a difficult and/or easy experience (for intervention) with one or several. They have been asked to provide brief descriptions of the setting, the strategy they used during the episode and an anlysis of what they believed to be their underlying assumptions about effective intervention. The heart of the case study was several pages of descriptions, in scenario form, of what was said during the meeting (on the right-hand side of the page) and what the individual remembers feeling or thinking, but did not say (on the left-hand side of the page).

The reader may wonder if several pages of scenario are an adequate sample. Empirically, the answer to date is affirmative (Argyris and Schon, 1974). Why should so little data predict accurately? A definitive answer based upon empirical research is not yet available. However, we may suggest one possible answer. Recall that the theory-in-use is a programme that the individual uses to design and inform his actions. Recall also that it is inferred from actual behaviour. If actions are consistent with, and informed by, theory-in-use then only a small sample of actions is required.

Another question that arises is can the individuals consciously distort the data they give in their cases? Conscious distortion is a possibility but, to date, no one has presented distorted data. But this may be due to the skewed sample of respondents. These respondents have been interested in learning. However, if they were to distort their cases, the distortion will tend to be surfaced during the seminar when they try to help their fellow participants. Thus, if A writes a Model II scenario because he 'knew' the concepts, he will be faced, during the seminar, with the challenge of *behaving* according to Model II in dyadic relationships, group setting and large group settings where he may be the focus of diagnosis or where he is helping others. Finally, it is doubtful that people can consciously distort the data (short of copying it directly from some source book) because even imagined scenarios are informed by theories-in-use.

Experimentation with how best to start an effectiveness seminar suggests that they should *not* begin with a social vacuum characteristic of T-group practice. Vacuums produce behaviour from which the theories-in-use produced are micro-theories about behaviour in social vacuums. These are important learnings, but not central to longitudinal effectiveness in going from Model I toward Model II. The non-contrived world is not full of vacuums; it is full of Model I episodes and behavioural settings.

The primary reason for the vacuum in a T-group is to generate, as early as possible, directly observable behaviour about the participants, from which all can learn. This need is filled in effectiveness education with the case material (typed or taped). Individuals are given their and others' cases as sources for learning.

In a T-group the early emotions are generated by the ambiguity of the vacuum, the lack of data with which to learn, the magnified importance of membership in the group, etc. For example, the T-group literature is replete with the assertion that the basic problems of group development include (a) who am I in this group, (b) what are my needs in this group, (c) who will have power in this group and (d) how adequate will we be in forming close and intimate relationships (Bradford, Gibb and Benne, 1964; Golembiewski, 1972; Schein and Bennis, 1965).

Under these conditions emotions surfaced during the early phases become a critical learning catalyst. Emotions are crucial because (a) many Model I people, who have suppressed their feelings, may be surprised and impressed with rediscovering their feelings and (b) emotions are the key, non-deniable, directly observable data generated by the group. According to Model I, the participants have learned to be very wary of expressing feelings lest they upset others and themselves. The public expression of feelings has been associated with immaturity and weakness in our society. These states, in turn, have been correlated with interpersonal rejection. Hence group membership and group cohesion are critical issues in a T-group.

Group membership and group cohesion are not, at the outset, critical issues in an effectiveness group and never, so far, become as important as they do in a T-group. In an effectiveness group, the first learning settings the individual faces are with his or her own behaviour, generated outside the group, and yet providing much data about him to this group. The initial questions are less

'How can I get along and find membership in this group.' The initial concerns are more toward analysing their own cases in terms of understanding their theories-in-use. Given the faculty, the cognitive maps available, and the exercises utilized, each individual realizes that much can be learned without having to be close to anyone or without generating a cohesive group. The individuals' concerns are more on how they can become more effective and less on how they can be trusted and loved. Moreover, the emotions that are experienced are related to feelings of ineffectiveness and incompetence *not* on the issues of membership in the group.

Emotions are expressed in effectiveness groups, but they are based more on reading one's own case; reading others' cases and seeing the incompetent behaviour; feeling failure; becoming competitive; etc. Emotionality in these groups, right from the outset, is related to personal competence and effectiveness in problem-solving.

B. Diagnosing one's present theory-in-use and ascertaining the degree to which it approximates Model I. The next phase of the transition process is for individuals to diagnose the extent to which their theories of action are programmed with Model I governing variables and behaviour. In preparation for this phase Models I and II are discussed thoroughly with them. An important part of this discussion is to illustrate the concepts in Model I and Model II with the behaviour of the participants (including the faculty). There are several sources of data on the behaviour. They are (1) the tape recordings of back-home meetings, (2) the scenarios written by the participants in the cases described above and (3) the tapes of the behaviour manifested during the seminars.

There are also several ways to relate the behaviour from these three sources to the models. One is to ask the participants to take episodes of the here and now behaviour within the seminar and relate it to either model or, if it does not seem relatable, to raise questions about new possible models. A second strategy is to ask the individuals, by working alone, to attempt to relate their case material to Models I and II. Once each individual has made his analysis, he describes it to the other group members to obtain their confirmation or disconfirmation and thereby to rewrite it so that it becomes more comprehensive and accurate.

We have been impressed with the trepidation expressed by people when asked to analyse their own cases. They appear to doubt their competence to perform well at a 'private' cognitive mapping activity that is to be discussed by their peers. However, we have been equally impressed with how quickly the trepidation is reduced once the individuals (usually with little help) are able to construct their own theory-in-use. Success in this phase appears to generate confidence in each person's ability to be reflective about and to generate their theories-in-use.

It also appears that this sense of increased personal competence may increase the probability of a successful group experience. Apparently, the increased self-confidence may reduce the individual's anxieties about whether or not they can learn in the seminar. This tends to reduce their dependence upon others which, in turn, may make them more open to hearing the confirmation or disconfirmation from others. This greater openness reduces the probability of defensive reactions which helps all parties to be less uptight about their capacity to learn and to help others to learn. Finally, this appears to be a factor in creating conditions of psychological safety for experimentation.

C. Awareness that being programmed with Model I tends to limit the quality of new options that can be designed. Once the individuals begin experimenting with new behaviour, they begin to find out how much they are prisoners of their present theories of action. Their learning may be summarized as follows:

(1) I am programmed with a theory of action that leades me to feel competent and confident when I articulate clearly my purposes; I advocate effectively my views; I control others in order to win and not to lose.

(2) I now see the unintended negative consequences of this behaviour upon others and myself.

(3) Therefore I will experiment with new behaviour. What is new behaviour if one holds a Model I theory of action? New behaviour is the opposite of the old behaviour. For example, low advocacy, less controlling over others, less focus on being articulate and a decrease in competitiveness.

(4) One important reason why the new options I am able to generate are those that are opposite to Model I is related to the type of learning that is possible under Model I conditions. Model I learning is privately tested, self-sealing and single-loop learning.

(5) Although Model I does not help me to learn Model II (or other possible models), Model II does not prevent me from utilizing Model I or exploring the creation of options other than Models I or II.

The individuals who experiment with behaviour that is opposite to Model I, soon experience a sense of frustration because they are still governed by Model I values (succeed, achieve the task by myself or under my control). Consequently, they tend to feel frustrated that the group is not performing effectively; that the discussion seems rambling or slow; that a thrust seems to be lacking in the problem-solving process; and perhaps more importantly that they have withdrawn or become more passive.

Simultaneously the others experience the 'new' behaviour of the individual experimenting as a withdrawal. They may become bewildered and mistrustful of the new behaviour. Consequently, they may also behave cautiously which would reinforce the sense of 'slowness' of the problem-solving processes and another self-sealing process is created.

The learning activities of the members, under these conditions, seem to become characterized by three processes. The importance and frequency of each process depends upon the mix of Model I theories-in-use held by the participants. Sometimes, the group processes appear to be dominated by members experimenting with the new behaviour described above. The result is that key people appear to have withdrawn; to under-control others; to strive to ask others questions in as much a non-directive manner as they can muster. A norm may develop that inhibits members from taking proactive stances as urging action; making decisions; making difficult choices. (The processes may be caricatured as overly non-directive and dealing with each other with kid gloves.)

At some point, the personal frustration of several members may become so high that they decide to behave more proactively. Since they are still programmed with Model I, they begin to over-control and dominate others. Those being dominated regress to a Model I reciprocal position which is to submit and to point out, with a sense of I-told-you-so, that the dominator is behaving according to Model I. Those doing the over-controlling tend to be aware of their behaviour and justify it by accusing the group of getting nowhere. The result appears to be a cyclical process of under-control to over-control to under-control, etc.

It should be pointed out that these reactions of withdrawal, over- and under-control, and the resulting quasi-freedom of others (the non-directive approach used to suppress personal directiveness) has also been found in the experiences of the participants in their back-home situation. For example, a group of company presidents who began to experiment in the above ways *within* the seminar also tried to do the same in their back-home situation. They began by withdrawing, under-controlling and becoming more non-directive followed by a period of directive and over-controlling behaviour. The results in the back-home situation were equally marginal. However, the presidents, in keeping with the learning strategy, taped these attempts and studied them when they met as a learning group.

It appears that as individuals come to the end of this phase they are usually relatively convinced that Model I tends to programme them to seek alternatives that are opposite to Model I; that these alternatives are not effective; and that significantly new behaviour is going to be needed. It is as if the participants must go through a phase to disabuse themselves of the cherished hope that learning will occur with all the conditions being at the low ends of the continua described in Figure 4. They appear to have to go through much experimentation to prove that new behaviour will require that they learn to become more tolerant of their own and others' behaviour that deviates from existing norms; that they cannot be effective through high advocacy and autonomy-through-control-of others but that they will have to learn to advocate their views through a relationship where they invite confrontation, challenge; a relationship of interdependence.

D. The discovery of fears about being effective with Model II. Once the individuals accept the fact that the transition will require some basic changes in their theories-in-use, in the theories-in-use of others, in existing conceptions of effective groups and organizations, and in societal norms about competent behaviour, they are ready to experiment with genuinely Model II behaviour.

To their surprise, many begin to experience feelings that range from a personal set of disquiet, to fear, to a generalized anxiety. One reason that they are surprised may be that most of those who have participated in our seminars are relatively successful in their careers. Consequently they have rarely felt a sense of fear and inadequacy about achieving a goal that they have set for themselves.

The second surprise is the degree to which they are fearful about experiencing fear. It appears that one of the ways of coping with the world and becoming successful was to suppress the experiencing of fears. Now, in a Model II learning environment, they are not only surfacing fears but they are asking themselves and others to be accepting of these fears. It is this acceptance that produces fears because, as many come to realize, they have conceived of their strength as not having (more accurately not permitting themselves to experience their own) fears and/or that anyone who accepts fears will tend to be controlled and immobilized by those fears.

The way they have dealt with these fears is to place all their energies into succeeding in their chosen careers. The key to success has been to satisfice the governing values of win don't lose; achieve one's own purposes by maximizing the behaviour of high on-task orientation; advocacy and the unilateral control over others. Since (or because of this) they work very hard and since, in order to make hard work imperative (i.e. rational to selves) they set very high goals, which, in turn, means they are seen by others as task-masters and not influence-able on discussions about reducing levels of aspiration. Again, the participants have sent us tapes where the same issues existed in their back-home situations.

In short, the participants tend to experience a set of fears or anxieties that they must eventually resolve. One fear is related to their doubts; now that they have understood the requirements of Model II, can they learn Model II behaviour? These fears, are after all realistic since, as has been pointed out above, during the early stages no-one seems to be able to produce Model II behaviour (at best they produce behaviour that is opposite to Model I).

The second fear is related to the others in their lives, especially those in the back-home situation. Will their subordinates trust them that they are trying to effect genuine changes? Is it possible to overcome the historical relationships of dependency and over-control? Moreover, will their subordinates be genuinely interested in learning Model II behaviour (otherwise there will be little chance that the superiors' learning can be useful or can be maintained over time).

E. The development of new behavioural strategies. As these questions and fears become surfaced and dealt with *within* the learning environment the participants begin to feel (1) an increased sense of cohesiveness (we need each other to learn), (2) a more realistic level of aspiration as to how long it will take to behave more effectively (five years or more are realistic levels of aspiration) which, (3) reduces the need to 'look good' in front of one's peers, which, (4) increases the experimentation of new behaviour.

It is during this phase that the learning of new behaviour and the development of new skills appears to begin in earnest. Unfortunately, we have yet to understand this phase enough so that we could articulate a theory of skill learning and acquisition. We are more certain than ever that it is an error to look upon skill practice, as has been the case, with disdain. The learning of skills is a problem whose depth has yet to be appreciated.

At the moment, we are at the stage where we are experimenting with many different types of exercises to produce skill learning. For example:

Individuals take sections of their taped cases or their scenarios and rewrite them in accordance with Model II behaviour strategies.

Discussion, within the seminar, is cut-off and the actors are asked to redesign it so that it approximates more Model II behavioural strategies. They then attempt to re-enact the scene just interrupted.

Individuals bring to the group a problem that they will be facing within the next few weeks. With the help of the group they design their behaviour. The discussion does not stop until the person can generate spontaneously actual scenarios as to how he would behave to fulfil the new design. The group members act as difficult subordinates trying to raise all the types of resistances that the individual may experience when he returns to the back-home situation.

F. The questioning of new organizational designs and managerial policies and practices. In the description of anxieties and fears one type of fear was excluded that now must be introduced. Not only do participants generate doubts about themselves and others but they also raise questions about the feasibility of managing systems with Model II behaviour when most of the structures, control mechanisms and management information systems are based upon Model I values of behaviour.

These questions lead to preliminary experimentation with new designs for organizational structures, reward and penalty systems, long-range planning practices, etc. It is not long before the participants learn that there is very little available from informed practice or research to help them in their deliberations. This insight does not have the depressing effect it might have because the participants also begin to realize that the way to design and introduce changes into their back-home settings is to involve the people in those settings.

G. Introducing Model II concepts and behaviour into the back-home setting. As the participants begin to gain some confidence that they understand Model II, they begin to explore how to introduce the concepts into their back-home organization. One group that has progressed to this stage is composed of a group of presidents. Their first reactions to this challenge varied. Some of them wanted to wait and, as one person said, 'Spring it on them when I know what I'm doing.' These individuals were confronted by others; was this not an indication that they were not using Model II behaviour because they were still acting in accordance with the Model I value of win, don't lose and the behaviour of being an effective advocate?

Some members concluded that the most effective strategy, if one were to follow the requirements of Model II, was to be open with one's subordinates. For example:

I am trying to learn how to behave in ways that are less controlling yet, I am not very good at it and I have qualms that unless I control certain work won't get done.

The initial reaction of most of the presidents was that they should not surface the fact that they did not feel competent in their new behaviour or that they had questions about its effectiveness. Presidents, they argued had to be strong and portray an image of confidence and certainty.

Why do they have to behave in these ways, asked several presidents. They soon concluded that one reason they 'had' to behave thus was that they were afraid of being vulnerable. Another reason was that they had, by now, probably educated their subordinates to expect them to exude confidence and certainty.

The presidents eventually concluded that if they could resolve the first question they could be more ready to deal with the second. But asking why does one fear being vulnerable leads them to a recursive set of dilemmas. In order to understand the abhorance of feeling vulnerable, the individuals must surface the very fears that create the feeling of vulnerability.

Next the presidents began to realize that the fears of losing control over others and being vulnerable combined to make them control others; to induce others into accepting being controlled and being followers. Such reactions by the others will decrease the probability that the presidents could deal with their qualms about vulnerability with their subordinates. This awareness, in turn, reinforced their lack of confidence and trust in others which fed back to justify and reinforce their competitive, unilaterally controlling behaviour.

The result of such insight has been, to date, for the participants to begin to experiment with new concepts of leadership behaviour. For example:

(1) How to be strong yet be open about dilemmas.
(2) How to behave openly yet not controlling.
(3) How to advocate yet encourage confrontation of one's views.
(4) How to respond effectively to subordinates' (others') anxieties when I have my own.
(5) How to respond effectively to others' doubts when I have my own.

Hopefully, the above has provided the reader with a view of the transition processes, so far observed, as individuals attempt to move from Model I to Model II. There is much that has been omitted primarily because so little is known and secondarily because of space limitation.* Figure 4 may help to illustrate a major thrust of the transition process.

Model I represents a high advocacy–low inquiry theory of action (box 2), where inquiry means learning of the double-loop variety. Model II represents a high advocacy–high inquiry theory of action (box 1).

The objective of effectiveness education is to help individuals learn to behave in accordance with the requirements of box 1. The transition processes seem to be a complex combination of movements toward boxes 3 and 4 before moving

*The reader is referred to Argyris and Schon, 1974.

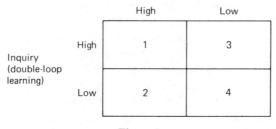

Figure 4

toward 1. The transition process seems to require frequent learning experiences where the individuals are high on double-loop learning but low on advocacy (box 3) coupled with, or sequentially connected with, withdrawal (box 4).

Effective movement toward box 1 requires the rejection of box 4 and the realization that (a) box 3 is not an adequate end result (box 3 may be an adequate end result in many T-groups), (b) that the transition toward box 1 requires striving to be cognitively clear and emotionally as unconflicted as possible about what one advocates, and (c) that advocacy is coupled with inquiry.

Although the learning environments are designed in order to help people learn to behave consistently with Model II requirements it should not be interpreted that Model II is advocated as the only theory of action. Model I, for example, may be an effective theory of action for unimportant issues or under extreme crises. Also, it may be possible that other theories of action can lead to increased effectiveness. Research on this possibility is to be encouraged. We need to generate as many different options as possible.

VII. *Examples of performance results in the back-home situation*

Although the effectiveness seminars are still in the primitive state, there is evidence that they are instrumental in leading to behavioural change and more effective problem-solving and performance in the back-home situation.

As the individual member's competence increases and as the group dynamics become more supportive of Model II values, behaviour and learning, the presidents have been able to design actions that have led to:

(1) Further personal effectiveness with their back-home top group.

(2) Increased interest on the part of the subordinates to choose to explore Model II theories of action.

(3) Increased confrontation of the subordinates of their president's behaviour in ways that the president found helpful.

(4) Increased predisposition of the top group (who have not participated in the seminar) to begin to confront each other as well as the effectiveness of their problem-solving and decision-making processes.

(5) The resolution of difficult problems hitherto not openly resolvable. For example:

(a) One organization was able to cut nearly 20 % of its operating budget with the entire top management group participating in the process.

(b) The need for an executive position that the president believed the vice presidents wanted was eliminated when, after a more open discussion, the presidents and the vice presidents developed a new set of operating procedures which did not require the proposed executive vice presidency.

(c) The relationship between a chairman of the board (and owner of the company) with the president (whom the former had appointed personally) began to deteriorate because of the latter's less than expected performance. The problems were discussed openly and solutions were generated that pleased both men but, more importantly, did not place the vice presidents into a squeeze between requesting a loyalty oath toward the owner or the president.

(d) An unprofitable venture that the president hesitated to close down (because he had originally decided to creat it) was cancelled with the help of the vice presidents who had become more open with the president.

VIII. *The faculty Model—a Model II concept of advocacy*

In closing, let us discuss briefly the role of the faculty. As has been pointed out above, participants who attend the learning environments (a) soon learn that they are programmed to behave in Model I ways, (b) that the instructors know other ways to behave and (c) if the instructors taught them the new concepts, they (the instructors) would be behaving in accordance with Model I. On the basis of our experience to-date, many of the participants seem to experience this dilemma as follows:

I know that there is something that I do not know, but I don't know what it is.

I am frightened (or feeling uncomfortable) to know that there is something that I don't know that I should know.

So I pretend to know it, but since I don't know what I am supposed to know, I have to pretend that I know everything. That is nerve-racking.

I can focus on whether I feel wanted, loved, accepted in the group and upon whom I want, love and accept in the group. This is a cop-out to untying the knot just defined.

One way to attempt to resolve the dilemma is for the participants to act as if they know how to behave in accordance with Model II. But this alternative is not viable because people programmed according to Model I cannot behave according to Model II. They will therefore be unable to maintain such an act for very long. Another strategy, more typical of encounter and personal growth environments, is to focus on generating love, warmth and acceptance to respond to the tensions produced (Argyris, 1967, 1970). This focus could lead the individuals to become more aware of the strength of their affiliation needs. Indeed, it could actually increase their need for affiliation and thereby feed back to make the need for love, warmth and acceptance even more meaningful.

Another way to deal with the problem is for the faculty members to state early in the seminar (or confirm) that they *do* know something and that the something is Model II; that Model II is learnable and teachable; and that the choice of learning and internalizing Model II, however, is up to each individual. If, as has always been the case to-date, most of the members' behaviours tend to approximate Model I, then the members also learn that the reason they do not know Model II is *not* necessarily because of some personal incompetence or incapacity but because our society does not tend to teach Model II as a theory-in-use. This could have the impact of reducing the individuals' guilt about not knowing Model II, and free them to make the fact more public, thereby increasing the probability for public testing of hypotheses and reducing self-sealing processes.

The faculty therefore admit and own up to the paradox. They (a) make explicit the model toward which they are prepared to help the individuals to move; (b) invite genuine confrontation of the model; (c) invite genuine shared planning in the development of the learning episodes that will lead toward forward movement; and (d) encourage the freedom to reject or stop the learning process as long as the rejection is requested and accomplished openly so that again, all individuals may choose.

Individuals programmed with Model I will understandably tend to resist learning Model II as a theory-in-use (although they may admire it as an espoused theory). They may react by returning to their present theories-in-use as being more appropriate. The faculty may encourage this continual testing, thereby helping the individuals to learn more about the effectiveness of their present theories-in-use. The testing may be designed in such a way that the participants cannot assign responsibility for their behaviour to anyone or any phenomenon excepting themselves. Then, if they find their behaviour to be ineffective, they may choose to consider new behaviours.

However, if they discover that their old behaviour is ineffective and they do not know, as yet, a new and appropriate behaviour, they will experience compounded dilemmas. The first dilemma is related to their awareness of ineffectiveness; the second is that the dilemma will tend to become public; and third, their success in learning will come precisely when they experience a sense of failure in their present degree of competence. Moreover, if, as is the case, they strive to maintain their Model I behaviour by creating tests to prove it can be effective, and if (as also tends to happen) they fail to generate such proof, they will find themselves in the dilemma of experiencing success that comes from the courage to learn about one's degree of incompetence.

Such learning can be frustrating and perplexing to people with Model I theories-in-use, because self-esteem has come from behaving effectively, but 'effectively' has meant satisficing on winning, controlling, creating self-sealing processes, etc. It can be predicted that the individuals may build up anger, hostility, competitiveness, fear, toward the faculty as well as toward the others in the learning environment. If so, one may also predict that the predisposition will be to suppress these feelings. First, the individuals may feel that it is 'their fault' that they are not behaving effectively. Second, the individuals will tend to be guided by Model I values and so may see such expressions of feelings as violating the values (e.g. expressing negative feelings and losing).

To date, these suppressed feelings lead to much energy being expended and a great deal of defences being built to prevent them from surfacing. This, in turn, reduces the energy for learning as well as the probability of double-loop learning. Soon the members will find themselves in a new dilemma. They are committed to learning Model II; the group setting does not seem to be productive; they have no other alternative for such learning; yet to surface their feelings could bring rejection and condemnation from the group.

The faculty may become the logical target for such 'attack'. One action may be to require the faculty to behave in Model II ways. Unlike the T-group, the faculty in an effectiveness group gladly does so (just as a tennis pro shows how to serve, a swimming coach how to stroke, etc.). If the faculty are able to show a Model II solution in a setting for which the participants have not been able to do so, their competence may become even more intimidating. A frequent reaction of participants is to condemn an effective Model II role-play by a faculty member by responding that such behaviour would be foolish and ineffective in the present world. The faculty member's response is to confirm a prediction, indeed to point out that Model II behaviour in a Model I world would tend to be seen as foolish. The participants then must come to grips with the very basic question of whether or not they want to begin the journey toward Model II, whether or not to learn by surfacing dilemmas publicly, by focusing on personal causation in cooperative modes, etc.

In closing, a few comments about some of the limits of the learning processes of effectiveness education that are created by the competence, motivation and capacities of both instructors and participants. Our approach makes certain requirements of both groups and succeeds only in so far as both groups meet these requirements.

First, instructors should be able to exhibit Model II behaviour under conditions of mild to moderate stress; that is, their theories-in-use must be consistent with their espoused theories. To the extent that their theories-in-use are consonant with Model II, participants will be exposed to Model II behaviour. At first, participants will observe, question and confront the instructor's behaviour. Later, they may begin to experiment with Model II behaviour. They may go through a transition period in which they openly acknowledge that they are trying to mimic the instructor's behaviour. Such a statement may be an attempt to make the instructor responsible, thereby making it safe for the participant to experiment with new behaviour. The instructor might discuss these possibilities after several such attempts have been made, pointing out the limitations for internalization if behaviour is performed without full responsibility for risks.

Modelling behaviour is not easy, and some people are better at it than others. Instructors should be as realistic as possible about their competence, admitting both their limitations and the effect these limitations may have on participants' learning.

Minimum standards of instructors' competence have yet to be determined, but we can suggest some guidelines. The instructor should (1) not take up more time for learning about his own behaviour than any other participant would; (2) his response to participants' defensive behaviour should not be compulsive; (3) he should be able to provide accurate cognitive maps of Models I and II; and (4) he should be able to design non-coercive learning environments. Instructors should have internalized Model II to the point that they are unconflictedly committed to it and to testing the model publicly and raising questions that challenge its foundation (double-loop learning).

Intense commitments and the excitement of confrontation and confirmation or disconfirmation helps instructors remain effective, especially during the difficult phases when most participants are questioning Model II and the instructors' commitment to it. Note that the model itself asks for enthusiastic exploration of the possibility that parts of the model may be incorrect and ineffective or that we are not behaving according to the model.

This stance at first appears especially bewildering to participants and may be attacked as being arrogant. Although it is a firm stance—which depends on the individual's confidence in his openness to confrontation—Model I is actually the more arrogant model because it requires the individual to win, manipulate, control and hide these strategies from others.

This does not mean that there will not be episodes in which the instructor may also become unintentionally controlling. Instructors are human beings and, especially under great stress such as attack from many class members with minimum support from others, may behave defensively.

Highly competitive participants who fear failure may feel guilty early in the seminar. Given their low sense of self-esteem (usually associated with extreme fear of failure and competitiveness), the guilt may become intolerable. One strategy that would be consistent with Model I would be to seek out any limit in Model II and condemn the entire model on the basis of that limitation. For example, some people have insisted Model II is useless because racists do not respond to or value the factors in the model. Others may condemn Model II because openness is not possible with people who are neurotic and psychologically brittle. We acknowledge the latter case as a limit of our perspective. We would never recommend openness toward others that would harm others. We have repeatedly stated that such actions as openness are, in Model II, designed bilaterally, not unilaterally.

Finally, there are limits posed by the participants. For example, some individuals cannot diagnose their behaviour because they have such strong defence mechanisms against failure that the diagnostic process may be too painful. These difficulties must be respected and the individuals be helped to leave the seminar if it should become too painful. Leaving the seminar would be in everyone's best interests when a participant displays these signs: (1) inability to produce directly observable behaviour (through cases or role-playing); (2) compulsive negative evaluation of incompetent behaviour (especially during the early phases), guilt feelings and a predisposition to punishing oneself or others; (3) denial of validity and usefulness of the diagnostic phases to an extent that he (a) prevents others from further exploration, (b) compulsively berates others for small but genuine progress and (c) consistently reacts to non-achievement with great guilt or anger.

References

Argyris, C. (1967) 'On the future of laboratory education.' *Journal of Applied Behavioral Science*, **3**, 2, 153–209.

Arygris, C. (1970) *Intervention Theory and Method*. Reading, Mass.: Addison-Wesley.

Argyris, C. and D. Schon (1974) *Theory in Practice*. San Francisco: Jossey-Bass, Inc.

Back, K. (1973) *Beyond Words*. Harmondsworth: Penguin Books.

Bennis, W. G. and H. Shepard (1956) 'A theory of group development.' *Human Relations*, **9**, 415–437.

Bradford, L. P., J. R. Gibb and K. D. Benne (1964) *T-Group Theory and Laboratory Method*. New York and London: John Wiley and Sons.

Golembiewski, R. T. (1972) *Renewing Organizations*. Ithaca, Illinois: F. E. Peacock Publishers, Inc.

Lakin, M. (1972) *Interpersonal Encounter: Theory and Practice in Sensitivity Training*. New York: McGraw-Hill Book Co.

Lippitt, G. (1969) *Organizational Renewal*. New York: Appleton-Century-Crofts.

Schein, E. and W. G. Bennis (1965) *Personal and Organizational Change Through Group Methods*. New York and London: John Wiley and Sons.

Simon, H. (1969) *The Science of the Artificial*. Cambridge, Mass.: M.I.T. Press.

Chapter 3

Towards an Applied Theory of Experiential Learning

David A. Kolb
Ronald Fry

Massachusetts Institute of Technology

The experiential learning model and its practical counterpart, the action-research method, are among the most seminal of the many contributions made by Kurt Lewin and his associates in their early work on group dynamics. From these ideas came the laboratory training method and T-groups, one of the most potent educational innovations in this century. The action-research method has proved a useful approach to planned change interventions not only in small groups but also in large complex organizations and community systems. Today this methodology forms the cornerstone of most organization development efforts.

The underlying insight of experiential learning is deceptively simple, namely that learning, change and growth are best facilitated by an integrated process that begins with (1) here-and-now experience followed by (2) collection of data and observations about that experience. The data are then (3) analysed and the

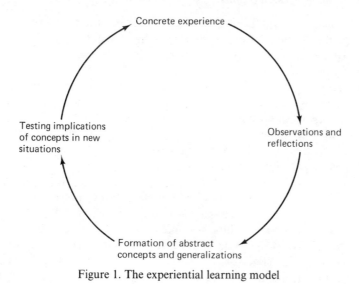

Figure 1. The experiential learning model

conclusions of this analysis are fedback to the actors in the experience for their use in the (4) modification of their behaviour and choice of new experiences. Learning is thus conceived as a four-stage cycle as shown in Figure 1. Immediate concrete experience is the basis for observation and reflection. These observations are assimilated into a 'theory' from which new implications for action can be deduced. These implications or hypotheses then serve as guides in acting to create new experiences.

Perhaps because of the practical face validity of the experiential learning model there has been relatively little serious scientific research directed towards understanding the dynamics of the learning process from this perspective. While the model has become a pivotal tool in training design and consulting practice, there has been little attention given to the exploration of how learning takes place and why experiential learning techniques and action-research methods work. For the past several years we have been engaged in a research programme aimed at answering these questions. In this chapter we will report some of our findings and conclusions from our attempts to explore the scientific implications of the experiential learning model. More specifically, we will seek to elaborate four implications of the experiential learning process:

(1) The integration of the cognitive and socio-emotional perspectives on learning.

(2) The role of individual differences in learning style.

(3) The concept of growth and development inherent in the experiential learning model.

(4) A model of learning environments that is commensurate with the experiential learning process.

Learning as an integrated cognitive and socio-emotional process

Since its inception and the classic studies by Lewin, Lippitt and White (1939) on leadership, the field of group dynamics has been dominated by a socio-emotional perspective, a perspective generated in a large measure by the insights of Freud and psychoanalysis. As a result the models of learning and change in group theory have tended to greatly emphasize the role of feelings and interpersonal relationships; such factors as trust, identification, inclusion, control, affection, interpersonal perception and communication. Even those specialized areas of group theory concerned with more cognitive activities such as problem-solving and creativity (e.g. Gordon, 1961) have in the end placed great emphasis on emotional, motivational and social factors.

The experiential learning model, however, emphasizes that learning and change result from the *integration* of concrete emotional experiences with cognitive processes: conceptual analysis and understanding. Thus learning involves the labelling or relabelling of immediate existential experience. Leavitt and Doktor (1970) have used developmental-cognitive terminology to explain (relabel) seemingly 'mystical' existential experience with meaningful results. To understand the learning process we must understand not only the factors which enable the person to gain contact with his own experience but also the cognitive processes which enable him to make sense of his experience.

This insight is illustrated no better than in the actual historical event that spawned it; the 'discovery' of the T-group (see Marrow, 1969). In the summer of 1946 Lewin and his colleagues, most notably Ronald Lippitt, Leland Bradford and Kenneth Benne set out to design a new approach to leadership and group dynamics training for the Connecticut State Interracial Commission. The two-week training programme began with an experiential emphasis encouraging group discussion and decision making in an atmosphere where staff and partici-pants treated one another as peers. In addition the research and training staff collected extensive observations and recordings of the groups' activities. When the participants went home at night the research staff gathered together to report and analyse the data collected during the day. Most of the staff felt that trainees should not be involved in these analytical sessions where their ex-periences and behaviour were being discussed for fear that the discussions might be harmful to them. Lewin was receptive, however, when a small group of participants asked to join in these discussions. One of the men who was there, Ronald Lippitt (1949), describes what happened in the discussion meeting that three trainees attended.

'Sometime during the evening, an observer made some remarks about the behavior of one of the three persons who were sitting in—a woman trainee. She broke in to disagree with the observation and described it from her point of view. For a while there was quite an active dialogue between the research observer, the trainer, and the trainee about the interpretation of the event, with Kurt an active prober, obviously enjoying this different source of data that had to·be coped with and integrated.'

'At the end of the evening, the trainees asked if they could come back for the next meeting at which their behavior would be evaluated. Kurt, feeling that it has been a valuable contribution rather than an intrusion, enthusiastically agreed to their return. The next night at least half of the fifty or sixty participants were there as a result of the grapevine reporting of the activity by the three delegates.'

'The evening session from then on became the significant learning experience of the day, with the focus on actual behavioral events and with active dialogue about differences of interpretation and observations of the events by those who had participated in them.'

Thus the discovery was made that learning is best facilitated in an environ-ment where there is dialectic tension and conflict between immediate, concrete experience and analytic detachment. By bringing together the immediate ex-periences of the trainees and the conceptual models of the staff in an open atmosphere where inputs from both perspectives could challenge and stimulate the other, a learning environment occurred with remarkable vitality and creativity.

Of central importance here is the idea that learning is by its very nature a tension and conflict-filled process. New knowledge, skills or attitudes are achieved through confrontation among the four perspectives in the experiential learning model. The learner, if he is to be effective, needs four different kinds of abilities—*Concrete Experience* abilities (CE), *Reflective Observation* abilities (RO), *Abstract Conceptualization* abilities (AC) and *Active Experimentation*

(AE) abilities. That is, he must be able to involve himself fully, openly and without bias in new experiences (CE), he must be able to reflect on and observe these experiences from many perspectives (RO), he must be able to create concepts that integrate his observations into logically sound theories (AC) and he must be able to use these theories to make decisions and solve problems (AE). Yet this ideal is difficult to achieve. How can one act and reflect at the same time? How can one be concrete and immediate and still be theoretical? Learning requires abilities that are polar opposites and the learner, as a result, must continually choose which set of learning abilities he will bring to bear in any specific learning situation. More specifically, there are two primary dimensions to the learning process. The first dimension represents the concrete experiencing of events at one end and abstract conceptualization at the other. The other dimension has active experimentation at one extreme and reflective observation at the other. Thus, in the process of learning one moves in varying degrees from actor to observer, and from specific involvement to general analytic detachment.

Most cognitive psychologists (e.g., Flavell, 1963; Bruner, 1960, 1966; Harvey, Hunt and Schroder, 1961) see the concrete/abstract dimension as a primary dimension on which cognitive growth and learning occurs. Goldstein and Scheerer (1941, p. 4) suggest that great abstractness results in the development of the following abilities:

(1) To detach our ego from the outer world and from inner experience.
(2) To assume a mental set.
(3) To account for acts to oneself; to verbalize the account.
(4) To shift reflectively from one aspect of the situation to another.
(5) To hold in mind simultaneously various aspects.
(6) To grasp the essential of a given whole: to break up a given whole into parts to isolate and to synthesize them.
(7) To abstract common properties reflectively; to form hierarchic concepts.
(8) To plan ahead ideationally, to assume an attitude toward the more possible and to think or perform symbolically.

Concreteness, on the other hand, represents the absence of these abilities—the immersion in and domination by one's immediate experiences. Yet as the circular model of the learning process would imply, abstractness is not exclusively good and concreteness exclusively bad. To be creative requires that one be able to experience anew, freed somewhat from the constraints of previous abstract concepts. In psychoanalytic theory this need for a concrete, childlike perspective in the creative process is referred to as regression in the service of the ego (Kris, 1952). Bruner (1966) in his essay on the conditions for creativity further emphasizes the dialectic tension between abstract detachment and concrete involvement. For him the creative act is a product of detachment and commitment, of passion and decorum, and of a freedom to be dominated by the object of one's inquiry.

The active/reflective dimension is the other major dimension of cognitive growth and learning. As growth occurs, thought becomes more reflective and internalized, based more on the manipulation of symbols and images than overt actions. The modes of active experimentation and reflection, like abstractness/ concreteness, stand in opposition to one another. Reflection tends to inhibit action and vice versa. For example, Singer (1968) has found that children who have active internal fantasy lives are more capable of inhibiting action for long periods of time than are children with little internal fantasy life. Kagan (1964) has found on the other hand that very active orientations toward learning situations inhibit reflection and thereby preclude the development of analytic concepts. Herein lies the second major dialectic in the learning process—the tension between actively testing the implications of one's hypotheses and re-flectively interpreting data already collected.

The experiential learning model depicts learning as a process of conflict confrontation and resolution among four basic adaptive modes or ways of relating to the world; Concrete Experience *vs* Abstract Conceptualization and Active Experimentation *vs* Reflective Observation. Individuals as a result of their experiences come to develop characteristic styles of resolving these con-flicts—consistent preferences for one adaptive mode over another. It is to this question of individual differences in learning styles we now turn.

Individual learning styles and the Learning Style Inventory

As a result of our hereditary equipment, our particular past life experience and the demands of our present environment most people develop learning styles that emphasize some learning abilities over others. Through socialization experiences in family, school and work we each come to resolve the conflicts between being active and reflective and between being immediate and analytical in characteristic ways. Some people develop minds that excell at assimilating disparate facts into coherent theories, yet these same people are incapable of, or uninterested in, deducing hypotheses from their theory. Others are logical geniuses but find it impossible to involve and surrender themselves to an ex-perience. And so on. A mathematician may come to place great emphasis on abstract concepts while a poet may value concrete experience more highly. A manager may primarily concerned with the active application of ideas while a naturalist may develop his observational skills highly. Each of us has, in a unique way, developed a learning style that has some weak and strong points. We have developed a simple self-description inventory, the Learning Style Inventory (LSI), that is designed to measure an individual's strengths and weak-nesses as a learner. The LSI measures an individual's relative emphasis on the four learning abilities—Concrete Experience (CE), Reflective Observation (RO), Abstract Conceptualization (AC) and Active Experimentation (AE) by asking him, several different times, to rank-order four words that describe these different abilities. For example, one set of four words is 'Feeling' (CE), 'Watch-ing' (RO), 'Thinking' (AC), 'Doing' (AE). The inventory yields six scores, CE, RO, AC and AE plus two combination scores that indicate the extent to which an individual emphasizes abstractness over concreteness (AC–CE) and the extent to which an individual emphasizes active experimentation over reflection (AE–RO).

The LSI was administered to 800 practising managers and graduate students in management to obtain norms for the management population. In general these managers tended to emphasize Active Experimentation over Reflective Observation. In addition, managers with graduate degrees tended to rate their abstract (AC) learning skills higher.* While the individuals we tested showed many different patterns of scores on the LSI, we have identified four statistically prevalent types of learning styles. We have called these four styles—the Converger, the Diverger, the Assimilator and the Accommodator.† The following is a summary of the characteristics of these types based both on our research and clinical observation of these patterns of LSI scores.

The *Converger*'s dominant learning abilities are Abstract Conceptualization (AC) and Active Experimentation (AE). His greatest strength lies in the practical application of ideas. We have called this learning style the 'Converger' because a person with this style seems to do best in those situations like conventional intelligence tests where there is a single correct answer or solution to a question or problem (*cf.* Torrealba, 1972). His knowledge is organized in such a way that, through hypothetical-deductive reasoning, he can focus it on specific problems. Liam Hudson's (1966) research in this style of learning (using different measures than the LSI) shows that convergers are relatively unemotional, preferring to deal with things rather than people. They tend to have narrow interests, and choose to specialize in the physical sciences. Our research shows that this learning style is characteristic of many engineers (Kolb, 1973).

The *Diverger* has the opposite learning strength of the converger. He is best at Concrete Experience (CE) and Reflective Observation (RO). His greatest strength lies in his imaginative ability. He excells in the ability to view concrete situations from many perspectives and to organize many relationships into a meaningful 'gestalt'. We have labelled this style 'Diverger' because a person of this type performs better in situations that call for generation of ideas such as a 'brainstorming' idea session. Hudson's (1966) work on this particular learning style shows that divergers are interested in people and tend to be imaginative and emotional. They have broad cultural interests and tend to specialize in arts. Our research shows that this style is characteristic of persons with humanities and liberal arts backgrounds.

The *Assimilator*'s dominant learning abilities are Abstract Conceptualization (AC) and Reflective Observation (RO). His greatest strength lies in his ability to create theoretical models. He excells in inductive reasoning; in assimilating

---

*The details of the inventory construction along with preliminary reliability and validity studies are described in Kolb (1973). The inventory itself along with management norms appears in Kolb, Rubin and McIntyre (1971) *Organizational Psychology: An Experiential Approach*. Englewood Cliffs, N.J.: Prentice-Hall.

† The reason that there are four dominant styles is that AC and CE are highly negatively correlated as are RO and AE. Thus individuals who score high on both AC and CE or on both AE and RO with less frequency than do the other four combinations of LSI scores.

disparate observations into an integrated explanation (Growchow, 1973). He, like the converger, is less interested in people and more concerned with the practical use of theories. For him it is more important that the theory be logically sound and precise. As a result, this learning style is more characteristic of the basic sciences and mathematics rather than the applied sciences. In organizations this learning style is found most often in the research and planning departments (Kolb, 1973).

The *Accommodator* has the opposite strength of the Assimilator. He is best at Concrete Experience (CE) and Active Experimentation (AE). His greatest strength lies in doing things; in carrying out plans and experiments and involving himself in new experiences. He tends to be more of a risk-taker than people with the other three learning styles. We have labelled this style 'Accommodator' because he tends to excell in those situations where he must adapt himself to specific immediate circumstances. He tends to solve problems in an intuitive trial and error manner (Growchow, 1973) relying heavily on other people for information rather than his own analytic ability (Stabell, 1973).

These differences in learning styles can be illustrated graphically by the correspondence between their LSI scores and their undergraduate majors. This is done by plotting the average LSI scores for managers in our sample who reported their undergraduate college major (only those majors with more than 10 people responding are included) (see Figure 2). The distribution of undergraduate majors on the learning style grid is quite consistent with our theory.* Undergraduate business majors tend to have accommodative learning styles while engineers on the average fall in the convergent quadrant. History, English, political science and psychology majors all have divergent learning styles. Mathematics and chemistry majors have assimilative learning styles along with economics and sociology. Physics majors are very abstract falling between the convergent and assimilative quadrant. What these data show is that one's undergraduate education is a major factor in the development of this learning style. Whether this is because individuals are shaped by the fields they enter or because of the selection processes that put people into and out of disciplines is an open question at this point. Most probably both factors are operating— people choose fields which are consistent with their learning styles and are further shaped to fit the learning norms of their field once they are in it. When

*Many of these differences in LSI scores among disciplines are highly statistically significant especially when they are grouped into physical sciences, social sciences and the arts (see Kolb, 1973 for details).

Some cautions are in order in interpreting this data. First, it should be remembered that all of the individuals in the sample are managers or managers-to-be. In addition most of these people have completed or are in graduate school. These two facts should produce learning styles that are somewhat more active and abstract than the population at large. (As indicated by total sample mean scores on AC–CE and AE–RO of +4·5 and +2·9 respectively.) The interaction between career, high level of education and undergraduate major may produce distinctive learning styles. For example, physicists who are not in industry may be somewhat more reflective than those in this sample. Secondly, undergraduate majors are described only in the most gross terms. There are many forms of engineering or psychology. A business major at one school can be quite different than that at another.

40

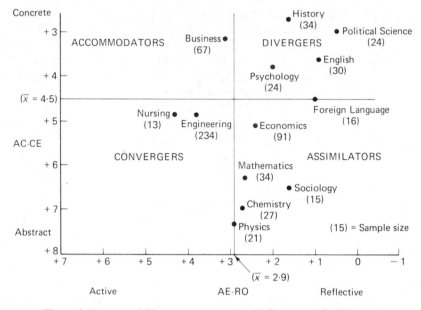

Figure 2. Average LSI scores on Active/Reflective (AE–RO) and Abstract/Concrete (AC–CE) by undergraduate college major

there is a mismatch between the field's learning norms and the individual's learning style, people will either change or leave the field.

Growth and development in the experiential learning model

In addition to providing a framework for conceptualizing individual differences in styles of adaptation to the world, the experiential learning model suggests more normative directions for human growth and development. As we have seen in the previous section individual learning styles affect how people learn not only in the limited educational sense but also in the broader aspects of adaptation to life such as decision-making, problem-solving and life style in general. Experiential learning is not a molecular educational concept but rather is a molar concept describing the central process of human adaptation to the social and physical environment. It is an holistic concept much akin to the Jungian theory of psychological types (Jung, 1923) in that it seeks to describe the emergence of basic life orientations as a function of dialectic tensions between basic modes of relating to the world. As such it encompasses other more limited adaptative concepts such as creativity, problem-solving, decision-making and attitude change that focus heavily on one or another of the basic aspects of adaptation. Thus creativity research has tended to focus on the divergent (concrete and reflective) factors in adaptation such as tolerance for ambiguity, metaphorical thinking and flexibility, while research on decision-making has emphasized more convergent (abstract and active) adaptive factors such as the rational evaluation of solution alternatives.

From this broader perspective learning becomes a central life task and how one learns becomes a major determinant of the course of his personal development. The experiential learning model provides a means of mapping these different developmental paths and a normative adaptative ideal—a learning process wherein the individual has highly developed abilities to experience, observe, conceptualize and experiment. In what follows we will describe our current thinking about these developmental paths and the process of growth toward this adaptive ideal.

The human growth process is divided into three broad developmental stages. The first stage, *Acquisition*, extends from birth to adolescence and marks the acquisition of basic learning abilities and cognitive structures. The second stage, *Specialization*, extends through formal education and/or career training and the early experiences of adulthood in work and personal life. In this stage development primarily follows paths that accentuate a particular learning style. Individuals shaped by social, educational and organizational socialization forces develop increased competence in a specialized mode of adaptation that enables them to master the particular life tasks they encounter in their chosen career (in the broadest sense of that word) path. This stage, in our thinking, terminates at mid-career although the specific chronology of the transition to stage three will vary widely from person to person and from one career path to another. The third stage, *Integration*, is marked by the reassertion and expression of the non-dominant adaptive modes or learning styles. Means of adapting to the world that have been suppressed and lay fallow in favour of the development of the more highly rewarded dominant learning style now find expression in the form of new career interests, changes in life style and/or new innovation and creativity in one's chosen career.

Through these three stages growth proceeds from a state of embededness, defensiveness, dependency and reaction to a state of self-actualization, independence, pro-action and self-direction. This process is marked by increasing complexity and relativism in dealing with the world and one's experiences and by higher-level integrations of the dialectic conflicts between the four primary adaptive modes—Concrete Experience, Reflective Observation, Abstract Conceptualization and Active Experimentation. With each of these four modes a major dimension of personal growth is associated. Development in the Concrete Experience adaptive mode is characterized by increases in *Affective Complexity*. Development in the Reflective Observation mode is characterized by increases in *Perceptual Complexity*. Development in the Abstract Conceptualization and Active Experimentation modes are characterized respectively by increases in *Symbolic Complexity* and *Behavioural Complexity*.

In the early stages of development, progress along one of these four dimensions can occur with relative independence from the others. The child and young adult, for example, can develop highly sophisticated symbolic proficiencies and remain naive emotionally. At the highest stages of development however the adaptive commitment to learning and creativity produces a strong need for integration of the four adaptive modes. Development in one mode precipitates development in the others. Increases in symbolic complexity for example refine and sharpen both perceptual and behavioural possibilities. Thus complexity and the integration of dialectic conflicts among the adaptive modes are the hallmarks of true creativity and growth. Albert Einstein in his personal account of his own development illustrates well the dialectic nature of the states of adaptive functioning in scientific inquiry.

'For me it is not dubious that our thinking goes on for the most part without use of signs (words) and beyond that to a considerable degree unconsciously. For how, otherwise should it happen that sometimes we "wonder" quite spontaneously about some experience? This "wondering" seems to occur when an experience comes into conflict with a world of concepts which is already sufficiently fixed in us. Whenever such a conflict is experienced hard and intensively it reacts back upon our thought world in a decisive way. The development of this thought world is in a certain sense a continuous flight from "wonder"...'

'I see on the one side the totality of sense experiences and, on the other, the totality of the concepts and propositions which are laid down in books. The relations between the concepts and propositions among themselves and each other are of a logical nature, and the business of logical thinking is strictly limited to the achievement of the connection between concepts and propositions among each other according to firmly laid down rules, which are the concern of logic. The concepts and propositions get "meaning", viz. "content", only through their connection with sense-experiences. The connection of the latter with the former is purely intuitive, not itself of a logical nature. The degree of certainty with which this relation, viz., intuitive connection, can be undertaken, and nothing else, differentiates empty phantasy from scientific "truth".' (Schilpp, 1949.) (From *Albert Einstein—Philosopher Scientist*, by permission of Open Court Publishing Co.)

Figure 3 graphically illustrates the experiential learning model of growth and development as it has been outlined thus far. The four dimensions of growth are depicted in the shape of a cone the base of which represents the lower stages of development and the apex of which represents the peak of development— representing the fact that the four dimensions become more highly integrated at higher stages of development. Any individual learning style would be represented on this cone by four data points on the four vertical dimensions of development. Thus a converger in developmental stage two (specialization) would be characterized by high complexity in the symbolic and behavioural modes and lower complexity in the affective and perceptual modes. As he moved into stage three of development his complexity scores in the affective and perceptual modes would increase. With this broad overview of the model let us now examine in more detail the processes of development in each of the three developmental stages.

While we have depicted the stages of the growth process in the form of a simple three layer cone, the actual process of growth in any single individual life history probably proceeds through successive oscillations from one stage to another. Thus a person may move from stage two to three in several separate sub-phases of integrative advances followed by consolidation or regression into specialization.

Stage one—Acquisition

We have found significant parallels between the experiential learning model

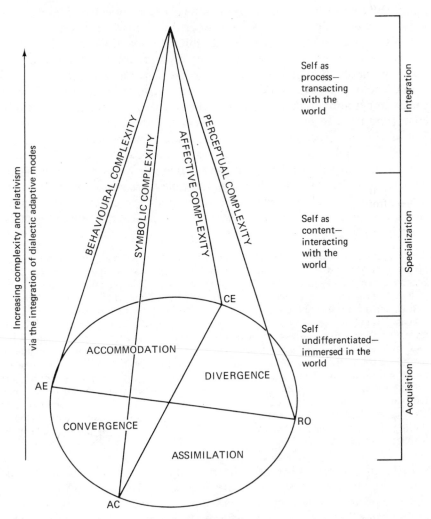

Figure 3. The experiential learning theory of growth and development

and the theory of learning implicit in Piaget's theory of cognitive development. By examining the characteristics of the stages of early cognitive development we can obtain a more complete picture of the acquisition stage of the experiential learning process. Piaget's work has identified four major stages of cognitive growth that occur from birth to about the age of 14–16. In the first stage (0–2 years) the child is predominantly concrete and active in his learning style. This stage is called the sensory-motor stage. Learning is predominantly *enactive* through feeling, touching and handling. Representation is based on action, e.g., 'a hole is to dig'. Perhaps the greatest accomplishment of this period is the development of goal-oriented behaviour. 'The sensory-motor period shows a remarkable evolution from non-intentional habits to experimental and exploratory activity which is obviously intentional or goal-oriented' (Flavell, 1963, p. 107). Yet the child has a few schemes or theories into which he can assimilate events and as a result his primary stance toward the world is accommodative. Environment plays a major role in shaping his ideas and intentions. Learning occurs primarily through the association between stimulus and response.

In the second stage (2–6 years) the child retains his concrete orientation but begins to develop a reflective orientation as he begins to internalize actions, converting them to images. This stage is called 'the representational stage'. Learning is now predominantly *ikonic* in nature, through the manipulation of observations and images. The child is now freed somewhat from his immersion in immediate experience, and as a result is free to play with and manipulate his images of the world. At this stage the child's primary stance toward the world is *divergent*. He is captivated with his ability to collect images and to view the world from different perspectives. Consider Bruner's description of the child at this stage:

'What appears next in the development is a great acheivement. Images develop an autonomous status, they become great summarizers of action. By age three the child has become a paragon of sensory distractibility. He is victim of the laws of vividness, and his action pattern is a series of encounters with this bright thing which is then replaced by that chromatically splendid one, which in turn gives way to the next noisy one. And so it goes. Visual memory at this stage seems to be highly concrete and specific. What is intruiging about this period is that the child is a creature of the moment; the image of the moment is sufficient and it is controlled by a single feature of the situation. The child can reproduce things that were there before—in the form that was there before. He can reproduce a pattern of nine glasses laid out in rows and columns with diameter and height varying systematically. Indeed, he does it as well as a seven year-old. But he can only reproduce the order the way it was—with height increasing from left to right and diameter from top to bottom. The likeness of equivalent patterns (for instance, with diameter varying from left to right) is lost on the younger child. He can copy but not transpose.' (Bruner, 1966, p. 13.)

In the third stage (7–11 years) the intensive development of abstract symbolic powers begins. This first symbolic developmental stage Piaget calls the stage of concrete operations. Learning in this stage is governed by the logic of *classes and relations*. The child in this stage further increases his independence from his immediate experiential world through the development of inductive powers. 'The structure of concrete operations are' as Flavell (1963, p. 203) suggests, 'rather like parking lots whose individual parking spaces are now occupied and now empty; the spaces themselves endure, however, and leave their owner to look beyond the cars actually present towards potential, future occupants of the vacant and to-be-vacant spaces.' Thus, in contrast to the child in the sensory-motor stage whose learning style was basically accommodative the child at the stage of concrete operations is basically *assimilative* in his learning style. He begins to develop concepts and theories which select and give shape to his experiences.

Piaget's final stage of cognitive development comes with the onset of adolescence (12–15 years). In this stage the adolescent moves from symbolic processes based on concrete operations to the symbolic processes of *representa-tional logic*. He now returns to a more active orientation but it is an active orientation that is now modified by the development of the reflective and abstractive powers that preceded it. The symbolic powers he now possesses enable him to engage in hypothetical-deductive reasoning. He develops the possible implications of his theories and proceeds to experimentally test which of these are true. As such his basic learning style is *convergent* in contrast to the divergent orientation of the child in the representational stage.

'...formal thought is for Piaget not so much this or that specific behavior as it is a generalized *orientation*, sometimes explicit and sometimes implicit, towards problem-solving; an orientation towards organizing data (combinatorial analysis), towards isolation and control of variables, towards the hypothetical and towards logical justification and proof.' (Flavell, 1963, p. 211.)

From this brief summary of cognitive development theory we can see the outlines of those basic developmental processes which shape the basic learning process of adults. The essential accomplishments in this stage of development are the acquisition of basic cognitive structures and the emergence from im-mersion in one's experience where self and world are undifferentiated to a sense of self and self-control.

Stage two—specialization

Although the child in his early experiences in family and school may have already begun to develop specialized preferences and abilities in his learning style (cf. Hudson, 1966), in the later years of secondary school and beyond the individual begins to make choices which will significantly shape the course of his development. The choice of college *vs* trade apprenticeship, the choice of academic specialization, and even such cultural factors as the choice of where to live begin to selectively determine the socialization experiences the individual will have and thereby influence and shape his mode of adaptation to the world. The choices an individual makes in this process tend to have an accentuating, self-fulfilling quality that promotes specialization.

In the experiential learning theory of adult development stability and change in life paths are seen as resulting from the interaction between internal personal-ity dynamics and external social forces in a manner much like that described by Super (Super *et al.*, 1963). The most powerful developmental dynamic that emerges from this interaction is the tendency for there to be a closer and closer match between self-characteristics and environmental demands. This match comes about in two ways—(1) environments tend to change personal character-istics to fit them, i.e. socialization, and (2) individuals tend to select themselves into environments that are consistent with their personal characteristics. Thus development in general tends to follow a path toward accentuation of personal characteristics and skills (Feldman and Newcomb, 1969; Kolb, 1973) in that development is a product of the interaction between choices and socialization experiences that match these choice dispositions such that resulting experiences further reinforce the same choice disposition for later experience. Most adult life paths follow a cycle of job, educational and life style choices that build upon the experiences resulting from previous similar choices. Indeed the common stereotype of the successful career is a graded ladder of similar experiences on which one climbs to success and fulfilment.

Some examples from our research will serve to illustrate this process of specialization in learning style as a result of accentuation. In a first attempt to examine the details of this process, Plovnick (1971) studied a major university department using the concepts of convergence and divergence defined by Hudson (1966). He concluded that the major emphasis in physics education was on convergent learning. He predicted that physics students who had convergent learning styles would be content with their majors whereas physics majors who were divergent in their learning styles would be more uncertain of physics as a career and would take more courses outside of the physics department than their convergent colleagues. His predictions were confirmed. Those students who were not fitted for the convergent learning style required in physics tended to turn away from physics as a profession.

In another study currently in progress Plovnick (1974) is attempting to identify a correspondence between the learning style of medical students and their choices for career specialization. In addition he is attempting to identify relationships between learning styles and the process these students go through in making these choices. Initial data indicate that the different medical career paths (e.g. academic medicine, private practice, public health, etc.) attract people with different characteristic learning styles. Those that have styles that do not 'match' their chosen career path indicate great uncertainty about whether they will continue to pursue that path. Further, students with different styles seem to be utilizing different sources of information and influence in the career development process. For example, concrete students seem to do more 'identification' with attractive role models while abstract-reflective students are influenced more by course work. These 'choices' about sources of influence then act to accentuate the learning style that led to the choice, since courses are inclined to be more abstract/reflective while close personal relationships are inclined to reinforce a more concrete style.

In another unpublished study we examined the accentuation process as it operated at the molecular level of course choice. This research examined the choice of sensitivity training by MIT graduate students in management. When we tested the learning styles of students who chose an elective sensitivity training laboratory, we found that they tended to be more concrete (CE) and reflective (RO) than those who chose not to attend the lab. When these individuals with divergent learning styles completed the training sessions their scores became even more concrete and reflective, accentuating their disposition toward divergent learning experiences.

As part of a large survey of MIT seniors (Kolb and Goldman, 1973) we selected for intensive case study four university departments whose learning style demands matched the four dominant learning styles. The four departments chosen and their learning style demand as measured by several criteria were Mechanical Engineering = Accommodator, Humanities = Diverger, Mathematics = Assimilator and Economics = Converger.

To study the career choices of the students in the four departments each student's LSI scores were used to position him on the LSI grid with a notation of the career field he has chosen to pursue after graduation. If the student was planning to attend graduate school his career field was circled. If the accentuation process were operating in the career choices of the students we should find that those students who fall in the same quadrent as the norms of their academic major should be more likely to pursue careers and graduate training directly related to that major while students with learning styles that differ from their discipline norms should be more inclined to pursue other careers and not attend graduate school in their discipline. We can illustrate this pattern by examining students in the mathematics department (Figure 4). Ten of the thirteen mathematics students (80%) whose learning styles were congruent with departmental norms chose careers and graduate training in mathematics. Only two of the thirteen students (15%) whose learning styles are not congruent plan both careers and graduate training in math (these differences are significant using the Fisher Exact Test $p < 01$). Similar patterns occurred in the other three departments.

To further test the accentuation process in the four departments we examined whether the student's choice/experience career development cycle indeed operated as an accentuating positive feedback loop. If this were so then those students whose learning style dispositions matched and were reinforced by their discipline demands should show a greater commitment to their choice of future career field than those whose learning styles were not reinforced by their experiences in their discipline. As part of a questionnaire students were asked to rate how important it was for them to pursue their chosen career field. In all four departments the average importance rating was higher for the students with a match between learning style and discipline norms (the differences being statistically significant in the mechanical engineering and economics departments). Thus it seems that learning experiences that reinforce learning style dispositions tend to produce greater commitment in career choices than those learning experiences that do not reinforce learning style dispositions.

From the above research we draw two main conclusions. First the experiential learning typology seems to provide a useful grid for mapping individual differences in learning style and for mapping corresponding differences in the environmental demands of different career paths. As such it is a potentially powerful tool for describing the differentiated paths of adult development. Secondly, the above data present enticing if not definitive evidence that early career choices tend to follow a path toward accentuation of one's learning style. Learning experiences congruent with learning styles tend to positively influence the choice of future learning and work experiences that reinforce that particular learning style. On the other hand, those students who find a

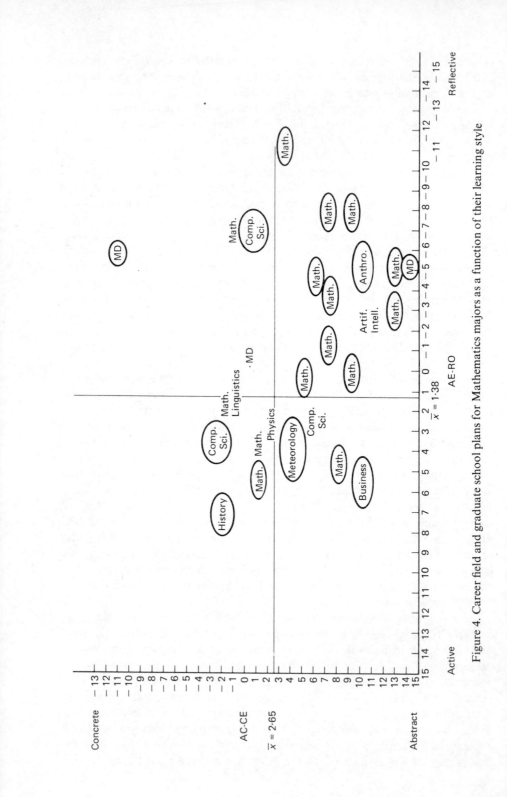

Figure 4. Career field and graduate school plans for Mathematics majors as a function of their learning style

learning environment incongruent with their learning style tend to move away from that kind of environment in future learning and work choices. The research to date suggests that accentuation is the most powerful force in early adult development. The primary reason for the strength of the accentuation forces in early career seems to stem from identity pressures to choose *a* job and *a* career. Fulfilment needs seem to be second priority at this time.

Thus in the second stage of development the individual achieves a sense of identity through the acquisition of a specialized adaptive competence in dealing with the demands of his chosen 'career'. His sense of self-worth is based on the rewards and recognition he receives for doing his 'work' well. The self in this stage is defined primarily in terms of *content*; things I can do, experiences I have had, goods and qualities I possess. The primary mode of relating to the world is *interaction*—I act on the world (build the bridge, raise the family) and the world acts on me (pays me money, fills me with bits of knowledge) but neither is fundamentally changed by the other. The radical educator Paulo Freire describes this stage-two sense of self and the 'banking' concept of education which he feels serves to prevent development beyond stage two:

'Implicit in the banking concept is the assumption of a dichotomy between man and the world: man is merely *in* the world, not *with* the world or with others; man is spectator, not re-creator. In this view, man is not a conscious being; he is rather the possessor of *a* consciousness; an empty "mind" passively open to the reception of deposits of reality from the world outside ....

It follows logically from the banking notion of consciousness that the educators role is to regulate the way the world "enters into" the students. His task is to organize a process which already occurs spontaneously, to "fill" the students by making deposists of information which he considers to constitute true knowledge. And since men "receive" the world as passive entities, education should make them more passive still, and adapt them to the world. The educated man is the adapted man, because he is better "fit" for the world.' (Freire, 1974.)

Stage three—integration

Paulo Freire's sense of frustration and pessimism about the destructive effects that societies, socializing institutions have on personal fulfilment has been a continuing theme of Western thought, particularly since the Enlightenment. The transition from stage two to stage three of development is marked by the individual's personal, existential confrontation of this conflict.

In 1826 the German poet and historian, Friedrich Schiller wrote:

'When the commonwealth makes the office or function the measure of the man, when of its citizens it does homage only to the memory in one, to a tabulating intelligence in another, and to a mechanical capacity in a third; when here, regardless of character, it urges only towards knowledge while there it encourages a spirit of order and law-abiding behavior with the profoundest intellectual obscurantism—when, at the same time, it wishes these single accomplishments of the subject to be carried to just as great an intensity as it absolves him of extensity—is it to be wondered at that the remaining faculties of the mind are neglected, in order to bestow every care upon the special one which it honours and rewards?' (Schiller, 1826.)

Later, Freud and his followers in psychoanalysis developed the socio-emotional dimensions of this conflict between individual and society—libidinous instincts clashing with repressive social demands. In modern organization theory this conflict has been most clearly articulated by Argyris (1962).

Yet it is Carl Jung in his theory of psychological types, whose formulation of this conflict and the dimensions of its resolution have the most meaning for the experiential learning theory of development. The Jungian theory of types, like the experiential learning model, is based on a dialectic model of adaptation to the world. Fulfilment, or individuation as Jung calls it, is accomplished by higher-level integration and expression of non-dominant modes of dealing with the world. This drive for fulfilment, however, is thwarted by the needs of civilization. Commenting on the passage by Schiller cited earlier Jung says:

'The favouritism of the superior function is just as serviceable to society as it is prejudicial to the individuality. This prejudicial effect has reached such a pitch that the great organizations of our present day civilization actually strive for the complete disintegration of the individual, since their very existence depends upon a mechanical application of the preferred individual functions of men. It is not man that counts but his one differentiated function. Man no longer appears as man in collective civilization: he is merely represented by a function—nay, further, he is even exclusively identified with this function and denied any responsible membership to the other inferior functions. Thus, the modern individual sinks to the level of a mere function, because this it is that represents a collective value and alone affords a possibility of livelihood. But as Schiller clearly discerns, differentiation of function could have come about in no other way: "There was no other means to develop man's manifold capacities than to set them one against the other. This antagonism of human qualities is the great instrument of culture; it is only the instrument, however, for so long as it endures man is only upon the way to culture"'. (Jung, 1923.)

It is the personal experience of this conflict between social demands and personal fulfilment and the corresponding recognition of self-as-object that precipitates the individual's transition into the integrative stage of development. The experience can develop as a gradual process of awakening that parallels specialized development in stage two or it can occur dramatically as a result of a life crisis such as divorce or losing one's job. Some may never have this experience, so immersed are they in the societal reward system for performing their differentiated specialized function.

With this new awareness the individual experiences a shift in the frame of reference he uses to experience life, evaluate activities and make choices. The nature of this shift depends upon the specifics of the individual's dominant and non-expressed adaptive modes. For the reflective person the awakening of the active mode brings a new sense of risk to his life. Rather than being influenced he now sees opportunities to influence. He can shape his own experience rather than observing and accepting experiences as they happen to him. For the person who has specialized in the active mode the emergence of his reflective side broadens his range of choice and deepens his ability to sense implications of his actions. For the specialist in the concrete mode the abstract perspective gives new continuity and direction to his experience. The abstract specialist with his new sense of immediate experience finds new life and meaning in his constructions of reality.

The net effect of these shifts in perspective is an increasing experience of self as *process*. A learning process that has previously been blocked by the repression of the non-specialized adaptive modes is now experienced deeply to be the essence of self. Carl Rogers in his description of the peak of human functioning describes this state as well as anyone:

'There is a growing and continuing sense of acceptant ownership of these changing feelings, a basic trust in his own process. Experiencing has lost almost completely its structure bound aspects and becomes process experiencing—that is, the situation is experienced and interpreted in its newness, not as the past. The self becomes increasingly simply the subjective and reflexive awareness of experiencing. The self is much less frequently a preceived object, and much more frequently something confidently felt in process. Personal constructs are tentatively reformulated, to be validated against further experience, but even then to be held loosely. Internal communication is clear, with feelings and symbols well matched, and fresh terms for new feelings. There is the experiencing of effective choice of new ways of being.' (Rogers, 1961.)

The key to this new sense of self-as-process lies in the re-establishment of the reciprocity between the dialectic modes of adaptation. Jung in his analysis of Schiller's work expresses it this way.

'...the idea of a "reciprocity" between the two instincts, a community of interest or *symbiosis*, as we should perhaps prefer to call it, in which the waste products of the one would be the supply of the other. Schiller himself says that "the reciprocity of the two instincts consists in this, that the effectiveness of the one both *restricts* and *establishes* the other, and that each in its own separate sphere can reach its highest manifestation only through the activity of the other." ' (Jung, 1923.)

With this overview of the three stages of development we now turn to an analysis of the learning environments that shape the growth process.

Towards a new view of learning environments

In this section we want to share some of our notions about learning environments, particularly as they relate to experiential learning theory. These ideas come from our work in trying to relate learning to the environment and represent an initial statement of where we are now. Our efforts to understand and further develop learning theory will be fruitful if the results eventually affect the deliberate use of models (based on theory) to design and implement more effective learning situations. We must therefore consider the basic paradigm posed by Lewin: $B = f(P,E)$. Any theory of learning must deal with person–environment interactions in order to be useful. More exactly, environmental differences must be expressed in a form commensurate with individual differences so that meaningful statements about the consequences of person–environment interactions can be made. Our current objective is to understand how people with different learning styles react to and interact with which environmental factors and with what results.

As Dubin and Taveggia (1968) found in their summary of research on lecture methods *vs* discussion methods, nothing can be concluded regarding this level of environmental analysis (comparing educational approaches) except that a given method was helpful to some students some of the time for some specific test. Unless we have a model of an environment that can be related to both inputs (different learning styles) and outputs (different learning goals) we can do little to understand or help shape effective learning situations. To have such an 'applied' model of environments, the three theoretical implications of experiential learning discussed so far in this chapter suggest the following:

(1) 'Environment' must be more broadly defined than its current meaning—formal educational approaches—in the educational research literature.

(2) Observable and controllable factors in the environment can be related to individual differences as expressed in behavioural learning styles.

(3) To be 'commensurate', person–environment interaction must be related in the context of growth and development goals for the learner.

We turn first to the concept of environment. The broader view of learning as an adaptative process has great implications for what is viewed as an educational setting. Learning, in the adaptative sense, is central to all life settings. The experiential model described in Figure 1 is much akin to problem solving which occurs everyday and everywhere. Because of their unique task and environmental demands, for instance, most work groups develop characteristic ways of thinking and working together, different styles of decision making and different approaches to solving problems. In one study (Kolb, 1973), we found that the members of functional groups of an organization had different characteristic learning styles that seemed to match the environmental demands of that particular group. Marketing managers tended to have accommodative learning styles, engineers had convergent learning styles, personnel managers had divergent learning styles and those in research departments had assimilative learning styles. Thus there seem to be styles that are best suited to particular task demands. And the interaction between learning styles and environmental demands occurs *outside* the typical educational setting. Even within traditional educational systems, the notion of environment has typically been bounded by the classroom or a subject/course where the key factors are either methods (e.g. lecture *vs* discussion) or climate variables (e.g. teacher/leadership style, seating structure, grading/reward system). Yet most classroom or course experiences are but a fraction of a total experience involving many classes, many courses, many activities outside of classrooms and so on. A teacher who sees a group of students four hours per week for twenty weeks, along with four other teachers, has a different effect on his students than if he taught them alone, twenty hours per week for four straight weeks, even if his methods and classroom climate factors remained the same. In an accelerated management curriculum for Master's students where thirty students took six courses over ten weeks, Fry and Rubin (1972) found that factors external to the classroom/courses played a key role in changing student expectations and behaviour. Factors including peer group norms, informal study groups, orientation to the programme, and general feedback sessions to the entire programme staff had major impacts on students' ability to benefit from individual courses.

Having expanded our view of what constitutes a setting wherein learning takes place, the challenge is deciding *what* it is in the environment that we should look at. One needs to understand the environment in terms that relate to learning styles—the way learners behave in situations. The four styles described earlier have been useful in distinguishing some features of the environment. A survey of over one hundred students who had completed an introductory, experientially oriented course in human factors in management at the M.I.T. Sloan School of Management indicated some trends such as the following: Accommodators found the classroom sessions most helpful (contributed most to their learning from the course) because of its lack of structure, high amount of peer-interaction, and lack of any authority figure; Assimilators least preferred the course in general because of the classroom emphasis but did find those activities requiring some conformity to directions or rules helpful as well as assigned readings and theory inputs; Divergers reported the open-ended, unstructured homework papers and self-diagnostic activites to be helpful and least preferred peer interactions in class and course requirements (e.g. number of required papers, deadlines); Convergers found instructor/expert inputs and reading linking classroom activities to the 'real world' helpful and least preferred open-ended peer discussions and group autonomy. Although far from conclusive or generalizable about person–environment interactions, this data points to the need for a more specific, micro-level analysis of environmental factors. It would not have sufficed in this case to have asked students to evaluate the 'seminar format' or the 'experiential mode' of teaching. At this level of environmental analysis, most everyone liked it, but for different reasons. Divergers liked the opportunity to watch and learn from it; Convergers liked the discussions relating it to the business world; Accommodators preferred the interactive, autonomous nature of the sessions; and Assimilators liked the role plays. Similarly in other surveys, we have found that although both Divergers and Assimilators prefer lectures, it is probably for different reasons. Both are comfortable in more passive, reflective situations but Divergers seem to be reacting most to the lecturer as a person (they also prefer faculty conferences, talks by experts and faculty feedback on papers) while the Assimilators seem to be reacting to the presence of an authority figure *per se* (they also prefer assigned readings, exams and being given a task). The fact that such data is highly interpretive only convinces us that superficial definition of environmental factors is meaningless. There needs to be a systematic exploration of how learners see situations. It is not enough to know that a lecture or lecturer was helpful or not. We need to know why. Only then can we begin to understand the person–environment interface.

Our interpretation of data like the above has led to a tentative typology of environments in terms of the personal growth dimensions discussed earlier: affective complexity, perceptual complexity, symbolic complexity and behavioural complexity. The kinds of environmental factors we now believe to be key in differentiating learning styles and stimulating growth within these styles are indicated by the following:

(1) *Affectively complex* environments are characterized by:
    (a) focus on here-and-now experiences,
    (b) legitimization of expression of feelings and emotions,
    (c) situations structured to allow ambiguity,
    (d) high degree of personalization.

(2) *Perceptually complex* environments are characterized by:
    (a) opportunities to view subject matter from different perspectives,
    (b) time to reflect and roles (e.g. listener, observer) which allow reflection,
    (c) complexity and multiplicity of observational frameworks.

(3) *Symbolically complex* environments are characterized by:
    (a) emphases on recall of concepts,
    (b) thinking or acting governed by rules of logic and inference,
    (c) situations structured to maximize certainty,
    (d) authorities respected as caretakers of knowledge.

(4) *Behaviourally complex* environments are characterized by:
    (a) responsibility for setting own learning goals,
    (b) opportunities for real risk taking,
    (c) environmental responses contingent upon self-initiated action.

We are currently in the process of clarifying and elaborating upon this typology. We are using this model in one study, for example, to understand if and how the ability to design is learned in graduate schools of architecture. In order to design, it appears that one needs both convergent skills (e.g. deductive problems solving within constraints, solutions expressed in practical terms) and divergent skills (e.g. creative or inductive thinking, ability to envision larger entity or total 'gestalt' from a subpart). Given this, how do learners with either style acquire the other? What factors in these schools contribute to either type of skill development and for which type of learner? Are there events or structures that help convergers become more divergent (enable them to integrate) and vice versa? If our typology above is useful in answering these kinds of questions then we will have taken a major step towards understanding learner–environment interactions. To test its applicability we hope to find that learners with similar styles report similar environmental factors as preferable and that these trends correlate positively with preferred events in their educational settings, events that have been independently rated or typed using the above dimensions.

Knowing 'what' to be concerned with in the environment is still, however, insufficient to be able to deliberately design learning situations. For environmental factors to be 'commensurate' with learning styles one must also consider the 'for what' question. As Hunt (1974) points out, matching environments to learners can be done on the basis of a compensatory model or a preferential model. The growth and development implications of experiential learning discussed earlier add insight to the choice between these two models. If, for example, the goal were one that involved acquisition or further specialization of knowledge, skills or attitudes that required a particular learning style, then one would try to design environments to match the preferences of that kind of learner. Most of the current research in educational environments seems to assume these goals (acquisition or specialization) because students are asked what they liked or preferred about a situation. We would speculate, for example, that a graduate school of mathematics would be designed to include those factors Assimilators 'like' because they have acquired that style as undergraduates and now want to specialize. If, on the other hand, the goal is to integrate styles by acquisition of less-preferred or least-dominant styles, then one must determine what factors are compensatory or needed to de-emphasize the preferred style of the learner and help him acquire new ways of learning. For example, Divergers who *prefer* open-ended, self-directed acitivities have reported *needing* time limits and constraints in order to learn more in a given situation where the goal was to apply and test ideas and theories they had already internalized. The point to be made here is that in addition to typical educator or employer goals in terms of desired knowledge, skill or attidude outcomes, the learner's growth and development needs must also be taken as goals. The distinction between what a learner likes, wants, needs or prefers now becomes very crucial in any effort to determine and measure environmental factors.

To summarize our model of learner–environment interaction, it is helpful to return to the previously mentioned study of an introductory, experientially based, master's-level course in human factors in management. The learning styles of the participants were predominately convergent and assimilative since most had come from engineering (e.g. chemical, aeronautical) or basic science backgrounds (physics, chemistry, mathematics). In relation to both their styles and the other courses they were taking (economics, statistics, marketing, finance) this course emphasized their non-dominant, less preferred learning skills. The course was centred around here-and-now experiences and reflective discussions in the classroom with minimal instructor leadership or conceptual input. It was thus an Affectively complex environment and varied at times from being Behaviourally complex in the class session to Perceptually complex in open-ended and introspective writing assignments. For the Convergers and Assimilators, this course had a compensatory goal to help them acquire new learning skills in order to learn and experience knowledge, skills and attitudes related to the course topic. For those who were Divergers or Accommodators, the course became more of a preferred learning situation wherein they could specialize and further develop learning styles they already had. The existence of these two goal models is born out by the fact that the Assimilators disliked the course in general and that those who took subsequent courses in organization behaviour tended to be Accommodators or Divergers.

Although the Assimilators (and some Convergers) least preferred the course, they did report that some degree of learning had taken place. Looking at the specific environmental factors they reported as contributing to their ability to learn gives us some insight into the integrative stage of learning growth and development. Some of the helpful factors included those events where there was a definite point of closure or summary, those situations where there were clear rules to be adhered to (such as how they perceived role plays), written introductions and summaries to experiential sessions, and opportunities to conform to authority figures. These factors did not typify the general environment in the course but they did seem to make the Assimilators comfortable enough to get something from the course. This suggests that a certain degree of 'psychological safety' must be attained before a learner can acquire non-dominant skills and constructs (e.g. move to the integrative stage of growth). The factors that lead to such safety may not be universal, however, for all learners. What seems to have made Assimilators comfortable was similar to what Accommodators least preferred and would not be likely to learn from without some of their preferred environmental factors present.

Summary

We have sought in this chapter to more systematically elaborate the scientific and practical implications of the experiential learning model first formulated by Lewin and his colleagues. We have seen that the model, in addition to being a very practical tool for use in training design, has much wider applications. Chief among these is that it provides a framework for the integration of the cognitive and socio-emotional perspectives of the learning process. In the integration of these perspectives lies the possibility of a holistic approach to the learning process that recognizes both the emotional and intellectual components of the learning act. Experiential learning theory also allows for the recognition and description of individual differences in learning styles. These styles shape behaviour not only in traditional educational settings but shape an individual's basic mode of adaptation to the world about him.

Thirdly, the experiential learning theory of growth and development describes the life cycle of human development through the stage of acquisition of basic cognitive structures, the stage of specialization in dominant learning style and matching career path, and the stage of integration of non-dominant modes of dealing with the world. Finally, we have addressed some of the issues involved in the deliberate design of learning environments. In the end, the basic conflicts between man and his social institutions will only be resolved through scientific understanding of these socializing environments that shape human development and through the enlightened design and management of these environments.

References

Argyris, C. (1962) *Interpersonal Competence and Organizational Effectiveness.* Homewood, Illinois: Dorcey.

Bruner, J. S. (1960) *Essays for the Left Hand.* New York: Atheneum.

Bruner, J. S. (1966) *Toward a Theory of Instruction.* New York: W. W. Norton.

Dubin, R. and T. C. Taveggia (1968) *The Teaching–Learning Paradox: A Comparative Analysis of College Teaching Methods.* C.A.S.E.A., University of Oregon.

Feldman, K. and T. Newcomb (1969) *The Impact of College on Students,* Vols: I and II. San Francisco: Jossey-Bass.

Freire, P. (1974) *Pedagogy of the Oppressed.* New York: The Seabury Press.

Fry, R. and I. Rubin (1972) 'The accelerated summer program: analysis and evaluation.' M.I.T. Sloan School Working Paper No. 624-72.

Flavell, J. (1963) *The Developmental Psychology of Jean Piaget.* New York: Van Nostrand Reinhold Co.

Goldstein, K. and M. Scheerer (1941) 'Abstract and concrete behavior: an experimental study with special tests.' *Psychological Monographs,* **53,** No. 239.

Gordon, W. J. (1961) *Synectics.* New York: MacMillan.

Growchow, J. (1973) 'Cognitive style as a factor in the design of interactive decision-support systems.' Ph.D. Thesis, M.I.T. Sloan School.

Harvey, O. J., D. Hunt and H. Schroder (1961) *Conceptual Systems and Personality Organization.* New York: John Wiley.

Hudson, L. (1966) *Contrary Imaginations.* Harmondsworth, England: Penguin Books Ltd.

Hunt, D. E. (1974) *Matching Models in Education,* Toronto: Ontario Institute for Studies in Education.

Jung, C. G. (1923) *Psychological Types.* London: Pantheon Books.

Kagan, J., B. L. Rosman, D. Day, J. Alpert and W. Phillips (1964) 'Information processing in the child: significance of analytic and reflective attitudes.' *Psychological Monographs,* **78,** No. 1.

Kolb, D. A. (1973) 'On management and the learning process.' M.I.T. Sloan School Working Paper No. 652-73.

Kolb, D. A. and M. Goldman (1973) 'Toward a typology of learning styles and learning environments: an investigation of the impact of learning styles and discipline demands on the academic performance, social adaptation and career choices of M.I.T. seniors.' M.I.T. Sloan School Working Paper No. 688-73.

Kris, E. (1952) *Psychonalytic Explorations in Art.* New York: International Universities Press.

Leavitt, H. J. and R. Doktor (1970) 'Personal growth, laboratory training, science and all that: a shot at cognitive clarification.' *Journal of Applied Behavioral Science,* **6,** 2, 173–180.

Lewin, K., R. Lippitt and R. K. White (1939) 'Patterns of aggressive behavior in experimentally treated "social climates".' *Journal of Social Psychology,* **10,** 271–299.

Lippitt, R. (1949) *Training in Community Relations.* New York: Harpers.

Marrow, A. J. (1969) *The Practical Theorist: The Life and Work of Kurt Lewin.* New York: Basic Books.

Plovnick, M. S. (1971) 'A cognitive theory of occupational role.' M.I.T. Sloan School of Management Working Paper, No. 524-71.

Plovnick, M. S. (1974) 'Individual learning styles and the process of career choice in medical students.' Doctoral Thesis in progress, Sloan School of Management, M.I.T.

Rogers, C. (1961) *On Becoming a Person.* Boston: Houghton Mifflin.

Schiller, F. (1826) *Uber Die Asthetischa Erziehung Das Menschen.* Cotta'sche Ausgabe, Bd. xviii.

Schilpp, P. A. (1949) *Albert Einstein—Philosopher Scientist.* La Salle, Illinois: Library of Living Philosophers Open Court Publishing Co.

Singer, J. (1968) 'The importance of daydreaming.' *Psychology Today,* **1,** 11, 18–26.

Stabell, C. (1973) 'The impact of a conversational computer system on human development perspective.' M.I.T. Sloan School of Management Master's Thesis.

Super, D. E., R. Starishevsky, N. Matlin and J. P. Jordaan (1963) *Career Development: Self Concept Theory.* New York: CEEB Research Monograph, No. 4.

Torrealba, D. (1972) 'Convergent and divergent learning styles.' M.I.T. Sloan School of Management Master's Thesis.

Chapter **4**

Process, Effects and Structure in Intensive Groups: A Theoretical– Descriptive Analysis

G. T. Barrett-Lennard

University of Waterloo

Intensive groups are an exceedingly complex phenomenon, obviously occurring in many specific forms, in a wide variety of settings, time frameworks, compositional and leaderships arrangements, involving a range of process patterns and usually lacking specificity in regard to goals and outcome effects. They may be likened to a pregnancy, in which the general character of the growth process and species nature of the offspring is known while its particular characteristics are only evident after birth has taken place—and still lie, in large measure, in the realm of potentialities.

As in the case of pregnancy, the general character of the developmental-'growth' process in a group can be looked at in various ways—in terms of elements or part-aspects and proportions of each, or properties of the whole and the ways these unfold and change, or in terms of subsystems and their balance and relationships, or in regard to relevant exterior conditions. By casting one's net widely enough and in salient directions it should encompass factors involved in a broad range of outcomes, including the case where things go seriously wrong, as they sometimes do even in the essential lifestep of pregnancy.

The writer's purpose is, first, to define the 'species-nature' of intensive 'experiential learning groups'. Most group experiences occurring under the headings of human-relations training (T) or learning (L) groups, sensitivity groups, encounter groups and closely related designations fall under the generic heading of experiential learning groups, within the author's general definition.

The second and principal aim is to present a framework designed to contribute to systematic thought and enquiry in regard to small-group phenomena and experiential learning groups in particular. The centrepiece is concerned with ways of looking at the within-group *process*, and ranges over several complementary perspectives and levels of analysis. An original examination of issues and approach in the study of outcome follows. Variations in group composition and context that can be expected to have a bearing on process emphases and effects are examined. The chapter ends with a brief overview and drawing together of a number of broad implications for practice and research.

A. Definition and species-characteristics of experiential learning groups

By way of brief definition, an experiential group is a small, temporary collection of persons, varying in salient individual and combinational characteristics, who meet intentionally within a planned time framework and usually with a designated leader–facilitator, with the general aims of interpersonal and self enquiry and of personal learning, growth or discovery. The meeting process stresses expression and exploration of present feelings, personal meanings and interperceptions *and* of the difficulties, ingredients, effects and meaning of such sharing.

As this definition implies, the process is multilevel. It includes, for example, (i) the content and sharing of immediate felt experience (self-focused and relational) in the group context, (ii) the 'how' of communication on the first level, as a concern and focus in its own right, (iii) the broader meaning or importance to group members (for example) of experiencing fuller 'connection' and capacity to be connected, with others, and (iv) the awareness of qualities, such as trust, in the overall group atmosphere and process, that appear reciprocally linked to movements in content, other qualities of the process, and its larger meanings. In experiential groups, such levels complement each other and the process falters if one level remains quite dominant in the experiencing and communication of members, for an extended period.

As a class, experiential groups can additionally be identified by the following properties:

(i) *In size, each group ranges from 8–14 persons altogether.* Larger or smaller numbers are possible, but generally associated with differences in other species characteristics. The range cited appears narrow but is actually a very broad one seen from one of the main perspectives advanced here, concerned with the mosaic of communicational and relational systems within an intensive group.

(ii) *A group includes one or (less often) two designated leader-facilitators.* 'Leaderless' experiential groups have been reported, but generally organized under the auspices of experienced leaders who assist indirectly (Berzon *et al.*, 1972; Farson, 1972).

(iii) *Groups typically have a 15 to 50 hour in-session life-span.* Even in two-week residential workshops, scheduled intensive group meetings are unlikely to total more than 50 hours. Weekend 'marathon' groups generally run to 15 contact hours, more or less.

(iv) *Membership is self-chosen and from populations not identified as disabled in their personal or interpersonal functioning.* Members generally are seeking enrichment, positive learning, growth, etc., rather than recovery from dysfunction.

(v) *Group meetings are without formal agenda or predictable, specific content.* Interchange is largely in terms of what members *find themselves experiencing,* eliciting in one another and wanting to express, explore, work out and respond to.

(vi) While the group leader usually has an important influence he/she does not direct or literally orchestrate the process. *Responsibility is vested in all the group members*, although the matter of how to exercise this responsibility is unclear, not susceptible to rapid consensus, and has itself to be found out within the group.

(vii) *There is implicit or explicit sanction to experiment* and try out self-expression, exploration and response to others that one is not used to and not at home with.

B. The in-group process: complementary perspectives

The central phenomenon of intensive groups is the in-group process—in its various aspects. By definition and general description, this process is a means to ends beyond the lifetime and context of the group itself. However, to the extent that the group experience has aspects that are intrinsically rewarding, or valued in their own right, some relevant outcomes may be said to lie in these interior qualities. Thus, while the writer's treatment of outcome will focus on change, such an approach may not exhaust the realm of relevant effects.

Effects only have knowledge-meaning in the context of being results of something that can be *recognized* when it exists or happens. Study of effects only has *strong* meaning when the nature of and variations in this 'something' are fully identified. And the something can be varied by intention with greater assurance the more fully its nature is known. Such at least is part of the rationale for giving priority here to the consideration of process. Another part is simply the challenge and fascination of the phenomena involved.

At least six main perspectives or levels of viewing the process in experiential groups are of interrelated salience, although some of these invite fuller elaboration than others. The six approaches involve (1) the level of basic 'elements' not necessarily distinctive to small groups, (2) broader normative qualities or characteristics which, taken together, are distinctive, (3) the group 'life-cycle' or sequential properties, (4) individual experience and self-learning processes, (5) the process from an interactionist/interpersonal perspective and (6) 'the group' as a phenomenon and system.

(1) *Constituent elements in the process*

As in chemical analysis, looking at the constituent elements reduces the phenomena to widely occurring familiar components, and potentially allows the greatest range of direct comparison with other personal/interactional contexts viewed on the same level. Some distinctive features of intensive groups in terms of the range of basic elements, or the amounts or proportions of particular components would be expected—and may be useful to explore. The author's aim is to provide a fuller picture (logically and conceptually) and add to the foundation for developments to follow, through this present step. The salient elements fall into at least three classes:

(a) *Experience* in the sense of on-going awareness, ranging from sharply differentiated perceptions or meanings to unclear emerging 'sensings', comprises a major category of elements. The various kinds and contents of experience fall especially in the realm of feelings and self-awareness, personal meanings, 'interpercepts' (interpersonal/relational perceptions), and participant observations of movement, flow, pattern or atmosphere in the group. Significantly included are such elements as wishes, desires, longings, hungers (perhaps more openly felt than in other contexts); anxieties, uncertainties, worries, confusion, conflict (both 'inner' and relational); feelings of closeness or distance from others, of loneliness or of contact and connection; feeling of inner freedom, purpose, confidence, strength or trust (e.g. in self or present others); many aspects of immediate perception and felt response to particular others; experiences of clarification, discovery, fresh awareness or understanding; and consciousness of *shifts* in attitude, feeling, purpose or behaviour.

(b) A second major category of elements consists of various aspects, modalities and contents of *international communicative behaviour*—forming the major sphere of visible activity in the group. Communicative acts are nearly as varied as the experiencing of members, which they express and reflect—directly or indirectly and fully to very incompletely.

(c) A third class of elements encompasses a variety of kinds and levels of behaviours in the group (non-verbal and verbal) which are expressive and generally communicative although not intentionally or deliberately so. Included, for example, are reactive responses and patterns that the reacting person does not distinguish, at least as they happen, but that have expressive—communicative meaning and impact for other group members; *and* spontaneous expressive activity within awareness but in effect having its own motivation aside from any immediate purpose of communication to others present.

Additional basic categories in similar vein might be discriminated and certainly this outline leaves much room for identification of further specific elements. Any of the elements and classes of elements referred to can be found in many life situations, especially in social–interpersonal contexts. Experiential groups are made out of the same basic stuff as other social life experiences, while possessing higher-order qualities and patterns that are relatively distinctive or unique. Commonalities between experiential groups and other life-contexts are fundamental to their useful outcomes in these contexts, although mere duplication of familiar situations and patterns would add nothing new and not facilitate change.

(2) *Normative characteristics of experiential groups*

The following qualitative features appear to characterize effectively function-ing experiential groups. They are not necessarily 'norms' of group members but characteristic of what in fact happens for a group to fully belong in the category under consideration.

(a) People *attend* particularly to their own and each other's feelings, personal meanings and attitudes, and personal styles and communication. There is also attention, in varying measure, to multiperson and group-wide interactional qualities, sequences and relationships.

(b) The attention to immediate felt experience and process is active, moving, enquiring and has a searching or exploratory quality. There is sanction, if not direct encouragement, to be venturesome and experimental, especially in such areas as self-expressive acitivity, direct communication, contact and shar-ing, and being a catalyst or enabler (on various levels) in relation to others.

(c) The vehicle and substance of interchange is the experience that happens when members are with each other in the group. Effectively, the focus is on what is found to be present and which unfolds and evolves as it is focused on and 'worked on'. In some respects, this is not dissimilar from many social groups, but it is quite distinct from most situations intended to be of an educa-tional–learning nature; and it is the source of the term 'experiential' learning.

(d) Members tend to 'own' or take primary responsibility for their own experience in the group, while also recognizing mutual influence. The idea of interdependence, or its equivalent, typically emerges but usually not in ways that reduce the experience of self-responsibility.

(e) There is a quality of down-to-earth honesty, directness, realism; a concern for getting at the truth of what *is* going on, inwardly and relationally, in the group.

(f) Consistent with and partly impled in other qualities, members 'work' (much more than in most social situations) at listening, turning into and sensitively picking up each other's felt meanings and messages, and checking out what they hear.

(g) Personal feedback communication in its various forms, occurs to a substantial extent. Often, one or more members directly share *their* 'pictures' of another person in the group, in a way which is personally involving and important to the giver(s) and receiver of this feedback, and in various ways to others in the group as well. Less often, the feedback is two-way, between two members on the same occasion, perhaps facilitated, encouraged or added to by other members.

(h) The intensity is uneven, with peaks that usually follow some spontaneous catalytic action by one or more members that 'spark' or help to bring about a release of energy, a feeling of some block or barrier being dissolved and very active or deeply felt experiential/communicative interplay within the group. One form of peak involves a shared, strong experience of contact with self (perhaps a 'surfacing' of deep-lying feelings) and others at the same time.

Implicit in such a peak is a lowering of 'guards' and a relatively high level and strengthening of trust among the members of the group.

(i) Significant shifts in level, focus or texture of the process tend to be acknowledged or somehow made explicit. A major characteristic example of such shifts is the change from emergent, immediate or spontaneous feelings and their expressions (where this is a fusion of experience and its expression), to a looking at experience and communications (in which 'meta'-communications become explicit), to reflections on or reactions to the 'looking at' level.

(j) The designated leader of the group 'works' as a facilitator by engaging him or herself personally over most of the same spectrum as other members but with a special purpose, concern or felt responsibility to further the kind of qualities and patterns outlined, in the group. The facilitator tends to be attentive to all members in ways that are a genuine expression of his or her observational perceptions and feelings, and to play a part in each person's feeling of connection and opportunity in the group. The specifics of each leader–facilitator's way of being and working in the group are varied and individual, not standard. As a group proceeds the leader's involvement and contribution typically becomes less distinct and he/she is increasingly 'assimilated' in a relational–attitudinal atmosphere of shared responsibility *and* fuller acceptance of individuality in contribution, needs and goals.*

(3) *The process as a sequence or life-cycle*

In so far as experiential groups are eventful, different from other social situations and a definable class of phenomena occurring within a restricted time frame, it is plausible to expect that they would be patterned over time in a more or less consistent way. There should tend to be natural order of progression, although differing compositional structure, leadership orientations and temporal arrangements may produce significant variations in this order, or in the qualitative nature of particular phases or transitions.

One way of establishing sequential characteristics is to work from transcripts, recordings or samples of interaction data, from actual groups. Content analysis of members' statements, interchanges and/or larger 'episode' units or themes is one example of this approach (e.g. Bebout, 1972). Another example involves the use of rating schedules filled in by members at the end of each group meeting or session from which member perceptions of the same perceived qualities or aspects of the group may be tracked, charted and compared, over the group's lifetime (Barrett-Lennard, 1967 and 1972).

Carl Rogers' first major paper on encounter groups (Rogers, 1967) is a particularly well-known portrayal of the process, using the form of a developmental sequence of characteristic steps or stages during the group's life span. Rogers' careful description is based mainly on his own personal observation

---

*Fuller statements along the same lines but presented in a more informal and personal form, and intended especially for prospective group members, have been published by the writer (Barrett-Lennard, 1973 and 1974b).

from the intensive groups and related experiences he had participated in up to that time. Some 15 overlapping elements are distinguished, which the writer in turn organized into three broad groupings or phases (Barrett-Lennard, 1974a). Additional adjustments to accord with other aspects of the author's thought in this presentation means that the following picture is a modification of Rogers' portrayal.

The first broad phase is termed *engagement*. It differs in specific quality and extent as between 'stranger' groups, groups made up of persons who have established outside relationships and groups whose members are drawn from very distant or conflicting social factions or reference cultures. It differs according to the 'experiential fluency' and general interpersonal trust level of members. However, it is always present as members strive to move beyond their initial self-consciousness and discover the possibilities and ways of being themselves in an active, personal, exploratory mode; in an arranged situation with others who are not known, at least in their combination and with the particular expectations or aims that each has. The engagement phase involves significant testing, trial and error and discontinuity in communication, concern in various forms and levels about the safety and meaning of dropping one's guard and being open in the group, more readiness (often) to express past feelings and there-and-then occurrences than highly immediate feelings and meanings.

Anxiety or frustration may surface during part of this phase, such that the first strong, immediate feelings to be expressed are quite often negative ones— directed to specific other persons or the process. Expression of such feelings, however, already implies some measure of felt connection and safety, and near-readiness to go further.

As the members become an experientially connected, self-active group which has a felt 'pregnancy' and special meaning, a second broad phase of *trust development and active exploration* characteristically occurs. Here-and-now feelings are increasingly expressed. Members speak not to address others but to be in contact with them. Active listening, strongly communicative self-expression, sustained exploration in various forms, are all more pronounced than in the first phase. Members become valued resources to one another in various ways and combinations. (In Rogers' terms, a healing capacity develops in the group.) A general (further evolving) climate of trust, candid exchange, a quality of immediacy and active, unfolding 'self-generating' exploration on various levels, appear to be principal ingredients of this phase. There continue to be back-and-forth swings and if the group settles to a steady state the third potential phase does not occur.

In the third phase of full-fledged *encounter and change*, some members at least actually feel differently about themselves—in such directions as a significantly increased sense of worth as a person or greater confidence in relating openly and effectively with others. Shifts in relation to personal attitudes or values may be implicit or clearly visible. Confrontational demands to drop residual fronts or facades may occur more sharply in this phase than before. With or without such confrontation, personal feedback processes are prominent. Helping or supportive relationships and further relational exploration outside group sessions often occur between members, especially when members are in residence together in a full-time workshop or laboratory. Episodes of deep sharing occur while vigorous, active exploration may taper off. Very warm and close feelings between group members are usually experienced and expressed whether or not there is any expectation of contact beyond the group. Changes in behaviour outside the individual's previous repertoire, style, associated consciousness, etc., tend to become noticeable in this phase.

Earlier descriptions of the sequential development or life-cycle of intensive groups are included in Tuckman's (1965) review. Empirical studies are outlined in the same source and by Stock (1964) and Cooper and Mangham (1971, Chapter 7). In principle, a sequential developmental perspective is uniquely useful—even though not sufficient for a comprehensive view.

(4) *Individual experience and process within the group*

Viewing the group directly as a vehicle or context for things to happen and evolve on an individual, person-by-person level differs from the other perspectives in respect to focus and emphasis while overlapping substantially in content. The focus includes individual self-activity and experience, and changes on these levels within the group context. In the small-group setting, explicit relational interaction and encounter is the lesser part (quantitatively) of each person's activity. The larger part includes silent participant observation and experiencing plus expressed self-enquiry and exploration.

The clearest, visible aspect of individual process in the group is that of self-focused exploration—stimulated, assisted, even provoked by others and the total group context but centring on qualities of inner and relational life that surface in the group, as an instance. Such exploration involves needful, active, searching and unfolding; integrative or 'opening' processes in the person as well as interactive events and changes between persons. For a given member, for example, this aspect of the process may focus on gaining a clearer view of self in some important respect (so that the question 'who am I' is further answered); on exploring felt insufficiency and achieving a more (genuinely) positive sense of self ('*I am* worthwhile' or, simply '*I* am a person'); facing 'pieces' that have not fitted together and gaining a greater sense of wholeness; letting in, touching and exploring loneliness or disconnection, angers, fear or other deep feelings; or looking directly and with question at (previously) implicit personal meanings, values or directions. Self-exploration can shade into a process of exploring the kind of world (or a broad sphere within this world) that has deeply experienced meaning and value, and working out action implications of a commitment or working orientation to this world.

Why is the *group* a context for distinctive *individual* (intrapersonal) process? A major reason applies indirectly to its distinctive impact on other levels as well. Experiential groups lack defined pathways or clear structure while their general norms or ethos (a) sanction and encourage qualities of human interchange unlike those in most social/interpersonal life and (b) place the individual in a position of having to find his or her way, with others (without 'maps' and with limited example and very broad guidelines) to a meaningful, group-specific realization of the general intention. Under these circumstances, members are thrown onto use and development of their personal resources in an unusual way. It is not possible to simply use one's established and familiar repertoire or to recycle or 'coast' in such a context.

One possible metaphor is that of a life-raft in a large body of water, where the crew either are strangers or don't know each other's capacities, tolerances or desires in this type of situation, where the usual navigation instruments are lacking or won't work, where there is a 'facilitator' but no captain, and where it is known (in a general way) that coming to terms with oneself and the other crew members is the key to a safe and fruitful outcome.

Specifically, one rule or aspect of the group ethos is that it is a place to break new ground, and another that it's particular nature, content and process emerges from its own membership. The individual must help to fashion the group (although he cannot fashion it to his will) and is there, in part at least, for the sake of personal learning. He virtually cannot avoid trying himself out in new or unfamiliar ways; and cannot rely, for example, on his self-presentations being preserved by the cooperation of others. Each also has a stake in contributing and learning through assisting others in self-enquiry and learning. In short, the individual must explore and part of this is a self-expressive inward search, stimulated and assisted by others.

A large proportion of events in a group can (in principle) be viewed through a lens that focuses on each person, one at a time, and projects a moving image of that individual person's experience and actions in the group. The image has a pattern and overall trajectory related to the individual outcome effects of the group. For each person, the group experience is a part, small in duration, of the larger journey of their life, in retrospect part of 'my history' of experience, action and relationships—often with episodes vividly recalled. What each person engages in, and the motion and unfolding of this engagement, forms a large part of this total picture of the 'group' process—and, by implication, of the analysis of outcome. Experiential groups are principally concerned with persons and their development; and direct consideration of individual process need not be at odds with (and potentially enhances and complements) the other perspectives advanced.

(5) *The process as a mosaic of interacting, developing relational subsystems*

The writer is developing a particular kind of interactionist perspective on the intensive group process. While it has some elements (or ideas) in common with a cluster of recent perspectives on therapy, communication and family interaction (e.g. by Laing, Phillipson and Lee, 1966; and Watzlawick, Beavin and Jackson, 1967) it is distinct from any of these in origin and scope. In systematic outline, the main features are:

(*a*) (i) The two-person system or *dyad* constitutes the most basic unit in interpersonal communication and relationship. As a small group of *n* members develops, each individual is a partner (in varying degree and quality) in *n*–1 dyadic systems. Typically in an experiential group each person becomes increasingly aware of the presence and qualities of each other member, and a principal aspect of any given person's experience is the mutual awareness, interaction and evolving relationship with every other person. Each dyadic association is a *potential* avenue for new experience, visible or implicit exploration and movement in awareness and resource.

(ii) The term *interchange* is a convenient one to refer to a short episode of communication or exchange of messages. A substantial *proportion* of the (explicit) process in a group consists of two-person interchanges, during which other group members are involved participant–observers.

(iii) Specifically, besides his or her direct involvement in *n*–1 dyads, each person is potentially an involved observer of the interchanges and evolving relationships between all *other pairs* of individuals in the group. There are $\frac{1}{2}(n-1)(n-2)$ such pairs ($=36$, in a 10-person group), offering a variety of participant observational experience of human interchange that is often highly evocative or meaningful in its own right, and potentially a significant further source of learning.

(iv) In total, or as viewed from the outside, there are $\frac{1}{2}n(n-1)$ pair combinations in the group as a whole ($=45$, in a 10-person group). In a low-structure, sustained intensive group it can be expected that episodes directly involving every one of these dyad combinations will occur during the group's lifetime. Relatively small differences in group size make a very big difference to complexity, in terms of 2-person systems. For example, 8 persons generate 28 dyads whereas 12 give rise to 66 pairs (and 16 individuals to 120 pairs).

(v) While in practice some dyad relationships will be much more eventful and salient than others, this perspective implies that some of the less salient ones may be an untapped resource in most groups. Also group size is probably a sensitive contributing determinant to the *proportion* of 'yeasty' two-person combinations.

(*b*) (i) At any moment during a dydic interchange a third person (prior to that moment, a silent observer) may become an active participant in response to that interchange in some way that involves and relates to *both* prior participants (rather than simply following on in response to one of them). The immediate process has then become a *triadic* interchange. A group member might engage in this way with any other active pair so that the pool of *possible* triad systems for any given person is the same as the range of observer/pair combinations indicated in (a)(iii) above ($=36$, in a 10-person context).

(ii) One principal and clear form of triadic system is manifest when two persons are into something together (in an overt interchange) and a third actively steps in in some way that is reactive or responsive to what is going on between them. In a productive group, the ongoing communication and experience of the first pair may be enhanced or furthered by the third person, who in any case, is probably attentive to the effects of his or her contribution. The paradigm of a three-person system is to be found in family interaction, especially between two parents and a child, or two children and a parent. In such systems, the relational interaction between any two members is often greatly influenced by the participation (or even the presence) of the third. Triadic interchanges and systems also occur frequently in friendship and work groups and other everyday contexts. They appear to be more difficult to manage and to be at home in than 2-person or larger systems—and potentially more damaging (see, for example, Haley, 1967)—and the group provides an even wider range of potential avenues for new experience and learning at the level of triadic associations than in 2-person contexts.

(iii) Viewed as a whole, a group contains $n(n-1)(n-2)/2 \times 3$ possible triad combinations and systems ($=120$, in a 10-person group). Unlike the situation in regard to dyadic relationships, it is quite *un*likely that examples of all possible triadic interchanges would occur in a group; and even less likely that each member would feel his or her way into a consciously discriminated association with each other *pair* of members. The extent to which triadic interchanges and systems actually occur and develop is a potentially significant measure of group differences, reflecting varied levels of use of an important avenue of interpersonal learning.

(iv) Experience in aiding communication, understanding or other important aspects of interchange and relationship between *other persons*, especially where one is also relationally involved in a direct way with each of the others, is one major avenue of potential new experience and learning via triadic systems within the group. The importance of real gains in this regard may be as great as change on any other level.

(*c*) (i) A triadic interchange may be followed by a fourth person responding to the third person's response in a way that is also inclusive of the first two; or to the first two directly but in a way that includes a message to the third person. Not counting the referent person, there are a great variety of *possible* triadic contexts for that person to enter: 84 in number in a 10-person group ($(n-1)(n-2)(n-3)/2 \times 3$).

(ii) A 4-person system may effectively contain 'imbedded' dyad and triad groupings. For example, three different sets of couplets (temporary pairs) are possible: A and B *vs* C and D; A and C *vs* B and D; and A and D *vs* B and C. Family systems, including two parents and two children, again provide a major paradigm. Friendship groups or temporary interchanges involving two man–woman couples occur frequently in everyday life. Other 4-person groups or interchanges are relatively common.

(iii) In an experiential group of typical size, the total number of *possible* 4-person systems (or 'quads') is larger still than the range of triad combinations. In a 10-person group there are 210 such possible systems ($n(n-1)(n-2)(n-3)/2 \times 3 \times 4$). Some of these will be manifest and (again) their actual extent *and* the consciousness of group members of distinctive, interactional and relational associations on this level may be an important dimension of group differences.

(iv) Communicating personally as a pair, with another pair, especially where the 'pairing' could be done in different ways and may shift around as one goes along is *one* important modality of process and potential learning in the 4-person system context that has significant relevance in family and other life contexts. Such configurations in experiential groups probably do not occur with high frequency, and are less often recognized. They constitute a sphere of potential further development, especially in terms of discrimination and intent.

(*d*) Relational–interactive groupings larger in number than four exist in latent and sometimes visible form. There is more overlap in membership among the larger, potential groupings and, with some exceptions, they appear to be of less interest and salience than the subsystems outlined. One such exception involves each individual person's relationship and interaction with the group as a whole (or, more exactly, with everyone else seen as a collective). At times, for any member, everyone else in the group appears as a single or largely undifferentiated entity with a collective attitude, intention, etc. There is always potential for this because there is one 'myself' and a group of 'others', for any member. Particularly at moments of intense and difficult absorption in oneself, 'others' may tend to blur together; and their casting as an undifferentiated collective may even help to elicit a relatively uniform response from them. In any case, the individual–group relationship is an important aspect of a bounded, face-to-face group with which each member needs to come to terms.

(*e*) (i) A further important mode of subsystem formation and interaction occurs when 'factions' arise in the group as a whole—as they nearly always do at some stage(s) in the life of an experiential group. Such factioning minimally involves felt, expressed commonality among members of a subgroup which distinguishes them from some or all others in the group, who in some degree then feel *their* shared identity in contrast to the first subgroup. Division (usually temporary) into subgroups, with for and against feelings in relation to some process or quality, attitude or outlook, or particular behaviour or goal, is a typical form.

(ii) Factional interaction may not involve everyone in the group in either faction. Those not 'aligned' may still be active participants in cross-factional interchanges, contributing distinctively to the overall movement in the group. A faction may be a dyad, triad or quad, etc., system (as already portrayed); and an emergent factional structure and process may only survive a short sequence of interchanges, or it may continue and evolve over a large part of the group's life-time.

(iii) Factioning with social groups and organizations is common in everyday life. Its occurrence in the special conditions of an experiential group provides another avenue for potential discovery of important ingredients of human affiliation and interchange, and further awareness of one's own make-up. *One* significant step in exploring the personal meaning of factional conflict within a group may be that of discovering that basic elements of *both* sides are represented in one's own feeling or attitude, although one holds stronger sway.

What are some of the operational values of this perspective? In the author's case, it has influenced what he sees, his concerns and some of his initiatives, within on-going groups. The effect is something like that of using a diver's mask under water: new aspects of the process environment spring into focus; and one is conscious of patterns, dimensions and possibilities not formerly in view or only discerned in vague outline. Further, the whole perspective suggests numerous possibilities for research, particularly in the sphere of comparative study of process in different groups; process development in the same group over time, and individual differences among members of a group in salient interpersonal aspects of exploration and within-group development.

Some groups probably concentrate particularly on dyadic communication and relationships augmented by triadic interchange patterns where the third person (often the leader) is primarily contributing in a direct facilitating mode. In others, interactional/relational patterns range freely over most of the spectrum outlined here. Sometimes, to judge from communication patterns, the relationship of each person to the group as a whole, is a prominent concern. And so forth. Such differences probably reflect compositional and leadership differences, and even varying time structures and settings—later considered.

The theoretical analysis suggests, for example, that a group of 8 or more people need more time than is often available (for example, in weekend marathons) to exploit at all fully the potentiality of their learning experience together. It is plausible that fairly explicit modes of working in the interpersonal avenues outlined can bring groups closer to problems and potentialities in everyday life, and enhance interpersonal values of the group experience. Further possibilities would occur to readers stimulated by this analysis; and the writer will be touching further on these and other implications later in this paper.

(6) *The group as a total phenomenon and system or 'team' in motion*

The group itself, in its totality, is a phenomenal entity for participants and has overall characteristics to an observer. Comparisons between groups and— as might be relevant in multi-group workshops—an organized perspective on intergroup relations, depend on things that can be said about the group as a whole. One approach to considering such overall properties is to derive them from the activities of individual members, interactive episodes, subsystem processes, etc., and obtain a 'group' result by some form of averaging. Another broad approach is to conceive of the group as an emergent entity in its own right, and to discriminate salient aspects and motion of its activity in this light. While it is difficult, in practice, to maintain a sharp distinction between these two approaches (and each is important) the in-principle difference between them is fundamental.

The members of a voluntary, intensive experiential group obviously hold overlapping views regarding the nature and purposes of the situation they are in together, and these views typically converge further as the group proceeds via extensive exchange, exploration and relational development. Even in the process of conflict or confrontation (and more obviously so in most other modes), members are cooperating in sustaining a context in which such processes are taken as part of the life and meaning of the group. Thus the group has the character of a purposive self-aware system or 'team' as this term is developed by Pentony (1970), drawing on Goffman's work (1959).

An experiential group is a special type of team, with qualities and process characteristics that would set it apart from many others, in the broad and integrative sweep which Pentony offers. A particular group has only a short history, formalization occurs but to a much lesser extent than in most teams (which usually have an external task or mission), it evolves rapidly and does not stabilize, and it may develop a very high level of cohesion but does not usually try to preserve itself beyond the span planned. Yet it is like an institution in having value for its own sake, rather than resembling a strictly functional organization (cf. Pentony, 1970).

The *process* of the group, or team, refers to its functioning and movement in salient qualities. The writer's outline of the process as a sequence or life-cycle (in 3, above) may be viewed in these terms, although as a special case. (For example, it rests heavily on aspects derived from part-processes—the 'first' approach—rather than a holistic view of the group—the 'second' approach.) Judgements regarding process properties of the group require longer time units than those involved in discriminating component process events and qualities focusing on particular members, interchanges and interpersonal subsystems. Most groups do not stay in session continuously for more than two hours or so at a time, and individual meetings are a convenient referent when participants are called on to make judgements about their group as a whole. The writer, for example, has made fairly extensive use of short questionnaires answered session by session by each participant in reference to the group atmosphere and process (Barrett-Lennard, 1967 and 1972). In a number of groups the questionnaire was in semantic differential form, containing bipolar items such as Harmonious/ Conflicting, Close/Distant or Caring/Hostile; Superficial/Searching, Turbulent/ Calm, Fast/Slow and Open/Closed. Each person's judgement was in effect an estimate of a 'group' characteristic during the referent interval. Pooling such judgements from everyone in the group increases the reliability of this estimate.

While it is feasible to generate group qualities based on personality concepts (as, for example, in Bion's pioneering work—Bion, 1961), the more literally this is done the less the group is being regarded as a unit with properties of another order than those applicable to its individual members. At least three clusters of process qualities that do appear to apply directly to emergent properties of a group occur to this writer.

(i) The aspect that has probably received the most attention and study—in a wide range of small-group contexts—is the extent to which a group is cohesive in its functioning; the degree to which it is firmly bonded, unified and close-knit—reflected in part by the level and quality of 'we' feeling among the group members. (See, for example, Deutsch, 1968 and Bedner and Lawlis, 1971.)

Cohesion probably develops most strongly in full-time, residential workshops or laboratory groups, where members share a common environment and relatively continuous contact. In these circumstances the participants may literally become a band of explorers for whom each scene is new, directly experienced by themselves but no others, who see themselves in and through each other and see the other through that person's searching and their own discoveries. Interdependence is, or becomes, a fundamental condition for progression and discovery; and each person's hunger for connectedness with others is released and joined in a rare and often powerful combination. The member's engagement, existence and activity *together* tends to stand out as 'figure', in intense relief, while the rest of the world may become, for the time, a shadowy 'ground'.

To the distant observer, the group has become a strange body, self-absorbed and pre-occupied, moving and breathing almost as one, locked together in a pattern of activity unlike that of 'normal' human interchange or other social groups. The image of a capsule moving in space by its own mystifying laws catches the aspect of cohesion, the idea of the group as a unity, and the potential distinctiveness of its motion. The degree and quality of cohesion differs of course from one group to another, and the growth and variation in cohesion during the course of a single group would be literally a feature of that *group*'s process.

(ii) A second aspect is the extent to which the group, in its total motion displays a high tempo of activity, vigour, flow, development and released or 'kinetic' energy. Variations in this aspect would also involve both degree and quality. The movement of the group may be rapid and in a relatively even, continuous flow, or it may be intermittently very active, moving in staccato bursts with relative quiescence between. Or the motion may have a surging, wavelike or cyclical quality.

A generally active, fast-moving group is likely to differ qualitatively from one session to the next—although not *necessarily* in a strongly cumulative, developmental fashion—and marked shifts or transformations quite often happen within a meeting session. The group may seem to 'run' or spin, with or without periodic 'braking'. There is probably little stillness, relative absence of a halting or explicitly uncertain quality, no 'waiting', few silences except those filled with inner activity through which the group moves or shifts in some discernible way. A less active group would tend to linger, perhaps with intermittent surging movement, to display a lower 'free' energy level, and to evolve more slowly. However, its general direction might be more continuous than the highly active one; and no direct or simple relationship between activity tempo and 'productivity' or outcome is implied.*

*In task-oriented groups a closer relationship between tempo and productivity would tend to occur than in the case of experiential groups, which are by nature inward-focused and where the most important outcomes are on an individual–interpersonal development level.

In a particular group, the tempo of activity, as an aspect that could be discriminated by participants and/or careful observers, would vary in wide or narrow range from session to session and within sessions. Its level and variation is potentially a central feature of the *group's* motion and identity, connected with a great many other process aspects and tracing a pattern over time effectively distinguishing one group from another.*

(iii) The further aspect is that of group intensity level. This is connected with the extent to which interaction is directly personal, immediate, self-disclosing and open in terms of directly shared mutual impressions or personal feedback. Wilkinson (1972, 1973) has significantly contributed to the conceptual delineation and assessment of group intensity levels. In Wilkinson's view the predisposition of members to be trusting of others in a personal sense is the key to the intensity level achieved in a group, given appropriate group leader modes and resources. This writer feels that other compositional and contextual factors might be equally important.

While a high intensity level would appear unlikely to be associated with a low tempo of activity, and may also imply at least moderate cohesion, it has its own attributes differing from those of these two other broad factors. A group may be very active but not strongly engaged in direct exchange and exploration of personal, immediate, owned feelings and perceptions—as can be observed in the early stages of some experiential groups. The process may be intense, given the personalities and circumstances of a particular group, without the membership being bonded in a highly cohesive unit.

As with the two other aspects, in any given group, the process will vary in intensity, within and between meeting sessions—following an individualized 'signature' over each group's history. 'Warm-up' periods imply lower intensity while times of strong involvement *and* interplay of candid, open, self- and other-focused exploration and sharing imply higher intensity. Individual meeting sessions can have clear 'peaks' in this regard although, as a group attribute, such peaks would necessarily resemble a tidal motion rather than individual 'surfing' waves. As a group goes on the tidal intensity level could be expected to rise to its maximum (early) in the third broad phase earlier portrayed, assuming this perspective is a good approximation to the group's actual sequence of development.

As mentioned earlier, the position taken here is that the *value* of the multi-level phenomenon and process described lies mostly in effects beyond the limited life and special context of the group itself. How to think of these potential effects, in the mainstream of each person's life experience and activity, is the next challenge-point and focus of this paper.

---

* While the writer has touched on this aspect in research, via participant end-of-session ratings (Barrett-Lennard, 1972), it appears not to have been a direct focus in any intensive group process investigation. Viewed as a broad, major dimension or feature of group functioning various refinements and operational translations are possible; and this statement stands as an introduction and first approximation only.

C. Outcome effects: approach and implications

To meaningfully consider and investigate the effects of experiential groups—or any other experience expected to have personal learning outcomes—a contextual body of thought is involved, which may be cast in the form of a set of key assumptions or working principles. In the present case, the group experience is seen as an episode of a qualitatively exceptional, personally eventful nature occurring within the larger context of the individual's life journey. This journey undoubtedly includes other 'nodal' episodes, of varying nature but in each case exceptional, vivid, personally eventful, and with bearing on the person's future course—occurring against a background of relative continuity, reception with small variation, the preservation of familiar 'programmes' of activity and experience and gradual (perhaps unnoticed) progression or change.

Expressed more systematically and fully, the assumptions and propositions offered as basic contextual guidelines for the study of outcome are as follows:

(i) Life-long development and change are part of the natural order in human (and other) life. Growth, maturation, learning, progression in the life cycle, all imply change. Adaptation to the rapidly changing environment that so many of us live in, implies change. Human beings by nature are not static in their consciousness and behaviour patterns, but mobile, unfolding, altering—gradually and sometimes swiftly—on many levels and in varying direction.

(ii) Deeper levels of personal and relational learning, important developments in one's consciousness, shifts in orienting goals, significant values, attitudes or commitments seem not to occur in an even, continuous flow, especially in adults. Such changes tend to happen, or at least to become apparent, in climactic spurts, an emergent sense of a new focus or of many 'bits' falling into place, a motivational metamorphosis, a dawning awareness that crystallizes in the 'right' context, or a decision that changes the subsequent context and texture of one's life.

(iii) The periodic, visible shifts or movement in self-identity, purpose, meaning, energy and personal sources, qualities and choice of relationships and other life-patterns can arise from intensely involving experience that the person is somehow 'ready' for. They probably result from the combination of relatively continuous change and the received impact of unusually potent, personally eventful experience.

(iv) Change or 'growth' associated with an experiential learning context such as an intensive group or personal therapy is often more significant in regard to the doors that are opened than those which are immediately passed through. Tendencies toward integration, self-actualization, mutually enhancing relationship with others, etc., are released or triggered but not consummated; the person changes gear but his main journey and much of the discovery is yet to come and depends partly on the terrain that lies ahead.

(v) Voluntarily and purposefully taking part in an intensive group is itself an outcome, in part, of prior formative influences and learnings. Its significance is similar in principle to the group experience serving as a (contributing) cause of later directions, choices and undertakings.

(vi) It follows that change effects of an experiential group cannot be adequately investigated simply by measuring immediate outcomes and determining whether before-to-after differences are sustained during a follow-up period. While this approach catches, as it were, one two-dimensional slice of the total sphere of potential change it implies no recognition that it is a 'sphere' and would be insensitive to a great part of the content of this sphere. Far more relevant in principle would be to look for shifts inferred both from within the group *and* before-to-after data which may have immediate value but also would lay the ground (or be likely conditions) for subsequent development in keeping with the same broad goals; this development in turn being a contributing foundation in later personally formative experiences or turning points.

(vii) In formal terms, the outlined assumptions and perspective can be represented in the following schematic form (Figure 1), where A, A1, etc., stand for the aspects or pattern of functioning being considered at successive points in time:

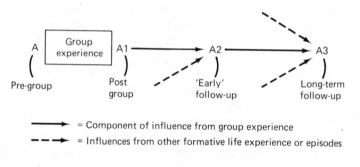

= Component of influence from group experience
= Influences from other formative life experience or episodes

Figure 1

(viii) Literally viewing the group experience as one key episode in a developmental life-journey (that includes many other critical episodes and turning points) complicates the study of outcome effects. Such 'complication' seems certain to include issues and aspects beyond those introduced here and probably is part of any real search for an extended vision.

Consistent with the presented views of the process and with the above considerations in mind, the range of actual outcome effects *should* include the following:

(a) Interpersonal resource development, including enhanced sensitivity or empathy in relation to others, an increased repertoire or skill in *personal* communication and greater expressiveness and openness with others are prospective aspects of immediate (or relatively early) outcome effects.

(b) Enrichment of interpersonal communication and deepening of affiliative contact in life relationships outside the group is an expected *indirect and possibly delayed* outcome. In the case of groups composed of members from the same affiliative community, or containing subgroups already in close relationship (such as couples, personal friends or immediate colleagues) immediate as well as longer-range effects on these relationships would be expected. Such effects should include at minimum changes in mutual awareness and in communication boundaries and process outside the group context.

(c) Change in attention, awareness and responsiveness to one's own and other people's *feeling life* is another likely principal aspect or focus. Such effects may reach a peak at the end or soon after the group experience, and can be expected to decline in some measure in 'outside' life contexts. The emphases and intensity of the group are of a kind to leave members enlivened and more at home with their own subjectivity and the feeling life of others. The change would tend to have temporary, enduring *and* potentiating aspects. While the immediate level of 'charge' in this respect is expected to diminish, former members know experientially what it is like to be more vibrant, attuned or expressive on a feeling level (than their own previous or usual norms) and something of how this came about. A 'meta effect' would be increased discrimination of and inclination toward further experience that would be similarly (or more deeply) enlivening.

(d) Increased personal unity, integration or congruence, in its various aspects and definitions, is a basic area of potential affect, both immediate and (more significantly) in a longer-range sense. Besides the core idea of wholeness, this aspect implies greater openness to experience (or increased 'experiential fluency') and more differentiated and reflexive awareness of self. Such an effect should tend to build on itself, for example, so that the individual *learns more* from subsequent personally involving experience, is more adaptive in contexts of crisis or stress, and is able to increase his or her actual connection with others.

(e) Content change in self-concept is a likely, related outcome presumably stemming from the personal understanding and feedback aspects of the group experience and also fron the aspect of experiencing oneself in action in new ways. Increased actual self-regard or esteem (or feeling of self-worth) is an example of such content change. Perhaps *more* important still is the associated aspect of modification in the *process* by which members define or form images of self. Potentially, there is a shift in balance toward discovering oneself *in* and through experience and away from depending (as much) on an established image of self to regulate awareness and action.*

(f) Increased cognitive/experiential awareness of interpersonal and group system influence processes, self and other control patterns and motives, and

*This aspect might be said to imply a more existential quality of living. Coupled with aspects (c) and (d) it also expresses a more 'organismic' mode of functioning and valuing (cf. Carl Rogers, in various writings) and, in particular, a more active, functional monitoring and responsiveness to feelings, personal meanings and other facets of subjective experience.

facilitation or enabling processes, from another level and cluster of potential outcomes, *perhaps* more marked in groups taking place in an educational and training context than those involving more exclusively personal motivation. The extent of such change would depend also on confirming follow-up experience, as the life and scope of the group may not suffice as a sole source of new, generalized cognitive learnings.

(g) Developmental change in personal priorities and social attitudes and purposes is an important sphere of potential effect. This implies modification in choices and decisions in personal, social and (potentially) vocational or public life. The inner aspects of such change are likely to be immediate but provisional—perhaps requiring to be confirmed by subsequent experience. They may not be immediately visible to others; or they may be partially visible but seen as put-on phoney. Groups of more diverse membership may provide greater potential for change in this sphere than relatively homogeneous groups. In any case, changes in the *processes* of value-formation and development may be a more significant and durable outcome than particular content changes.

(h) Depending on the composition of the group *and* its impact on other levels, members may go away wanting to initiate and/or lead experiential groups themselves, or to seek further experience and preparation with this end in view. Such an effect may also be delayed as other outcomes 'gel' or further evolve in interaction with new experiences. In either event, a potential effect is to become active in a contributing sense in the small group field or associated work in the human relations/human potential sphere.

(i) Organizational, community relations or social system change are potential long-range outcome effects of individual, relational and attitude change associated with experiential groups. This level of effect plausibly depends (for example) on how extensively the outside organization or system is represented in the groups, whether individuals at all levels have taken part, and (beyond individual learning) the development of communication, actual respect and shared values and awareness that occurs among organization or community members via the group experience.

The fairly extensive research on change effects of experiential groups includes or relates to some aspects of each of these proposed areas of outcome. Generally the work has not been guided by assumptions of the kind set forth here, and the groups investigated would not all have the process qualities outlined. Thus the evidence is for the most part suggestive rather than strongly relevant for present purposes.

Substantial reviews of the work actually done (relating to outcome) include those by Gibb (1971), Mangham and Cooper (1969) and Babbage (1973). Books that include a research (or research and theory) focus *include* those by Cooper and Mangham (1971), Lieberman, Yalom and Miles (1973) and Solomon and Berzon (1972). The present writer's research relates at least to aspects (a), (b), (e) and (f) above (e.g. Barrett-Lennard, 1967; and Barrett-Lennard, Kwasnik and Wilkinson, 1973/74).

D. Structural conditions as contributing determinants of process and outcome

Structural conditions in the present context are features that are built-in or exist as 'givens' when a group begins, and that can be expected to influence the process (and, hence, the outcomes) of the group experience. Aspects of group composition, leadership, and temporal arrangements and setting are the main categories considered.

(a) *Group composition*

At least five component aspects of composition are potentially relevant. These are:

(i) The numerical *size* of the group.

(ii) The presence/absence and nature of *prior outside relationships* among members.

(iii) The expectations, goals and other salient aspects of motivation and personality of members; and the 'mix' of these within the group.

(iv) The sex composition and age/generation composition of the group.

(v) The ethnic and language, educational and social class, and religious or personal value characteristics and mix of the participants.

Implications of group size have been mentioned in several places and flow particularly from the interactive/relational subsystem perspective on the group process, discussed in B5, above. Both this analysis and other comments are in keeping with the view that 'stranger' groups, where all or most relationships start from the beginning and are not continued afterwards, are a special case; and in the (different) case where people know each other beforehand and, in some significant sense, will be living together afterwards, important differences in process emphasis and development can be expected. One broad aspect is a different quality of relational focus associated with the *direct* importance of relational development in life-connected groups, as against stranger groups. In stranger groups, members may concentrate relatively more fully and freely on self-expression and development, and on relational experimentation in a more literal and wide-ranging sense. Life-connected groups would have more immediate relevance for possible changes in the human relations systems to which the members jointly belong.

The general strength and quality of motivation of members, particularly toward common or interrelated goals, is of obvious importance in principle although difficult to tease out in practice. Particularly in regard to personality and motivational qualities, ways in which groups are homogeneous or heterogeneous in composition have received a good deal of attention, in terms of process and outcome effects (Harrison, 1965, and later work). Persons who go to a great deal of trouble to take part in a group will have a differing quality of motivation than those who virtually 'fall into' it. (Anyone who feels pressured or implicitly 'required' to participate will begin with a still different attitude.) Voluntary participation in a group whose intent and expected characteristics have been clearly portrayed in advance would tend to result in significant commonality on the part of members, while leaving room for differences that are likely to be advantageous, providing members are quite strongly committed and motivated toward the kind of journey a group can provide. From the process perspectives advanced, diversity in the context of broadly shared values and comparable readiness for experiential involvement and exploration, would provide the *potential* for breaking more new ground than would a high degree of homogeneity. In the case of life-connected groups, oriented toward a relational focus, the homogeneity/heterogeneity issue has less potential relevance.

(b) *Formal leadership*

'Formal' in this sense simply implies a focus on pre-arranged, designated or official leader–facilitators and not on informal 'leadership' participation by other members. Built-in aspects of leadership tie in with some of the compositional features mentioned and include at least four aspects:

(i) The presence/absence and number of designated leaders in the group.

(ii) The orientation, style and purposes of the leader(s), for example, in terms of kind and degree of initiative in the group, personal sensitivity and openness, degree of attunement to self *vs* interpersonal *vs* group process exploration, and inclination to meld into the group *vs* maintaining a role distinct from others.

(iii) The attributes of the formal leader(s), in terms of general standing or status *and* particular expertise in the small-group context vis-a-vis other members; especially as perceived by members and the leader(s).

(iv) The role and responsibility the leader(s) present, in the initiation and advance organization of the group experience.

By example and the direct effects of their sharing, responsive and observing communications in the group, and by what they do not do, skilful, enabling leaders (e.g. in terms relevant to the normative characteristics earlier described) would substantially influence and contribute to the process, most distinctly in the initial, 'engagement' phase. The perceived standing and expertise of the leader is also most (visibly) important at the beginning, and can work in different ways as the group proceeds. If the leader's distinction or status is high and members see themselves on a substantially lower level, feelings around authority, achievement, success and related areas may be involved (more strongly than otherwise) but difficult to express and explore freely in here-and-now ways. The degree of difficulty would interact with the second numbered aspect above, such that a potentially important area of learning and discovery may either be realized *or* bypassed in the group. If the leader's role in organizing the group has been central, and especially if group members find themselves collectively stuck in some way, the leader/group relationship would tend to become a focus, unless actively avoided.

Two leaders potentially can provide a valuable example from their own inter-action, or complement each other in their contributions. However, if leaders are not very free and secure with one another, either may inhibit the other and the effect can be a neutralizing one. Or, their interaction may become a distraction rather than a freeing or evocative example. Multiple leaders can be played off against one another (usually without conscious intention) and respond either in ways that assist some valuable learning or that simply or largely perpetuate familiar patterns. Thus, the presence of more than one leader could influence the process in varying directions and, other things being equal, would add to its complexity. 'Leaderless' groups, in the terms earlier mentioned, in fact have a leader–organizer, initiator or model who is not present but indirectly in-fluential. Effects would depend greatly on the form and thrust of this indirect leadership, coupled with the resources and composition of the group.

(c) *Time structure, setting and associated activity*

The length, spacing and context of a group experience involve several inter-related aspects that can be expected to have important bearing on the process and effects:

(i) The time structure itself, in terms of total in-session meeting time and the way that this group time is distributed over total time, is one main aspect.

(ii) The degree and kind of direct involvement and activity (if any) of members with one another between the small-group sessions naturally would affect relational qualities and development within the group.

(iii) The extent to which members are involved between sessions in their on-going life activities and relationships affects immediacy of application or 'practice' of new meanings *from* the group and what members may bring back *to* it.

(iv) A further related aspect is the actual setting of the in-group experience: whether it is conducive to informality and lack of distraction, the personal associations that it has for members, whether there is 'surrounding' contact with nature and/or human artistic and creative expression, and the extent to which it fosters between-session association of members.

(v) Last in order of mention, is the extent to which collateral groups are going on in a larger workshop or laboratory community, and the scope of organized and informal intergroup experiences.

The typical alternatives in practice are (a) the full-time residential experience, away from the member's life environment and running for a weekend up to two or even three weeks; (b) a series of meetings spaced up to a week or more apart, and sometimes interspered with all-day or weekend full-time sessions, to which members converge from their separate life-contexts; and (c) meetings on a daily to weekly basis of members who belong to the same 'host' organization or affiliative community.

From observation *and* inference it is this writer's view that groups whose in-session life span is in the upper half of the range earlier cited (15–50 hours), meeting over a week or longer, provide the experiential–interactional 'space' for development of process and effects more in keeping with the total analysis presented here than do briefer groups. As mentioned, the continuity and contextual aspects of full-time groups make possible greater momentum and intensity than in spaced groups; and the effects of what happens directly within the group can be expected to be greater in 'continuous' groups than through equal time in spaced, discontinuous groups. This is not to say that the latter is always less valuable, for under some conditions it may work to augment or trigger a development process rather than being the principal vehicle for it even during the group's lifetime.

In general, full-time group experiences are plausibly a more effective as well as more feasible context in the case of stranger groups; while the reverse may be true for life-connected groups whose members place high priority on development in their communication, interawareness and relations. Full-time groups make possible greater selectivity of setting, increase the feasibility of being in a larger community of similar purpose and involvement, and may extend opportunity for intergroup observations and experiences that add to the self and interpersonal learning dimensions.

E. An overview

This paper has presented a view of the domain of phenomena involved in intensive experiential groups. The writer has worked to sort out principal features within this domain and offer interlocking descriptive/theoretical perspectives in regard to these features. He has been as much concerned with *how* to form an adequate picture as with its specific content; and although each of these levels helps to validate the other they are partially independent. Some components of the picture actually presented are programmatic, exploratory, new even to the author, while others are more anchored in earlier thought. The totality is fresh, ripening in the writing.

The group process is seen as an emergent, unfolding, multilevel complex of happenings that grows out of what the group participants (including the leader) are like and what they are up to—individually and in combination—where they are with each other to begin with and in their outside lives, how many are present, the setting of the group experience, how much time they have together and how it is arranged, and other aspects of composition, purpose and context. In consequence experiential groups differ significantly, each is unique, and their commonalities are definitional as well as descriptive.

The combination of relevant prior and initiating conditions and emergent events and qualities are necessarily complex in their separate and interactive influence; and some act more as a 'yeast' from which new properties emerge and flow than as direct causes. Simple linear models of cause and effect seem not to be plausibly applicable to the process itself and, still less, to its effects.

Each person comes to a group with an individual history that is likely to include deeply personally eventful and formative episodes or turning points. He or she is, or has been, already developing, changing, learning. The group experience is another potentially nodal episode probably unique in some of its qualities and effects but in no way unique in having important personal effects. It is a step, perhaps a major turning stride in that person's total developmental journey. Its eventual influence is a product of the past and future, as well as the present; and it is at once an outcome, a movement in itself and an entry to new possibilities.

Numerous implications both for the searching practitioner and research investigator can be drawn from the overall perspective offered here. Broad examples (first) with a practical emphasis are:

The intensive group context is enormously rich in the possibilities for exploration, learning and development that it offers. A great deal is happening on several fairly distinct levels and, like that part of the iceberg that rises above the surface, much of what is there no doubt passes unnoticed in the ongoing process of most groups. Put more positively, the boundaries to actual discrimination, discovery and development are probably set more by what participants want to, can (in the exact circumstances) and do actually attend to, than by the phenomenon itself; and there is potential for extending the spectrum in any given case—by such means as carefully prepared advance information for participants, allowance of sufficient in-group time and for 'augmenting' between session and follow-up activity, and enhancement of the group leader's 'reach' and contribution.

The leader–facilitator's role, sensitivity, consciousness and skill is likely to be *most* influential in the earlier parts of a group's lifetime; but important throughout, to a degree that depends partly on the individual and combinational qualities of other members. The leader potentially can 'facilitate' on *several connected* levels—including those of self-inquiry, interpersonal communication, consciousness and exploration of multiperson interactional/relational patterns, and awareness and evolution of the group's activity as a total system. The *range* in this sense of the leader's active, non-impositional awareness and responsiveness would complement the *quality* of his resourcefulness on any given level.

Group composition, over the range of aspects considered, is highly relevant to the process potentialities and outcomes of the group experience. Size alone and, especially, in combination with the duration of the group experience, is closely related to the degree to which members can utilize potential interpersonal and multipersonal avenues of exploration and learning. Particular implications are that groups of shorter duration should be kept to smaller size than those that run for a longer period; and that under any conditions a *low-structure intensive* group of more than a dozen persons is enormously complex, and potentially less satisfactory than groups not above this size. Life-connected *vs* stranger groups have differing potentialities and each can be a more favourable avenue for congruent purposes. Groups can be homogeneous and heterogeneous in many different ways, again with corresponding variation in potential. By and large, moderate diversity would be expected to be more fruitful than a *high* level of homogeneity.

Durational structure and setting contribute to the boundaries *and* potentialities of the group experience. The perspective advanced strongly suggests that a weekend provides too short a time to explore, develop and utilize at all fully the potentialities of an intensive group (although it may provide 'space' for a useful part of this spectrum). Full-time residential contexts are probably optimal (considering for example, the relevance of cohesion, intensity and tempo) for 'stranger' groups. For life-connected groups, spaced meetings with time for substantial in-between experience may be more valuable, particularly in conjunction with one or more extended sessions (all-day or weekend) to provide greater opportunity for *group* development and potentially deeper levels of interpersonal/communicational exploration.

From the perspective advanced, wide variation in outcome effects from group to group (and person to person) is inevitable. Part at least of this variation is potentially advantageous. There are plausible grounds in theory (augmented in some areas by research) for planning groups to *emphasize* certain levels or classes of outcome. Consistent with the species and normative characteristics outlined the proposed purpose of such planning would not be to narrow the range of learning possibilities, but to responsively arrange conditions within the range portrayed, according to the known goals, on-going relationships (if any) and active concerns and resources of participants.

Many relevant, potential outcomes of experiential groups (particularly intensive full-time groups) would be at the level of altered potentialities rather than immediately manifest effects. It is suggested that this perspective or issue be in some way brought into the group for exploration, for example, in the later or ending stages. In the same way (in principle) that coming to the group is a step and destination from the former course of a much larger journey, the group experience is an episode whose immediate impact is a prelude to wider significance it can turn out to have in the individual's total development and unfolding future.

Principal, broad areas of research need and potential include the following:

Investigations that help to specify the particular characteristics and patterning of the *in-group process*, particularly, on a multi-level basis that permits broad, conceptually anchored comparison of one group with another, are of leading importance in the present state of knowledge and of descriptive/theoretical systems—as illustrated here. Research-based generalizations regarding the effects of intensive groups mean very little without clear and salient specification of what the particular sample of groups was in fact like.

To the extent that identified process characteristics are linked empirically with known compositional, leadership, durational and/or contextual features (section D factors in this analysis), a major level of serious explanatory work is under way. Linking the same, or similar, process characteristics with short- and long-range outcome effects would be the other side or half of a potentially very powerful total sphere of connected investigation and meaning. The system presented stands as a resource, not a set of boundaries, to such development and integration.

The type of conceptual approach in regard to outcome effects offered here (section C) needs further translation into a research model that provides a fully-fledged alternative to prevailing models. The latter typically imply a steady-state beforehand, a change effect *during* the group experience (if it *is* effective) and a steady-state afterwards in the sense of the 'treatment effect' being maintained or increased during the follow-up period. This model is considered at best sensitive to a single 'slice' within a broad sphere of potential change effects.

A myriad of specific aspects for further descriptive examination, hypothesis testing, and areas of exploratory correlational study—including a number directly suggested at earlier points—could be drawn from the step-by-step content and linkage portrayed throughout this presentation. Existing research, including and beyond studies and sources mentioned, would in some cases be directly helpful.

In concluding this paper, the writer is well aware that it could evolve into a book rather than a chapter. Much of it is condensed and rather formidable to read; and some sections could almost stand alone. While the reader's interest naturally would be sparked more by some parts or aspects than by others, hopefully the individual trees and the wood they stand in emerge in complementary relationship—at least for the reader who makes it all the way through, or only skips here and there. It will be evident to such readers that the author is very seriously interested in experiential groups *both* on a theoretical level *and* at the level of practice. This statement is a hard-working attempt to provide at least a scaffolding for serious inquiry and further development in regard to one of the most fascinating, potent and hopeful forms of personal/social experience and learning in contemporary life.

References

Babbage, L. (1973) 'Personal change as a result of sensitivity training: A review of the literature.' *Group Process Studies Papers*, No. 7, University of Waterloo (Mimeo—Dept. Human Relations and Counselling Studies).

Barrett-Lennard, G. T. (1967) 'Experiential learning in small groups: The basic encounter process.' *Proceedings Canadian Assn. University Student Personnel Services*, Nov. 1967, 2–12.

Barrett-Lennard, G. T. (1972) 'Group process analysis from post-session and follow-up data.' *Group Process Study Papers*, No. 5, University of Waterloo (Mimeo—Dept. Human Relations and Counselling Studies).

Barrett-Lennard, G. T. (1973) 'The intensive group experience: General process description and guidelines.' *Canada's Mental Health*, **21**, Supplement No. 73.

Barrett-Lennard, G. T. (1974a) 'The client-centered system: A developmental perspective.'

In F. J. Turner (Ed.) *Social work practice: Interlocking theoretical approaches*. New York: Free Press.

Barret-Lennard, G. T. (1974b) 'Experiential learning groups.' *Psychotherapy: Theory, Research and Practice*, **11**, 71–75.

Barrett-Lennard, G. T., T. P. Kwasnik and G. R. Wilkinson (1973/74) *Interpersonal Development*, **4**, 35–41.

Bebout, J. (1972) *Personal Communication and Group Interaction Analysis Schedule*, T.I.E. Project. Berkeley, California: The Wright Institute.

Bedner, R. L. and G. F. Lawlis (1971) 'Empirical research in group psychotherapy.' In A. E. Bergin and S. L. Garfield (Eds.) *Handbook of Psychotherapy and Behaviour Change*. New York: Wiley, Chapter 21.

Berzon, B., L. N. Solomon and J. Reisel (1972) 'Audio-tape programs for self-directed groups.' In L. N. Solomon and B. Berzon (Eds.), *New Perspectives on Encounter Groups*. San Francisco: Jossey-Bass.

Bion, W. R. (1961) *Experiences in Groups, and Other Papers*. London: Tavistock Publications.

Cooper, C. L. and I. L. Mangham (Eds.) (1971) *T-groups: A Survey of Research*. London: Wiley.

Deutsch, M. (1968) *Field Theory* (Concepts of group dynamics). In D. L. Sills (Gen. Ed.) *Encyclopaedia of the Social Sciences, Vol. 5*, pp. 412–417. New York: McMillan and Free Press.

Farson, R. E. (1972) 'Self-directed groups and community mental health.' In L. N. Solomon and B. Berzon (Eds.), *New Perspectives on Encounter Groups*. San Francisco: Jossey-Bass.

Gibb, J. R. (1971) 'The effects of human relations training.' In A. E. Bergin and S. L. Garfield (Eds.), *Handbook of Psychotherapy and Behaviour Change*. New York: Wiley.

Goffman, E. (1959) *The presentation of Self in Everyday Life*. New York: Doubleday.

Haley, J. (1967) 'Toward a theory of pathological systems.' In G. H. Zuk and I. Boszormenyi-Nagy (Eds.) *Family Therapy and Disturbed Families*. Palo Alto, California: Science and Behavior Books.

Harrison, R. (1965) 'Group composition models for laboratory design.' *J. Applied Behavioral Science*, **1**, 409–432.

Laing, R. D., H. Phillipson and A. R. Lee (1966) *Interpersonal Perception: A Theory and Method of Research*. London: Tavistock Publications.

Lieberman, M. A., I. D. Yalom and M. B. Miles (1973) *Encounter Groups: First Facts*. New York: Basic Books.

Mangham, I. L. and C. L. Cooper (1969) 'The impact of T-groups on managerial behaviour.' *J. of Management Studies*, **6**, 53–72.

Pentony, P. (1970) 'Persons as teams: An analogy.' *Comparative Group Studies*, **1**, 211–268.

Rogers, C. R. (1967) 'The process of the basic encounter group.' In J. F. T. Bugental (Ed.) *The Challenges of Humanistic Psychology*. New York: McGraw-Hill.

Solomon, L. N. and B. Berzon (Eds.) (1972) *New Perspectives on Encounter Groups*. San Francisco: Jossey-Bass.

Stock, D. (1964) 'A survey of research on T-groups.' In L. P. Bradford, J. R. Gibb and K. D. Benne (Eds.) *T-group Theory and Laboratory Method*. New York: Wiley.

Tuckman, B. W. (1965) 'Developmental sequence in small groups.' *Psychological Bulletin*, **63**, 384–399.

Watzlawick, P., J. H. Beavin and D. D. Jackson (1967) *Pragmatics of Human Communication*. New York: W. W. Norton.

Wilkinson, G. R. (1972) 'The application of differentiated small-group processes to developmental learning in an educational setting.' Unpublished doctoral thesis, University of Waterloo.

Wilkinson, G. R. (1973) 'A manual for conducting small groups at three levels of interpersonal intensity (Manual for group leaders).' *Group Process Study Papers*, No. 9, University of Waterloo (Mimeo—Dept. Human Relations and Counselling Studies).

Chapter 5

Consciousness-raising: A Five-stage Model for Social and Organization Change

Samuel A. Culbert

University of California, Los Angeles

'Power to the People', the radical chant of the sixties, could well be considered the moderate maxim of the seventies. More and more people are trying to come up with alternatives and now seem willing to work for change within the system. We seek ways of living and working which involve fewer personal compromises.

All societal roles and practices are open to suspicion. Conventional sex roles are questioned for the limitations they place on individual expressiveness. The Anglo's domination of industry and education is questioned for racist practices and elitist control. Government and the courts are suspect. Formulas and principles of welfare and taxation are challenged. No longer are conventional marriages and single careers the norm; private medicine doesn't work; the environment is deteriorating at an unacceptable rate; and all hidden forms of influence, whether from the private sector or from the government, are being viewed for the limitations they pose to individual freedom and democratic values.

Much of the critique and change results from the work of consumer and citizen's advocacy movements led by experts and lawyers. An increasing amount results from individuals and self-help groups, who through techniques of consciousness-raising, are able to see how the system conflicts with their interests, ideals and self-expression. The process by which individuals—sometimes on their own, usually with the support of a group—recognize conflicts between their interests and the expectations of the system, formulate alternatives that reduce the extent and the number of the compromises they make, and work for change, is termed consciousness-raising. One model by which this process can proceed provides the subject of this paper.

Consciousness-raising

Consciousness-raising takes place gradually with one insight paving the way for others. Usually its goals are the formulation of alternative ways for people to live and work in a social or organization system. However it is one thing to formulate an alternative which can improve our situation, and it is still another to put it into practice. Consequently, in the model I'm about to describe, alternatives we initiate which lead to our improved functioning in the system are considered but the *by-products* of consciousness-raising. It is the actions we can support others to take, based on their own ideas of what constitutes an improved situation, which constitute the *real products* of consciousness-raising.

Consciousness-raising has two components, the personal and the system. The personal component depends on our developing sufficient understanding of who we are naturally, that is, without our adaptations to the system, to recognize which parts of the system fail to fit our needs. The system component involves both our seeing what the system really is and how it actually works—as contrasted with how we've been conditioned to see it—and our thinking about the well-being of others who are also part of the system. Social theorists, like Paulo Friere,* caution us not to accept solutions that free us from our oppression with actions that oppress others. Those we oppress will also need to escape and the pattern may never be broken. For instance, the women's movement made its most important gains only after those involved could look beyond their own oppression to see how the social structure oppressed men as well.

Most of the issues encountered in consciousness-raising have their roots in what we were conditioned to believe about our role in the social system, the social institution or the organization that is the subject of our inquiry. Usually we began our relationships with these systems from a position of low personal power. We were marginal members who felt a strong need to establish ourselves by winning approval and acceptance from those who had power. We conformed to what we felt they expected of us and set our goals on accomplishments which we thought they would value. Had we been able to approach the system from a position of greater internal security and less exaggerated needs for external acceptance, then more of our behaviour might have been more tailored to accomplishing goals which had intrinsic value and interest to us. Instead we submitted to an intense process of socialization and neglected important aspects of ourselves. Unwittingly we contributed to our domestication in the system thereby supporting the status quo.

Hypothetically the system to which we tailored our behaviour worked well under conditions which were present when the system originated. Usually, the system evolved as our needs were articulated and undeniably recognized so that those who played key roles had to let the system change. In some systems, like the Catholic Church in the 1960s, those in power were insufficiently responsive to the basic needs of the people and the system underwent decay. The populace determined that what they wanted was a natural expression of who they were and decided to hold out indefinitely against opposition. In contrast, in the 1970s, we see many instances of social systems, institutions and organi-

*Freire, P. (1970) 'Cultural action for freedom.' *Harvard Educational Review*, Monograph series 1.

zations giving in to meet the demands of minorities who are no longer willing to compromise.

But large-scale change begins with our simplest feelings that something in our relationship with the system is 'off'. Only when we pay attention to the feelings which signal that something is off, can we hope to discover what needs to be improved. But knowing what is off does not necessarily tell us what we need to know to formulate an alternative that actually improves our situation. Oftentimes what we think is off is merely a symptom of an as yet unidentified ill. Until we develop greater understanding about ourselves, the system and our relationship to the system we are likely to make illusionary changes which remove us further from seeing what is wrong. Dealing with the surface problem makes it less likely that we will come to grips with the fundamental ill. Eventually we need a structure or a model that insures our progress is real. Of course relying on a single model can put us in the worst kind of trap.

The consciousness-raising model I'm about to describe was developed to help people who work in large organizations to formulate and put into practice alternatives which better fit their needs and interests than current organizational practices.* However, subsequent experiences with consciousness-raising groups in a variety of settings have convinced me that this model also applies to interactions we have with just about any social system or social institution.

The model has five stages, an overview of which is portrayed in Figure 1. The outputs of each stage provides the inputs for the next, so it is important to carry out these stages in sequence. The model directs our reconsideration of the relationship we have with the social or organization system which is the focus of our inquiry. One part of this reconsideration depends on our indentifying and coping with unnatural and destructive components of the system. Another part depends on our viewing and coping with the immature and self-defeating components of our own personality. A support group is necessary or we can get bogged down by our preoccupation with either part and fail to take constructive steps towards putting our relationship with the system on a higher plane of inquiry.

The support group

Some brief comments about the characteristics and formation of the support group should prove useful in envisioning the five stages of consciousness-raising that follow. Keep in mind, however, that I intend these comments as suggestions rather than as fixed rules. When it comes to consciousness-raising, each person is different, therefore each group is different, and all procedures must remain open to modification based on the experiences of the people involved.

---

*The theory from which this model derived, as well as the model itself, is described in a book I wrote on its application to large organizations: *The Organization Trap and How to Get Out of It*. New York: Basic Books, 1974.

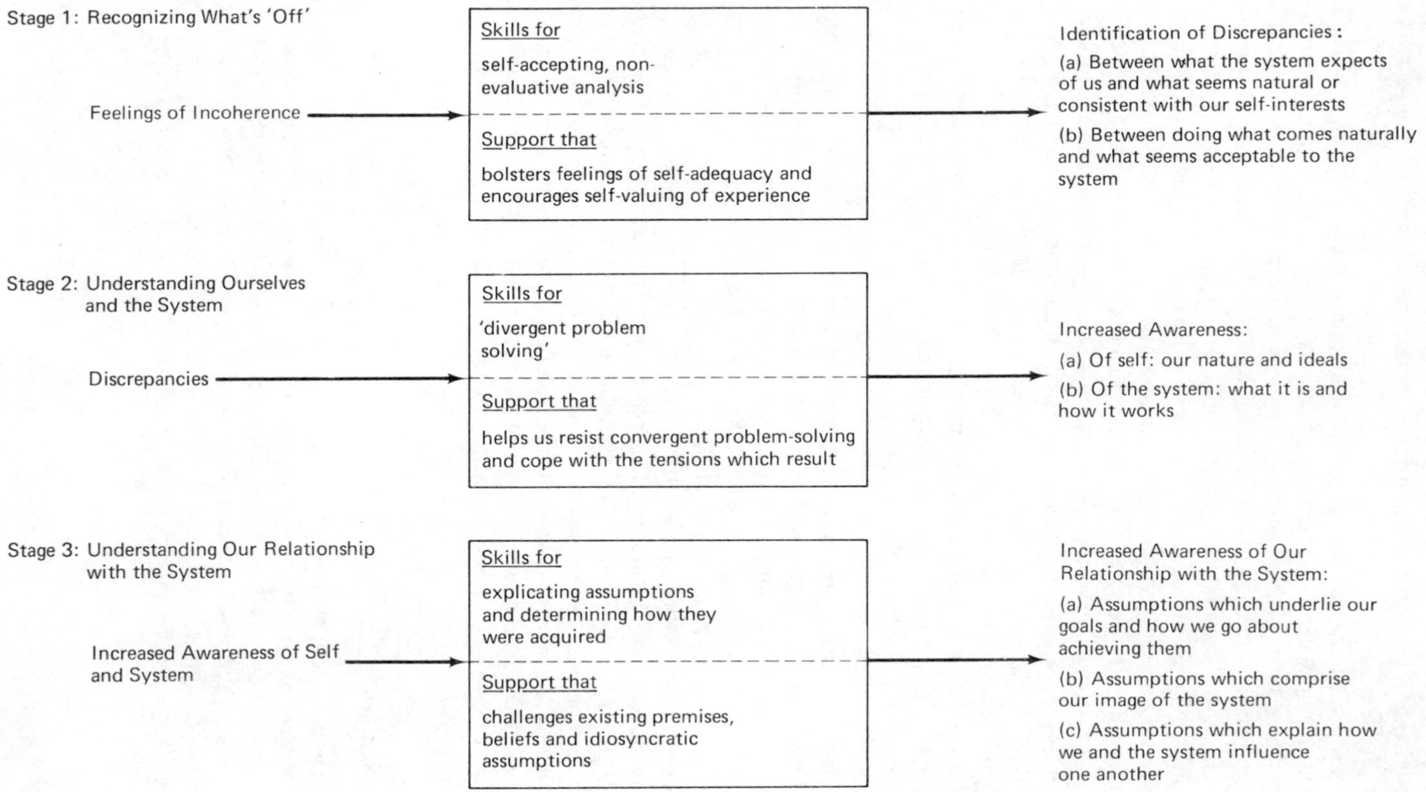

Stage 1: Recognizing What's 'Off'

Feelings of Incoherence

Skills for

self-accepting, non-evaluative analysis

Support that

bolsters feelings of self-adequacy and encourages self-valuing of experience

Identification of Discrepancies :

(a) Between what the system expects of us and what seems natural or consistent with our self-interests

(b) Between doing what comes naturally and what seems acceptable to the system

Stage 2: Understanding Ourselves and the System

Discrepancies

Skills for

'divergent problem solving'

Support that

helps us resist convergent problem-solving and cope with the tensions which result

Increased Awareness:

(a) Of self: our nature and ideals

(b) Of the system: what it is and how it works

Stage 3: Understanding Our Relationship with the System

Increased Awareness of Self and System

Skills for

explicating assumptions and determining how they were acquired

Support that

challenges existing premises, beliefs and idiosyncratic assumptions

Increased Awareness of Our Relationship with the System:

(a) Assumptions which underlie our goals and how we go about achieving them

(b) Assumptions which comprise our image of the system

(c) Assumptions which explain how we and the system influence one another

Figure 1. Consciousness-raising model for social and organization change

Composition. The people who form a support group should have a common relationship to the social system or structure serving as the focus of their discussion. To include others runs the risk of having additional issues raised which, however interesting, will diffuse the group's focus. If it's a group of married women examining their relationship to the demands of family life, then it's advisable that the group not include single women or any men. If it's a taxpayer's group examining the relationship members have to government and the economy, then it's best to include only people who are roughly in the same tax bracket. Homogeneity of composition reduces the possibility that someone will play the expert, oppressor or novice, any one of which are roles that compromise group productivity. Wherever possible the differences which exist between members' age, experience, status; etc. should have no meaning in terms of the relationships members hold to the social or organization system serving as the focus for their discussion.

Size. Support groups need to be small enough for individual pictures of reality to be shared comfortably and large enough for members to construct a fairly accurate perspective on how the system under discussion sees reality. I have been in consciousness-raising groups with as few as five members. With them I enjoyed intimacy but also a troublesome feeling when one person couldn't attend a meeting that our loss was too great to continue without him. On the other hand, I've been a member of groups as large as twenty-two and, while I could always count on someone understanding exactly what I meant, it was a struggle to get a turn to talk.

Commitment. It's important that group members hold a common expectation for how many sessions their group is going to have and when these will be held. I recommend that a group agree to a beginning set of three meetings with time reserved in the middle of the third to discuss whether or not group members feel there should be additional sessions and, if so, how many? Having the expectation of a specified number of meetings provides members the structure they need to articulate problems that group participation is causing them and not just to drop out silently. It also gives members who are opening up a topic which cannot be resolved in a single meeting assurance that they will have another chance to complete their thoughts. If in the course of discussion the group exhausts its concerns with the system they've been discussing or interest shifts to another area, then I recommended that the group dissolve and reconstitute itself with a majority of new members. In this way old members get the benefits of fresh perspectives and new members don't have to contend with group patterns which they lack the history to appreciate.

Group roles. While support groups have no leaders there are some coordination, moderator and recorder roles which need to be performed and it is best that these be traded off from meeting to meeting. We want to avoid anyone feeling overly responsible for group progress or using his or her role to avoid free and active personal involvement.

The model

Stage 1: Recognizing what's 'off'

Consciousness-raising begins with feelings that something is off in our interaction with some social or organization system. Usually these feelings are vague and we are hard-pressed to specify exactly what is bothering us. Specifying what it is constitutes the output of the first stage of consciousness-raising.

The first obstacle we face in raising consciousness lies in our self-suspicions that we are making a big deal out of something minor with which we live daily. However, until we specify the *discrepancy* causing our *feeling of incoherence*, we can't say with confidence whether we live with it daily because it is minor or because we've been socialized to think 'It can't be changed so what's the use of bothering with it?'.

Analysing what's off usually turns up a discrepancy in our relationship to the system on which we're focusing. We can discover what it is by asking ourselves some simple questions:

In what ways could this feeling be a clue that the system expects something from me that doesn't seem natural or consistent with my self-interests?

In what ways could this feeling be a clue that something which seems natural enough to me is considered inappropriate or inadequate by the system?

Asking ourselves these questions brings us to the next obstacle. When something is off in our relationship with an established system, we have a tendency to think that the cause can be traced back to some deficiency in us rather than in the system. We require support to overcome this intimidation and to analyse the exact nature of the conflict.

Group support for Stage 1

When it comes to self-criticism, each of us has something deep and unique to overcome. However, within a support group, these obstacles can be at least temporarily sidestepped. First we can create a conceptual structure that helps us explicate discrepancies in relatively factual, non-judgemental terms. Reflecting on the two questions mentioned above seems to work quite nicely. These questions focus us on incompatibilities not judgements. Second, we can create a milieu of acceptance which encourages support group members not to blame themselves nor judge one another. Such a milieu develops merely by people with similar concerns acknowledging their commonality of interests. It is strengthened as members hear others describe their conflicts with the system and see that more was involved in the conflict than met the eye initially.

However, groups can reach a point where the early supportive momentum is exhausted and members talk as if greater discipline or adequacy on their parts could have avoided some of the problems which got the best of them. When this happens it's advisable to implement a small exercise that gets people back on a track of self-acceptance. For example, members can take turns relating instances where they accepted the blame or responsibility for something that went wrong only to receive a later indication that they were not at fault.

The consciousness-raising process develops momentum as members take turns converting feelings of incoherence into crisp statements of discrepancies. A discrepancy for a participant in a woman's group was between her desires to feel more in control of her body and the paternalistic treatment she receives from doctors. Her realization was sparked by feelings of anger she experienced in the waiting room of her new gynecologist. She reflected, 'There's a familiar note to what I'm feeling.'

As the process of articulating discrepancies gets rolling one person's report and realizations will trigger personal insights in others. These insights need to be recorded and it saves time to have some mechanism for doing this planned in advance. Group members will use their list of discrepancies in the next stage of consciousness-raising.

Stage 2: Understanding ourselves and the system

Recognizing discrepancies offers us an immediate opportunity to take action and set the system straight. However, if we do so, we will miss fundamental problems. Our fantasies of improvement will be circumscribed by the discrepancies which we now want to resolve. A chance to improve something fundamental as opposed to symptomatic is possible only when we delay taking corrective action and use the discrepancies we have noted to increase our understanding of ourselves—how we work and what we need—and our understanding of the system with which we're interacting—what it is and how it actually operates.

Probing for this understanding requires that we resist our usual convergent approach to problem-solving and, at least for a while, engage in a period of divergent analysis. *Convergent problem-solving* involves accepting a problem more or less as it has been stated and systematically directing our thoughts and actions towards solving it. The word convergent refers to our focus on taking steps that sequentially bring us closer to a solution. It does not refer to the number of alternative approaches considered in the process of coming up with a solution.

On the other hand, *divergent problem-solving* requires a different set of thought processes, which all of us know but which few of us can be counted on to use skilfully. They are the inductive thought processes we use when viewing a situation as if it were the symptom rather than the basic ill and then going on to inquire what ailment this symptom might signal. We use these processes when we inquire into the reasons which explain why we have a difference with someone, rather than presenting our case and arguing why our perspective is better than the other person's. In essence, these are the inductive skills which allow us to deepen the level at which problems are conceptualized and strike closer to the basic issues underlying what has been 'problematized'.

Group support for Stage 2

Our support group helps us develop and use our divergent problem-solving skills. Correspondingly, it helps us resist convergent problem-solving and cope with the tensions which result. Not only are we living with unresolved conflicts but we don't even seem to be progressing towards a resolution. Delaying action and thinking divergently requires both discipline and the anticipation of benefits.

There are any number of questions we might raise to approach a discrepancy divergently. We might ask 'If this discrepancy were a symptom of a more basic conflict, what would that conflict be?'. Or we might ask 'What combination of human qualities and organization attributes could have produced conflicts such as the ones we've identified?'. For example, consider the students who got together to discuss their relationship with a graduate programme in psychology. They concerned themselves with discrepancies between their interests in having a good deal of out-of-class interaction with faculty and the non-availability of their faculty. Thinking convergently they wrote a 'constructive' note to the department chairman describing this problem and asking that the situation be changed. Thinking divergently the students might have asked themselves several questions which could spark deeper understanding prior to engaging the academic system. They might have asked:

What does this situation tell us about the pressures our faculty face?

What can we learn about ourselves from the fact that we waited this long before taking action?

What does the way our faculty are conducting themselves say about the professional role we'll be taking once we get our degrees and take jobs teaching?

Have any of the ways we've been acting in relation to one another contributed to our problems with the faculty?

What assumptions are we making that prevent us from directly approaching the faculty with whom we want to talk?

Why haven't individual faculty members also been bothered by this problem? Etc.

Understanding developed through divergent analysis allows us to learn some of the essentials we need to know prior to thinking about a solution. We have the opportunity to upgrade the picture we hold of ourselves, both in terms of making it more realistic and in terms of making a stronger personal commitment to our ideals. We also have the opportunity to see the system, institution or organization with which we experience discrepancies from the standpoint of its goals, priorities and assumptions about how effective operations are carried out. In this way we gain a more realistic picture of both parties involved in the conflict.

The discrepancies we submit to divergent analysis will come from the list our group generated in the first stage of consciousness-raising. Some will be discrepancies about which a large number of group members feel strongly and some will be ones with which only one or two members identify. Discrepancies with which only a few people identify usually reveal more about the individuals experiencing them than about the systems involved. While learning specific to each individual is important, it comes most easily after the group has spent some time analysing discrepancies with which many people identify.

The group discussion proceeds most smoothly when arrangements have been made for recording what is learned from the divergent discussion. I have found it useful to have two easels with newsprint, one of which is used to record insights about the system and the other to record what is learned about the needs and interests of group members. Just how much members ought to debate differences in perception and interpretation is open to question. On one hand we can reasonably expect defensiveness in any situation where consciousness is being raised and we may not get very far unless defences are challenged and differences in opinion are openly discussed. On the other hand, struggling through every difference as if reality were not open to individual interpretation is unrealistic and will weaken group process. At this stage of consciousness-raising it's probably best to argue through some differences and leave others alone once it has been determined that the discussants aren't getting anyplace or what they are debating isn't all that important. Sometimes we can eliminate arguments by formulating small experiments or surveys that people can use in getting added information about a disputed issue. For instance I know a recently promoted shipping manager who was able to verify his colleagues' suspicions that this promotion was the last he would be likely to receive. He went out and surveyed all the other shipping managers in the company and saw that company history was against him.

Group members continually need to caution one another about acting precipitously. For one thing there is more we need to understand about the basis of our relationship with the system, and for another, once we take action we usually stop searching and begin focusing convergently. In the example above, the shipping manager did not know all he needed to know in order to confront his boss intelligently. He was in danger of using the hat-in-hand approach which consistently had gotten him nowhere. His support group helped him to see this.

Stage 3: Understanding our relationship with the system

Increased understanding of ourselves and of the system helps us to recognize parts of the system that suit our self-interests and to resist other parts which try to contain us. We sense a new personal freedom. However, getting carried away with this 'freedom' proves to be a short-term strategy for gaining control. It puts us underground, 'working' the system. But eventually those who seek to influence us will discover that we've eluded them and we'll be back playing cat and dog again.

Real freedom depends on our ability to address the underlying conflicts that produce discrepancies. In order to see these conflicts we need to increase our understanding of how we've been interacting with the system. We can use what we now know about ourselves and the system to produce this understanding. We need to explicate the assumptions on which our inter-actions with the system are based and examine how these assumptions were formed. We'll also need to distinguish between those assumptions which are the result of our own experience and those which are the result of social condi-tioning.

For those assumptions which we determine to be the direct result of our experience we'll want to decide whether or not they remain applicable to current conditions. We can update our assumptions where we find conditions have changed and we can respond with renewed confidence where we find conditions are more or less the same.

The greatest opportunities for learning are found in re-examining assump-tions which were acquired implicity through our conditioning in the system. They provide us a chance to see what the system would like us to believe and to decide for ourselves whether or not this is valid. They also allow us to view in retrospect the processes used to indoctrinate us in false beliefs. Viewing these processes gives us a better handle on how we're vulnerable to external controls without knowing it.

Basically there are at least three areas of our relationship to the system where we'd do well to search out assumptions. The first area involves the goals we hold for our interactions with the system and the means we use for achieving them. Along these lines I once listened to a group of people planning for their retirement recognize how they'd been programmed by the society to hold the goal of eventually leaving their city life and routine for an old-age community in the country. They further realized that the uncertainties connected with this move caused them to have a corollary goal of parsimony. They now felt badly about having become overly-conservative spenders who deprived them-selves of luxuries in their fifties so that they'd have sufficient funds for the years ahead.

The second area involves assumptions we make about the system: its purpose, values, roles in society and, in particular, its way of viewing us. Along these lines I once listened to a group of unmarried 'cohabitators' reflect on the social institution of marriage and how it impacts on their desires to have children. The learnings were diverse. One woman realized that she believed every child deserved married parents and that she was using her unmarried state as a means of hiding her own ambivalence about having children. A man from a second couple realized how his being brought up with the ethic of 'children should be seen but not heard' was spoiling his relationship with the child of the woman he was living with. A third couple spent a good deal of time focusing on the legal rights of children who are born out of wedlock.

The third area involves assumptions that explain the ways we and the system influence one another. Along these lines I once listened to a group of university researchers discuss how they and the foundations which grant research monies influence one another. They realized that more often than not they were taken in by the 'unimportant' modifications they were making to fit their research proposals within the parameters of what they thought a granting agency would fund. They also acknowledged how it is sometimes necessary to reinterpret their data in order to present a valid case for why they should be awarded additional funds. Several of these researchers themselves sat on funding panels and they reflected that their own 'working' of the system caused them to view other people's findings with suspicion.

Group support for Stage 3

Support group members can help one another to explicate the assumptions they make. They can help by listening to one another talk about each of the three areas mentioned above and identifying the 'as-if' and 'if-then' messages contained in what they hear. For instance, in the first area members are asked to state their goals for personal success and fulfilment in relation to the system with others inquiring why these goals are personally meaningful and questioning how each speaker plans to go about accomplishing them. Each person's assumptions are recorded and later on others are asked to register their identification with what they have heard. Once members have declared their connection with an assumption, then they can join the person who mentioned it in searching out when and how that assumption was formed.

Figuring out when an invalid assumption was acquired proceeds most smoothly when members trade stories about where they first acted on the assumption being examined. However we won't always be able to track an assumption back to its origin. In instances where we can't, it may be sufficient to think of current situations in which the assumption plays a prominent role in determining how we act. In either case, we'll want to recall the people who strongly advocate the assumption, the roles they play in the system, what the assumption does for the system and the conditions under which the assumption seems to be most applicable.

Assumptions with which only one or two members identify offer special opportunities to learn about the people involved. These assumptions probably have idiosyncratic origins and may often play an important role in a person's relationships with other social systems. Whether or not constructive personal learning emerges from exploring these assumptions will depend on the trust and support that has been built up among the members of the group.

When it comes to individual learning in a group, especially where emotions are involved, I have been a longtime advocate of the simultaneous presence of support and confrontation. I'm for the type of support that accepts the person's difficulties in actively reflecting on a certain topic or on accurately hearing what has been said to him or her, not insincere support for his or her point of view. I'm for the type of confrontation that engages the person's resistance to considering what's been said and inquiring into his or her defensiveness, not confrontation aimed at getting the person to agree with what's been said. Both of these roles are difficult for a single individual to assume simultaneously, which of course is the advantage of having the help of several persons in a group.

Stage 4: Formulating alternatives

New understanding about ourselves, about the system, and about the assumptions which link us to the system provide us with what we need to know to formulate alternatives that improve our relationship to the system. We do this by noting how assumptions which have been characterizing our relationship with the system are inconsistent with that we have learned about our own needs, interests and ideals. Reflecting these inconsistencies against what we now know about the system allows us to assess the practicality of alternatives which occur to us now.

Focusing on inconsistencies, rather than reflecting only on our nature, provides a contrast that helps us to envision alternatives. Inconsistencies stimulate thoughts about what would constitute a better situation. Basically there are two types of alternatives we might formulate: those which improve the way the system works and those which change our relationship to it. For instance, a group of nurses considered requesting permission to present their views on reforms needed in the staffing of post-operative recovery rooms to the administrative staff of their hospital. But this type of request would have reinforced their subordinate position in the medical hierarchy. Alternatively they decided to call a strike for hospital reforms with special attention to not making any demands for personal benefits that might cause others to see them as only out for themselves. In this instance they wanted recognition as professionals capable of representing the public's interest.

Overall this fourth stage of consciousness-raising involves re-examining how we've been socialized by the system. In a sense it can be likened to a self-directed process of resocialization.

Group support for Stage 4

Group members help us spot where our relationship to the system conflicts with our self-interests and nature. They also help us reflect how these conflicts fit within the priorities of what matters to us and to conceptualize alternatives which can be put into practice without undue personal hardship. However, before group members can advise us intelligently, we have to spend some time filling out their pictures of who we are and where we want to go. With a more complete picture, they can spot when we're going off to fight a battle that doesn't need to be won and when we're involved in changing something that might cost us more than we're receiving in exchange.

While we can't tell others everything, there is much we can cover in the course of an hour by addressing ourselves to essentials. In particular we need to relate those life events and personal feelings which will help support group members to understand why the inconsistencies on which we plan to focus carry so much meaning for us. For instance, if we're someone who is interested in the public's access to coastal recreation areas, our group needs to know why we place so much importance on beaches, our history in fighting for public rights, or whatever they need to hear to appreciate why this issue grabs us the way it does.

Group members can help us to consider a broader range of alternatives than we can formulate for ourselves. For example, if an inconsistency results in our formulating an alternative that proposes a change in the system, group members might ask us if we can think of an alternative that involves our changing our relationship to the system. If we can't, they might suggest one that occurs to them. They do so not because they expect us to use it but because they want to open up an entirely new avenue of possibilities for our consideration.

When it comes to our relationship to social systems there are few alternatives we can formulate that won't impact on others. Accordingly, our support group can help us think through the types of reactions we're likely to receive and think up ways to pose our alternatives so that we will evoke minimum resistance in others. When the issue is crucially important to us, and we can predict in advance that we're going to incite counterforces, our support group can help us plan how to cope with these forces and bolster us when we're under stress. Additionally, group members can help us monitor our progress. They can point out when we're making more headway than we think we are, perhaps because it is being accomplished in a slightly different form than we expected. They can also caution us not to be taken in when others whom we are trying to influence change their words but not their actions.

Stage 5: Affecting the lives of others

Thus far I've given the impression that consciousness-raising is something we can do on our own and doesn't necessarily involve our getting the cooperation of those whom we see as blocking us. This is true to a point, but eventually we'll do much better if others in the system develop empathy for what we are trying to achieve. To develop this empathy, we will need to approach people who see things differently and we will get furthest when we approach them from the standpoint of what's in it for them rather than from the standpoint of what's in it for us.

We must keep in mind that each person has a different view of reality and from that view most all of his or her actions make sense. Thus, while we're ardently focusing on the problems a system creates, we can expect that there will be others who only talk about the benefits. In all likelihood these will be the very people whose cooperation we are going to need if things are to change peacefully. We will need to find a way of approaching them so that they can join us in the search for reforms.

If we go on the assumption that there is an objective reality, which will be rationally perceived by anyone who puts his or her mind to thinking things through, then we are likely to approach others by advocating a specific plan and seeking their explicit support. However, if we assume that people will resist converging on a single picture of reality, that they will proceed differently once they have grasped what is at stake and that maximum benefits are possible only when people holding different perspectives pool their ideas of how the system can be improved, then we are better off approaching the system open-endedly without advocating specific improvements. The latter approach reflects my beliefs about how to bring about change in the majority of situations. We broaden out from our parochial viewpoint to consider the well-being of all members of the system and in the process act like a statesperson might behave. Accordingly, I refer to the thinking used in this approach as 'statespersonlike'.

The statespersonlike approach begins after we've raised our consciousness about what's off in our relationship to a given social system and have figured out how that system is based on misassumptions about our needs and interests. We not only have a specific alternative in mind, but we also have sufficient grasp of the fundamentals to recognize alternate proposals that appropriately address our concerns.

We put this approach into action by developing a friendly dialogue with people we see playing a key role in our dilemmas. In sequence: we want to point out the problems we face in our functioning in the system (not the solutions we've envisioned); we want to support these people in identifying discrepancies they experience which either are comparable to our own or are created for them by our experiencing the discrepancies we have noted; and we want to acquaint them with the process of divergent problem-solving and encourage them to use it in reflecting on the discrepancies they have conceptualized. Throughout, our emphasis is on helping them identify the discrepancies which are present in their own life in the system. In doing this we need to remember that what these people learn from divergent thinking about their discrepancies is far more important than the specific phrasing they give a discrepancy.

If in using this approach we involve ourselves in discussing specific actions, then we're likely to cross the thin line that separates a statesperson from a partisan. Consciousness is political. People are likely to become reactionary if they sense our collaborative attitude is a guise for indoctrinating them in our political beliefs. They are almost certain to feel this way if they judge the changes they are considering more likely to improve our lot than their own.

At some point we want to tactfully suggest to the people we are approaching that they begin to divergently discuss these issues with people who have similar roles in the system as themselves. Only when they are supported by a peer group of their own can we count on our discussion with them to be perceived as sufficiently fairminded so that their perspectives can be pooled with ours to create a third, more enlightened and synergistic, reality. Wherever possible we want to stay away from a modality of negotiating on the basis of 'If you do this for me, I'll do this for you'. We want to create an attitude of mutual cooperation. The most significant changes will come about when all parties are looking for ways to improve the overall functioning of the system and where each party can support changes which bring other closer to a more fulfilling existence in the system.

Idealistic? To be sure. But it can happen. It's the kind of tactic a group of enlightened students used in a consciousness-raising session with policemen in the spring of 1970. They did this in the aftermath of police intervention to stop unauthorized rallies protesting the United States Army's incursion into Cambodia. It is the kind of tactic I've seen human relations experts use when helping high-level managers realize the consequences their assumptions about control and orderly managerial processes hold for initiation throughout the ranks of their company's workforce. And it's the kind of tactic my colleagues and I use when approaching the UCLA administration with proposals for field and laboratory courses which involve little reading.

Group support for stage 5

By the time we've gotten to this stage our needs for support are subtle. We need an occasional pat-on-the-back and someone who will point out that we're caught up in our own picture of things. By now we're out on our own contacting people whose viewpoints must be encountered for the system to change. Our interactions are quite complex. We are only indirectly addressing our needs for change and the very people we're talking with supportively are the ones we'd like to confront. Our support group will need to keep us directed toward long-term fundamental change as contrasted with the short-term situational change that is easiest for us to pursue. The group helps us work off the tensions which result from keeping our own ideas of how the system might be improved out of the divergent discussions we're attempting to have with those we seek to influence. Once we insert our ideas, it's we, not the people we're contacting, who are talking convergently.

To this point I have not explored the most powerful change tactic a support group can use. It is a tactic which we all know—banding together to overpower the opposition through a variety of mechanisms from civil disorder, to disruptive strikes, to peaceful petitions, to constructive discussions. I've avoided going into this because it is also the riskiest tactic a group can use. It can polarize and politicize the opposition and it can produce tunnel vision and attitudes of righteousness within us. In the model I use, it is dialogue and openminded thinking that count. As a matter of principle I'm willing to sacrifice the immediate gain—but then there are always exceptions. If we can't get enough of what we need to sustain ourselves in the present, then we may feel little recourse but to indulge our desires for action. Hopefully we'll get enough nourishment from our support group to sustain our collaborative approach to meaningful change in the system.

Conclusion

In some ways consciousness-raising can be considered the next generation of encounter-groups and sensitivity training. It pits the human dimensions of group process against problems which have substance beyond the feelings and realities of the people discussing them. It views conflicts people have with a system as an interaction of personal needs and system structure. These are problems which cannot be solved by the creative use of emotional energy alone. Rather, these are problems which have deep substantive components requiring intellectual muscle and conceptual skills. Nevertheless, without group members to give emotional support and exercise interpersonal sensitivity we will not develop the means of sustaining ourselves in working for funda-mental and lasting change.

But change is evolutionary. Our best ideas today are just that. We can count on learning more tomorrow and this will mean new, improved visions of what is possible. Thus it's important that we do not become complacent with the changes our consciousness-raising leads us to seek today. Eventually we must return to areas we have already covered and once again ask ourselves the questions which led us to see new possibilities.

Chapter 6

Group and Organizational Team Building: A Theoretical Model for Intervening

Robert R. Blake
Jane Srygley Mouton

Scientific Methods, Inc.
Austin, Texas

Organizations are segmented into hierarchies of departments, division, sections and individuals. At many levels, particularly above the lowest, those reporting to the same boss have more or less well defined jobs with different specialized responsibilities. Yet no manual of position descriptions can possibly foresee all day-by-day contingencies. Under such arrangements, then, valid communication, mutual understanding and teamwork are indispensable if coordinated effort and productive achievements are to result. Otherwise it becomes a virtual impossibility to meld the separated activities in ways that produce either meaningful operational results or a sense of personal accomplishment. Even non-traditional designs such as matrix and project structures, in so far as they offer no solution to the fundamental problem, quickly return to hierarchical arrangements.

Hierarchical systems of organization predispose against long-term continuity of good teamwork. For example, in pyramidal structures—whether static or expanding—vacancies are forecasted or may unexpectedly occur. This entails some members being chosen for advancement over others. Also, available positions become fewer and fewer toward the top. Finally there is only one. Since not all can get the nod, choice of one person for advancement involves the implied or explicit rejection of others.

At the other end of the career continuum is termination. Often those who join organizations look forward to decades-long tenure within them. Yet not all are to earn and retain the organization's respect. Some are asked to leave. Many who don't get along well do so of their own accord. No-one—either as a boss or colleague—can be sufficiently objective to evaluate in every case the most qualified person for advancement or for year-by-year employment continuity.

The basic realities of organization life cannot help but stimulate competitive feelings, invidious comparisons, jealousies and antagonisms. Where there are, for everyone, incessant branching possibilities either of going up, being side-lined or squeezed out, people feel a necessity to 'play their cards close to the chest' and withhold the kinds of actions which, no matter how much 'objec-tively' needed by the organization, might involve risks of misinterpretation by others, or of not succeeding. Blots like these on one's track record increase the likelihood of being passed over or even terminated. Yet when these individual 'personal safety' considerations predominate because of peer-competition pres-sures, needed cooperation, mutual understanding and teamwork are at stake and often sacrificed.

There is another aspect too. No matter whether the advancement route is mostly up-from-the-ranks or from some moderatly high platform for pro-fessionals and university graduates, little attention may have been given to aiding future managers to become knowledgeable about their personal behavi-our options and preferences and the impact of these upon other people. Other than in the school of hard knocks, there may be little opportunity to learn to become effective in problem-solving interactions involving two or more in-dividuals. Although some human relations training might be provided, educat-ing individuals in the theory and skills of teamwork is lacking. Thus many organizational situations are managed poorly because people enter management with insufficient teamwork skills, particularly for dealing creatively with the inevitable conflicts that arise when managers who are in man-to-man competi-tion try to put their heads together to arrive at a best decision or solve a given problem.

One of the most significant organizational improvement developments in the late 1950s was the emergence of Team Building as a way of strengthening interpersonal effectiveness (Blake, Mouton and Blansfield, 1962). Since that time, the general idea has been widely applied, with consultants interpreting the 'team building' concept each according to his assumptions of the best way to go about it.

At least five distinct approaches to team building are currently being engaged in. These respectively involve cathartic, catalytic, confrontational, perspective and theory interventions. Those to be described here are derived from a broader study of interventional approaches (Blake and Mouton, 1975a). Although dealing with different aspects of team dilemmas, each of the five approaches has the same ultimate purpose, namely, to aid individuals, during their inter-actions, to make better organizational contributions while also gaining greater personal gratification from the exercise and strengthening of their productive capabilities.

In this chapter, attention focuses on the *team* and its members as interacting participants who have a common boss and organizational responsibility. Thus, other interventions which also may take place in a *group* setting—but not a structured and purposive organization—and which have as their purpose in-creasing individual awareness and understanding of one another's thoughts and emotions (Lieberman, Yalom and Miles, 1973), are not dealt with.

In the sections that follow, case examples will illustrate what the consultant does, what client problem is most pertinent from the consultant's viewpoint, and what the expected or unexpected outcomes of intervention are. Thus, a comparative theory of team building is to be presented. This is an abridged version of a longer study available elsewhere (Blake and Mouton, 1975b).

Cathartic team building

Catharsis is a technical word. The core idea is of a process of 'cleansing' that brings about a release from tensions. The key concept is that the consultant aids team members to experience and 'work through' emotions and feelings that are hampering performance or disturbing behaviour in unwelcome ways. Then after catharsis, as the approach predicts, the particular problem situation facing team members can be dealt with in an objective, problem-solving fashion.

The basic proposition is that either organizational hierarchy inevitably arouses interpersonal tensions and lack of mutual understanding or that some particular organization's members are currently deficient in their teamwork. The approach of cathartic team building is to aid team members to express their feelings of tension, frustration, anxiety, insecurity and bewilderment. This is to be done within a climate of sympathetic acceptance and non-evaluative appreciation by those with whom they work. Such circumstances permit feelings which have prevented effective cooperation in the past to be discharged and dissipated, perhaps being replaced by understanding of each person's innately good intentions. Catharsis provides the background for building a climate of trust, openness, respect and intimacy which is essential for collaborative effort. After such cathartic release, team members are expected to get to a basis of thinking that is unencumbered by disabling emotions. Then work problems of team members can be dealt with in a more objective, problem-solving fashion.

An episode involving hierarchy-based tensions is reported by Margulies and Raia who describe cathartic interventions with clerical workers and their supervisors in a large organization in the southern United States (Margulies and Raia, 1968).

The company problem that led to consultants being engaged related to excessive personnel turnover. As the consultants interviewed to learn more about it, however, they found that people in the employment office wanted to talk about their *own* immediate problems. The intense emotions associated with these, in turn, served as the beginning of the cathartic process as employees told of how a high degree of supervisor–worker control, imposed on a one-to-one basis, resulted in low trust, enforced isolation of employees who needed to cooperate, lack of instruction and the rejection of improvement ideas. This is a clear example of where the 'client problem', as initially formulated, was not the 'real' one.

Viewing these interpersonal problems as barriers to any genuine problem-solving efforts, Margulies and Raia proposed and got agreement to conduct 'family group' laboratory sessions for team development. These were initiated by feeding back summaries of data gathered during earlier interviews. These summaries centred attention on the 'low trust' climate existing among participants. Though the summary feedback dismayed participants, it generated a high degree of motivation to do something, and a plan to have one four-hour meeting per week for a period of several weeks. Nick, the common boss of both the recruitment and selection supervisors and their sections, attended the meetings but mostly in a silent role.

In the first session,

'There appeared to be a good deal of anxiety and nervousness in the group. The participants, seated in a circle, clustered in small sub-groups. Barbara, Joann, and Judy, all of whom had come to the employment office less than six months ago, sat next to each other. A second sub-group included Louise, Lorraine, and Pauline. These were the "old-timers" who had worked in the office for a number of years. Jerri and Sandy, who had come to the employment office from another department, seemed to be uncommitted to any sub-group and resisted overtures from the other participants. Mary, the selection supervisor, sat tapping a pencil on the notebook on her lap and seemed generally unconcerned.

Most of the session was spent struggling with ways to express feelings toward the supervisor.

"Mary," Judy said at one point, "I wish I could tell you how difficult you make it for me around here. And I know that some of the others feel the way I do, but just won't say it."

"O.K.," Mary replied, "Go ahead and say what you want to, all of you. It's your meeting."

"Well, it's *that* kind of comment and the way you look right now that makes it awfully hard for me to say how I feel," said a somewhat flushed Judy. Suddenly she cried to the rest of the group, "Where are the rest of you in this! Doesn't anyone else care about what goes on around here?"

Barbara offered some support. Hesitantly, she said, "Yes, Judy, I do feel the way you do about Mary's behavior. I just wonder if it's worth exposing myself. But I'm willing to try if it will do any good." Several others, in a very detached way, shared some of their impressions of the supervisor's behavior.' (Margulies and Raia, 1968, pp. 5–6.)

The catharsis started a process among the girls of expressing and sharing emotions. At the next session,

'With some help from the trainers, a few of the participants were able to explore their relationships with the supervisor. Much of the discussion centered around the feelings of frustration and dependency, aroused in the newer girls by what appeared to them to be Mary's persistent need to know everything and to control everyone. Barbara told of how she had cried at home the night before after being "scolded" by the supervisor earlier in the day.

"I only stopped in to ask Judy a question about the interview form," she said to her supervisor, "I was only in there a couple of minutes when you came in and chewed me out."'

Mary gave Barbara a technical procedures-oriented reply. During the remainder of the session, in which she was the target of more emotional expressions by other subordinates of hers, she seemed to stay composed; but immediately afterwards,

'"I didn't know they felt this way," she said to one of the trainers, "I didn't know I was such a terrible supervisor."' (Margulies and Raia, 1968, p. 6.)*

Suffice it to say that morale subsequently perked up, and with a more open, trust-based set of relationships, it became possible to focus on and successfully solve some significant work-related issues.

Many other examples of 'unblocking' through cathartic release of emotions are described in the literature (Kuriloff and Atkins, 1966; Fordyce and Weil, 1971, pp. 129–131).

Many times the need for change is recognized, yet it does not occur because of undefined fears people have. Fear of the unknown has the effect of saying, 'Better not risk it', and so needed innovations may be sacrificed. Releasing participants from the 'blind' consequences of fear is a first step toward progress. Gibb (1972) describes a situation which is pertinent to this point. Team building is about to get started in an organization, but there is a resistance to full participation. This is diagnosed as 'fear', and Gibb explains why it must be worked through rather than being ignored or ridden over roughshod. His contention is that failure to work such feelings through could result in 'foot dragging', absenteeism from the team-building sessions, participation but with low involvement, and so on.

The several top men who are to participate in team-building sessions come together in a pre-team-building session. They are provided with the opportunity to share with one another and then to explore as many of their fears about team building as they are able to ventilate. The consultant helps get the fears into the open by assisting participants to share with one another their doubts and reservations. For example, managers might express the fear that team building may reduce their power to deal with subordinates. Initially it is felt that if they, the managers, begin to act in ways that permit subordinates to have more involvement and participation, poorer decisions might result than under one-to-one decision making. After full exploration and working through of such feelings, group members begin to see that some of these fears are unrealistic or imaginary. Other fears are identified and found to be obstacles to excellence that need to be faced and surmounted. Thus a number of intra-team constraints and barriers which might have doomed the team-building programme to failure can be removed. Other cases using a cathartic approach to uncorking long-standing frustrations and hostilities have been reported (David, 1967; Levinson, 1973, pp. 166–167).

Two kinds of team situations that seem to have been approached by cathartic interventions have been described in this section. The first was one characterized by tensions that various team members felt regarding their boss. The other example involved tensions shared among equal-rank colleagues concerned with engaging in proposed activity that presently seemed risky.

As was illustrated in these team situations, the cathartic consultant con-

*Reproduced from Newton Margulies and Anthony P. Raia (1968) 'People in organizations. A case for team training.' *Training and Development Journal*, **22**, 8, by permission of The American Society for Training and Development.

tributes in two ways. First, he encourages participants to express their feelings in an unfiltered, authentic way. They can do this more easily when the consultant accepts whatever the client says in a non-evaluative, non-judgemental manner, thereby inviting the client to put his defences aside and to give expression to his deeper-lying feelings. Defensive kinds of behaviour such as rationalizations, justifications, denials and projections—all of which are inappropriate to the situation—tend not to be provoked because the consultant is neither 'attacking' nor 'prescribing'. The other consultant contribution is through ensuring that participants in the team-building process 'share' with one another by listening understandingly and appreciating what is really being said. When team participants do this, they facilitate one another in expressing their feelings and emotions. Thus, the emotional expression is taken at full value—those who hear it accept it as the person's authentic feelings and thereby take a less judgemental attitude than they otherwise might have done. The consultant himself, by providing an ongoing example of non-defensive behaviour, helps to reduce the likelihood that others will react in ways that block cathartic release.

The purpose of cathartic interventions is to aid in releasing emotional tensions and misunderstandings that stem from feelings and emotions which people either have 'bottled up' or in some other way have felt a reluctance to express. Feelings that prevent team members from thinking through to decisions or solutions in objective ways have to be resolved before progress can occur. The consultant's rationale is that after releasing the dammed-up emotions through cathartic interventions, the problem causes can then be identified and rectified.

Catalytic team building

The word *catalysis* describes a kind of chemical reaction. When placed in conjunction with certain other substances a catalytic agent causes a change or reaction to happen; one which either would not have occurred had this agent not been present, or would have occurred more slowly. The term also is used to describe a particular way of bring about changes in teamwork. A consultant enters a situation with the intention of catalyzing a new 'process' or of increasing the rate at which 'process' is presently occurring. The client's situation is taken at face value by the consultant. Rather than working toward any fundamental alteration of the *status quo*, his goal is to assist those operating within it to be more effective in their customary team activities.

The catalytic approach concentrates attention of team members not so much on the emotional undercurrents in their relations but rather upon their need to reduce pluralistic ignorances. Examples of the latter can be shared lack of understandings of the situation or of one another. Greater understanding can be facilitated through gathering data about the situation itself, the reactions of each individual to the others and self-perceptions. These empirical facts, summarized and presented with logical analysis, are the 'agents' that the consultant uses to catalyze the client's situation and facilitate his change efforts.

Such data often consist of *social* facts such as the existing state of the client's attitudes and emotions. Bringing into awareness empirical facts that presently are not shared or have been 'misunderstood' aids in *perceptual* clarification. The catalytic assumption is that once team members 'see' their shared situation more objectively they can then take the needed steps to improve it.

The data gathered by the consultant are usually obtained from preliminary inquiries addressed to individual team members, either through interviewing or the use of survey instruments. The consultant then studies the replies and summarizes them into a number of categories.

At the first subsequent team-building session, discussion is likely to be initiated by the consultant, who 'feeds back' his summary of findings. He avoids revealing the identity of which members said what. This is made possible by grouping different reactions into categories so that in each case more than one person will have made the same or similar point. A recognizable point of view which is held by one person only is likely not to be reported. Furthermore, when feeding back about members' behaviour, the catalytic-oriented consultant usually specifically quoting verbatim reactions that he got when he asked the question, 'How would you describe the management style of Mr X? How do you think he could be more effective?'. He avoids this because to present such information exposes Mr X to data that he reacts to without knowing its source.

A U.S. State Department project in team building that used a catalytic approach to intervention is described by its team leader, Crockett, who at the time was Deputy Under Secretary of State for Administration. The interventions were led by Ferguson and Seashore. They initiated the project through interviewing all twelve team members, with the anonymity of each respondent ensured.

The first session was started by Ferguson, who reviewed the agenda and procedures to be employed during the next two days. He indicated that he would present interview-based data on a man-by-man basis first. Then each of the pictured persons could react to the feedback data, with others later joining the discussion.

The interview data for each man were presented on a large board. They were arrayed anonymously, to keep hostility or embarrassment at a minimum, and categorized so that each distinctive description of a personal characteristic was indicated with the frequency with which it had been reported by other participants. As an example, these are the reactions posted to describe Crockett.

'. . . For example: "He doesn't delegate properly." "He gives contradictory instructions to different people so that there are binds within the group." "He makes unilateral decisions relating to our responsibilities without first talking them over with us." "He takes action in our areas without telling us." "We are not generally informed about what's happening in the whole group." "We are kept ignorant about one another's activities." "He doesn't like confrontation and conflict." "He can't make tough (people) decisions." "We can't get in to see him." "He sees the wrong people." "He doesn't give us his attention when we do see him." "He has too many irons in the fire at one time." "He confuses us about priorities." "He is manipulative."' (Crockett, 1970, p. 297.)

Then participants informed one another of the meanings to them of the posted data.

'...But here again the consultants tried to give us understanding of the deep difference between a cold, hard, objective, critical "appraisal" by the boss on one hand and a legitimate (even if critical) "feedback" that is given in a climate of trust and warmth and caring, on the other. We discussed the obligations which were imposed upon all who opted into such a group; specifically, we were reminded of the obligation of "caring" for other group members. Members who "cared" had obligations both individually and collectively to help the others to understand how they "came through" and "were seen," how they were "felt" and "perceived," how they "looked," and how their actions and conduct and attitudes were helpful or were hurtful in their communications. Each had an obligation to give and to receive feedback, and to give coaching to the others.' (Crockett, 1970, p. 299.)

How it worked out in practice is illustrated by Crockett's description.

'For example, where one had said I did not delegate, I denied it by saying, "I am the best delegator in the Department. You all have authority. You have responsibilities in your area. And it is up to you to get them done." And then the anonymity would disappear because the person who had put this item on the list would come in hard to justify his stand. And so with illustration of time and place and circumstance he would prove when I had not delegated properly or how I would fall back after I had given them authority, or how I had made a decision unknown to them or how, before evidence had come in, I had changed their decision, and so on. This kind of confrontation only started the conversation. Chuck would not let any of us off so easily. He probed deeply. How did my action make them feel? How did they see me? What were my motives? How did this affect the group's work together? This and many more questions that he asked would give me the opportunity to reply, "Yes, but you don't realize the pressure I am under from the White House ... or from the Congress ... or from the Secretary ...." And the whole complexity of relationships, the pressures upon me, and explanations for my seemingly erratic behavior would come out. From such explanations and probings came understanding and a sense of sharing that had never before existed in the group.' (Crockett, 1970, p. 300.)*

Such feedbacks under the 'relationships-as-facts' approach did much to reduce the pluralistic ignorance existing within the group as to how each was seen by the others, and helped to reduce or eliminate each individual's 'blind spots' within his self-perception.

A team-building project relying on survey research feedback has been reported by Baumgartel (1959). First, survey instruments were filled out by members of six accounting departments in various operating components of a large company. These survey instruments focused on three aspects: work, human relations and the organization. Sixty supervisors and 640 non-supervisory employees participated. Then four departments received data feedback, and discussion of them took place over a 12-month period. Two departments received no feedback. All six departments completed research instruments both before and after the survey research instruments were completed, regardless of whether or not they were later to receive feedback. This strategy permits an answer to the question, 'What effect did the feedback from survey research produce?'. Members of departments who received feedback and discussed it felt:

*Reproduced by special permission from William J. Crockett (1970) 'Team building—one approach to organizational development.' *Journal of Applied Behavioral Science*, **6**, 3.

Their supervisors better understood their point of view.
Their supervisors got along better with each other.
They understood better how their supervisor sees things.

As Baumgartel concluded,

'The result of this study suggest that the creative use of new information for conferences and meetings at all levels of departmental organization may be one of the best and most dynamic avenues to management development and organizational growth.' (Baumgartel, 1959.)

The key element in the catalytic approach is that in some way or another all the consultant's interventions are part of an endeavour to get participants to see the situation from one another's points of view. Until this prerequisite perceptual clarity is attained, needed actions for improving the situation cannot be taken. So the motivation for catalytic team building is a felt need to gain improved perception of the situation now facing the group. By the consultant operating within the client's felt needs, defences such as rationalization, justification, projection and denial are not aroused. The consultant, in other words, avoids doing anything which would provoke defences.

The consultant sees himself as a change 'agent', as someone who can increase the information flow, whether this be of impersonal facts or the summarized facts of feelings. His techniques of strengthening information flow vary with the situation. Sometimes he gathers information by interview, sometimes by survey research, action research, or the use of simple tests and questionnaires. Later he aids people to sort into categories that clarify their perceptions of the situation, what they have earlier said or felt. He may do a number of things to keep the discussion 'objective' and away from personalities. One way is to group the data and only feed back what has been said by several. Another is to promise anonymity in data gathering and not to reveal sources during feedback. A third is to 'edit' strongly hostile or provocative remarks which, if fed back in the literal manner in which they were expressed, would be likely to wound. A fourth way is to place himself in the role of intermediary and in this way to provide a buffer between those who, for example, if they were to confront one another, would become adversaries. A final way is by the consultant offering procedural suggestions which permit the client team to gather 'neutral' data and then to assist them in categorizing and interpreting these. At the present time, this approach to team building appears to be the most widely represented in the literature (Davis, 1969, p. 292; Daw and Gage, 1967, p. 184; Drinkwater, 1972, pp. 116–117; Fordyce and Weil, 1971, pp. 140–141; French, 1972, pp. 36–39; Harvey and Boettger, 1971, p. 164; Humbel, 1967, p. 60; Jacques, 1964, p. 362; Miles et al., 1970, p. 357; Schein, 1969, p. 106; Schmuck and Runkel, 1972; Varney and Lasher, 1973, pp. 75–82).

Team building by confrontation

Some of the most important value-based assumptions underlying organizational hierarchy, segmentation and specialized responsibilities involve the uses and misuses of organizational power in problem solving and decision making. These range from deference to the boss's authority to dictate what is to be done, even when he is wrong, to an underlying rebelliousness that crops out whenever the boss uses his rank to control subordinates' behaviour no matter how 'right' his actions may be.

The value-based assumptions people hold guide them in what they do or do not do. Sometimes the guidance is 'sound'. Things go smoothly and results are good. Sometimes values and assumptions cause 'trouble'. To begin solving such difficulties, the value-based assumptions must be explicitly identified and understood. A consultant who operates in a confrontational mode identifies to team members, in a way they can understand, the extent to which their value-based assumptions are invalid or unjustified, or valid and sound; but he stops short of prescribing the values by which they should interact. His purpose is to aid team members to break through their rationalizations, justifications, explanations or the unspoken and unwritten 'rules' of behaviour that keep them from having an objective view of their situation; while, at the same time, avoiding creating defensive behaviour through his interventions causing team members to feel they are being attacked.

Argyris provides an example of a confrontational intervention. The team described here included a corporate president and his vice-presidents. The consultant had just asked, 'Is there anything you do that may make it more difficult for marketing people?'. Before the marketing vice-president could reply, the president cut in and said, 'I'm sure that A (the marketing vice-president) can answer that better than anyone, but let me try.'

The consultant listened. When the president had finished, the marketing vice-president partially agreed, then the president and he explored their differences and the event was over. But not for the consultant, who said:

> '"May I ask why you felt that you had to answer for A even though you stated A could answer it better than anyone else?"
> President: "I don't know. That's a good question. I do that an awful lot with A."
> A: "Yes, you do."
> Consultant: "How did you feel when he answered for you?"'

The marketing vice-president described how he felt when the president did this. He concluded that he felt angry at himself whenever this happened.

Then the president asked if this was dominating behaviour, and went on to say,

> 'President: "I wonder if others feel that way. No, I don't think so because they know me well and would say so."
> Consultant: "I can't confirm or disconfirm your view. Perhaps you can check your view some day by asking them directly."' (Argyris, 1970, p. 168.)*

*Reproduced from C. Argyris (1970) *Intervention Theory and Method*. Reading, Mass.: Addison-Wesley, by permission of Addison-Wesley Publishing Company, Inc.

This episode is a useful illustration of confrontational interventions that focus on hierarchy-based values. The president was acting on an authority–obedience premise between himself and his subordinate. His value-based and probably implicit assumption was that it was his prerogative to cut off the subordinate to whom the question was addressed and by whom it might best have been answered. Not only was this one of his hierarchical 'rights'; he doubtless thought that important questions got answered more quickly and—despite his compliment to A—*better* that way. Furthermore, the president's presumption of prerogative was matched by the subordinate's presumption of obedience: he let himself be cut off. One of the 'costs', though, was the anger and lack of creative involvement apparently felt by A, and probably by other subordinates as well. Yet the president seemed unaware of this until the consultant intervened and some evidence was produced.

These confrontational interventions go far beyond the emotional cleansing made possible by cathartic interventions and the data gathering-feedback-planning cycle, based on 'felt needs', which characterizes catalytic interventions. Instead, contemporary influences, particularly in the authority–obedience area, are pointed to so as to bring them into sharpest possible clarity; albeit without 'telling' participants what they should do to solve their problems.

A use of confrontation strategies based on psychoanalytic formulation (Ezriel, 1950) but applied in the context of 'businessmen as students', is described by Rice. Its character is revealed in the following excerpts from the first meeting of such a study group. Someone said, 'Let us introduce ourselves'. But after the introduction an embarrassed silence fell on the group. While Rice was pondering what to say, a member spoke, 'Well, we didn't learn much from that—in fact I've forgotten most of the names already. I seldom pick them up the first time.' This remark stimulated another round robin of mutual introduction which ended again in embarrassed silence. Someone slapped his hand on the table and exclaimed, 'Well, that's cleared the decks'.

In the nautical spirit of the moment, Rice weighed anchor and sailed in with a confrontational intervention, referring first to the 'clearing of the decks'. He commented that the decks may have been cleared for a fight against him for not giving the kind of leadership that was expected. He pointed to their hostility, shown by lack of support, to others who had tried to take a lead. The members individually and collectively denied they had any such feelings:

> '"I don't feel hostile, but I do feel afraid of what is going to happen. If only we had a clear purpose."
> "We need to establish formalities to enable us to discuss."
> "We're trying to find a common denominator. This is an unnatural situation. The trouble is that nothing is happening. There is nothing to study. We're not competing for a job or anything ... (a pause, in which tension in the groups could be felt to mount). We all look at Mr. Rice ... (then another pause). For God's sake somebody else talk!"'

And then the tension was broken by laughter.

Rice's intervention focused attention on his non-traditional leadership behaviour, indicating that in his view, his 'refusal' to engage in the typical implicit rules of cooperation had put members on the spot; to which in turn, they had reacted with hostile feelings toward him. Interestingly, this is the same reaction as subordinates have to a boss whose unfamiliar 'leadership through delegation' leaves them nonplussed. Rather than critical fingers being pointed inward, they tend to be pointed at the boss as 'cause' of their trouble.

Rice comments upon aspects of his role as a confrontational consultant working with a group.

'The consultant's job is to confront the group, without affronting its members; to draw attention to group behavior and not to individual behavior; to point out how the group uses individuals to express its own emotions, how it exploits some members so that others can absolve themselves from the responsibility for such expression.

As a group fails to get its consultant to occupy the more traditional roles [authority–obedience relationship] of teacher, seminar leader, or therapist, it will redouble its efforts until in desperation it will disown him and seek other leaders. When they too fail, they too will be disowned, often brutally. The group will then use its own brutality to try to get the consultant to change his task by eliciting his sympathy and care for those it has handled so roughly. If this manoeuvre fails, and it never completely fails, the group will tend to throw up other leaders to express its concern for its members and project its brutality onto the consultant. As rival leaders emerge it is the job of the consultant, as far as he is able, to identify what the group is trying to do and to explain it. His leadership is in task performance, and the task is to understand what the group is doing "now" and to explain why it is doing it. Drawing attention to interesting phenomena without explanation is seldom used.' (Rice, 1965, pp. 60, 65–66.)*

The above is an example of a learning situation where confrontational interventions can be made with the object of helping business leaders to study the extent to which values and assumptions regarding authority and obedience are embedded in their own behaviour. Such self-examination, in turn, often points toward consideration of what the alternative possibilities of an involvement–participant–commitment model might be.

The confrontational consultant focuses on those aspects of the boss's hierarchy-based values which are adverse to team effectiveness and member gratification, as well as on the characteristics of each team member's reactions to the boss. When values held by the boss are challenged under ordinary conditions such as by his own subordinates, such questioning is likely to be seen as insubordination or at least as arrogance. It is equally unlikely that an internal consultant would be more effective when confronting a person higher in the organization's hierarchy.

The necessary factor in effective confrontation is for an expert who has no 'vested interests' to be able to pierce participant defences directly in a way that precludes rationalization, justification or team members falling back on their prerogatives. Thus, a confrontational consultant's strategy takes cognisance of the likelihood that any team member is likely to rationalize and justify his present value-based assumptions, thereby explaining away difficulties, rather than actively setting about discovering in a factual way what his presently

*Reproduced from A.K. Rice (1965) *Learning for Leadership*. London: Tavistock Publications, by permission of Tavistock Institute of Human Relations.

unperceived problem is. Team members can be helped to see their value-based assumptions in a more objective light if they are challenged to explain the 'whys' of their present behaviour. If the consultant can point to here-and-now examples as they occur in interactions among team members it is likely that defences can be pierced.

Prescription-based team building

The prescription-oriented approach rests on the idea that difficulties of teamwork could have been avoided if members had the understandings and skills essential for operating in organizations. But often they don't. So there is recourse to solving problems of team effectiveness through members implementing advice from experts.

Having been called in, the prescription-oriented consultant accepts it as given that he has been employed to come up with answers. Like the confrontational consultant, his entering advantage is that he can see objectively what team members can't, either because they are too involved in the situation or incompetent to deal with the problem at hand. Or they may be at their wits' end. Whatever the circumstances, the prescription-oriented consultant's aim is to give to the boss or team the guidance needed for them to take action.

Herman (1972, pp. 42–45) pictures the prescriptive character of Gestalt-based interventions in the setting of a high-level corporate team. The boss had developed strong commitment to what he called 'OD Values', requiring him to be fair, rational and helpful. Being a man who customarily used his position in the hierarchy with great personal forcefulness as well as occasional moodiness—aspects not consistent with 'OD Values'—he was in conflict with himself. For the most part, teamwork under his leadership proceeded routinely, but from time to time this manager would 'blow his stack' and pin several of his staff to the wall. His logic was excellent, but his vehemence led to subordinates feeling steamrollered. Some defended themselves with counter-logic; one would react by cracking jokes; another would wilt because of feeling punished. Then, as he became aware of these individual reactions which indicated to him that he must have breached his ideal standards, the boss would 'clam up', and this in turn resulted in issues being left unresolved.

The consultant happened to be present when one of these incidents occurred. A proposal for a policy change was being suggested, and it had received some support from two team members. The boss's initial reaction was negative, and he accused the proponents of unrealism. Then after some back-and-forth discussion, he went glum.

In this kind of situation, a consultant has several options. He could focus attention, in a confronting way, on the deadening effects produced by the top man's reaction. Or, in a catalytic way, he might intervene to encourage the team to investigate their shared perceptions of the situation. But in this case the consultant intervened in a prescriptive way, pushing the manager to follow through on his initial comments, to get it all out. The manager acted on the expert advice—at first clumsily, but, as he warmed up, with gusto. He tore into a number of his subordinates. Those whom he attacked, counterattacked. Soon everyone was shouting back and forth.

Later, these participants critiqued what had transpired and concluded that this consultant-directed episode had produced in them a greater sense of vitality, excitement and relatedness than had been experienced previously. Some members had also learned not to buckle under, but to stand their ground. The top man also formed a new respect for both them and himself.

Herman's prescriptive approach was structured in terms of the Gestalt concept of 'closure'. The manager needed to 'complete' himself, rather than only to go halfway. This could be done by first overcoming his typical impulse to cut himself off after an initial outburst. By going further into his frustrations, the boss got himself and others stirred up to a pitch where all of them could react authentically to one another.

The next illustration presents a quite different kind of prescriptive inter-action. It relates to the handling of crisis situations. Crises can occur within teams and larger institutions whenever an unexpected event over which control cannot be established prevents important objectives of theirs from being realized. Although some organization-centred crises may be more easily pre-ventable—in a 'managerial foresight' sense—than are famines, floods and epidemics, these crises can still occur with comparably disastrous results, leaving 'casualty' persons affected with the sense of being powerless to respond to the situation. Prescriptive interventions can provide a basis for restoring individuals' and teams' capacities to address the crisis situation in a problem-solving way. The consultant, who is not 'involved' in the crisis as a participant, can exercise initiative and direction that group members are presently unable to muster among themselves.

A case study involving just such a crisis intervention has been reported by Thomas, Izmirian and Harris (1973, pp. 1–3). For some time before the crisis incident they had been working with an organization training team on a com-petency-building programme. The training team had just scheduled its work for the year ahead when it learned that necessary funds for implementing this programme would not be forthcoming. The day after the announcement, team members' conversations with one another, as well as with others in the larger organization, had the effect of further blurring whatever 'facts' were as yet available. Team members came to feel victimized and reacted with a sense of hopelessness.

Under these conditions the consultants' prescriptive interventions were based on the following assumption:

When the Client Group	*The Consultant*
1. . . . is unable to provide leadership.	. . . assumes group leadership.
2. . . . is unable to stay with any one task.	. . . keeps the group on the task.
3. . . . assumes it knows less than it really does know.	. . . provides a method for the group to look at things clearly.

4. ...assumes all power has been taken away.	...provides a method for the group to look at reality.
5. ...therefore doesn't know what it is doing or how to function.	...tells rather than asks the group how to function but not what to function on.
6. ...(fears) conflict will erupt internally unless movement/success occurs rapidly.	...speeds up the movement.*

So the consultant intervenes to:

1. Stop reactive and self-destructive behaviour.
2. Lead the evaluation of what the current situation actually is.
3. Focus attention on new goals.
4. Identify steps—within the 'new' circumstances—by which these goals can be reached.
5. 'Supervise' the step-by-step actions needed for movement.
6. Ensure that steps are taken.

In the situation described, confusion, anger, frustration and fear led to emotional contagion, which in turn prevented team members from focusing on a task and coalescing around it. The consultant stepped in to prescribe an agenda topic dealing with how planned and previously scheduled activities would now have to be changed and new goals formulated. With this meaningful and pertinent agenda focus, the consultant was thereafter able to lead the team's analysis and evaluation of its situation. This in turn permitted the members to collect current facts and to analyse them in the light of altered conditions. With these new findings as to what they *now* needed to do, it was possible to define the available resources for taking next steps and to set concrete priorities for taking these steps. A problem-solving basis had been restored, and the consultant could then 'return' leadership to its 'rightful' team owner. The effort proved to be successful, largely because of the timeliness of these interventions which took place the day after the fund-cut catastrophe occurred and because of its prescriptive character when the consultant filled the power vacuum left by the 'natural' leadership's demoralization.

Prescriptive consultation can provide the answers that team members are unable to agree on or reach among themselves. Sometimes their inability to move is because of decision-making impasse. Sometimes it is a power vacuum, in which all authority has gone out of the team. Sometimes team members are faced with a problem of such technical complexity that they cannot solve it (Taha, 1971, pp. 1–2). Or it may be felt that the possibilities for disorder during team deliberations make necessary an external source of 'control via procedure'. Thus it comes about, for example, that an industrial organization's top-team members may conduct their meetings under the aegis of a long-dead prescriptive 'authority' (Robert, 1876) or use a manual of procedure which has been

*Reproduced by special permission from Ann Thomas, Bonnie Izmirian and Jacke Harris (1973) 'Federal cutbacks: An external crisis intervention mode.' *Social Change*, **3**, 2.

evolved, over many years, within their nation's *legislative* chambers (May, 1946; see also Finer, 1961, pp. 474–476).

There are four key features of situations where prescriptive consultation appears to make a positive contribution. The first has to do with a situation facing a client. He may have reached an impasse where he is unable to impose his will on other team members and they are unable to move without his concurrence. A second is where the solution to the problem is beyond the reach of team members who simply don't know what to do. They may have thrown up their hands in despair. A third is a situation where a team is immobilized resulting from some traumatic event which is experienced as such a total defeat that no team member is able to redefine the problem in construc ve terms. Under these conditions, defences are at a low level. Rather than resenting prescriptions, people are receptive to them because of the positive alternatives that they offer. The fourth feature involves availability of a consultant who is prepared through prescription to assert his will based on his expert authority as it relates to the difficulty facing the group. His expectation is that they will comply. When such client needs and receptivity are appropriately addressed by consultant prescriptions, situations that might otherwise continue to produce chronic difficulty or even tragedy can be averted. However, rather than trying to reduce authority-and-obedience and make it less arbitrary and coercive— the basic theme that underlies so many confrontational interventions—prescription rests on the use of authority–obedience to get a problem solved. That is, authority is exercised by the consultant, while the client's 'obedience' in carrying out the consultant's recommendations is presumed.

Theory-based approach to team building

Inherent conditions of organization hierarchy, divisional segmentation and individualized responsibilities, coupled with tensions related to competition for promotion, fear of termination and so on, were referred to at the beginning of this chapter. These have taken on their present character under two sets of historical conditions. Under *economic-survival* conditions of scarcity, men have always been more or less ready to do what they were told and to avoid trouble by swallowing resentment towards arbitrariness, exploitation and coercion. Under *industrial-survival* conditions of ensuring profitability, organization leaders have designed systems having primary focus upon needs for productivity with secondary attention, if any, on needs of personnel as mature and competent individuals capable of much wider involvement, participation and personal commitment to effective decision making and problem solving. Both management and the worker have been underutilized to the detriment of the corporation as an institution of society. Many organizations continue to be run today in ways that 'fit' the past but that are severely maladapted to societies where economic scarcity and survival pressures present less of an immediate threat. As a result people are less ready to buckle under and swallow resentments to protect an economic security which is available in other ways. Thus, older approaches to managing, premised on historical conditions, are failing more and more to bring about desired and needed operational outcomes.

One significant approach to solving this dilemma has been for entire managements to learn to manage according to theory-clarified models that bring *involvement*, *participation* and *commitment to the task* to replace traditional ways of pressuring for results. Behavioural science-based theories and principles are fundamental for assisting such a change-over from historical practices to operations conducted under an approach that is more congruent with deep-lying human motivations.

A theory-based approach to team building rests on the premise that teamwork, like any other aspect of human experience and conduct, can be learned about in a systematic way. Perspectives shared among members provide insights into oneself and others. By making alternative actions comparable in terms of predicting 'less' and 'more' favourable consequences, theory constructs enable team members to operate in a more effective manner. Thus, team members are able to integrate their efforts more effectively than if these conditions are not present or are only 'assumed'.

There are a number of reasons why behavioural theory approaches to management are such powerful aids to changing behaviour toward improvement along personal and team-synergy dimensions. One is that theories can be written out so that they are explicit. They can then be tested for their validity in predicting consequences which become discernible in research and experimental evidence. As they do, they qualify as 'objective' in the sense of being based on external proof. The authority they may eventually carry, therefore, is derived from empirical evidence. Persons engaged in theory-based team building use these models to observe their own conduct, and to predict its consequences instead of engaging in intuition-oriented exchanges. Theory aids behaviour change in the following ways.

(1) Theory, with its explicit formulations, brings individuals face-to-face with their subjective *values*.

(2) Theory-based understanding of personal modes of managing and the consequences of them reduces or eliminates *defensiveness* when a person can see and understand that what he previously took for granted as 'right' or 'sound' or 'valid', now appears untenable.

(3) Theory provides individuals *perspective* through supplying a social microscope for seeing what is actually going on in the present as well as a social telescope for seeing how the past and possible future is affecting here-and-now behaviour.

(4) Theory-based language enables people to *communicate* with their subordinates, colleagues and bosses, in definite mutually understood terms, as to best approaches for getting results through people.

(5) A model of excellence can be designated by theory that makes it possible for a person to see what is possible and to provide the *motivation* for him to want to do better.

(6) *Creativity* is stimulated when theory aids people to be more curious and more imaginative in pursuing solutions to managerial problems.

(7) An individual's capacity for self-direction and *autonomy* can be increased by theory because it is less necessary to consult with others when a person can consult with himself as to the implications of various actions being considered.

(8) Theory specifications for sound team management provide criteria for evaluating whether or not *teamwork* is synergistic in the sense that $1+1=3$, or that 'two heads are better than one'.

The above are general statements as to why theory is an important basis of intervention. But not all theories are of equal significance. Some are overly simple in the sense that so few categories are used that dissimilar behaviours are artificially grouped together and therefore predictive value is severely limited. Others are so over-elaborate that people lose their way in attempting to understand them, and as a result dismiss theory as academic and therefore irrelevant. Still others, although called theories, are little more than philosophical speculation as to the nature of man.

Two examples demonstrate how theories have been used for team building.

McGregor (1960) posited two theories of management, 'X' and 'Y'. The characteristics of each theory are summarized in Figure 1.

Using these two models McGregor then developed a set of scales for use in team building. The left side of each scale represents X, the right Y.

	X	Y
Trust	High suspicion	High trust
	1 2 3 4 5 6 7	
Support	Every man for himself	Genuine concern for each other
	1 2 3 4 5 6 7	
Communication	Guarded, cautious	Open and authentic
	1 2 3 4 5 6 7	
Listening	We don't listen to each other	We understand and are understood
	1 2 3 4 5 6 7	
Team Objectives	Not understood	Clearly understood
	1 2 3 4 5 6 7	
Conflicts	Deny, avoid or suppress	Accepted and 'worked through'
	1 2 3 4 5 6 7	

Assumptions

Theory X	Theory Y
(1) Work is inherently distateful to most people	(1) Work is as natural as play if conditions are favourable
(2) Most people have little ambition or desire for responsibility and prefer to be directed.	(2) For achieving organizational goals, self-management is often indispensable.
(3) Most people have little capacity for creativity involving organization problems	(3) Creativity for solving an organization's problems is widely distributed throughout its membership
(4) Motivation occurs at a bread-and-butter survival level	(4) Rewards which satisfy ego and social needs, as well as bread-and-butter needs, conduce to self-control in line with organizational objectives
(5) Most people must be closely controlled and often coerced to achieve organizational objectives	(5) The capacity for creativity is under-utilized in organizations

Implications for Teamwork

Theory X	Theory Y
(1) Authority flows unilaterally from superior to subordinate	(1) Authority flows from formal and informal sources, up, down and across the team
(2) Span of control is narrow and supervision is close	(2) Span of control is wide, with supervision being general rather than detailed
(3) The individual is considered as an isolated unit, and work is organized primarily in terms of his physiological being	(3) The individual is considered as a social–psychological–physiological being and the structuring of his work does not ignore the fullness of man
(4) Work is routinized	(4) The task is a meaningful whole, providing some variety and requiring some skill and judgement

Figure 1. McGregor's theories X and Y

Members rate their team on these seven-point scale. Then the team-as-a-whole discusses the situation indicated by average scores for any item of less than 5, or for any scales where there is a wide range of individual ratings. Finally team members are asked to consider and identify 'why' the situation is as they have pictured it.

In using scales such as these, McGregor points out that '. . . it is important to agree in advance on a ground rule that there will be no attempt to ferret out the "author" of any individual rating, although any member may *volunteer* comment about his own rating.' (McGregor, 1967, p. 174.)* If the consultant

*Reproduced from D. McGregor (1967) *The Professional Manager*, McGraw-Hill Book Company. Used with permission of McGraw-Hill Book Company.

knows the team by virtue of having worked with it previously, he may complete the scales and his rating may also be used as data, either as a part of the statistical summary or as a basis of comparison in order to give the team the benefit of his 'expert' but outsider view. McGregor comments that his experience is that ratings by most groups using these kinds of scales tend to be unrealistically high, particularly when such an attempt is first made. He therefore suggests that after an initial discussion it is often better to wait a week or two and then readminister the scales, but this time to a regular meeting which deals with normal operating problems.

One of the advantages of such a set of scales is that the consultant, by the items he includes in it, can ask the team to deal with issues that it might not recognize as being important prior to the consultant-initiated discussion of them. For example, McGregor's scales include questions concerned with mutual trust and mutual support, communications, listening, team objectives, conflict, use of member resources, how control is exercised and about 'organization climate'. Significant as these are known to be as barriers to team effectiveness, most of them are not issues that managers spontaneously raise in day-by-day work meetings in such clear-cut and undisguised terms. These particular questions are not the only ones that might be asked; and indeed, a team might be invited to invent the scales which it then applies to itself. However, he points out that to do so can cause managers to become preoccupied with mechanics rather than data. The main purpose is to provide each member with information about how others perceive the team in comparison with the way he does, and clues as to how group effectiveness can be improved.

Another example uses Grid© theories (Blake and Mouton, 1964) as the model against which to examine and perfect teamwork. The Grid identifies thirteen theories which make different approaches to management explicit. Five are basic; the other eight are combinations of two or more 'pure' theories and are less common. Thus, how a manager goes about planning, directing, controlling and staffing can be identified in terms of Grid styles and the consequences of using it.

The Conflict Grid is key for identifying basic problems underlying team behaviour. It is to be understood in the following way. Whenever a man meets a situation of conflict, he has at least two basic considerations in mind. One of these relates to the *people* with whom he is in disagreement. Another focuses upon *production* or *results*. The particular degrees of emphasis he places on these respective concerns determine how he deals with conflict.

Basic attitudes toward people and toward results are represented on the nine-point scales, the horizontal one denoting *Concern for Production or Results* and the vertical one *Concern for People*. 'Concern for . . .' does not necessarily refer to results produced but rather denotes the degree of emphasis placed on getting results or having to do with people. The *1* end of each scale represents low concern, and the *9* represents the highest possible concern. There are 81 possible coordinate intersections between numbered points on the two scales, and each represents a particular fusion of degrees of the two concerns. But there are only five that are basic.

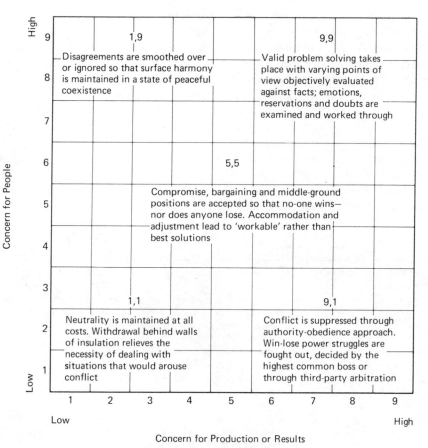

Figure 2. The conflict grid. Reproduced by special permission from Robert
R. Blake and Jane Srygley Mouton (1970) 'The fifth achievement.' *Journal of
Applied Behavioral Science,* **6(4)**

When these basic styles are understood, one can *predict* how a person operating under any style is likely to handle conflict, as well as the consequences that
can be expected from dealing with it in that way. No one style need be exclusively characteristic of a given person, although one style may be dominant in that
person's actions, with others being used as backup behaviours. Furthermore,
even though one particular Grid style may be dominant for a time, it can be
abandoned and replaced by another as and when the earlier one is found
ineffective.

Some of the more basic ways of dealing with conflict are briefly depicted in
the positional statements given in Figure 2.

In Grid team building, various topic items such as teamwork objectives,
planning, communication, traditions, precedents, past practices, critique,

initiative, facing-up, standards of excellence, profit and so on, are probed into for analysing the effectiveness of team action. But team self-study does not stop there. It also examines and critiques with each individual his personal characteristics in terms of his decisions, convictions, conflict, temper and effort. In its concluding phase this 'total' team study is re-examined in the light of what 'ideal' teamwork for that particular team would be and what changes for each member and the team-as-a-whole are required to shift from the way it has been operating to the way it should operate. Implementation steps and check points to evaluate progress are decided upon as the final step.

An example of how team building takes place follows. Team members rank various Grid style approaches to each of several items in terms of what is the actual situation and what would be the soundest way for their team to operate. An example of such a scale is included in Figure 3.

INDIVIDUAL COMPLETION			TEAM AGREEMENT	
Soundest	Actual		Soundest	Actual
A————	A————	The boss makes the decisions based solely on his personal thinking. (9,1)	A————	A————
B————	B————	Frequent pleasant discussions result in little action. (1,9)	B————	B————
C————	C————	Minimum discussion occurs; each man is more or less on his own. (1,1)	C————	C————
D————	D————	The boss leads us, but he usually concurs with majority decisions; much action takes place on a one-to-one basis. (5,5)	D————	D————
E————	E————	Synergism is exploited—issues are talked through and solutions and decisions based on facts are fully thrashed through to understanding and agreement. (9,9)	E————	E————

Figure 3. The use of grid theory to diagnose teamwork

Organizational team building for strengthening effectiveness

One or another of five basic approaches are present in various modes of team building. Most of these are 'pure' but, as practised, some interventions may involve more than one of them, depending on the particular aspect of team building being worked on and the consultant's strategy choices.

These basic processes are

Intervention mode	Key words	Indicated when
Catharsis	Emotional release	Pent-up feelings are blocking thought and action; 'immobilizing tensions' are barriers to constructive action
Catalysis	Strengthen perception	Poor communication has resulted in pluralistic ignorance about what's going on
Confrontation	Value identification	Values, often hidden, are having negative effects and must be brought into focus before the causes of problems can be worked on
Prescription	Giving answers	There is impasse, hopelessness, or despair, and yet immediate action is imperative to avoid further negative consequences
Theory	Concept based insight	Team members are ready to diagnose and to solve problems systematically, using pertinent theory as the basis for contending with future problems

Team building is not a simple affair. While all approaches have the objective of contributing to the effective achievement of performance goals, there are different ways of trying to bring about team development in terms of this objective. The different approaches sometimes tend to be mutually exclusive, but this need not be so.

The cathartic approach is premised on a concept that tensions presently existing among members are the principal 'cause' of their ineffectiveness, and that a necessary and sufficient step toward *effectiveness* is to aid participants to express their emotions and in this way to gain relief from them. The more cognitive development steps that could well follow such catharsis and the building of team effectiveness skills up from what—even post-catharsis—is 'ground zero', are usually not emphasized.

The catalytic approach rests on the working hypothesis that conditions of ineffectiveness at the team level arise from 'pluralistic ignorance'. This means usually that among team members there are at present insufficiently developed perceptions of problems that need to be dealt with, even though various members may be somewhat aware that such problems defeat the objectives of teamwork. Thus, the goal of catalytic team building is to aid members to strengthen their perceptions of situations in which they are currently embedded. As is true of the solely cathartic approach, team effectiveness skills are unlikely to be emphasized. Rather, they are likely to be subtly coached toward improvement by the consultant in order to permit better communication while he is present, whithout his thereby aiding team members to exercise such skills on their own initiative when he has departed.

The confrontational approach focuses on values inherent in organization hierarchy-based privilege, power and prerogative, reinforced by authority–obedience; all of which can, under certain conditions, be at cross-purposes to valid teamwork. With the crumbling of authority–obedience in modern times as the basis for organizing and controlling, it has become generally recognized that sole reliance on this and the aforementioned cluster of related factors nowadays provides an inadequate basis of team leadership and membership. Authority–obedience can be replaced by an approach that arouses involvement, participation and commitment of all team members to carrying out those activities of the enterprise for which they are distinctively responsible. In addition team members can find better ways to pull together toward achieving superordinate team goals that each person shares in common and on a more voluntary basis with the others. Again, like the cathartic and catalytic approaches, if a consultant has adopted this one as a *sole* methodology with his rationale for using it tailored to fit, involvement, participation and commitment are expected to follow almost as an automatic result of rejecting authority–obedience. But in fact, unless the confrontations are followed by active and positive-toned team building steps, there may be outcomes that are non-coercive on the one hand but bureaucratic or political on the other.

The prescriptive approach uses an expert to study the situation, to evaluate individuals in it and to design a more functional arrangement of the team. This includes specifying what each person on the team is expected to do in terms of his own responsibility as well as how members are expected to work together to accomplish shared objectives. Of significance in evaluating this 'efficiency' approach is the fact that no matter how precise a prescription is in the sense of detailing what is to be done, the anticipated consequences are unlikely to be realized if people lack the behavioural skills for implementation. Cooperation is not the automatic result of edict. Beyond this inherent limitation, even though his prescriptions may be 'right', to the degree that they cause a departure from the status quo, they are likely to arouse resistances among those for whom the prescription would cause lost status, position, rank, pay or title. By the same token, even 'wrong' prescriptions are likely to receive endorsement by those who would benefit from their implementation.

The theory-based comparative approach assumes first that individual team members need clear concepts about fundamentals of teamwork effectiveness. This is viewed as basic to their acquiring the personal skills essential for strengthening their own capacity to participate as team members. It then becomes possible for them to engage in designing a model of how they *should* function, and from it to derive consequences and implications for team building. In such team self-examination, traditional practices that have become inadequate can be replaced by problem-solving approaches that are more likely to promote effective results.

In the perspective of science it is a self-evident truth that when *theories* can illuminate why things happen as they do and what must occur to cause change and improvement, and when such theories are clearly understood by those who use them, then innovative and creative actions under model-tested *principles* can be taken. The theory and principles approach to team building is the most encompassing and widely applicable of any of the five approaches that have been described. Its major weakness is that, for some, the fascination that ideas can stimulate can result in concepts becoming ends in themselves rather than means to more effective team performance. Also, the introduction of a theory-based approach may be impractical unless and until a period of cathartic intervention has permitted team members to ventilate their present emotional tensions. Then there is at least a possibility, if not yet a clear likelihood, that members may see the opening directions toward improvement of the kind that theory and principle-based learning may offer as the basis for integrating effort. The statement also applies to other approaches. For example, a catalytic approach that aids a team to strengthen and widen its team-based perceptions may be an essential step for aiding members to see discrepancies between its current effectiveness and that which is potentially available. Readiness to engage in theory-based team building is a possibility once the discrepancy is clear.

The reverse sequence—that is, starting with theory, and then getting into one or another of the remaining modes—is of no less significance. Once theory identifies a gap, say, between desired candour and actual closedness, a cathartic phase of team building may ensue, with aroused feelings and emotions being expressed that 'clear the air' by relieving pent-up tensions. Next steps may be catalytic or confrontational, or may rely on derivation from theory as the basis for building toward effectiveness.

As circumstances vary in the conditions facing one team *vs* another, particular sequence predictions are not possible in any concrete situation. They must vary in terms of specifics that are unique to each particular team. Yet, in considering the entry issue of 'where to begin' in team building, having regard to finding out what the actual present circumstances and dynamics of one's own team are and what would be involved in building and implementing a strategy of improvement, recourse to *theory*—either of an unrecognized one that is the 'sum total' of personal predilections, or of an explicit science-based one—is a practical inevitability.

The generalization can be made, however, that cathartic, catalytic, confrontational or prescriptive consultant approaches constitute short-term means toward subsidiary ends rather than providing a borad and versatile strategy for reaching a superordinate goal of organization excellence. As means they can create facilitating conditions, but the strategy most likely to result in effective overall teamwork is one that uses sound theory and principles clearly understood by those who interact and cooperate as the basis for increasing effectiveness.

References

Argyris, C. (1970) *Intervention Theory and Method.* Reading, Mass.: Addison-Wesley.

Baumgartel, H. (1959) 'Using employee questionnaire results for improving organizations.' *Kansas Business Review,* **12,** quoted in W. G. Bennis (1969) *Organization Development: Its Nature, Origins, and Prospects.* Reading, Mass.: Addison-Wesley, p. 9.

Blake, R. R., J. S. Mouton and M. G. Blansfield (1962) 'How executive team training can help you.' *Journal of the American Society of Training Directors,* **16,** 1, 3–11.

Blake, R. R. and J. S. Mouton (1964) *The Managerial Grid: Key Orientations for Achieving Production Through People.* Houston: Gulf Publishing Co.

Blake, R. R. and J. S. Mouton (1975a) *Consultation* (to be published).

Blake, R. R. and J. S. Mouton (1975b) *Organizational Team Building* (to be published).

Crockett, W. J. (1970) 'Team building—one approach to organizational development.' *Journal of Applied Behavioral Science,* **6,** 3.

David, G. (1967) 'Building cooperation and trust.' In A. G. Marrow, D. G. Bowers and S. E. Seashore (Eds.), *Management by Participation.* New York: Harper and Row.

Davis, S. A. (1969) 'An organic problem-solving method of organizational chance.' In W. B. Eddy *et al.* (Eds.), *Behavioral Science and the Manager's Role.* Washington, D.C.: NTL Institute for Applied Behavioral Science.

Daw, R. W. and N. L. Gage (1967) 'Effect of feedback from teachers to principals.' *Journal of Educational Psychology,* **58,** 3.

Drinkwater, A. (1972) 'Group training and consultancy approaches in IBM UK Ltd.' In M. and P. Berger (Eds.), *Group Training Techniques.* Epping: Gower Press.

Ezriel, H. (1950) 'A psycho-analytic approach to group treatment.' *British Journal of Medical Psychology,* **23.**

Finer, H. (1961) *The Theory and Practice of Modern Government.* London: Methuen.

Fordyce, J. K. and R. Weil (1971) *Managing WITH People.* Reading, Mass.: Addison-Wesley.

French, W. (1972) 'Organization development: objectives, assumptions and strategies.' In N. Margulies and A. P. Raia (Eds.), *Organizational Development: Values, Process, and Technology.* New York: McGraw-Hill.

Gibb, J. C. (1972) 'TORI theory: Consultantless team-building.' *Journal of Contemporary Business,* **1,** 3, 33–41.

Harvey, J. B. and C. R. Boettger (1971) 'Improving communication within a managerial workgroup.' *Journal of Applied Behavioral Science,* **7,** 2.

Herman, S. (1972) 'A Gestalt orientation to O.D.' In W. W. Burke (Ed.), *Contemporary Organization Development: Conceptual Orientations and Interventions.* Washington, D.C.: NTL Institute for Applied Behavioral Science.

Humble, J. W. (1967) *Improving Business Results.* Maidenhead, Berks.: McGraw-Hill.

Jacques, E. (1964) 'Social-analysis and the Glacier project.' *Human Relations,* **17,** 4.

Kuriloff, A. H. and S. Atkins (1966) 'T-group for a work team.' *Journal of Applied Behavioral Science,* **2,** 1.

Levinson, H. (1973) *The Great Jackass Fallacy.* Boston: Harvard University Press.

Liebermann, M. A., I. D. Yalom and M. B. Miles (1973) *Encounter Groups: First Facts.* New York: Basic Books.

McGregor, D. (1960) *The Human Side of Enterprise*. New York: McGraw-Hill.

McGregor, D. (1967) *The Professional Manager*. New York: McGraw-Hill.

Margulies, N. and P. Raia (1968) 'People in organizations: A case for team training.' *Training and Development Journal*, **22**, 8, 2–11.

May, T. E. (1946) *Parliamentary Practice*. London: Butterworths.

Miles, M. B. *et al.* (1970) 'Data feedback and organizational change.' In R. T. Golembiewski and A. Blumberg (Eds.), *Sensitivity Training and the Laboratory Approach*. Itasca, Ill.: F. E. Peacock.

Rice, A. K. (1965) *Learning for Leadership*. London: Tavistock Publications.

Robert, H. M. (1876) *Robert's Rules of Order*. Glenview, Ill.: Scott, Foresman, 1970.

Schein, E. H. (1969) *Process Consultation: Its Role in Organization Development*. Reading, Mass.: Addison-Wesley.

Schmuck, R. A., P. J. Runkel *et al.* (1972) *Handbook of Organization Development in Schools*. Palo Alto, Cal.: National Press Books.

Taha, H. A. (1971) *Operations Research: An Introduction*. New York: Macmillan.

Thomas, A., B. Izmirian and J. Harris (1973) 'Federal cutbacks: An external crisis intervention model.' *Social Change*, **3**, 2.

Varney, G. H. and H. J. Lasher (1973) 'Surveys and feedback as a means of organization diagnosis and change.' In T. H. Patten, Jr. (Ed.), *OD—Emerging Dimensions and Concepts*. Washington, D.C.: American Society for Training and Development.

Chapter 7

The Centrality of Interpersonal Trust in Group Processes

Robert T. Golembiewski
Mark McConkie

University of Georgia

Perhaps there is no single variable which so thoroughly influences interpersonal and group behaviour as does trust, on this point ancient and modern observers typically agree. In this spirit, Deutsch observes (1973, p. 143): 'If we examine the writings of learned men throughout the ages, we find that, while they often disagreed whether to trust or not, they did agree that the topic was important.' Of late, in addition, this agreement has triggered a major research effort. The burgeoning literature pounds home one major point: trust acts as a salient factor in determining the character of a huge range of relationships. Moreover, the same literature also indicates that trust is critical in personal growth and development as well as in task performance.

The centrality of trust in much thought and comentary may be illustrated economically. Thus to some observers, trust appears to be a major (perhaps *the* major) foundation upon which healthy personalities are built. Moreover, other observers see trust as key facilitator in group accomplishment; as one of the most significant elements in managerial problem solving; and as among the most important components of effective labour relations and collective bargaining (Nigro, 1969). Nor do these samples begin to exhaust the fuller catalogue. Thus the efficacy of high levels of trust is emphasized in relationships between therapist and client (Seeman, 1954), as well as between parent and child (Baldwin *et al.*, 1945). Moreover, trust is seen as a necessity for professionals involved in corrections (Hardman, 1965), public management (Jennings, Cummings and Kilpatrick, 1966) and community mental health (Ilfeld and Lindeman, 1971). And still others seek clues about social trends in attitudes of trust among college students (Rotter and Hochreich, 1970) or international managers (Harnett, 1971).

That trust plays such a central role in so much social thought and commentary is easy enough to understand, in general terms. From one perspective, as Gibb convincingly argues (1964), low trust induces defensive behaviour, which is perhaps the basic block to any learning. That is, learning or growth depends essentially on understanding and acceptance of self and others, and defensiveness inhibits both. Hence experience with trusting relationships, especially early in life, can be a very powerful determinant of an individual's ability to adapt learningfully throughout life (Deutsch, 1962; Fullmer, 1971). More broadly still, perhaps Hartmann has been *primus inter pares* in his stress on the fundamental significance of trust or faith in human life. He notes (1932, p. 294):

> 'All human relationships, from external "credit" up to the highest forms of delegated powers in public life and of personal trust, are based upon faith. All strength derived from cooperation consists in men's reliance upon one another . . .'.

Hartman concludes powerfully: 'The distinctively moral value of life begins in the sphere of those who trust one another.' Other observers like Rotter (1971, pp. 443–444) agree, and emphasize that the lessened impact of religious and political creeds merely increases the need to rely on interpersonal trust as a major social adhesive.

It is far more difficult to be convincing *and* specific about trust and its effects, however. Everyman has a personal conceptual definition of interpersonal trust, and these often differ profoundly. Efforts to measure trust, moreover, are so variegated that the results of any two or more studies are not necessarily comparable.

The challenge to be more convincing and more specific about interpersonal trust motivates this paper. Specifically, this paper directs atention to three emphases, in turn. They are:

A conceptual clarification of interpersonal trust.

A brief survey of alternative operations for measuring trust.

The development of a theoretical network of interpersonal trust and its covariants, as far as that is possible, and the development of research priorities where such a network cannot presently be specified with even preliminary precision.

I. Interpersonal trust as concept

In a few words, the study of interpersonal trust comprises a set of widely accepted certitudes that often nestle gently in designational and denotional gossamer. The study of trust is rooted in a paradox, that is to say. Briefly, diverse conceptualizations of 'interpersonal trust' coexist with intense convictions that the various somethings described are central in all of human life.

The immediate purpose is to come to grips with conceptual diversity, whatever its underlying *raison d'être* so as to work toward central tendencies in thought and research about trust. Four emphases are required to do the job. First, a number of central features in concepts of trust will be distinguished, relying on an extensive literature while seeking to transcend it. Second, the duality of trusting/risking in these central conceptual features will be highlighted. Third, the 'spiral' character of trusting/risking will be described and analysed. Fourth, two basic models of trusting/risking linkages will be distinguished, in which linkages critical elements of theory and practice will be located.

A. *Some central features of trust*

Despite manifold variations, it is possible to isolate several central features of 'trust' concepts. For working purposes, at least, in common usages:

Trust implies reliance on, or confidence in, some event, process or person.

Trust reflects an expectation about outcomes based on perceptions and life experiences.

Expectations or decisions about trusting and trustworthiness seem an interface between two realities, one internal and the other external to the person choosing. To illustrate, trust is a function of 'the congruence between actual and perceived intentions' in Clifford's (1971) terms.

Trust implies that something is being risked in the expectation of some gain:

(a) pleasant consequences will result if the expectation is fulfilled: the trusting person is better off than if trust had not been extended;

(b) unpleasant consequences will result if the trust is unfulfilled: the trusting person will be worse off than if trust had not been extended;

(c) the loss or pain attendant to unfulfilment of the trust is sometimes seen as greater than the reward or pleasure deriving from fulfilled trust.

Trust implies some degree of uncertainty as to outcome.

Trust implies hopefulness or optimism as to outcome.

From a positive perspective, then, 'trust' is strongly linked to confidence in, and overall optimism about, desirable events taking place. Looked at from the standpoint of what trust is not—to rely on a basic distinction made by Deutsch (1973, pp. 148–169)—trust-as-confidence needs to be differentiated from trust-as-

Despair, in which the option of not trusting is so noxious that an individual may choose to behave in an apparently trusting way as the clearly-lesser of two evils.

Social conformity, in which case apparently trusting behaviours are so effectively demanded that the individual is more coerced than trusting.

Innocence, in which trusting behaviour is based upon a lack of appreciation of its dangerous or negative possibilities.

Impulsiveness, in which case the individual gives inappropriate weight to the consequences of his apparently trusting behaviour.

Masochism, in which the individual performs apparently trusting behaviours in the expectation of the pain or punishment derivative from the trust's probable or inevitable consequence.

Faith, in which the negative consequences of some trusting behaviour are eliminated, or very substantially reduced, by a belief that outcomes have been determined by some superior force and hence are unalterable and/or to be welcomed rather than chosen.

Gambling, in which case the individual is willing to bet that desirable outcomes will happen, however slight the realistic probabilities.

These central conceptual features are usefully illustrated by considering in detail two perspectives on trust concepts as sun and rain, as it were. To simplify, trust is seen as central in growth relationships and, to extend the organic analogy, such growth can be enhanced by the socio-emotional equivalents of sun and rain.

(1) *Trusting as nurturant sun.* Without doubt, the prime emphasis in trust concepts is on warmth, nurturance and acceptance that basically free the individual. For example, trust is commonly perceived as a giving up by one person of control of influence over another, as in the case of a deep love or friendship.

These enfolding, reaching-out and enabling qualities of trust are both subtle and explicit. Gently, that is, most concepts emphasize that trust is in the acceptance of the perceiving person rather more than in the objective reality (McGregor, 1967, p. 163), that is, it is something in the minds of individuals based on their perceptions and life-experiences which are taken to be relevant to a person or group about which a decision-to-trust must be made or whose trustworthiness must be estimated (Rotter, 1967, p. 651). The nurturant quality of trust is perhaps most explicit in the formulations of Gibb. Witness the central role he assigns to what is for him *the* critical human process in growth: the movement from fear to trust. The Gibbs explain (1969, p. 43) that 'latent fear' derives from lack of trust, and its consequences are constricting and inhibiting. They sample its dreary consequences: 'Latent fear predisposes individuals to build social structures around role relations, develop strategies for mask maintenance, attempt to manage motivations by various forms of persuasion, and maintain tight control systems.' The reasonable individual reacts in predictable and distancing ways, the Gibbs continue. 'The individual camouflages his fears to himself by building role barricades; he camouflages his humanness with an idealized presenting self; he reacts to imposed motivations by attempting to impose motivations on others; and he protects himself from intimacy by defending or rebelling.' More trusting environments allow the individual to unfold and flourish, in contrast. The individual, we are told, 'tends to be more personal; he replaces facades with intimacy and directness; he becomes more search-oriented and self-determining; and he develops the capacity for making interdependent relationships with relevant and significant others.'*

Based on such notions, increasingly comprehensive models of interpersonal trust and its consequences have been evolving. Especially noteworthy is a

*Reproduced from J. R. Gibb and Lorraine M. Gibb (1969) 'Role freedom in a TORI group.' In A. Burton (Ed.), *Encounter The Theory and Practice of Encounter Groups*. San Francisco: Jossey-Bass, 42–57, by permission of Jossey-Bass Inc., Publishers.

recent effort by Zand (1972), which breaks new ground while being nestled securely in the context of a long developmental history. Basically, Zand develops a fourfold concept of trust, drawing especially on the contributions of Deutsch (1962) and Gibb (1964). Zand integrates six conceptual emphases:

The *intention* of self to be trusting.
The *actual behaviour* of self as it is consistent/inconsistent with such intention.
The *expectation* of other about self's trustworthiness.
The *perception* of other that self's behaviour is trustworthy.
The nature of the *problem-situation* or context in which self and other are located.
The hypothesized *consequences* of high-trust *vs* low-trust.

These several emphasies are linked as in Figure 1.

To elaborate briefly on the conceptual emphases in Figure 1, Zand distinguishes the intention of a sender, as well as behaviour. The model thus admits the commonplace slippage between intent and action. The receiving actor at once *expects* a certain level of trustworthiness, as well as *perceives* a certain level. The possible richness encompassed by even these elemental components of the model is patent. For example, receiver's low expectation about trustworthiness might lead to a congruent perception of the sender's behaviour and intention, even though other observers might read high trustworthiness into both intention and behaviour of the sender. In this regard, the model seems faithful to major features of social life. Further, Zand's model emphasizes the relevance of the character of the problem-situation involving sender and receiver. Specifically, some issues involve a high degree of what Zand calls 'objective uncertainty'. Here the effects of trust are likely to be more pronounced, because low trust adds a 'social uncertainty' to whatever degree of objective uncertainty exists.

Figure 1 also sketches a number of major consequences that might be expected of high-trust conditions where the problem-situation has substantial objective uncertainty. Those consequences clearly touch much that is central in social and organizational life.

(2) *Trusting as necessary rain.* Less obtrusively but not no less decisively, trust concepts imply dark clouds as well as sunny skies. That is, implicit in any trusting attitude or orientation—of 'a person ... relying upon an object, event, process or another person'—is the notion that 'something is being risked by the trusting person' (Giffin and White, 1967, p. 2). Similarly, in noting that the 'trusting person is *hoping* to achieve some goal', they emphasize that achievement of 'this desired goal is uncertain'.

The emphasis on willingness to risk, hoping and uncertainty is consequential. Consider Deutsch's (1958, especially pp. 265–266) concept. He notes that most common usages include a significant point, explicitly or by implication: that the trusting individual 'perceives that he will be worse off if he trusts and his trust is not fulfilled than if he does not trust.' Deutsch cites the mother who

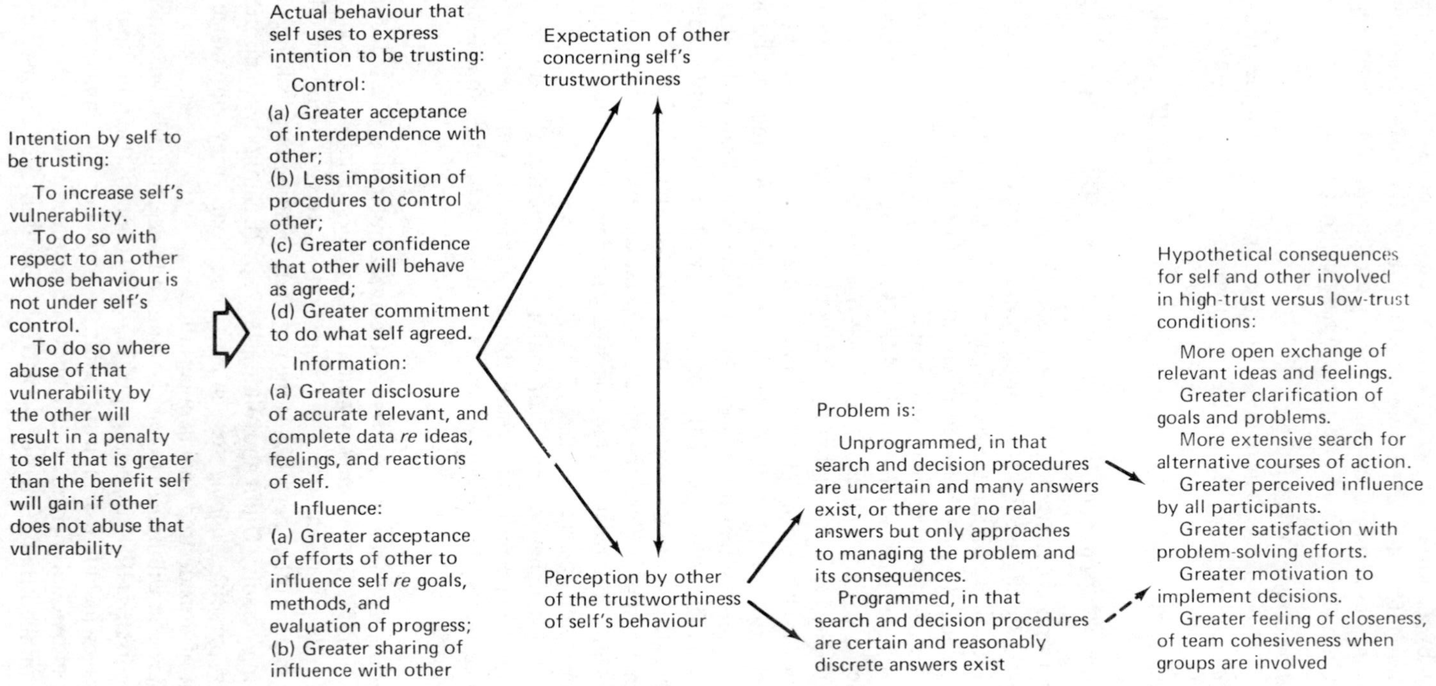

Intention by self to be trusting:

To increase self's vulnerability.

To do so with respect to an other whose behaviour is not under self's control.

To do so where abuse of that vulnerability by the other will result in a penalty to self that is greater than the benefit self will gain if other does not abuse that vulnerability

Actual behaviour that self uses to express intention to be trusting:

Control:

(a) Greater acceptance of interdependence with other;

(b) Less imposition of procedures to control other;

(c) Greater confidence that other will behave as agreed;

(d) Greater commitment to do what self agreed.

Information:

(a) Greater disclosure of accurate relevant, and complete data *re* ideas, feelings, and reactions of self.

Influence:

(a) Greater acceptance of efforts of other to influence self *re* goals, methods, and evaluation of progress;

(b) Greater sharing of influence with other

Expectation of other concerning self's trustworthiness

Perception by other of the trustworthiness of self's behaviour

Problem is:

Unprogrammed, in that search and decision procedures are uncertain and many answers exist, or there are no real answers but only approaches to managing the problem and its consequences.

Programmed, in that search and decision procedures are certain and reasonably discrete answers exist

Hypothetical consequences for self and other involved in high-trust versus low-trust conditions:

More open exchange of relevant ideas and feelings.

Greater clarification of goals and problems.

More extensive search for alternative courses of action.

Greater perceived influence by all participants.

Greater satisfaction with problem-solving efforts.

Greater motivation to implement decisions.

Greater feeling of closeness, of team cohesiveness when groups are involved

Figure 1. A conceptualization of trust and its consequences. —— Indicates dominant relationship, ----- indicates less-dominant relationship. Based on Dale Zand (1972) 'Trust and managerial effectiveness.' *Administrative Science Quarterly*, **17**, 230–233

entrusts her child to a babysitter. If the babysitter does not fulfil the trust-exception, the mother suffers unpleasant consequences—harm to her baby. Consequently, warns Deutsch (1958, p. 266), the potential costs of trusting and then having the trust unfulfilled are 'considerably greater than the advantages' of being able to do the things which she otherwise could not do. In a later version (1973, pp. 144–145), Deutsch affirms that trust may lead to either benefit or harm. He adds: 'the harm that may befall the trusting individual if his trust is unfulfilled is not a trivial harm in relation to the amount of benefit to be received from trusting and having his trust fulfilled.'

This perspective on trusting as a 'risking situation' also has generated associated theoretical networks, although these lack the pizzaz of many trust-as-sun versions. Consider the work of Lundstedt (1966), for example. His conceptualization 'involves an element of risk and utility, in addition to giving away influence and control' (1966, p. 4), which Lundstedt develops into an Interpersonal Risk (IR) Theory. He explains (p. 4):

'If one gives away influence and control of any kind one can find them used for one's own welfare, or against it. Such a risk factor always seems to be calculated by the individual on the basis of prior learning in which subjectively perceived risk is affected by the pattern of rewards coming from the exchanges in the interactions. If past experience has been rewarding, then the amount of subjective risk should be low. One should increasingly be apt to give away influence and control under this condition. The opposite would tend to be true if the amount of subjective interpersonal risk is high. There are many forms of personal control and influence that can be exchanged and given away.'

Lundstedt's model sketched in Figure 2 encourages three useful perspectives on trust-as-rain. First, the model implies that IR behaviour is rooted in individual life-experiences and—although an individual's IR propensity may vary for different classes of issue-areas—it is reasonable to inquire if individuals differ in what may be called IR orientation. Variations in IR, for example, might be systematically related to such antecedent conditions as those illustrated in Figure 2.

Antecedent conditions	Intervening variables	Consequences
(1) High IR behaviour with respect to personal control and influence over others[a]	Attitudes Cognitions Needs Motivation Personality variables: Self-esteem Level of aspiration Ethnocentrism Etc.	(1) Approach behaviour: mutuality, open communication, social exchanges, few serious conflicts
(2) Low IR behaviour with respect to personal control and influence over others		(2) Avoidance behaviour: less mutuality, lower amounts of communication poorer in quality, few exchanges, increases in serious conflicts

[a]The temporal order of the independent and the dependent variables can be reversed.

Figure 2. A schema of Interpersonal Risk (IR) theory. Reproduced by permission from Sven Lundstedt (1966) 'Interpersonal risk theory.' *Journal of Psychology*, **62**, 7

Second, Lundstedt's concept has important theoretical and applied features. Specifically, for example, Low IR individuals may exist, to whom the model of relationships sketched in Figure 1 might apply in lesser degree or not at all. Relatedly, at least in the abstract, Lundstedt's model implies that different learning development strategies or learning designs might be appropriate for Low *vs* High IR individuals.

Third, Lundstedt's basic perspective implies that risk and trust are reflexive in basic senses. To put the point in awful verse:

> Trust without risking can have
> few fruits;
> Risking without trust has
> shallow roots.

For some confirming if preliminary evidence, see Lillibridge and Lundstedt (1967).

(3) *Trusting as dysfunctional or even pathologic.* To extend the preceding analogy, trusting—whether viewed as sun or rain—can help produce curious fruit. This description goes against the grain of most commentary on trust, which has a decidedly positive/optimistic quality about it. Hence the especial value of the emphasis here. Directly, some kinds of trusting behaviour can be dysfunctional, or even pathologic.

The dark side of trusting can be sketched briefly, given two preliminaries. First, despite the uncommonness of the usage, it seems useful to distinguish a 'pathology of trust' as well as a 'pathology of suspicion'. Deutsch acknowledges that referring to the two pathologies may seem strange, since 'to be trusting' typically is considered 'good' while 'to be suspicious' is seen as 'bad'. He also acknowledges that for the recipient of behaviour, it is usually preferable to experience trusting rather than suspicious behaviour. However, Deutsch asks (1973, p. 170): 'from the point of view of the individual who initiates the behavior, can we hold that it is better to trust than to be suspicious?' That is to say, it is not possible to judge whether an individual should be trusting or suspicious, except given detailed knowledge of a specific set of conditions.

Second, the key to non-pathological trust and suspicion seems to lie in the degree of flexibility of responses to changing conditions. Again, Deutsch provides useful guidance (1973, pp. 170–171). He explains: 'Pathological trust or suspicion ... is characterized by an inflexible, rigid, unaltering tendency to act in a trusting or suspicious manner irrespective of the situation or the consequences .... . The pathology is reflected in the indiscriminateness of the behavior tendency.'

There is a major caution inherent in this brief reference to a pathology of trust, some specific attention to which will be given in the first section below dealing with clusters of covariants related to trust. The present goal is a limited one: to raise a caution about the optimistic 'metaphysical pathos' that infuses much of the discussion about trust.

(4) *Basic conceptual challenges to commentary and research.* Even these introductory conceptual notions imply major challenges for commentary and research that seeks to be specific, among which challenges three are paramount. Thus trust involves complex linkages of intention, perception and behaviour, which pose major problems for operational definition. Moreover, it seems necessary to think of trust as like the Chinese idiograph for 'change'. That idiograph is a composite of two others, the one for opportunity and the second for danger. Finally, distinguishing kinds of trust will require major sophistication and discipline from both social observers and researchers.

A greater sense of these challenges, as well as of progress toward clarifying them, can be achieved by considering the circular character of our conceptual quarry. Briefly, what follows suggests that trust is such an intractable subject because its specific analysis essentially requires some statement of the goals of human development as well as a theory of learning. These critical dependencies are too seldom emphasized.

B. *The circular character of trusting/risking*

Very near the heart of most trust concepts is a kind of self-heightening feature, as in the 'spiral reinforcement' quality of Zand's (1972) model. To illustrate, consider the interaction between a high-trust sender and a low-trust receiver. Because of low expectations about the trustworthiness of the sender, the receiver may misperceive the trustworthiness actually present in the behaviour of the sender. Hence receiver may read more malice into sender's behaviour than sender intends. The sender not only tends to get that message. In addition, sender might be concerned enough about misperceptions of his behaviour and misjudgements of his intentions to punish the receiver. As sender becomes defensive, or hostile, or non-communicative, clearly he also joins receiver in inducing low trust. This is the essence of spiral reinforcement. One cannot win for losing, bluntly. High-trust conditions trend toward opposite consequences, a kind of inability to lose for winning.

The self-heightening quality of trust concepts also is patent when the relationship with risking behaviour is taken into specific account. Although that relationship is complex and elusive, several probable linkages seem to stand out in available research. To wit:

Risk-taking signals a desire to trust and it frequently initiates a trusting relationship (Swinth, 1967).

Trust implies 'at least a minimal amount of risk to the trusting person' (Giffin, 1967, p. 105).

If a condition of mutual trust exists, risk-taking is more likely to occur than where there is a lack of mutual trust (Lillibridge and Lundstedt, 1967).

If risking behaviour occurs, it can serve 'to maintain or enhance mutual trust' (Lillibridge and Lundstedt, 1967, p. 120).

Such propositions attract more than they explain. They clearly deal with some central interpersonal dynamics, to be sure, but precisely how is pretty much still a mystery. For example, it is not known what degrees of risk-taking increase (decrease) trust. There seems no question that trust can be increased by substantial risk-taking behaviour. However, it also appears that in some circumstances trust can be established with moderate risk-taking, or even when the risks are slight. And clearly, some risk-taking can impede the development of trust, or even wither it. At the very least, then, there is no solid empirical justification for suggesting that risk and trust are high, direct covariants.

Although it is not possible to be very specific about trusting/risking linkages, it is a straightforward matter to suggest their central role. Three extended illustrations must suffice here, one in each of the following sections. The first reflects the sense of trusting/risking as paired-elements in self-heightening spirals. Relatedly, the second illustration places trusting/risking in the context of a relatively developed model of learning. A third following section will seek to relate the two illustrations of trusting/risking linkages.

(1) *Trusting/risking as self-heightening spirals.* Figure 3 reflects the centrality of trusting/risking linkages in a global but useful way. That is, trusting/risking behaviours are seen as reinforcing and escalating in both Figures 3(a) and 3(b). The graphics require little commentary, if they are taken to provide only a kind of general orientation, which is all they are intended to do.

Two general cases are dealt with in Figure 3. In one case—both when trusting is the starting point in Figure 3(a) as well as when risking is seen as providing the initial stimulus in Figure 3(b)—trusting/risking linkages can buoy the individual to increasingly masterful coping with the self and environment. Briefly, trusting/risking linkages can permit the individual greater freedom in responding to his world, and they can also provide greater support and more reliable information relevant to that effort at growth. But in seeking to find/ explore self, to introduce the second general case, the individual also can become lost. Similarly, that is, both figures imply that those trusting/risking linkages can entrap the individual in a rapidly accelerating spiral of fixated or frozen behaviour, which is at once compelling and costly. The total sense of it is a growing estrangement and aloneness: not trusting enough to seek guidance/ help; and not able to risk sufficiently to try to escape the downward-sucking vortex. Figure 3 also implies the crucial role of mutual risking/trusting, which is prominent in the observations of Argyris (1965, p. 9) and others.

Beyond such generalities, Figures 3(a) and 3(b) can do further duty, given some benchmarks for the notion of 'mature stages of development'. With no pretence at completeness, consider only these three components of 'maturity':

The individual increasingly sees others as accurately differentiated human beings, as opposed to we/they collections of individuals who are accepted/ rejected as categories.

The individual has an increasingly clear perception of self, which more closely integrates the self-perceived-by-others with the self-known-to-self.

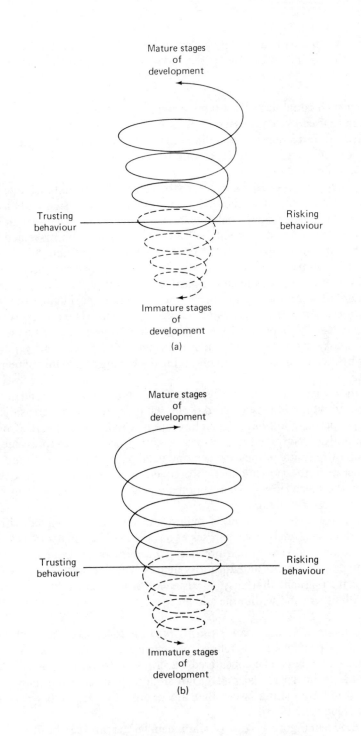

Figure 3. Four patterns of trusting/risking linkages

The individual is increasingly aware of feelings and reactions, and attaches them with growing precision to the inducing stimuli rather than projecting them onto scapegoats, etc.

Given such rough criteria, Figure 3 implies that each individual at various points in time can be characterized by several ascending and descending spirals relevant to different persons and different issue-areas. Moreover, the individual might tolerate even substantial incongruence between sets of such spirals, at least for a time.

Take the case of a teenager recently busted on a marijuana charge. Before the bust, despite frictions, much evidence supported the existence of an ascending spiral in the teenager's relationships with parents and other authority-figures. From their standpoint, substantial trusting/risking seemed appropriate because most signs pointed to the teenager's continuing development. At the same time, however, a trusting/risking linkage with peers in a new school was spiralling downward toward lessened maturity. Valuing the acceptance and affection of several others who were 'into marijuana', the teenager began to escalate a trusting/risking linkage with them. The process was rapid. From the teenager's point of view, these valued others inspired enough trust to risk smoking pot; the camaraderie seemed to heighten trust; and greater risking behaviour followed, as in observing the buying and selling of marijuana; etc.; etc.

For the teenager, the trusting/risking appeared to be liberating and growthful. But non-growthful effects also did occur. Thus the teenager increasingly came to see people as good/bad, depending upon whether they smoked pot. The perception was reinforced in part because other peers at school seemed to be increasingly rejecting of the teenager, and in larger part because of the common bond between the pot-smokers. Moreover, major incongruence developed between the teenager's self-perception and the self as perceived by parents and other authority-figures.

Finally, there occurred a rapid build-up of anxieties associated with maintaining the increasingly divergent selves as personally known and as known to 'square' others, anxiety which precipitated a number of unsatisfactory/angry encounters with parents and authority figures. The two spirals of development were so incongruent that easy coexistence became very difficult to manage, both with others and within the adolescent.

(2) *Trusting/risking as major elements in a model of learning.* The schema in Figure 4 provides more refined perspective on trusting/risking linkages. Indeed, that figure can be considered a useful start toward a model of learning applicable to interpersonal and group situations, despite the many still unresolved and conflicting issues that any eventually satisfactory model must resolve (Knowles, 1973).

The model in Figure 4 is that of Hampden-Turner, and can basically stand on its own. His starting-point is some specific developmental level, an individual's

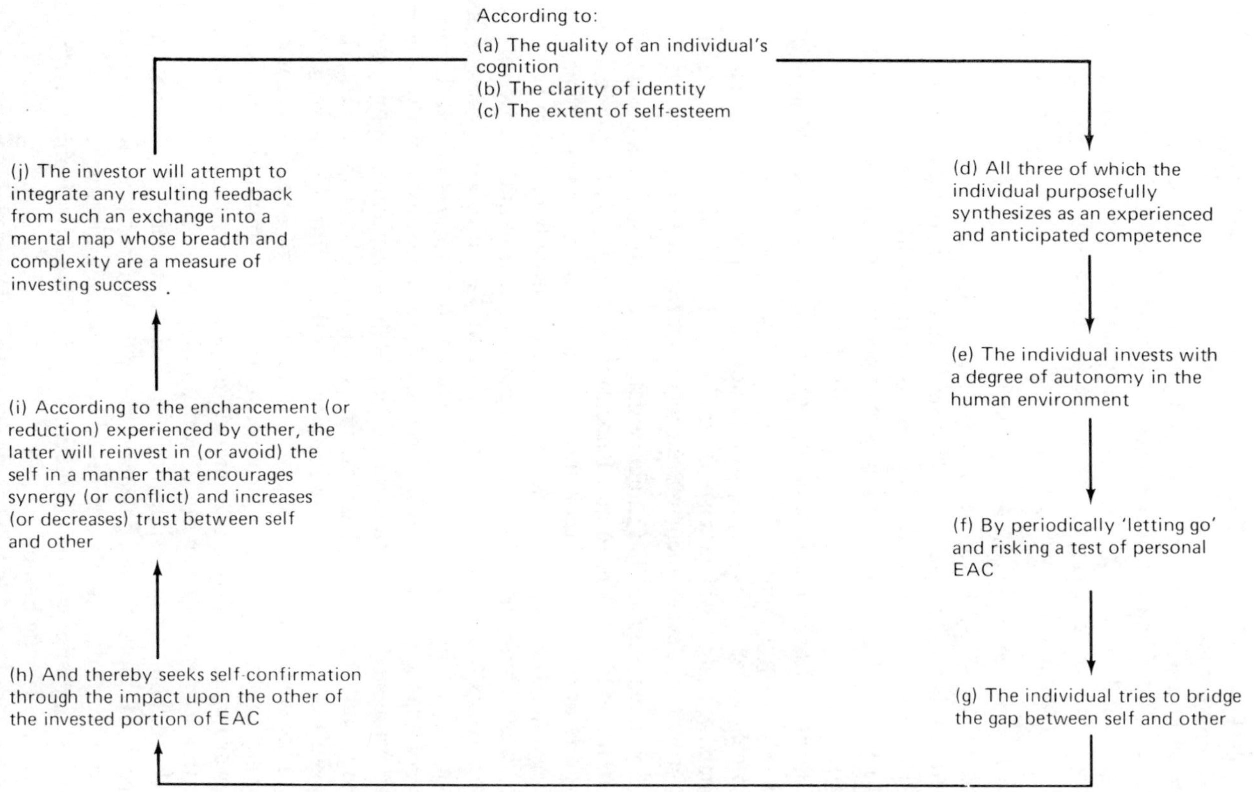

According to:

(a) The quality of an individual's cognition
(b) The clarity of identity
(c) The extent of self-esteem

(d) All three of which the individual purposefully synthesizes as an experienced and anticipated competence

(e) The individual invests with a degree of autonomy in the human environment

(f) By periodically 'letting go' and risking a test of personal EAC

(g) The individual tries to bridge the gap between self and other

(j) The investor will attempt to integrate any resulting feedback from such an exchange into a mental map whose breadth and complexity are a measure of investing success .

(i) According to the enhancement (or reduction) experienced by other, the latter will reinvest in (or avoid) the self in a manner that encourages synergy (or conflict) and increases (or decreases) trust between self and other

(h) And thereby seeks self-confirmation through the other of the invested portion of EAC

Figure 4. Trusting/risking linkages in a model of learning. Reproduced by special permission from Charles M. Hampden-Turner (1966) 'An existential learning theory and the integration of T-group research.' *Journal of Applied Behavioral Science*, **2**, 368

EAC quantum, an existing state of experienced and anticipated competence. The individual can risk a test of that EAC quantum, usually a part of it. Depending upon the consequences of that risky test, the EAC quantum can either swell or shrivel, and the tester's level of trust can either be heightened or diminished. In either case, a new EAC level is thereby established. If the individual experiences a disconfirmation of the invested portion of EAC, not only will the EAC level be reduced but so also will be reduced the individual's capacity for future trusting/risking which are necessary to re-establish that level. And so the game of life can take on a tragic quality.

(3) *Two major indeterminants in trusting/risking linkages.* Figures 3 and 4 tease more than satisfy, that much is clear in at least two senses. First, the two figures imply that individuals somehow seek 'desirable' outcomes and avoid others. However, 'desirable' can be defined in at least two senses, which are difficult for researchers let alone interacting persons to distinguish or even to be conscious of:

As somehow pleasurable or rewarding at an immediate, here-and-now level, as in 'that feels good'; and/or

As somehow serving/violating some ontological 'programmes' built into individuals, as in a set of needs like those sketched by Maslow on whose satisfaction growthful development is seen to be dependent in the long run.

This first indeterminacy has monumental import, although major efforts to finesse it are common. Kegan and Rubenstein (1972, pp. 179–180) deal with both aspects of the point. According to some interpretations of humanistic psychology, he explains, the relevance of goals for growth is obscured or even defined away. Those interpretations, Kegan explains, maintain that: 'if the individual trusts himself enough to be sufficiently open to experience of his organism—which in turn reflects experience of the world—he will discover whatever guidance and control is necessary for his healthy growth.' Kegan and Rubenstein are gentle with these 'assumptions or postulates' of humanistic psychology, but they insist that: 'At times it may be appropriate to accept these postulates and to try to live according to them. But ... the behavioral scientist may wish to question or test aspects of these theories.' And for such questioning and testing, it is at base necessary to have in mind as well as to work toward some set of goals of human development, as in the early Maslowian work with the 'hierarchy of needs'. From another perspective, research about trust/risk is difficult or impossible to interpret in the absence of some statement of the goals of human development and growth. What is trust for goals that stress short-run desirability/acceptability, epigrammatically, can well be pseudo-trust or pathologic trust in the context of goals that are somehow rooted in the essence of being human.

Figures 3 and 4 provide few details about this first crucial requirement for dealing specifically with trusting/risking linkages. Providing that detail constitutes one of the basic challenges in the study of trust, as well as in applications of that knowledge.

One further conceptual feature at once temporarily side-steps the subtle business of defining the 'desirable' and also illustrates its significance. An intervening variable—the favourability of the consequences of risking—seems to determine whether or not high risking will be a high positive correlate of high trust over the long run. That is, if the consequences of risking (trusting) seem desirable, the overall evidence suggests, then trusting (risking) behaviours will increase. If the consequences of risking (trusting) are contrary to the desires of the acting person, then trusting (risking) behaviour will not follow. In addition, an individual's perception of potential consequences, as well as his early experiences, will not only influence how trusting he will permit himself to become, but will also help determine whether or not he will venture to make the initial risk.

Note that the reference to 'favourability of consequences' is inconclusive in at least two senses. Thus the usage implies the need for, but does not provide, a definition of the 'desirable'. Moreover, the reference is moot on a central question: will specific degrees of risking lead to known degrees of trusting behaviour? No one knows, even though critical issues for both science and application are involved. Figure 5 provides a best-guess of the relationships, suggesting that risk-taking behaviour of several intensities will, if followed by favourable consequences, elicit trusting behaviour of like intensity. However, if the consequences of the risk are negative or unfavourable, then the probable result will also be a low level of trust. Trusting follows risking behaviour which leads to favourable consequences, in sum.

A figure similar to Figure 5 could be drawn with the vector-arrows being directed from trusting → risking, patently. Changes in the wording, but not the sense, of the three paragraphs above would be necessary to elaborate on this alternative figure.

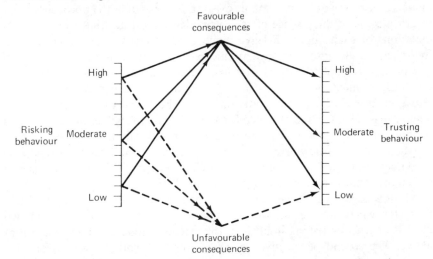

Figure 5. Schema of hypothetical relationships between levels of trusting and risking behaviours

Second, Figures 3–5 imply another critical indeterminacy for interpreting research about trust and its covariants, as well as for applying derivative knowledge. Recall the earlier discussion of the need for basic agreement about the ontologic goals of human growth and development. Patently, also, attempts to interpret and to apply findings about trust/risk will at least be chancy in the absence of a comprehensive model for learning which permits efficient pursuit of the goals of human development and growth. To put it baldly, an individual's behaviours can be evaluated as somehow functional or dysfunctional only under two conditions: given a definition of goals *re* the 'desirable' or 'growthful'; and given a model of learning which sketches the phases/processes by which individuals can approach such goals. A pedestrian example will have to suffice here to illustrate the value of such a model of learning. What would be functional freedom for individuals at mature stages of development, that is, might imply danger or wanton neglect at less mature stages of development.

(4) *Two essential challenges for commentary and research.* A comprehensive theory of trust, then, will evolve only as progress is made toward two macro challenges: the satisfactory specification of human goals as they relate to the 'desirable' or 'favourable'; and growing closure on a model for learning or change. These are at the heart of the intractability of trust as a focus for research.

The last couple of decades have been preoccupied with thought and research on related themes. That is, Hampden-Turner's model discussed in the preceding section illustrates progress toward a set of phases/processes for learning and growth. Moreover, much attention has been given to the alternative approaches in Maslowian 'growth psychology' and in Skinnerian 'behavioural psychology', both of which imply different goals of human development as well as alternative models of learning or change. While existing versions of both approaches seem to grasp some of the essence of reality, evidence indicates that available formulations of each approach leave much behavioural variance unaccounted for when put to more or less specific test. Efforts to integrate these two approaches (Diamond, 1974) are just beginning, moreover. There is an obviously immense value in such an integration, if it can be brought off. However, even if any such integrative model can be shown 'to work' empirically, a massive issue would remain open for some. Would the values implied in such a model define the 'good life', a personal and social order that is to be pursued because of its intrinsic worth? The relevant arguments take many forms, with a contemporary peaking of interest involving Jensen (1973), Shockley (1971) and many critical commentators (e.g. in Riegel, 1973).

Acknowledging where we need to go, the rest of this paper modestly seeks to sketch where we are, in two major senses. The first emphasis is on two models of trusting/risking implicit in the extended conceptual considerations above. The second perspective on where we are involves a review of trust and its covariants, as isolated by research or as suggested by extrapolations from it.

C. *Two models of risking/trusting in group processes*

These efforts at conceptual elaboration have significant practical import for the development of learning designs. Specifically, they imply two models for trusting/risking linkages in interpersonal and group contexts:

I. A somehow adequate   successful   heightened   increased risking ...
    level of trust ——————→ risking ——→ trust ————→ propensity

II. Somehow induced   heightened   increased   heightened ...
    successful ————————→ trust ————→ risking ——→ trust
    risking   propensity

The sense of it is that, within wide limits, there are several combinations of two basic ways of starting the engine of interpersonal exploration and perhaps growth. Figure 6 tries its hand at providing a schema of such combinations, along with examples of each.

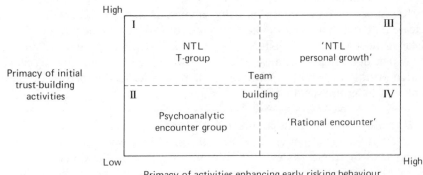

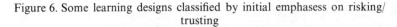

Figure 6. Some learning designs classified by initial emphasess on risking/ trusting

It is easy enough to illustrate these two approaches to starting the engine of growth and exploration. Thus a group experience might begin with either of two sets of instructions:

I. 'We are here to learn from one another. This learning is best established after a micro-society is established, after we learn what to expect from one another. There are many ways to begin. How would you like to start?'

II. 'You are husbands and wives here to learn from your partners and other couples. The sooner we get started, the more you will learn.

As a starter, without any preliminaries, please write 3 items on a slip of paper you would never dream of revealing to your partner ...

Done? Good.

Now who will be first to share with us one of the items on his or her list? It will only become harder to do if you resist.

Now, who's the bravest one?'

More broadly, the two approaches to revving up the engine are characterized by a substantial catalogue of differences, some differences in degree and some of kind:

I. *Trust-building activities*	II. *Activities that trigger risk-taking*
(1) The development of a supportive climate and norms	(1) Emphases on an early getting-down-to-business
(2) Building toward shared norms on the basis of perceived similarities in attitudes and experiences of participants, e.g. 'they won't hurt me because they like me in many basic ways'	(2) Building an early sense of the balance of benefits over costs in the situation, e.g. 'this experience can help me and negative consequences are unlikely'
(3) Relatively immediate, here-and-now, interventions which are more or less specific in focus and basically release material that is undisclosed but is easily available to participants	(3) 'Deep' interventions, which are macro in focus and often liberate materials below conscious thresholds, as by so-called 'non-verbal interventions' (Mill and Ritvo, 1969)
(4) The development of a we-ness, a shared identity that implies substantial direction by group members	(4) Basic direction by a charismatic leader/facilitator

With only somewhat less confidence, it is also possible to predict a catalogue of alternative consequences that are likely to be associated with learning experiences or trainer styles favouring one emphasis or the other. Five such alternative consequences will be detailed here. First, designs emphasizing the primacy of trust-building activities are likely to require more time and patience.

Second, where they 'work', risk-triggering activities are likely to be more impactful and emotionally arousing. Their effects also are more likely to be induced in a briefer time.

Third, trust-building activities no doubt run fewer risks of precipitating participants into learning situations for which they may not be ready, and which they may therefore be less likely to psychologically own or even manage successfully. This proposition clearly assumes (for example) similar participants, which assumption may not apply in many cases. Take a T-group laboratory, to illustrate. Given adequate pre-information and individuals who are in tune with their capacities and needs, participants may self-selectively gravitate toward learning designs or trainers having one emphasis or the other, as in the intriguing design of Heine *et al.* (1974).

Fourth, the two approaches may both create transfer problems, perhaps in different ways. Trust-building activities may build so much dependence on a nurturant group that transfer into rational–technical systems is seen by participants as inappropriate or too chancy (Winn, 1969, especially pp. 158–160). Emphasis on risk-triggering activities, in contrast, may encourage dependence on a charismatic leader or trainer. This dependence might create its own brand of transfer-problem. Following Argyris (1968), a trainer's style massively characterized by risk-triggering activities violates the presumed wisdom that the learner can and should basically influence and manage the learning process. Specifically, individual learners should have frequent opportunities to (Argyris, 1968, especially pp. 153–154): develop their own learning goals; develop their own approaches to their own central needs; and choose a level of aspiration that is at once challenging but not overwhelming.

Although it is not easy to draw the line, at some point the emphasis on risk-triggering activities can become so marked as to imply quite a different picture of the genotypic learner. Argyris (1968) makes the contrast sharply. The model of the learner implicit in the three features above is one seeking to acquire competence, as one intent on self-enhancement and more effective coping. As one moves away from these three features, so also does the image of the learner become survival-oriented or deficiency-oriented.

Fifth, although data about the point are hardly conclusive (Lieberman, Yalom and Miles, 1973; Golembiewski, 1972, especially pp. 228–242), available data and a reasonable line of surmise imply that higher 'casualty rates' can be provisionally assigned to trainer styles that emphasize risk-triggering activities. The same may be true of learning designs with the two emphases. It is sometimes difficult to distinguish a psychologic casualty from a learner who has had a particularly meaningful experience, of course. So some readers may conclude that the generalization here merely accentuates the value of trainer interventions or of learning designs that emphasize risk-triggering activities. That is not the intent. In any case, we are only just beginning to make some sense out of the cost/benefit trade-offs relevant to learning in groups, largely because the issues are fiendishly complicated.

II. Toward a network of relations: trusting/risking linkages and some of their covariants

These conceptual musings should amply demonstrate the elusiveness of trust as analytic quarry; and they are intended as tethers for any overexuberance that might creep into the efforts below to sketch a number of covariants of trusting/risking linkages. These covariants are offered as gross central tendencies only, for at least three reasons which at once help explain and also exacerbate the conceptual profusion discussed above. That is, individual studies use a wide variety of operational measures of 'trust'. Moreover, rigorous research has only begun. Finally, available research tends to deal with two or a few variables at a time. All these points require brief elaboration.

First, the diversity of operational measures of trust encourages a careful tentativeness in interpreting research. For example, one study may reveal that $trust_1$ is directly and strongly related to variable A; but a study of $trust_2$ may reveal no relationship at all with that variable. Only cautious interpretations of such 'results' are prudent, given the unknown congruence of the operational definitions.

Unfortunately, concern with the comparison of alternative operational definitions is quite unusual. Only a few major exceptions to this troublesome generalization exist (e.g. March, 1956; Eisman, 1959). The 'trust' literature is not one of these major exceptions (Kee and Knox, 1970; Kegan and Rubenstein, 1972). Illustratively, available research diversely defines 'trust' in terms of

What people report about their attitudes toward self or others as trusting or trustworthy.

How people seem to behave toward others, from which an external observer infers 'trust'.

Unobtrusive measures that infer trustfulness from observations of such acts as who locks their cars while attending church (TeVault, Forbes, and Gromoll, 1971).

The condition where 'behaviour conforms to commitment—when people do what they say they will' (Lieberman, 1964).

Situational features, that is, as when a prediction about trust or trustworthiness is derived from the specific behaviour and/or expressed attitude of a specific other.

A genetic predisposition to be trusting or suspicious, which is generalizable over a broad range of conditions and situations (Rotter, 1967).

A broad orientation toward institutions, as in a 'political trust' orientation (Michener and Zeller, 1972).

A direct response to a simple stimulus such as: How much do you trust X?

A resultant of statistical manipulations of a batch of items, as by factor analysis (Roberts and O'Reilley, 1974), which distinguishes a cluster of 'trust' items from a larger set of items.

Patently, it is incautious to believe that such diverse 'trust' operations are or should be consistently related to the same covariants. For example, as Allen (1973) reports, predictions of trustworthiness based on expressions of the attitudes of another can differ significantly from predictions based on the observed behaviour of that other.

In addition, these operational ambiguities are exacerbated by several common usages, which overlap in part but seem conceptually distinct. Thus a person may be said to 'trust', which can imply a state of confidence about a limited range of outcomes, or it may refer to a person's general predisposition or style of relating. Alternatively, an individual may be said to be 'trusting', by which is sometimes meant a broad predisposition but which can also refer to some specified behaviours in a specific situation. Or an individual may be called 'trustworthy', as one worthy of the trust of others because of appearance or behaviour. In other usages, to be 'trustworthy' carries the additional implication that one also trusts or is trusting.

Second, the literature to be reviewed has been developed only recently, which youth has patent implications for what follows. 'Despite the obvious significance of trust and other related phenomena,' Deutsch (1973, p. 144) reminds us, '[they] have largely been ignored by the social scientist.' Why this is the case need not detain us here, especially since observers such as Koestler (1967) have provided convincing explanations from various perspectives. That the literature is young should suffuse the following summary review with appropriate tentativeness and caution.

Third, the paucity of variables in most trust research implies especial dangers for tracing patterns of covariation. This is the heart of Rapoport's (1963) concern, for example, about the laboratory study of trust and suspicion in non-zero sum games, a popular variety of research. Rapoport emphasizes the 'outcome orientation' of such research, which typically neglects psychological variables. Rapoport discourages attempts to extrapolate any findings to real-life situations where, for him, psychological variables patently come into play in major ways. This is the case whether or not such variables account for much of the variance observed in short-term experimental groups. Evidence of both kinds exists, with students like Wallace and Rothaus (1969) reporting that personality variables had no predictive power in experimental situations, while opposed conclusions are offered by Noel (1963, p. 99) and Wrightsman (1966).

Similarly, Rotter (1971) notes that—although trust research is often done in interpersonal or group settings both in laboratories and the natural state—research seldom specifies the properties of the collectivities studied. Ample evidence (Golembiewski, 1962) urges that groups are not homogeneous with respect to either their character or the consequences they produce. Hence the general failure to specify group properties complicates interpretations of any results of research. This is a 'serious limitation', Rotter notes (1971, p. 444): 'it is not known whether the results could be generalized to other groups or, indeed, what variables in group selection are relevant in generalizing results.'

A. *Seven clusters of covariants: toward a comprehensive network*

Although the welter of operational definitions of 'trust' and the brief research history should properly encourage caution, they need not timidify. In this spirit, seven major clusters of the covariants of trust will be emphasized here. Sometimes the 'clusters' will be relatively precise mini-networks of variables. Usually, however, the 'clusters' will provide only a general gestalt or orientation to what seem significant and related phenomena.

(1) *Generic trust effects on personality development and learning.* Overall, limitations of existing research notwithstanding, trust seems to have profound effects on learning and development, whether in interpersonal encounters, in groups or in large organizations. That the effects which flow from trusting behaviour apparently permeate every segment of human activity may be illustrated from three points of view: some processes of trust; some proposed outcomes of trust; and an introduction to available research.

(a) *Some processes of trust.* There are numerous ways of conceptualizing the processes associated with trust in personality development and learning, among which Figure 7 is both revealing and convenient. Overall, that figure

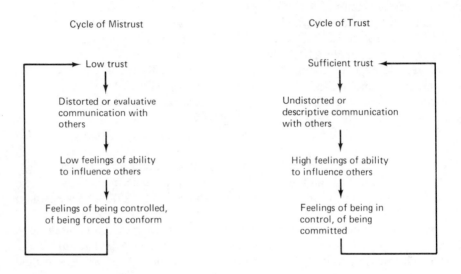

Figure 7. Two cycles for characterizing human relationships. Reproduced from Gordon L. Lippitt (1969) *Organization Renewal*. New York: Appleton-Century-Crofts, p. 90

implies, the individual caught in a cycle of mistrust is cut off from much information required for healthy development, and consequently must be either very guarded or often surprised. Neither condition is a desirable one, on balance. Witness the individual who responds in a frozen and maladaptive way to a 'climate which induces defensiveness', one of the unfortunate major products of a cycle of mistrust. Gibb emphasizes (1961, p. 144) that individuals in such a climate are too preoccupied to learn effectively. Such an individual 'thinks about how he appears to others, how he may be seen more favourably, how he may win, dominate, impress, or escape punishment, and/or how he may avoid or mitigate a perceived or anticipated attack ....' Only as these defences are reduced can the targets of communication 'concentrate on the structure, the content, and the cognitive meaning of the message.' To put it positively, the more 'supportive' or 'defence-reductive' the climate becomes, Gibb adds, 'the less the receiver reads into the communication distorted loadings which arise from projections of his own anxieties, motives, and concerns.'

(b) *Some outcomes of trust.* The outcomes of processes conceptually associated with different levels of trust are also susceptible to myriad illustrations. Implied in the description of processes above, for example, is some such general causal chain for high trust:

Trusting environment for personal development	High self-esteem of Individual A	High propensity to be trusting and trustworthy over the broad range of human encounters, but with the capability of being mistrustful and suspicious if situationally appropriate	Positive overall outcomes for personality development and learning of Individual A
$\longrightarrow$	$\longrightarrow$	$\longrightarrow$	

Given the earlier discussion of the linkages between trust and ontological goals of human development and maturity, of course, such references as 'positive overall outcomes' should be interpreted gently. A broadly humanist perspective underlies such judgements here.

Some evidence suggests that a similar chain for low trust is substantially more complicated. The position here relies on Deutsch (1973, especially pp. 169–176), who proposes that (p. 171) 'whenever there is a pathology of trust or suspicion with regard to others, there is an accompanying pathology with regard to oneself.' He explains (p. 171): 'Pathological overtrust of the other (gullibility) is usually accompanied by pathological undertrust of oneself; pathological oversuspicion of others (paranoia) is usually accompanied by pathological undersuspicion with regard to oneself.' Rotter (1967, p. 663) provides empirical evidence about the need to make some such distinction, which adds support to the preliminary effort in Figure 8. That figure seeks to highlight and summarize Deutsch's more extended development of a critical complexity in the role of trust in personality development and learning.

(c) *An introduction to available research.* Given the broad-brush treatment in the two sections above, it should come as no great surprise that available research only nibbles around the edges of a vast conceptual territory. However, given that vastness—both in significance and complexity—the general picture above is substantially supported by the details of numerous studies of the impact of trust on individual personality development and learning.

Some sense of the literature dealing with trust and personality development can be sketched briefly, to begin to supply evidence for the summary conclusion above. For example, Kegan and Rubenstein (1972) write that trust-in-self or self-esteem is one of the chief building blocks of a healthy personality. Ample evidence, in turn, seems to suggest that trust-in-self is associated with a developmental environment characterized by trust. Julian Rotter explains (1967, p. 651) that 'various writers' indicate that the presence of trust is an important variable in the 'development of adequate family relationships and of healthy

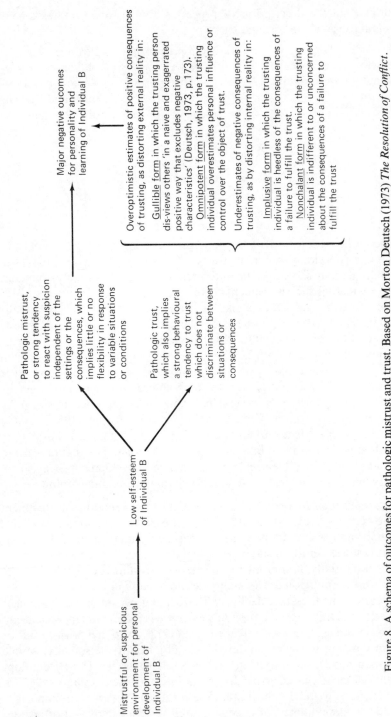

Figure 8. A schema of outcomes for pathologic mistrust and trust. Based on Morton Deutsch (1973) *The Resolution of Conflict.*
New Haven: Conneticut, Yale University Press, especially pp. 169–176

personalities in children.' In their report on efforts to retrieve children from the hell of personality disorders, specifically, Ganter, Yeakel and Polansky (1967) make a similar observation about the importance of trust.

Available clinical work supports a similar picture of the linkages of trust and personality development. Consider Lichtenberg and Norton's (1970) analysis of the experiences of the young, hospitialized schizophrenic girl who wrote *I Never Promised You a Rose Garden*. Three major issue-areas emerge from a content analysis of that book:

Honesty and trust in communications.
Trust and loyalty in social relations.
'Personality equality' between individuals.

The researchers conclude (p. 39): 'The findings may be summarized by saying that honesty, trust, and personality equality are therapeutic ingredients of the first order.' Moreover, the positive aspects of the three issue-areas are related to improved functioning in the adolescent, schizophrenic girls depicted in the volume.

On balance, the bulk of the literature also finds a broad range of expected linkages between trust and personality development, as variously defined. For example, Kenny (1969) demonstrates that 'paranoid schizophrenics' are rated less trusting than 'normals', when both are exposed to the Distrust condition in the Prisoner's Dilemma game.

The research literature is also dotted with many exceptions to, or modifications of, general expectations about trust and its effects. Sometimes this signals the limited generalizability of findings, as in Kenny's (1969) case. Thus Harford and Solomon (1969) show that patients classified as 'paranoid schizophrenics' seem to reflect different degrees of trusting and trustworthy behaviours in their relationships with individuals whose basic behavioural strategies are differentiated as 'reformed sinner' and 'lapsed saint'. The exceptions to, or modifications of, expectations about trust effects also derive from failure to isolate in nature what is assumed to exist. Johnson (1971) was not able to find consistent relationships between a measure of interpersonal trust, empathy and stage of ego development in adults, for example. She concludes that empathy and trust are basically independent of one another, as well as that trust is not positively correlated with ego development. Such 'exceptions' are impossible to interpret definitively. For example, Johnson's findings may tell us les about reality than they reflect problems with Rotter's Interpersonal Trust Scale, which she used. Evidence about the scale can be easily marshalled, both pro (Rotter, 1967) and con (Fitzgerald, Pasewark and Noah, 1970).

To conclude this review of available research on generic trust effects, much commentary suggests a strong if complex relationship between the level of trust and the facility with which people are able to learn. The underlying rationale is uncomplicated. Much learning by human beings is based on the verbal and written statements of others. How much we accept of what others have written and spoken is a function of how willing we are to accept their word as competent, or acceptable, that is, by how much trust we have in them (Rotter, 1967, p. 651). Similarly, Gibb (1964, pp. 308–309) writes that individual growth is a process of learning which is most effective when 'there is an appropriate degree of self-trust and acceptance ....'.

Such considerations relevant to learning have led insightful students like Schmuck (1972) to urge on professional educators the great importance of trusting relationships in schools, but only piecemeal research has tested the validity of the relationships sketched above. Some sense of the available literature can be economically conveyed by Figure 9, which is illustrative only and hypothetically conflates findings from several sources. Major proposed directional relationships are indicated by the solid vectors and feedback loops are designated by the broken lines. Figure 9 begins with a distinction between persons with reference to broad generalized expectancies (Rotter, Hamsher and Geller, 1968). 'Internalizers' are individuals who see their own behaviour as central in determining what happens to them and their lives; 'externalizers' are those who basically see their behaviour as a dependent variable, with 'fate' or 'luck' or 'the world' essentially determining what happens to them and to their lives.

Clearly, no available research relates to the full set of theory-fragments sketched in Figure 9, and the illustrative fragments here patently omit major intervening variables. Nonetheless, the bits-and-pieces of a number of studies do generally support that sketch. For example, some evidence implies that trust will vary with differences in internalization/externalization (Rotter, Hamsher and Geller, 1968). Still other research implies that trust will be associated directly with self-confidence (Lillibridge and Lundstedt, 1967) and with efficacy (Michener and Zeller, 1972) or perceived competence (Glenn, 1970), as well as indirectly with a generalized defensiveness (Rotter, Hamsher and Geller, 1968). Still other work implies that both generalized and situational efficacy or power are significant antecedents/predictors of the degree to which individuals will experience positive behavioural or learning outcomes. The effects seem to hold at all levels: for small groups (Archer, 1974), organizations (Miles, 1965, p. 219) and the macro-society as well (Seeman, 1971).

Many other such composite mini-networks could be sketched here, but their import would be very similar. A propositional trinity expresses this similarity. The relationships imply very critical issues indeed; and the bulk of relevant commentary reflects substantially the same pattern of relationships; but the available research is more tantalizing than definitive.

(2) *Trust effects on friendship and interpersonal association.* A broad range of research establishes that trust has broad-spectrum effects on the intimate bonds between humans. To illustrate, Giffin's (1967) review of the experimental literature concludes that the following variables tend to increase as trust increases:

Acceptance of influence of others.

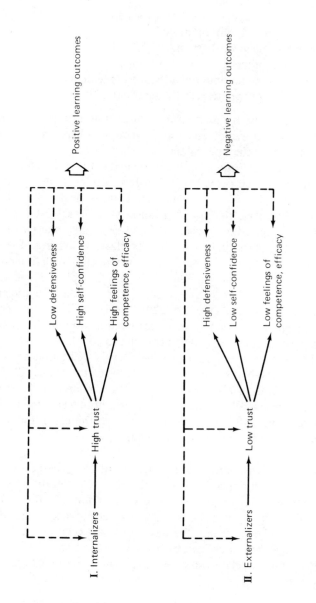

Figure 9. A schema of some hypothetical linkages of trust with learning outcome

Acceptance of motives of others.

Acceptance of diverse behaviour of others.

Acceptance of distrust by others.

Seeking control over process rather than over people.

Freedom to deviate from group opinion.

Offers from others to reciprocate trust.

Communication with others.

Communication of personal opinions or value judgements.

Positive affect or liking for parties to the interaction.

Similar effects also have been observed in natural-state groups, as well as in temporary learning collectivities such as T-groups. There the research is thinner, but no less convincing, on balance.

Some detail on the interaction between trust and the character of interpersonal association can be provided. Consider Rotter's (1967) attempt to measure trust sociometrically. He found that trust is negatively related to dependency, as in leaning on others for assistance. Moreover, trust is 'positively related to humour, friendship, popularity and especially trustworthiness.' Rotter is not alone in associating trust with the pleasant sharing of selves, as in personal friendship. Gibb has formulated a model dealing with four concerns which inhere in all social interaction. One of these is 'acceptance' which, Gibb (1964, pp. 280–281) points out, is a need satisfied only when people exercise trust. Zand concurs and writes (1972, p. 229): 'Trust facilitates interpersonal acceptance.' It appears that trust is a major cornerstone upon which friendship and human association in many contexts is built; to conclude.

Similar effects have been reported at macro-levels of human association, as well as at micro-levels. Not surprisingly, to illustrate, the quality of race and minority group relationships also has been frequently related to 'expectancies of one group that the verbal statements of the other cannot be accepted' (Rotter, 1967, p. 651). Credibly, that is, the perceived trustworthiness of the members of a group influences behaviour directed at them.

(3) *Communication* ↔ *trust interaction.* Significant linkages between trust/communication are commonplace, both in the research literature as well as in social commentary. Three emphases are necessary to outline these linkages. First, two popular expressions of the broad character of trust/communication interfaces will be sketched. Second, the interaction between amount of communication ↔ trust will be suggested by a brief review of available research. Third, the more complex relationships necessary in communication ↔ trust linkages will be sketched.

(a) *Some conceptual views.* The complex interactions between trust/communication in the literature can be economically elaborated by two illustrative approaches dealing with different levels of social organization. At a mciro-level, Gibb draws attention to four concerns that 'pervade all interpersonal relationships'. These four concerns are:

Acceptance of self and others, which is associated with trust formation and the reduction of fear.

The flow of data, both of information and of feelings.

Goal formation and achievement.

Implementation of mechanisms for control and organization.

Similarly, all of these focal concerns relate to the degree of trust within a group, and they all have powerful impacts upon the quality and degree of communication. As Gibb explains (1964, pp. 283–284):

'Data-flow is possible only within the limits of trust formation. A free flow of data is possible only with antecedent or concurrent reduction of distrusts and fears. Defense mechanisms and organizational demands prevent functional processing of data beyond the trust limits. A person can look at his goals only as he begins to trust himself. This growing self-trust makes self-awareness possible. Integration of group goals occurs only as rapidly as members build sufficient trust ... Premature goal formulation beyond the trust and data boundaries leads to unrealistic, overaspirational or formalized goals, the pursuit or lack of which leads to apathy or various other forms of resistance. Stable and functional organizational structure is possible only as goals have been achieved through adequate reality processing of data within the trust boundaries of the organization ... In early stages of organization, the structure is to some degree maintained by fear, strategy, persuasion, and power. In later stages, the structure comes to be maintained by trust, reality-data, intrinsic motivations, and interdependence of roles.'

Briefly, Gibb argues that increases in trust lead to more timely feedback, to more effective communication, and to constructive action.

Much the same gestalt is offered by students of large organizations, many of whom seem to have been influenced by Gibb's concept. Consider the formulation of a very influential commentator, the late Douglas McGregor. The last expression of his work is climaxed by a section prescribing how to ameliorate the differences which often exist between management and employees. There he comments, almost as if he were giving final testament, about the centrality and saliency of trust. 'Obviously, authentic communications cannot be produced by fiat, by an order, or even a plea from the leader', McGregor (1967, p. 192) begins. 'They depend on certain other related conditions', rather, among the most important of which is a climate of mutual trust and support among members of the organization. Given such a climate, he concludes, members can 'be themselves', and not be fearful of the consequences. 'They perceive', he explains, 'that even within the competitive struggle for power and status and the other rewards of corporate life, their fellow members and the leader will not take unfair advantage of their openness — and the attendant vulnerability.' McGregor does not let it go at that. He also includes a section (p. 163) arguing that trust induces communication while distrust retards communication. And he adds yet another section which maintains (especially pp. 163–164) that communication and trust area fundamental to managerial effectiveness.

McGregor's emphases find receptive audiences. Indeed, these emphases amount to a kind of orthodoxy among many observers of large systems, as in the analysis of Crockett, Gaertner and Dufur (1972, pp. 17–18). They write that trust is *the* basis for effective delegation, two-level communication, giving and receiving feedback, and team spirit.

(b) *Some early relevant research*. We begin with two broad conclusions, which will be illustrated briefly by considering one seminal line of research. That is, the research literature provides general support for the formulations above; but it will be a very long time indeed before that literature can provide a complete map to the trust/communication territory. That is to say, the territory is very rough and complex as well as significant. Hence the temptation to overinterpret available literature will be with us for a long time, for we need so much to know while there is so much that requires knowing.

All of these features are illustrated in an experimental setting by Loomis' pathfinding work (1958 and 1959). Using a simulation which permitted control over the amount of communication possible between participants, Loomis anticipated that the percentage of participants who perceived trust would increase with increments in the degree of communication permitted by the experimental design (1959, p. 312). Moreover, Loomis predicted that participants would act in trustworthy ways if they perceived trust, and that they would act defensively if they did not perceive trust. That is to say, amount of communication is directly related to degree of trust. Moreover, as Loomis extrapolated (p. 306), 'if the individual perceives mutual trust, he will cooperate, and if the individual does not perceive mutual trust, he will not cooperate.'

Loomis' research-targets are of central theoretic and practical significance. Overall, his experimental results show his predictions to be correct in four of five cases (p. 312), on the average. Specifically, three features of Loomis' study about the impact of communication on trust loom largest. First, amount of communication and perceived trust are directly related. Second, the 'percentage of perceived trust increased as communication increased.' Why perceived trust is so central to human behaviour is suggested by a third finding of the Loomis' study: 'about 80 per cent of all the subjects made choices [about cooperating and competing] consistent with their perception of the [trust] relationship' (p. 314). In other words, people tend to choose the association of those whom they trust, with the degre of trust being influenced in major ways by the amount of communication possible between them.

Some early natural-state studies, notably one by Mellinger (1956), also point to the significant impact of trust → communication. He studied 330 scientists in a large public research organization, with emphasis on these hypothetical linkages:

	A consequently tends to conceal attitudes and information from B,	B's perceptions of reality are consequently impaired, e.g.
A distrusts B ⟶	by communicating in ways that are:	B in cases may overestimate agreement with A.
	Evasive. Complaint. Agressive	B in cases may underestimate agreement with A

Questionnaire data generally supported these hypothecated linkages.

(4) *Factors intervening in communication ↔ trust interaction.* Given the need to know, and to know quickly, it is not surprising that such early research tended to inspire work having two features. Thus dominant attention was accorded to the communication → trust linkage, apparently because 'communication' was seen as more easily manipulable as an independent variable. Moreover, the temptation to make too much of results like Loomis' often was irresistible. Witness Newcomb *et al.* (1965, p. 247), who proposes that Loomis found 'that the development of perceived mutual trust was a function of the amount of communication permitted. ... The increased sharing of information regarding mutual problem solving activities resulted in an increase in shared acceptance of rules and in mutual trust.'

There was both good and bad in these biases, but progress beyond them was patently necessary. Hence it often has been necessary to whittle down to size overexuberant interpretations of amount of communication → trust interaction, to restrain optimism with the wet blanket of the complexity of nature. For example, a condition that is well known in organization life (Whyte, 1961, especially pp. 125–135) was reflected in some subsequent experimental studies (e.g. Pilisuk and Skolnick, 1968) that fail to verify the linkage between amount of communication and trust. That is, under certain conditions the opportunity to communicate can lead to reduced trust. Hence the most useful prescription in the face of some falling levels of trust may be to variously limit or preclude communication, not encourage it. Jackson provides a case in point. He reports (1960, especially pp. 454–456) that only some employees who receive frequent communications from their supervisors become accurately informed about their supervisor's real attitudes. For other employees, this is not true. The apparent reason: the supervisor does not trust the latter subordinates, and the more frequent the contact, the more patent that fact becomes and the less accurately informed are some subordinates about their supervisor's real attitudes.

Directly, the linkage between amount of communication and trust is neither simple, nor unidirectional, nor capable of standing without specification of intervening variables. To illustrate, Deutsch would agree with Newcomb, but only speaking quite generally. More specific agreement would, for him, require some important qualifications of the simple and direct relationship of the amount of communication and the level of trust. It is best to let Deutsch speak for himself, but essentially he notes that the quality of the communication shared can be as relevant as the amount. He summarizes the central thrust of his own research in these terms (1962, pp. 312–314):

'. . . An individual is more likely to trust another (a) if he believes the other person has nothing to gain from untrustworthy behavior and (b) if he perceives that he is able to exert some control over the other person's outcome.'

Some progress also has been made toward considering trust as the independent variable in research designs. Although the plain fact is that the required sophistication is the only beginning to develop, the available research does support two working conclusions. Thus the specific linkages between trust and the quality of communication cannot be spelled out in great detail, and they cannot yet be firmly rooted in a comprehensive network of theory. However, the outlines of the complex linkages required are becoming increasingly clear.

Two pieces of research usefully illustrate the emerging pattern of linkages between trust and the quality of communication. Based on expectations like those described above, to begin, Zand hypothecates that trusting behaviour leads to increases in the quality of communication. He explains (1972, pp. 251–252) that persons who trust one another will be:

Less fearful that any disclosures will be abused.

More receptive to the influence attempts of others.

More likely to accept interdependence with others.

Less likely to seek to impose controls on others.

More likely to provide accurate and timely information.

Less likely to misinterpret their behaviours and attitudes.

More likely to identify real problems and to solve them in mutually acceptable ways.

Zand's clever research design establishes the essential validity of these expectations.

A recent natural-state study by Roberts and O'Reilley (1974) adds substantial confidence that—despite the sparse research—the gestalt developed above also essentially applies outside of laboratory settings. Studying four organizations, these researchers sought linkages between the quality of upward communication and three classes of variables: trust by subordinate in superior; perceived influence of superior; and mobility aspirations of subordinates. Overall, the findings permit relatively unqualified summary. 'While the importance of trust as a facilitator of open information exchange was supported', Roberts and O'Reilley conclude (p. 205), 'this was less true of [the other two major classes of variables studied] influence of the superior and mobility aspirations.' More specifically, the prime interfaces between trust and the quality of communication may be summarized in this convenient way:

High trust between superior and subordinate	Low trust between superior and subordinate
(1) Subordinate estimates high degree of accuracy of information coming from superior	(1) Subordinate expresses doubts about the accuracy of information received from superior
(2) Subordinate estimates that superior has high degree of influence	(2) Subordinate discloses high tendency to withhold information
(3) Subordinate expresses high desire for interaction with superior	(3) Subordinate expresses lack of desire for interaction with superior
(4) Subordinate expresses high satisfaction with communication between self and superior	(4) Subordinate acknowledges major forces to distort upward communication

Roberts and O'Reilley provide data that confirm major anticipated effects of trust, while improving on much of the literature in one basic regard. That is, they develop a measure of trust, using factor analysis, and seek to account for variations in separate measurements. In contrast, as Giffin observes (1967a, p. 9), the conclusions of many classical trust studies 'must be viewed as inferential, since trust *per se* was never measured.' In one kind of common research, he explains, subjects 'were allowed to choose "risky" or "safe" alternatives' in a two-person non-zero sum game; the inference was made that trust was present when the risky alternative was chosen.

It is also necessary to highlight three major inconclusive features of the research of Roberts and O'Reilley. First, they sometimes only direct attention to critical points. Consider the evidence (e.g. Mellinger, 1956; Rekosh and Feigenbaum, 1966) that people of similar status or position tend to trust each other more. Roberts and O'Reilley implicitly deal with some negative consequences of the basic organizational strategy of differentiating superiors and subordinates, while demonstrating that trust can be a significant intervening variable between organization rank and communication outcomes. In doing so, however, Roberts and O'Reilley only help set some major research priorities, two of which are implied in these questions: Why are some superiors trusted more than others?; and What strategies or technologies can be used to increase trust, to counter the effects of differential status?

Second, as the researchers themselves note (p. 213), data about performance are not available for their study. Consequently, writing about the low trust condition, they can note (p. 213) only by inference that: 'Certainly in an ambience like this it is easy to envision groups operating with inadequate data flow and partial efficiency.' This inference is consistent with most available commentary (e.g. Gibb, 1964) and research (e.g. Friendlander, 1970; Mellinger, 1956), but that is not the same as being rooted in specific performance data.

Third, the findings of Roberts and O'Reilley are no doubt dependent upon the specific mix of persons in their sample. Other research (Deutsch, 1960; Solomon, 1961) suggests, that is to say, that had their population been heavily loaded with individuals with marked preferences for authoritarian relationships, Roberts and O'Reilley might have observed different patterns than those sketched above.

(5) *Trust ↔ cooperation interaction.* Clear linkages between trust and cooperation also have been widely anticipated in available conceptualizations, and these linkages often have been observed in nature. Thus Loomis' (1958, 1959) studies focus on the simplified causal chain below indicated by the solid lines. Loomis' research also provides general support for some important feedback loops, which are designated below by the broken lines.

A three-stage argument here will seek to show how commentary and research elaborate on this sketch of critical linkages. First, trust → cooperation is prominent in all relevant conceptualizations. Deutsch (1962), for example, argues that trust is *the* central prerequisite of cooperation. His rationale is straight-

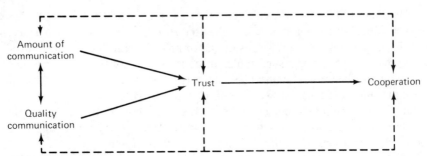

forward. Whenever individuals choose to cooperate, they essentially place their fate in the hands of others. This is a basic act of trust. Relatedly, Gibb proposes (1964, p. 287) that when a person experiences trusting and trustworthy behaviour, his concerns about controlling others become relatively minor, or may even disappear. Such a condition patently will facilitate cooperation, and may be an absolute prerequisite for it.

Numerous research efforts (Deutsch, 1960; Tedeschi, Hiester and Gahagan, 1969; Boyle and Bonacich, 1970) provide support for the trust → cooperation linkage, while they also extend it. Using brief experimental instructions to induce appropriate behaviours, to illustrate, Deutsch (1960, p. 138) expected that 'a cooperative orientation would lead to highly predictable trusting and trustworthy behavior, whereas a competitive orientation would lead to highly predictable suspicious and untrustworthy behavior over varied experimental conditions.' Deutsch concludes that for the 'most part' his experimental results are consistent with the theoretical expectations. Thus it appears that cooperative environments are trust-inducing, as well as that trust is a facilitator of cooperation, an effect also reported by Boyle and Bonacich (1970). Hence trust ↔ cooperation.

Second, many studies pinpoint the importance of trust in activities which require cooperation or are facilitated by it. The conceptual basis is transparent. Consider Fullmer, who concludes (1971, p. 32): 'Mutual trust and safety are antecedent to sharing anything, especially responsibility.'

Available research implies that trust ↔ cooperation linkages affect performance on certain kinds of tasks. To illustrate, Arnstein and Feigenbaum (1967) report that trust and cooperation are correlated 0·79, with some evidence that trust is an artifact of cooperation. Similarly, Kee (1970) observes that trust is critical in performing a task that requires bargaining. Based on past experience, to explain, Kee formed Trust and Suspicion groups. In the bargaining situation, major differences in performance emerged between the two kinds of groups. Thus a Trust group reached agreement in less time, and its members were active in exchanging information. Members of the Suspicion group refused to bargain, and their interaction was characterized by lies, threats and ultimata.

Third, the implications of such trust/cooperation linkages seem truly profound, over a broad range of contexts. Witness McGregor's extension of the research and its logic into managerial situations, especially those involving 'high technology', broad product lines and pervasive need to change. He notes (1967, p. 78) that increasingly the most appropriate managerial strategy is one in which management is able to help individuals achieve their goals by directing their efforts toward organizational goals. This contrasts sharply with an older, command/obey philosophy. As McGregor explains, this new kind of management necessitates the 'creation of a climate of genuine mutual trust, mutual support, respect for the individual and for the individual differences.' Moreover, McGregor notes (1967, p. 129), an environment of trust helps to induce commitment and to establish accepted standards.

A burgeoning research and descriptive literature testifies that McGregor's insight is acute, even if there seem many managerial situations in which more bureaucratic approaches are at least tolerable if not necessarily the most efficient or effective (Perrow, 1970, especially pp. 78–81). This literature will be briefly sampled here. Thus Harrison (1972, p. 11) reports that trust is necessary for effective problem solving in most or even all managerial situations, but especially in that growing proportion of cases in which it is necessary and/ or convenient to place reliance 'in the capacity of the individual to attain goals without specific programming regarding the precise steps to be taken.' More broadly still, Argyris (1970, pp. 47–48) argues that any managerial system behaves competently to the extent that it is able to solve problems and make decisions and then implement those decisions effectively. He proposes that norms of behaviour which emphasize trust (among other variables) 'will tend to increase the probability that the system will fulfill the competence criteria.' Argyris further emphasizes the fact that in order to provide minimal competence levels of a system, it is necessary to establish at least minimal conditions of trust. Finally, most observers see trust as intimately related to the degree of flexible change possible in organizations.

(6) *Trust effects on performance.* Conceptually, trust is often linked closely to performance, both by individuals and in groups. Gibb's (1964) formulation probably has the widest currency. His contingency hierarchy of developmental phases was introduced in section (3) above. Major gaps remain in the exploration of such trust/performance linkages, but enough work has accumulated to permit some confidence about four major features of the interaction.

First, individual performance seems related to trust. Consider the ability to learn, to illustrate. Rogers indicates that an increase in trust appears to be causally related to 'more rapid intellectual development, increased originality, increased emotional stability, increased self-control and decreased physiological arousal to defend against the threat' (Zand, 1972, p. 229). Some such catalogue of covariants also seems to underlie successful efforts in industry to facilitate learning at work (Fommersal and Myers, 1966). Relatedly, many observers (Rotter, 1967, p. 651) view trust as a major determinant of successful performance in a critical activity, psychotherapy. The rationale is direct, as Zand (1972) explains from the viewpoints of both therapist and participant in therapy. Thus trust in others at once facilitates the expression of vulnerability by seeking help; it can inhibit the abuse of that vulnerability by others; and it also implies lower expectations of such abuse. Moreover, self-trust increases one's willingness to control own behaviour, and heightens satisfaction and motivation.

Second, convincing if still sparse evidence implies major interactions between trust and problem solving. The linkages seem reasonable. As Zand (1972, p. 238) notes of low-trust groups, 'interpersonal relationships interfere with and distort perceptions of the problem. Energy and creativity are diverted from finding comprehensive realistic solutions, and members use the problem as an instrument to minimize their vulnerability.' Using an elegant design, Zand demonstrates experimentally that individuals exposed to instructions including high *vs* low trust levels generate significantly different patterns of behaviour. Illustratively, high-trust instructions are more likely to foster such features related to enhanced problem-solving:

More open exchanges of relevant ideas and feelings.
Greater clarification of goals and problems.
More extensive search for alternative courses of action.
Sharing influence more broadly among all participants.
Greater satisfaction among participants about their problem-solving efforts.
Greater motivation to implement decisions.
Greater feeling of interpersonal closeness, or team cohesiveness when groups are involved.

Notably, also, Zand's results are the same when data are gathered in two independent ways: via self-reports from participants; and via reports from observers who are not aware of the details of the experimental instructions.

Other studies in both natural-state and experimental contexts also support the conclusion that the performance of groups can be facilitated or inhibited by high *vs* low levels of trust. For example, Friedlander (1970) establishes that initial trust in natural-state groups is a key predictor of eventual accomplishment. Similarly, Kee (1970) finds that—at least for bargaining tasks—trust/suspicion are critical moderators or determinants of performance in experimental groups. His Trust groups reached agreement more quickly than Suspicion groups, which were more given to threats and lies than to the easy sharing of information. Evidence confirming such effects is common, as in the work of Rekosh and Feigenbaum (1966) or Pilisuk and Skolnick (1968).

Third, many open issues still exist about how and whether trust levels can be manipulated so as to influence performance in specified ways. Five emphases are required to barely sketch the character of the open-endedness appropriate about ways-and-means of affecting trust.

In experimental groups, experience seems to support a number of conclusions, albeit with variable force. To begin with the most certain conclusion, straightforward and broad instructions usually suffice to induce different degrees of trust or suspicion, with significant effects on group and individual performance. This implies that most individuals have latent trusting/suspicious responses in their repertoires which can be elicited without great difficulty, despite evidence that some variance in trusting behaviour is accounted for by broad orientations or predispositions that apply in most or all situations (e.g. Rotter, 1967). Down the certainty scale a notch or two, the experimental experience encourages agreement with Kee's (1970) conclusion that suspicion 'was more easily established than trust.' There patently is much fuel for speculation in this feature of experience. More troublesome is the strong probability that trust phenomena in experimental situations will be difficult to disentangle from other processes, a separation which can be significant for both theory and practice. For example, assume that a naive individual makes judgements on an experimental task very much like three other persons who are covert stooges of the experimenter. Alternatively, it is possible to explain the naive individual's behaviour in several different and partially exclusive ways:

As trusting in the senses defined above, with especial emphasis on the naive individual's specific intent to be trustworthy and thus to induce reciprocated trust.

As dependence on the stooges.

As the result of specific social influence, as in conformity pressures to behave like other group 'members'.

As the result of broad social influence dynamics, as in mimicking.

As a consequence of efforts to reduce dissonance between self and others, to increase general social comfort.

As a need for specific social approval, a condition of 'membership' in the experimental group.

As a consequence of broad social comparison processes, as in a lack of enthusiasm to be too different when it does not matter all that much.

As a result of the naive subject's ennui and lack of energy.

These alternatives are of patent significance when interpretations of research findings are attempted.

In experimental groups, many efforts have been made to test strategies or technologies for heightening trust, contributors/determinants that are both gross and fine. Some research on the amount and quality of communication has been reviewed above in sections (3)–(5). Other studies emphasize such specific features as the impact on trust of the degree of 'source credibility' (Giffin, 1967b), or of the discrepancy between the positions of communicator and communicatee, with relatively consistent findings that are not always easy to interpret. Thus Brehm and Lipsher (1959) report that communicators induce more trust when their opinional positions are supported by facts and arguments, and also that communicators induce less trust to the degree that their opinional positions are discrepant from those of communicatees. In addition, they report a kind of 'big lie' tendency. For very large discrepancies, communication *without content* produced perceptions of high perceived trust in communicators.

Still other studies focus on such broader strategies intended to increase trust as Osgood's proposal for international deescalation of tensions via small conciliatory moves preceded by honest prior announcements (Pilisuk and Skolnick, 1968). Derivative findings are difficult to interpret.

In temporary training groups, as in stranger T-groups, substantial increases in participant trust usually seem to occur, typically as a function of such variables as the length of interaction and confidence in trainers (Draeger, 1969). Most participants, that is, seem to be able to respond appropriately, at least during the period of training, to the values and norms that are variously programmed into the typical T-groups design (Golembiewski, 1972, especially pp. 59–110). Basically, the T-group technology rests on values and norms that emphasize such features as the following, which the typical piece of research ties generally to high levels of trust:

Extended and intensive interaction.
Helpfulness and cooperation.
'Levelling' or authentic communication in both self-disclosure and feedback.
An environment that is 'unstructured' and is intended to induce enough anxiety and risk to encourage disclosure and testing of the participating selves, but in a context which emphasizes the psychological safety of the participants.

In ongoing natural-state groups, the situation seems far more complicated. In a seminal study, Friedlander (1970) reports that a T-group experience was not successful in raising trust. He notes by way of explanation (p. 399), that the work units had been together for several years, during which period their various levels of trust or distrust had become so 'frozen' as to blunt the effects of laboratory training. 'Thus the level of trust within a group appears', he concludes, 'to be fairly enduring organismic state which does not change easily during short-term training.'

Other efforts have been more successful (Marrow, Bowers and Seashore, 1967; Seashore and Bowers, 1970; Golembiewski and Carrigan, 1973), in large part apparently due to their greater attention to on-the-job reinforcement of training and to tying the training into the command structure at work. Even there, as Friedlander implies, differences in the reactions of group members to training seem less favourable for established work units in stable or declining areas of the organization than they are for units that are relatively 'young' and in growth areas.

In start-up situations involving natural-state groups, the accumulating evidence strongly implies that it is possible to accelerate the development of trust and to facilitate performance. A review of numerous descriptions of team-building efforts supports this conclusion (Golembiewski, 1972, especially pp. 327–386), as does the scarce research literature (Golembiewski and Kiepper, n.d.).

Overall, then, the state of the science/art with regard to influencing levels of trust is both developing and undeveloped. On balance, applications are substantially ahead of the science: they often induce valued consequences as the result of processes which are still at a black-box state of understanding (Diamond, 1974, especially p. 142).

Fourth, evidence implies that some variation in trust is unmanipulable in that it derives from relatively stable properties of individuals. The classic demonstration is that of Deutsch (1960) with trust and the F-Scale (Adorno et al., 1950). Deutsch shows that those who tend to be 'more authoritarian, less intellectually sophisticated, less liberal in their political views, more cynical concerning human nature, and more prejudiced toward minority groups', tend at the same time to be more 'suspicious and untrustworthy' (p. 140). Deutsch's results are essentially corroborated by Solomon's (1961) simulation, which sought to determine relationships between different power and game strategies and the development of interpersonal trust. Of course, major methodological objections have been raised about the F-Scale instrument, as by Christie and Jahoda (1954).

Other research suggests similar linkages of trust with individual developmental experiences. Consider Rotter's (1967) Interpersonal Trust (IT) Scale, which purports to measure global predisposition to trust. Some research implies that individuals can be successfully characterized by differences in such predispositions. Schlenker, Helm and Tedeschi report (1973), for example, that individuals who score high on the IT Scale are more likely to believe the promises of an experimental stooge and to cooperate with the stooge than are low scorers. Similarly, other observers (Abramson, 1972; Wubberhorst, Gradford and Willis, 1971) relate differences in individual predispositions-to-trust to race, sex and socioeconomic variables.

Fifth, despite such findings of the explanatory value of genetic predispositions toward trust-suspicion, situational factors seem more powerful motivators of behaviour. Three kinds of evidence help establish the point. Paramountly, perhaps, trust experimentation would be impossible were most (many) subjects unable to respond to instructions intended to induce trust or mistrust.

More specifically, situational factors seem dominant when directly compared with broad predispositions toward trust/suspicion. Consider the study by Schlenker, Helm and Tedeschi (1973). They manipulated an important situational determinant of trust—the degree to which the promises of an experimental stooge are actually kept—and also determined their subjects' degree of generalized predisposition to trust, as measured by Rotter's IT Scale. The results are unequivocal. Differences in both IT Scores and in the probability of promise fulfilment are associated with differences in cooperation, in expected ways. The situational variable has much stronger effects on the cooperation of subjects than variations in the IT Scale, however. The dominance of situational factors also is demonstrated by a range of studies that observe the variably trusting behaviour of the same individual exposed to a range of situations, as in Henslin's (1968) study of cab-drivers and the factors influencing their trust in potential passengers.

Finally, substantial evidence implies that most individuals can respond appropriately to situations in which high-trust is valued/rewarded, as in sensitivity training groups. The anecdotal literature provides abundant evidence of the point (e.g. Todd, 1971); and available controlled research tends to support a similar conclusion, overall, in the eyes of such observers as Hampden-Turner (1966). Such a view is also consistent with the fade-out of the effects of a group learning experience, as when learners must return to an uncongenial macro-environment (Argyris, 1964, especially p. 71).

To be sure, this generalization must be qualified in several major senses. Each T-group experience will certainly not induce similarly high levels of trust between all or almost all participants. Such an effect does seem to occur more often than not, for most participants, even under very difficult circumstances (Bell, Cleveland, Hanson and O'Connell, 1969). But the effects may be very complex and variable (Gamez, 1970), or may not even occur at all. In addition, we assume that the typical T-group basically affects situational trust. The evidence is inferential, but is convincing to us. T-groups do not seem to trigger changes in basic personality orientations, based on a slim available literature (Kassarjian, 1965), as well as on the convincing proposition that temporary learning situations are not likely to induce lasting changes in attitudes/behaviours that have developed over many years.

(7) *Factors influencing levels of trust.* The full list of factors influencing trust would be a very formidable catalogue indeed, whose length and character can only be illustrated here. To sample from the broader literature, levels of trust have been shown to increase as:

The amount of communication increases.
The quality of communication emphasizes

a cooperative orientation,
timely and appropriate self-disclosure,
the sharing of feelings and values, as well as information,
acceptance of, but not necessarily agreement with, the content of communication.

Interacting parties clearly signal their intentions and expectations concerning their willingness to trust,

their approach to reacting to violations of their intentions/expectations.

Interacting parties have social power over each other, which apparently discourages violations of trust.

More specifically, research accords a substantial prominence to three classes of determinants. They are, following Giffin (1967a, p. 6): developmental or personality characteristics of the person doing the trusting; interpersonal expectations and perceptions of the parties to a trusting relationship; and situational conditions or features. Each of these three classes will be briefly illustrated in turn.

(a) *Developmental or personality characteristics.* Patently, it seems that trusting behaviour can be learned and enhanced. In one sense, then, some of the roots of trust can usefully be sought in the differing early developmental experiences of individuals. Hence also some researchers have felt justified in seeking linkages between orientations/affinities to trust and 'personality', that complex conceptualized product of developmental experiences.

Some observers see the roots of trust in the early development of the person. For example, Deutsch and Krauss (1965, p. 143) agree that even in the early stages of life, from 6 to 18 months of age, the child is beginning to have a 'developmental crisis of trust *vs* mistrust'. The outcome is a critical one: the infant establishes enduring, but not necessarily unmodifiable, dispositions to be 'more or less trusting or mistrusting of the outside world and of his own capacity' to cope with 'personal feelings and to elicit response from others'. Others basically agree (Gibb, 1964, pp. 300–301; Rotter, p. 658). In common, all such formulations imply that trusting behaviour is learned, and at least some of that learning will have deep genetic roots.

However, no set of linkages between trust and personality characteristics has been distinguished. Illustratively, Deutsch (1962, p. 303) observes that trusting behaviour can be induced by many different personal characteristics, given various circumstances and conditions. To illustrate, he notes several: 'despair, impulsivity, innocence, virtue, faith, masochism, or confidence'. If there are many different foundations upon which the feelings of trust are based, of course, this complicates research. But that finding has an intuitive attractiveness.

That different strokes for different folks seems to apply to trust relationships is usefully elaborated by considering self-disclosure, which implies communication of a particular quality. Briefly, self-disclosure involves an exposure by a person of his 'real self', warts and all, as it were. Self-disclosure involves many subtleties (Jourard, 1971; Golembiewski, 1972, especially pp. 221–227) but, in brief overview, it clearly relates to central human processes of growth and development. Figure 4 above, for example, sketches much of the sense of that centrality. Here, only two perspectives on the role of self-disclosure will be added. Broadly, as Egan (1970, p. 193) notes, 'a person who cannot love cannot reveal himself', and vice versa. An essential feature of the human condition, then, is that each individual 'make some efforts to reveal the person within' to others. Therein lies the very stuff of social life. Egan concludes: 'responsible self-disclosure is a kind of royal road to community. The sharing of the human condition—in its sublimity, banality, and deformity—pulls people together.' More narrowly, self-disclosure involves the key processes of confirmation/ disconfirmation, which are at the heart of individual development and growth. That is, there seem to be major reasons why a person should disclose, perhaps even must disclose. That is to say, following Culbert (1971, especially p. 75), the non-disclosing person faces added difficulties 'in obtaining information about the reality or objective aspects of relationships in which he participates.' Mowrer (1964) goes even further in arguing that the inability or failure to disclose induces a press against the consciousness, on which he bases a theory of pathology.

Figure 10 sketches some major probable linkages between self-disclosure and trust that have general support in the research literature (e.g., Swinth,

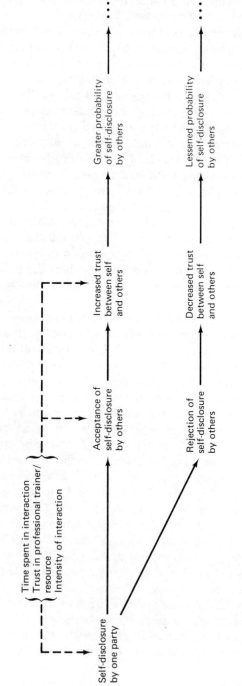

Figure 10. Some major interactions between self-disclosure and trust

1967; Johnson and Noonan, 1972). The basic relationships are indicated by the solid vectors. The broken vectors indicate conditions (e.g. Draeger, 1969; Walton 1969) that can reinforce that basic chain of covariation. Patently, such learning technologies as the T-group seek to provide experience with self-disclosure — acceptance — trust linkages. They also seek to generate the development of appropriate skills and attitudes to induce and heighten such linkages in the T-group, as well as in the broader world of relationships.

While such linkages seem appropriate enough in the general case, however, they hold only with major qualifications when individual predispositions to self-disclose are taken into account. Consider Benedict's (1971) comparison of low *vs* high self-disclosers. Low self-disclosers value people who are like themselves with regard to self-disclosure. They are described as strong, independent, well-adjusted, and socially skilful. When low self-disclosers are exposed to high self-disclosers, in contrast, they describe the latter as less well-adjusted, as socially inept and even as eccentric. That is to say, taking individual differences into account will require a more complex schema than Figure 10. Each person may have a preferred range of acceptable self-disclosure and/or others, for example. Within such a range, the schema in Figure 10 may apply. Given self-disclosure beyond that preferred range, however, the relationships in the figure may not hold. Experience in T-groups suggests that— under some conditions, at least—this range for most people is flexible and may be enlarged. But such a range does seem to exist.

(b) *Interpersonal expectations/perceptions.* Trust is powerfully influenced by perceptions of reality as well as by what exists. No doubt experience constitutes powerful feedback in the longer run (e.g. Kee, 1970), but trust seems basically more a matter of the perceived intentionality of the other to be trusting/trustworthy than it is of the intent of the other (Clifford, 1971). Trust is ineluctably 'subjective', then.

That trust is at the interface of internal and external realities has been variously demonstrated in the research literature. For example, the expectation/perception of trust tends to beget trust and the expectation/perception of mistrust begets mistrust. Deutsch (1960, p. 139; 1962) and others (e.g. Rotter, 1967) also find that experimental subjects who trust others expect to be trusted. Similarly, those who are suspicious and untrustworthy predominantly expect exploitative behaviour from others. In addition, individuals who are trusting typically are perceived as trustworthy and vice versa (Deutsch, 1960; Wrightsman, 1966; Tedeschi, Hiester and Gahagan, 1969).

The communication of intent seems central in these perceptions/expectations. As Kim Giffin observes (1967a, p. 8): 'There is experimental evidence to support the point that the trusted person's intentions are perceived as a separate variable.' The intent-to-trust attributed to a person seems a function of at least three kinds of communication involving: the promise of reciprocating trust; the conditions under which trust will be reciprocated; and the conditions under which efforts will be made to restore trust when it is violated. Further still, Boyle and Bonacich (1970) suggest that initial expectations about trust will change in the direction that experience indicates, and to a degree proportional to the difference between the actual experience and the initial expectations.

More or less, that is to say, people give what they expect to receive in the matter of trust; and they also tend to get what they give.

This is not to say that the skills/expectations of individuals are beyond influence or change; at least, they certainly do not defy description. Consider the way in which Gibb (1961, p. 144) elaborates on the centrality of intentions to both trust and trustworthiness. He argues that trust of persons by others tends to increase when their intentions are perceived to be:

Non-evaluative.
Problem-oriented rather than oriented toward control.
Spontaneous rather than planned or strategic.
Empathic or affect-filled rather than neutral.
Between persons of relatively equal status rather than unequals.
Provisional or tentative rather than certain.

Of course, these six features can be prescriptors as well as descriptors. That is, they help circumscribe the features of a trusting interchange. Moreover, they also specify features of interaction that an individual might seek to emphasize so as to help raise the trust-levels in various relationships.

The critical impact of perceptions on trust is also illustrated by some research at the University of Kansas concerning a listener's perceptions of a speaker. That research highlights the importance of such interpersonal variables as personal expertise, reliability, perceived intentions, personal dynamism and personal attractiveness. These five characteristics of a speaker are perceived directly by a listener, and 'each appears to influence interpersonal trust' (Giffin, 1967a, pp. 9–10).

(c) *Situational features*. Despite some research on general predispositions to trust/mistrust that have genetic roots, finally, evidence indicates that much trusting behaviour is situationally determined. In one explicit test of the relative potency of genetic *vs* situational factors (Schlenker, Helm and Tedeschi, 1973), for example, both sets of factors had an impact on the incidence of trusting behaviour. But a situational factor was substantially more powerful than a purported measure of a broad predisposition or orientation to trust/ mistrust. Many specific situational variables have been studied. Those factors which tend to increase trust include:

Little possibility of gain through trust violation (Giffin, 1967a, p. 6).
A unilateral promise by one of a set of interacting persons (Evans, 1964).
The power to influence other parties to a trusting relationship, which apparently reduces their incentive to engage in untrustworthy behaviour (Deutsch, 1958).
A display of 'justified self-interest' (Clifford, 1971).

A high credibility of intent, that is, when the intentionality attributed to the behaviour of another is the same as the other's stated intent (Clifford, 1971).

Similarly, research has also focused on a kind of reverse-list of contributors to mistrust or suspicion, as in the work of Komorita and Mechling (1967).

Perhaps the most powerful situational factors, however, inhere in the 'programme' or 'scenarios' of interaction that can be said to characterize any interactive or group situation. Given one such programme, trust is a likely consequence. Another programme can generate mistrust and suspicion.

Variations in these programmes or scenarios can be induced in a variety of ways, four of which will be illustrated here. First, many of the linkages of trust with other variables seem reflexive. As Giffin (1967a, p. 2) observes: 'the degree of trust one person has for another influences their communication behavior and interaction outcomes. The relationship between these variables is reflexive—as trust increases, certain interaction variables increase, and in turn, they tend to increase the degree of interpersonal trust, and so on.'

Such reflexivity implies great potential leverage for applied usage, as in variously stimulating the amount of interaction so as to increase trust. In a T-group, the reflexity is usually pronounced even though intervening variables will vary widely.

Second, even minimal instructions seem generally capable of inducing appropriate programmes or scenarios for interaction, especially in short-lived temporary groups. Thus Deutsch (1960) utilizes relatively straightforward sets of experimental instructions to involve his subjects in 'cooperative' and 'competitive' programmes or scenarios.

Individuals also seem to come variously programmed for feelings of trust and expectations of trustworthiness, a capability which is within broad limits subject to change throughout a person's lifetime. Indeed, Rogers writes (1962, p. 417) that people continually must earn trust, or the right to be trusted. The mechanism is direct yet profound: persons must be 'open' and be 'what they are', rather than hide behind a 'professional shield' or other defences. This seems another way of emphasizing the salience of risk-taking in building a trusting relationship. The 'open' person, that is, makes himself accessible to others, and therefore becomes potentially vulnerable to them. Hence, Argyris (1965, p. 16) views risk-taking as the 'major criterion of trust'.

Third, powerful determinants of trust inhere in group norms, which constitute ideal standards for conduct, beliefs and attitudes (Sherif, 1952). For example, variable such as cohesiveness (Schachter et al., 1968) or morale (Kahn and Katz, 1960) are not associated directly with such outcomes as high or low productivity. Rather, cohesiveness and morale act only through a group's norms concerning specific desirable levels of output, whether high or medium or low.

In a similar way, norms also can be significant reinforcers of trust, as well as determiners of it. Where group norms are favourable to trusting behaviour, patently, the levels of trust are likely to be high or individuals will feel a sense of failure or guilt. The avoidance of these feelings, of course, can motivate efforts to sustain trust at acceptable levels.

Experience indicates that quite specific sets of norms can with tolerable efficiency be induced in short periods of time. Such effects have been observed on 'cultural islands' of strangers responding to the apparent lack of structure in a T-group setting (Golembiewski and Blumberg, 1973), of course. Moreover, such norm-building is also possible, at least in substantial degree, among members of a formal work-unit who are quite mindful of their past and their future (Golembiewski and Carrigan, 1970 and 1970a). Moreover, the norms need not emphasize warmth and acceptance. If anything, indeed, it seems easier to induce hostility and rejection, even though they seem harder to manage in the sense of extracting useful learning. The classic demonstration is by Sherif (1952), and more contemporary versions include the 'power laboratories' pioneered by Oshry (1972).

Fourth, structure is another situational variable that often impacts on trust levels in organizations. McGregor comments (1967, p. 163) that the form of organization, 'particularly the stress on individual competition', affects the degree of trust. And easy extrapolations from the early work with 'group climates' (Lippitt and White, 1943) imply that the directive or autocratic supervisory style consistent with traditional notions for organizing work (Golembiewski, 1965, pp. 179–195) is more or less intendedly threatening and trust-inhibiting.

The message in such emphases has impacted on much organization practice. This is no place for a review of such efforts, but at least three classes of applications can be distinguished which seek to increase trust in organizations. They can be described briefly as:

Efforts to reduce mistrust by giving work-units major roles in influencing/controlling the worksite, as in group decision-making (Coch and French, 1953), following the rule-of-thumb that the best way of changing the behaviour of members of a group is to seek to change the norms of the group.

Efforts to increase trust by orienting the structure of organizations around work-flow or matrix models vs functional and process specilization (Golembiewski, 1965; Galbraith, 1973), which alternative structures encourage integration vs fragmentation, collaboration vs win–lose competition, etc.

Whether or not structural change is possible or convenient, efforts have been made to change norms and atmosphere so that open communication is valued, risk-taking is encouraged, and a problem-solving vs hierarchy-serving orientation is reinforced (Golembiewski and Carrigan, 1973).

Such efforts clearly presume that it is necessary or at least convenient to have high levels of trust at work, despite the lack of definitive research about 'bottom-line' effects. This essay begs off this question. In at least one common general case, however, it seems reasonable to expect a positive association between high trust levels and such factors as working relationships and effectiveness. This general case involves organizational change. It is a truism that all organizations must change sometime; and some organizations must change often and effectively, or die (Thompson, 1967). And here trust seems central. For example, Chris Argyris argues (1970, p. 70) that low levels of trust increase the probability of resistance to change. In fact, says Argyris, 'It is understandable that in a world relatively low in openness, trust, and risk-taking and high in conformity, mistrust, and crisis management, that participants will tend to be wary of change.' Hence one prime reason for high trust levels in organizations is the facilitation of change, which is an increasingly common challenge facing many organizations.

III. Conclusions

Despite the reliance here on laboratory research, with its consequent risk of overgeneralization, several conclusions seem safe enough.

(1) Trust seems a salient factor in influencing central dynamics in the full range of social systems: interpersonal, group and organization.

(2) This ubiquitous significance seems patent despite major conceptual and operational problems in available research. Hence there is perhaps no unqualified, relatively specific statement that may be made about trust relationships. But major central tendencies in the literature seem patent and significant nonetheless.

(3) A major part of the difficulty with trust concepts and operations is likely to be with us for a long time. Specifically, distinguishing trust from pseudo-trust, or distinguishing types of trust, will require two momumental developments. One such development is a model of the ontological programmes, or needs, or goals that specify the directionality of human development or maturation to which trust concepts/operations eventually must be tied. The second required development is a theory of learning or development, increasingly comprehensive approaches to which are necessary to permit efficient approaches to human needs or goals. Neither development seems immanent, but there is a healthy ferment in both areas, fortunately.

(4) Trust seems to act as one of the fundamental building blocks upon which the most basic human interaction is built. For example, all of these critical factors seem related to trust, or are relatable to it: the ability to learn, to communicate, to cooperate, to get along well with others, to establish friendships and to inspire the confidence of one's peers.

(5) It seems apparent that there is a general association between trusting behaviour and a substantial catalogue of significant variables, especially those related to communication and decision-making. These include: risk-taking, perceived trustworthiness, reliance on the words or actions of another, openness, owning of behaviour, expectations of what others will do, cooperation and so on.

(6) Trust appears to be part of a self-heightening cycle. That is to say, trusting behaviour begets trusting behaviour and mistrusting behaviour seems to foster more mistrusting behaviour. Similarly, a trusting person will often

be perceived as trustworthy, while a non-trusting person will not. This seems reminiscent of Lewin's notion that 'friendly fields are additive'. Perhaps unfriendly fields are subtractive, in addition.

(7) Trusting behaviour seems to generate a 'positive' valence which counters such 'negative' factors as anxiety, fear, suspicion and inaccurate perception.

(8) Trust may influence a range of organizationally relevant variables. These include: communication and feedback, managerial problem-solving, effective delegation, degree of social certainty, the relevance of information received, the acceptance of common goals and the sharing of responsibility. Appropriate research has only begun, however.

(9) Trusting behaviour is something which can be learned, lost and altered, although some individuals may have long-standing predispositions to trust or mistrust that are relatively fixed.

(10) It is possible to create a wide range of environments which foster experience with trusting relationships, and which also seem to permit the enhancement of attitudes and skills associated with trust, trusting and trustworthiness. For example, trust is more likely to grow in an atmosphere which is non-evaluative and problem-oriented rather than oriented toward social control, empathic rather than neutral and provisional rather than certain.

(11) Organization structure probably impacts on levels of trust, especially via the leadership styles consistent with specific structural alternatives.

Organizations with high levels of trust may increase efficiency because of the resultant increases in ability of people to work together, to communicate directly and accurately, etc. These effects are more likely in organizations with complex mixes of products and specialties, operating in turbulent environments.

(12) Trust seems central in change-processes in large organizations.

References

Aberach, J. D. and J. L. Walker (1970) 'Political trust and racial ideology.' *American Political Science Review*, **64**, 1199–1219.

Abramson, P. (1972) 'Political efficacy and political trust among black school-children: two explanations.' *J. Politics*, **34**, 1241-1269.

Adorno, T. W., E. Frenkel-Brunswik, D. J. Levinson and R. N. Sandford (1950) *The Authoritarian Personality*. New York: Harper and Bros.

Allen, B. P. (1973) 'Perceived trustworthiness of attitudinal and behavioral expression.' *J. Social Psychology*, **89**, 211–218.

Archer, D. (1974) 'Power in groups: self-concept changes of powerful and powerless group members.' *J. Applied Behavioral Science*, **10**, 208–220.

Argyris, C. (1964) 'T-groups for organizational effectiveness.' *Harvard Business Rev.*, **42**, 60–74.

Argyris, C. (1965) *Organization and Innovation*. Homewood, Ill.: Dorsey Press.

Argyris, C. (1968) 'Conditions for competence acquisition and therapy.' *J. Applied Behavioral Science*, **4**, 147–177.

Argyris, C. (1970) *Intervention Theory and Method: A Behavioral Science View*. Reading, Mass.: Addison-Wesley.

Arnstein, F. and K. D. Feigenbaum (1967) 'Relationship of three motives to choice in the prisoner's dilemma.' *Psychological Reports*, **20**, 751–755.

179

Back, K. W. (1972) 'The way of love and trust.' In K. W. Back, *Beyond Words*; *The Story of Sensitivity Training and the Encounter Movement*. New York: Russell Sage Foundation, 26–33.
Baldwin, A. L., J. Kalhorn and F. H. Breese (1945) 'Patterns of parent behavior.' *Psychological Monograph*, **58**, 268, 1–75.
Bell, R. L., S. E. Cleveland, P. G. Hanson and W. E. O'Connell (1969), 'Small group dialogue and discussion: an approach to police–community relationships.' *J. Criminal Law, Criminology and Police Science*, **60**, 242–246.
Benedict, B. A. (1971) 'The effects of self-disclosure on the development of trust.' *Dissertation Abstracts*, **(31-B)**, 5601.
Berzins, J. I., W. F. Ross and D. I. Cohen (1970) 'Relation of the A–B distinction and trust–distrust sets to addict patients' self-disclosures in brief interviews.' *J. Consulting and Clinical Psychology*, **34**, 289–296.
Boyl, R. and P. Bonacich (1970) 'The development of trust and mistrust in mixed-motive games.' *Sociometry*, **33**, 123–139.
Brehm, J. and D. Lipsher (1959) 'Communicator–communicatee discrepancy and perceived communicator trustworthiness.' *J. Personality*, **27**, 352–361.
Christie, R. and M. Jahoda (1954) *Studies in the Scope and Method of "The Authoritarian Personality"*. Glencoe, Ill.: Free Press.
Clifford, C. (1971) 'Cooperation, trust, and. perceived intentions in a 2 person game.' *Dissertation Abstracts International*, **32**, **(5-A)**, 2797–2798.
Coch, L. and J. R. P. French Jr. (1953) 'Overcoming resistance to change.' In D. Cartwright and A. Zander (Eds.), *Group Dynamics*. New York: Harper and Row, 257–279.
Crockett, B., B. Gaertner and M. Dufur (1972) 'OD in large systems.' A paper presented at the NTL Conference on New Technology in Organization Development, Washington, D. C.
Culbert, S. A. (1971) 'The interpersonal process of self-disclosure: it takes two to see one.' In R. T. Golembiewski and A. Blumerg (Eds.), *Sensitivity Training and the Laboratory Approach*. Itasca, Ill.: F. E. Peacock, 73–79.
Deutsch, M. (1954) 'Trust and cooperation—some theoretical notes.' New York: Research Center for Human Relations, New York University.
Deutsch, M. (1958) 'Trust and suspicion.' *J. Confl. Resolution*, **2**, 265–279.
Deutsch, M. (1960) 'The effect of motivational orientation upon trust and suspicion.' *Human Relations*, **13**, 123–139.
Deutsch, M. (1962) 'Cooperation and trust: some theoretical notes.' In M. R. Jones, *Nebraska Symposium on Motivation 1962*. Lincoln, Nebraska: University of Nebraska Press.
Deutsch, M. (1973) *The Resolution of Conflict*. New Haven, Conn.: Yale University Press.
Deutsch, M. and R. Krauss (1965) *Theories in Social Psychology*. New York: Basic Books.
Diamond, M. J. (1974) 'From Skinner to Sartori?: toward a social learning analysis of encounter group behavior change.' *J. Applied Behavioral Science*, **10**, 133–148.
Draeger, C. (1969) 'Level of trust in intensive small groups.' *Dissertation Abstracts*, **29**, **(10-A)**, 3457.
Egan, G. (1970) *Encounter*. Belmont, Cal.: Wadsworth Publishing.
Eisman, B. (1959) 'Some operational measures of cohesiveness and their interrelations'. *Human Relations*, **12**, 183–189.
Ellis, A. (1969) 'A weekend of rational encounter.' In A. Burton (Ed.), *Encounter*. San Francisco: Jossey-Bass, 112–116.
Evans, G. (1964) 'Effect of unilateral promise and values of rewards upon cooperation and trust.' *J. Abn. Soc. Psych.*, **69**, 587–590.
Farr, J. N. (1957) 'The effects of a disliked third person upon the development of mutual trust'. Paper read at the American Psychological Associaion, New York.
Fiedler, F. E. (1945) 'Quantitative studies on the role of therapists' feelings toward their patients.' In O. H. Mowrer (Ed.), *Psychotherapy: Theory and Research*. New York: Ronald Press, 296–315.

Fitzgerald, B. J., R. A. Pasework and S. J. Noah (1970) 'Validity of Rotter's interpersonal trust scale: a study of belinquent adolescents.' *Psychological Reports*, **26**, 163–166.

Friedlander, F. (1970) 'The primacy of trust as a facilitator of further group accomplishment.' *J. Applied Behavioral Science*, **6**, 387–400.

Fullmer, D. W. (1971) *Counseling: Group Theory and System*. Toronto: Canada International Textbook Company.

Galbraith, J. (1973) *Designing Complex Organizations*. Reading Mass.: Addison-Wesley.

Gamez, G. L. (1970) 'T-groups as a tool for developing trust and cooperation between Mexican-American and Anglo-American college students.' *Dissertation Abstracts*, **31**, (4-B), 2305.

Ganter, G., M. Yeakel and N. Polansky (1967) *Retrieval From Limbo: The Intermediary Group Treatment of Inaccessible Children*. New York: The Child Welfare League of America, Inc.

Garfinkel, H. A. (1963) 'A conception of and experiments with "trust" as a condition of stable concerted action.' In O. J. Harvey (Ed.), *Motivation and Social Interaction: Cognitive Determinants*. New York: Ronald Press, 187–223.

Geller, J. D. (1966) 'Some personal and situational determinants of interpersonal trust.' Unpublished doctoral dissertation, University of Connecticut.

Gibb, J. R. (1961) 'Defensive communication.' *J. Communication*, **11**, 141–148.

Gibb, J. R. (1964) 'Climate for trust formation.' In L. P. Bradford, J. R. Gibb and K. D. Benne (Eds.), *T-Group Theory and Laboratory Method: Innovation in re-education*. New York: Wiley, 279–309.

Gibb, J. R. (1972) 'Trust and role freedom: a TORI innovation in educational community.' *J. Research and Development in Education*, **5(2)**, 76–85.

Gibb, J. R. (n.d.) 'A framework for examining change.' *Research Reprint Series*, No. 6, National Training Laboratories, Washington, D. C.

Gibb, J. R. and L. M. Gibb (1968) 'Emergence therapy: the TORI processes in an emergent group.' In G. M. Gazda (Ed.), *Innovations to Group Psychotherapy*. Springfield, Illinois: Charles C. Thomas, 96–129.

Gibb, J. R. and L. M. Gibb (1969) 'Role freedom in a TORI group.' In A. Burton (Ed.), *Encounter: The Theory and Practice of Encounter Groups*. San Francisco, Calif.: Jossey-Bass, 42–57.

Giffin, K. (1967) 'The contribution of studies of source credibility to a theory of interpersonal trust in the communication process.' *Psychological Bulletin*, **68**, 104–120.

Giffin, K. (1967a) 'Recent research on interpersonal trust.' A paper presented to the Annual Convention of the Speech Association of America, Los Angeles. Published by the Communication Research Center, Lawrence, Kansas, University of Kansas.

Giffin, K. (1967b) 'Interpersonal trust in small group communication.' *Quarterly J. Speech*, **53**, 224–234.

Giffin, K. (1968) 'The trust differential.' Lawrence, Kansas: The Communications Research Center, University of Kansas Press.

Giffin, K. (1968a) 'An experimental evaluation of the trust differential.' Lawrence. Kansas: The Communications Research Center, University of Kansas.

Giffin, K. (1969) 'Personal trust and the interpersonal problems of the aged person.' *Gerontologist*, **9**, 286–292.

Giffin, K. and N. White (1967) 'An exploratory study of selected semantic differential scales for measuring interpersonal trust.' Lawrence, Kansas: The Communication Research Center, University of Kansas.

Gilbert, J. (1967) 'Interpersonal trust: implications for psychotherapeutic technique.' Unpublished master's thesis, University of Connecticut.

Glenn, A. D. (1970) 'Elementary school . . . trust, political efficacy and change.' *Dissertation Abstracts*, A-6401.

Golembiewski, R. T. (1962) *The Small Group*. Chicago: University of Chicago Press.

Golembiewski, R. T. (1965) *Men, Management and Morality*. New York: McGraw-Hill.

Golembiewski, R. T. (1972) *Renewing Organizations: The Laboratory Approach to Planned Change.* Itasca, Ill.: F. E. Peacock.

Golembiewski, R. T. and A. Blumberg (Eds.), (1973) *Sensitivity Training and the Laboratory Approach.* Itasca, Ill.: F. E. Peacock.

Golembiewski, R. T. and S. B. Carrigan (1970) 'Planned change in organization style based on laboratory approach.' *Administrative Science Quarterly*, 15, 79–93.

Golembiewski, R. T. and S. B. Carrigan (1970a) 'The persistence of laboratory-induced changes in organization styles.' *Administrative Science Quarterly*, 15, 330–340.

Golembiewski, R. T. and S. B. Carrigan (1973) 'Planned change through laboratory methods.' *Training and Development J.*, 27, 18–27.

Golembiewski, R. T. and A. Kiepper (n.d.) 'MARTA: toward an effective, open giant.' MS.

Gommersal, E. R. and M. S. Myers (1966) 'Breakthrough in on-the-job training.' *Harvard Business Rev.*, 44, 62–72.

Hampden-Turner, C. M. (1966) 'An existential "learning theory" and the integration of T-group research.' *J. Applied Behavioral Science*, 2, 367–386.

Hardman, D. G. (1965) 'The matter of trust.' *Crime and Delinquency*, 15, 227–237.

Harford, T. (1965) 'Game strategies and interpersonal trust in schizophrenics and normals.' Unpublished doctoral dissertation, Boston University.

Harford, T. and L. Solomon (1969) 'Effects of a "reformed sinner" and "lapsed saint" strategy upon trust formation in paranoid and non-paranoid schizophrenic patients.' *J. of Abr Psych.*, 74, 498–504.

Harnett, D. L. (1971) 'Risk, fate, conciliation and trust: an international study of attitudinal differences among executives.' *Academy of Management J.*, 14, 285–304.

Harrison, R. (1972) 'Developing autonomy, initiative and risk-taking through a laboratory design.' Paper presented at the NTL New Technology in Organization Development, Washington, D. C.

Hartmann, N. (1932) *Ethics.* New York: Macmillan.

Heine, C., B. Lubin, J. Perlmutter and A. Lubin (1974) 'Negotiating for group and trainers.' *Social Changes*, 4, 3–6.

Henslin, J. M. (1968) 'Trust and the cab-driver.' In M. Truzzi (Ed.), *Sociology and Everyday Life.* Englewood Cliffs, N. J.: Prentice Hall, 138–158.

Hochreich, D. J. (1966) 'A children's scale for measuring interpersonal trust.' Unpublished masters thesis, University of Connecticut.

Hochreich, D. J. (1973) 'A children's scale to measure interpersonal trust.' *Developmental Psychology*, 9, 141.

Hughes, E. C. and M. Helen (1952) *Where People Meet.* New York: The Free Press.

Ilfeld, F. W. and E. Lindeman (1971) 'Professional and community pathways toward trust.' *Amer. J. Psychiatry*, 128, 583–589.

Into, E. C. (1969) 'Some possible childrearing antecedents of interpersonal trust.' Unpublished Master's Thesis, University of Connecticut.

Issacs, K. S., J. M. Alexander and E. A. Haggard (1963) 'Faith, trust, and gullibility.' *International J. Psycho-Analysis*, 64, 461–469.

Jackson, J. (1960) 'The organization and its communication problems.' In A. Greshaw and J. Hennessey (Eds.), *Organization Behavior: Cases and Readings.* New York: McGraw-Hill.

Jennings, K., C. Cummings and F. P. Kilpatrick (1966) 'Trusted leaders: perceptions of appointed federal officials' *Public Opinion Quarterly*, 30, 368–384.

Jensen, A. R. (1973) *Educability and Group Differences.* New York: Harper and Row.

Johnson, D. W. and P. M. Noonan (1972) 'Effects of acceptance and reciprocation of self-disclosures on the development of trust.' *J. Counseling Psychology*, 19, 411–416.

Johnson, R. J. (1971) 'An exploration of relationships between and among empathy, trust and ego state development in the adult learner.' *Dissertation Abstracts*, A-5748.

Jourard, S. (1971) *Self-Disclosure.* New York: Wiley–Interscience.

Kahn, R. and D. Katz (1960) In D. Cartwright and A. Zander (Eds.), *Group Dynamics Research and Theory*. Evanston, Ill.: Row, Peterson, 554–570.

Kassarjian, H. H. (1965) 'Social character and sensitivity training.' *J. Applied Behavioral Science*, 1, 433–40.

Katz, H. A. and J. B. Rotter (1969) 'Interpersonal trust scores of college students and their parents.' *Child Development*, 40, 657–661.

Kee, H. (1970) 'The development, and the effects upon bargaining, of trust and suspicion.' *Dissertation Abstracts*, 30, (9-A), 4017–4018.

Kee, H. and R. T. Knox (1970) 'Conceptual and methodological considerations in the study of trust and suspicion.' *J. Confl. Res.*, 14, 357–365.

Kegan, D. L. (1971) 'Trust, openness, and organization development: short-term relationship in research and development labs and a design for examining long term effects.' *Dissertation Abstracts*, A-32, 3423–3424.

Kegan, D. L. and A. Rubenstein (1972) 'Measures of trust and openness.' *Comparative Studies*, 3, 179–201.

Kegan, D. L. and A. Rubenstein (1973) 'Trust, effectiveness, and organizational development: a field study in R & D.' *J. Applied Behavioral Science*, 9, 498.

Kelley, H. and K. Ring (1961) 'Some effects of "suspicious" versus "trusting" training schedules.' *J. Abn. Soc. and Psych.*, 63, 294–301.

Kenny, J. W. (1969) 'Performance in the prisoner's dilemma game as a measure of trust in schizophrenics and normals.' *Dissertation Abstracts International*, 30, 382–383.

Knowles, M. (1973) *The Adult Learner*. Houston, Tex.: Gulf Publishing.

Koestler, A. (1967) *The Ghost in the Machine*. New York: Macmillan.

Komorita, S. S. and J. Mechling (1967) 'Betrayal and reconciliation in a two-person game.' *J. Personality and Social Psychology*, 6, 349–353.

Kruglanski, A. W. (1970) 'Attributing trustworthiness in supervisor–worker relations.' *J. Experimental Social Psychology*, 6, 214–232.

Lawton, M. J. (1963) 'Trust as manifested by delay of gratification in a choice situation.' Unpublished Doctoral Dissertation, Northwestern University.

Lewin, K. (1958) 'Group decision and social change.' In E. Maccoby, T. M. Newcomb, E. L. Hartley (Eds.), *Reading in Social Psychology*. New York: Henry Holt and Company, 197–211.

Lichtenberg, P. and D. G. Norton, (1970) 'Honesty, trust, equality in the treatment of schizophrenia: an analysis of *I Never Promised You a Rose Garden*.' *Pennsylvania Psychiatric Quaterly*, 10, 33–40.

Lieberman, B. (1964) 'I-trust: a notion of trust in three person games and international affairs.' *J. Confl. Resolution*, 8, 271–280.

Lieberman, M. A., I. D. Yalom and M. B. Miles (1973) *Encounter Groups: First Facts*. New York: Basic Books.

Likert, R. (1967) *The Human Organization*. New York: McGraw-Hill.

Lillibridge, J. R. (1967) 'A test of a theory of interpersonal risk behavior.' *Dissertation Abstracts*, A28, 785.

Lillibridge, J. R. and S. Lundstedt (1967) 'Some initial evidence for an interpersonal risk theory.' *J. Psychology*, 66, 119–128.

Lippitt, R. and R. K. White (1943) 'The "social climate" of children's groups.' In R. G. Barker, J. S. Kounin and H. W. Wright (Eds.), *Child Behavior and Development*. New York: McGraw-Hill, 485–508.

Loomis, J. L. (1958), 'Communication and development of trust.' Unpublished Doctoral Dissertation, New York University.

Loomis, J. L. (1959) 'Communication, the development of trust and cooperative behavior.' *Human Relations*, 12, 305–315.

Lundstedt, S. (1966) 'Interpersonal risk theory.' *J. Psychology*, 62, 3–10.

McConkie, M. (1973) 'A view of trust and its relationship to selected organizational variables.' Mimeod paper, Athens, Ga.: University of Georgia.

Macdonald, A. P., V. S. Kessle, and J. B. Fullmer (1970) 'Self-disclosure and two kinds of trust.' Unpublished MS, Rehabilitation and Research Training Center, West Virginia University.

Mcgregor, D. (1967) *The Professional Manager*. New York: McGraw-Hill.

March, J. G. (1956) 'Influence measurement in experimental and semi-experimental groups.' *Sociometry*, **19**, 260–271.

Marrow, A. D., D. G. Bowers and S. E. Seashore (Eds.) (1967) *Management by Participation*. New York: Harper and Row.

Mellinger, G. D. (1956) 'Interpersonal trust as a factor in communication.' *J. Abn. and Soc. Psych.*, **52**, 304–309.

Michener, H. A. and R. A. Zeller (1972) 'A test of Gamson's theory of political trust orientation.' *J. Applied Social Psychology*, **2**, 138–156.

Miles, M. B. (1965) 'Changes during and following laboratory training.' *J. Applied Behavioral Science*, **1**, 215–243.

Mill, C. and M. Ritvo (1969) 'Potentialities and pitfalls of non-verbal techniques.' *Human Relations Training News*, **13**, 1–3.

Mowrer, O. H. (1964) *The New Group Therapy*. Princeton, N. J.: D. Van Nostrand.

Newcomb, T. M., R. Turner and P. Converse (1965) *Social Psychology: The Study of Human Interaction*. Chicago: Holt, Rhinehart, Winston.

Nigro, F. A. (1969) *Management–Employee Relations in the Public Service*. Chicago, Ill.: Public Personnel Association.

Noel, R. C. (1963) 'Evolution of the inter-nation simulation.' In H. Guetzkow (Ed.), *Simulation in Social Science*. Englewood Cliffs, N. J.: Prentice-Hall, 69–102.

O'Donovan, D. (1964) 'Detachment and trust in psychotherapy.' *Psychotherapy: Theory, Research and Practice*, **2**, 174–176.

Oshry, B. (1972) 'Power and the power lab.' In W. W. Burke (Ed.), *Contemporary Organization Development*. Washington, D. C.: NTL Institute for Applied Behavioral Science, 242–254.

Perrow, C. (1970) *Organizational Analysis*. Belmont, Calif.: Wadsworth.

Pilisuk, M. and P. Skolnick (1968) 'Inducing trust: a test of the Osgood proposal.' *J. Personality and Social Psychology*, **8**, 121–133.

Rapoport, A. (1963) 'Formal games as probing tools for investigating behavior motivated by trust and suspicion.' *J. Confl. Res.*, **17**, 570–579.

Rekosh, J. H. and K. Feigenbaum (1966) 'The necessity of mutual trust for cooperative behavior in a two person game.' *J. Social Psychology*, **69**, 149–154.

Riegel, K. F. (Ed.) (1973) *Intelligence: Alternative views of a paradigm*. Basel, Switz.: S. Karger.

Roberts, K. H. and C. O'Reilley III. (1974) 'Failure in upward communication in organizations: three possible culprits.' *Academy of Management J.*, **17**, 205–215.

Roberts, M. (1967) 'The persistence of interpersonal trust.' Unpublished M. A. Thesis, University of Connecticut.

Rogers, C. R. (1961) *On Becoming A Person*. Boston: Houghton Mifflin.

Rogers, C. R. (1962) 'The interpersonal relationship: the core of guidance.' *Harvard Educational Rev.*, **32**, 416–429.

Rotter, J. B. (1955) 'The role of the psychological situation in determining the direction of human behavior.' In M. R. Jones (Ed.), *Nebraska Symposium of Motivation*. Lincoln, Neb.: University of Nebraska Press.

Rotter, J. B. (1967) 'A new scale for the measurement of interpersonal trust.' *J. of Personality*, **35**, 651–665.

Rotter, J. B. (1971) 'Generalized expectancies for interpersonal trust.' *Amercian Psychologist*, **26**, 443–452.

Rotter, J. B., J. H. Hamsher and J. D. Geller (1968) 'Interpersonal trust, internal-external control, and the Warren Commission Report.' *J. Personality and Social Psychology*, **9**, 210–215.

Rotter, J. B. and D. J. Hochreich (1970) 'Have college students become less trusting?' *J. Personality and Social Psychology*, **15**, 211–214.

Rotter, J. B. and D. K. Stein (1971) 'Public attitudes toward the trustworthiness, competence and altruism of twenty selected occupations.' *J. Applied Social Psychology*, **1**, 334–343.

Sandler, D. (1965) 'Investigation of a scale of therapeutic effectiveness: trust and suspicion in an experimentally induced situation.' Unpublished Doctoral Dissertation, Duke University, Ann Arbor, Michigan, University Microfilms, No. 66-1382.

Schachter, S., N. Ellerson, D. McBride, and D. Gregory (1968) 'An experimental study of cohesiveness and productivity.' In A. Zander and D. Cartwright, *Group Dynamics, Research and Theory*, 3rd ed. New York: Harper and Row.

Schlenker, B., B. Helm and J. Tedeschi (1973) 'The effects of personality and situational variables on behavioral trust.' *J. Personality and Social Psychology*, **25**, 419–427.

Schmuck, R. (1972) 'Developing collaborative decision-making: the importance of trusting, strong and skillful leaders.' *Educational Technology*, **12**, 43–47.

Seashore, S. E. and D. G. Bowers (1970) 'Durability of organizational change.' *Amercian Psychologist*, **25**, 227–233.

Seeman, M. J. (1954) 'Counselor judgments of therapeutic process and outcome.' In C. R. Rogers and R. F. Dymond (Eds.), *Psychotherapy and Personality Change*. Chicago: University of Chicago Press, 99–108.

Seeman, M. (1971) 'The urban alienations: some dubious theses from Marx to Marcuse.' *J. Personality and Social Psychology*, **19**, 135–143.

Sherif, M. (1952) 'Group influences upon the formation of norms and attitudes.' In T. M. Newcomb, E. Hartley and G. E. Swanson, *Readings in Social Psychology*. New York: Henry Holt, 229–262.

Sherif, M. and C. Sherif (1953) *Groups in Harmony and Tension*. New York: Harper.

Shockley, W. (1971) 'Negro IQ deficit.' *Rev. Ed. Res.*, **41**, 227–248.

Solomon, L. (1961) 'The influence of some types of power relationships and game strategies upon the development of interpersonal trust.' *J. Abn. Soc. Psych.*, **61**, 223–230.

Strickland, L. H. (1958) 'Surveillance and trust.' *J. Personality*, **26**, 200–215.

Strong, S. R. and L. D. Schmidt (1970) 'Trustworthiness and influence in counseling.' *J. Counseling Psychology*, **17**, 197–204.

Swinth, R. L. (1967) 'The establishment of the trust relationship.' *J. of Confl. Res.*, **11**, 335–344.

Tedeschi, J., D. Hiester and J. P. Gahagan (1969) 'Trust and PD game.' *J. Social Psychology*, **79**, 43–50.

TeVault, R., B. Forbes and H. F. Gromoll (1971) 'Trustfulness and suspiciousness as a function of liberal or conservative church membership: a field experiment.' *J. of Psychology*, **79**, 163–164.

Thompson, J. H. (1967) *Organizations in Action*. New York: McGraw-Hill.

Todd, R. (1971) 'Notes on corporate man.' *Atlantic*, **228**, 86 ff.

Wallace, D. (1967) 'Group loyalty, communication and trust in a mixed motive game.' *Dissertation Abstracts International*, **27 (12-B)**, 4569.

Wallace, D. and P. Rothaus (1969) 'Communication, group loyalty, and trust in the P. D. game.' *J. Confl. Res.*, **13**, 370–380.

Walton, R. (1969) *Interpersonal Peacemaking*. Reading, Mass.: Addison-Wesley.

Weinstein, M. S. (1972) 'The role of trust in program evaluation: some guidelines for the perplexed administrator.' *Canadian Psychologist*, **13**, 239–251.

Whyte, W. F. (1961) *Men at Work*. Homewood, Ill.: Irwin-Dorsey.

Willis, F. N. (1968) 'Trust and personal characteristics.' Paper presented at the Annual Meeting of the Missouri Academy of Science, Kansas City, Missouri.

Winn, A. (1969) 'The laboratory approach to organization development: a tentative model of planned change.' *J. Management Studies*, **6**, 155–166.

Wrightsman, L. S. (1966) 'Personality and attitudinal correlates of trusting and trustworthy behaviors in a two-person game.' *J. Personality and Social Psychology*, **4**, 328–332.

Wrightsman, L. S. and N. J. Baker (1964) 'Where have all the idealistic, imperturable freshmen gone?.' *Proceedings of the 77th Annual Convention of the American Psychology Association*, **4**, 299–300.

Wrightsman, L. S., Jr., J. O'Conner and N. J. Baker (Eds.) (1972), *Cooperation and Competition*, Belmont, Calif.: Brooks/Cole.

Wubberhorst, J., S. Gradford and F. N. Willis (1971) 'Trust in children as a function of race, sex, and socio-economic group.' *Psychological Reports*, **29**, 1183–1187.

Zand, D. E. (1972) 'Trust and managerial problem solving.' *Administrative Science Quarterly*, **17**, 229–239.

Chapter **8**

Interpersonal Affection and Change in Sensitivity Training: A Composition Model*

W. Brendan Reddy

University of Cincinnati

Despite the early claims of some practitioners that a messianic movement was at hand and despite the calls of critics that sensitivity training and encounter groups would destroy the integrity of man, there are now considerable data (Gibb, 1971) that some participants learn from their experiences in groups. However, outcome studies in any area have rarely proved very useful in that they do not specify who learns under what conditions.

And so it is with sensitivity training. We are beyond the early claims of both 'cure-all' and 'condemnation', and technically we have advanced beyond the grossly measured outcome studies. While critics continue to bemoan the lack of research and theory, one wonders if they have read Bradford, Gibb and Benne (1964), Schein and Bennis (1965), Cooper and Mangham (1971), Lieberman, Yalom and Miles (1973) and a plethora of journal articles which are not all 'badly designed' and 'weak methodologically'.

The major research emphases in sensitivity training currently are intragroup dynamics and trainer/member relations, although the specific focus of this research varies widely. For example, Lieberman, Yalom and Miles (1973), Bolman (1971) and Lundgren (1974a, 1974b, 1971) are especially interested in the role of the trainer; Jacobs, Jacobs, Gatz and Schaible (1973) and Jacobs, Jacobs, Feldman and Cavior (1973) explored the effects of feedback. Cooper and Bowles (1973) studied self-disclosure and physical encounter; Gibbard and Hartman (1973) the relationship patterns in leaderless groups; Peters (1973), identification and modelling; and D'Augelli (1973), Harrison (1965), Cooper (1969), Smith (1974) and Reddy (1972) the impact of group composition.

All of these dimensions have been found to contribute to positive and negative change in sensitivity training. The present chapter focuses on one of these dimensions, namely, the impact of group composition on the learning and behaviour of participants in sensitivity training groups. The chapter has two

*The author is grateful to Drs Leonard M. Lansky and Leonard Oseas for their reading of the manuscript and for their helpful comments, and to Ms Carol Strohmaier for her typing and editorial assistance.

major sections: I. Definition and an examination of research; II. A specific model for group composition in sensitivity training.

Group composition and its variation will be defined first. Then, the influence of composition will be examined by a review of the research findings in the field. Finally, a preliminary theoretical model will be presented which accounts for the effects of a specific type of composition, interpersonal affection compatibility.

What is group composition? Simply, group composition denotes the individuals who make up a group, each with his own unique characteristics, needs, behaviours and personality traits. Connotatively, group composition implies the interactive effect of the group participants upon their relationships, productivity, task completion or learning.

Does it make any difference what combination of people are placed in a group? The answer is an emphatic, yes. For many years researchers have been inquiring into the effects of composition on different kinds of groups. In a recent text, Shaw (1971) reviews the findings to that date. Bednar and Lawlis (1971) and Yalom (1970) have looked at the influence of composition in group psychotherapy and Cooper and Mangham (1971) and Gibb (1971) in sensitivity training. The evidence is clear: if composition is manipulated, outcome is altered.

Before the literature is examined, a distinction must be made. Composition research usually focuses on homogeneous/heterogeneous variables or compatible/incompatible needs. This distinction is an important one. Homogeneity *vs* heterogeneity implies dissimilarity of traits or variables, while compatible *vs* incompatible implies non-complementary needs. Thus, while individuals may be homogeneous on a number of personality traits or variables, they may be quite incompatible in terms of their interpersonal needs. For example, ten group participants may be similar on a measure of self-confidence. However, five members may have a need for close interpersonal relations, and five may have a need to maintain interpersonal distance. The ten members are homogeneous with regard to self-confidence. However, in terms of interpersonal needs one subgroup of five members are compatible with each other (close interpersonal relations), and the second subgroup of five members are also compatible with each other (distant interpersonal relations). The two subgroups are incompatible with each other on the dimension of preferred interpersonal relations.

The concept of homogeneity/heterogeneity is more easily understood than the concept of compatibility/incompatibility. Schutz (1958), more than any other theorist, has refined the definition and measurement of compatibility.

Schutz postulates three interpersonal needs, inclusion, control and affection, to constitute a sufficient set of areas of behaviour for the prediction and explanation of interpersonal phenomena. That is, the interaction of two or more people is accounted for by the fit between what they express in these three areas and what they want others to express towards them. Schutz maintained that 'interchange compatibility' in these areas leads to mutual satisfaction of interpersonal needs. He presents evidence of greater goal achievement in more *vs* less compatible groups. Schutz has developed a test, Fundamental Interpersonal Relationship Orientation-Behavior (FIRO-B), which has enjoyed great currency in the field. It measures an individual's expressed and wanted behaviour in the three interpersonal areas of inclusion, control and affection.

Schutz (1958) defined compatibility as 'a property of a relation between two or more persons, between an individual and a task, that leads to mutual satisfaction of interpersonal needs and harmonious coexistence' (p. 105). Schutz further proposed the concept of 'interchange compatibility' which refers to the mutual exchange of the 'commodity' in a given need area. In the area of affection, low interchange indicates a preference for keeping affectional distance, while high interchange indicates a preference for maintaining close affectional relations. In order to be *compatible*, two or more individuals' scores on the FIRO-B affection dimension must be similar. That is, participants must agree on the degree of the affectional expression of distance or closeness. *Incompatibility* denotes disparity between those participants who wish close affectional ties and expression and those who prefer to keep an emotional distance regarding affection.

This distinction between homogeneity and compatibility is particularly important to keep in mind as we review the literature. While most compositional studies focus on interpersonal variables, some do not differentiate between homogeneity (similarity) and compatibility (need complementarity).

Early composition studies (Furst, 1951) focused on homogeneous *vs* heterogeneous personality traits in group psychotherapy participants. Gross (1959) in an early and extensive review of the group composition literature cited three major contributions: Powdermaker and Frank's (1953) book on group psychotherapy patients, Stock and Thelen's (1958) report on the National Training Laboratories, Group Development studies and Schutz's (1958) three-dimensional theory of interpersonal behaviour.

While the composition studies in small group research and group psychotherapy are of interest, they are not particularly crucial to our discussion of sensitivity training. The reader is referred to Shaw (1971) for an examination of small group research and Yalom (1970) for research in group psychotherapy. In the present chapter, we will focus on the research pertinent to experiential groups.

In order to keep the homogeneous/heterogeneous *vs* compatibility/incompatibility distinction clear, homogeneous/heterogeneous composition research will be presented first. The compatibility/incompatibility research follows since it is directly relevant to the composition model of learning to be presented.

Homogeneous/heterogeneous. The general questions asked by investigators are: (1) Does a given homogeneous composition of specific traits, characteristics, styles or needs promote more favourable learning conditions than different homogeneous composition? (2) Does a homogeneous composition promote more favourable learning conditions or specific learnings than a heterogeneous composition? The data seem to show that *heterogeneity* of composition leads to a greater array of alternative behaviours and that this enhances learning.

In an early study, Lieberman (1958) composed one group of participants who showed a preference for fight, pairing, dependency, counterdependency and flight. A second group was similarly composed except on the pairing dimension. He used the Reaction to Group Situation Test to compose the groups. The author found that counterdependent participants changed least in the group which excluded *pairers*. Lieberman concluded that heterogeneity of styles promoted more favourable learning conditions.

The first systematic investigation into the composition of training groups which focused on interpersonal factors was by Harrison and Lubin (1965).

Harrison and Lubin (1965) composed homogeneous groups based on an interpersonal or an impersonal/task orientation as measured by the Person Description Instrument III. The authors predicted that the ten-member, person-oriented group would learn more, develop a deeper level of personal relations, be more cohesive and expressive and understand interpersonal issues better than the ten-member, task-oriented group. While the personal group was indeed more expressive and attained a deeper level of personal relations than the impersonal group, the impersonal/task group members learned more. The authors speculated that the task group participants were confronted with disconfirmations and alternatives in the 'foreign' setting of the T-group culture which focused on interpersonal issues. Conversely, the personal group partici-pants were in a familiar and comfortable setting with little confrontation and alternative seeking. There was little expectation or challenge to change, and less opportunity to learn, in the latter group.

Two related investigations by Harrison (1965a, 1965b) are noteworthy. In the first study (1965a) Harrison reported an investigation in which laboratory members were placed in new groups based on their preference for low structure or high structure. One group was mixed, with half the members preferring low structure and half preferring high structure. Three groups were homogeneous in preference for moderate structure. While the heterogeneous group had more confrontations than homogeneous groups of low or high structure, the hetero-geneous group increased significantly more than homogeneous groups on measures of understanding of self and others.

In the second study (Harrison, 1965b), groups were composed of members who had been identified as 'problem members'. Passive, high-affect members were placed with active, positive-affect members. Passive, low-affect members were placed with active, negative-affect members. At times during the labora-tory, each group was divided into homogeneous subgroups in order to explore common issues. While the passive, high-affect members showed learning in being more active, passive, low-affect members were not as successful. It seemed that they were often influenced by the negative-affect members who generated a climate of fight and counterdependency. That is, when the level of fight in counterdependency was too high, passive members could not explore alternatives; when it was moderate, exploration of alternative behaviour took place.

Pollack (1971) studied group composition using Schutz's FIRO-B Scale and focused on the interpersonal behaviour dimension of control. The author composed four homogeneous groups around control, namely, high expressed, high wanted; high expressed, low wanted; low expressed, high wanted; and low expressed, low wanted. Twelve heterogeneous groups were formed by combining subjects who scored high, moderate or low on expressed and wanted control.

When the three need areas of inclusion, control and affection were combined, subjects of heterogeneous groups showed more positive change than subjects of homogeneous groups on reduction of the differences between expressed and wanted behaviour. While the confrontation variable was not examined in this study, the author speculated that heterogeneity did lead to more confrontation among members. In each study participants involved in heterogeneous interpersonal groupings demonstrated greater learning or change than those in homogeneous interpersonal groupings.

Five additional investigations further demonstrate the influence of homogeneous/heterogeneous interpersonal composition on learning climate and outcomes.

Powers (1965) found that groups which were homogeneous with respect to a high desire to give and to a high desire to receive showed a higher level of learning than groups with a low desire to give or receive.

Vraa (1971) demonstrated that the strength of members' interpersonal needs, measured by FIRO-B, was a major factor in group membership. With twenty-four graduate students randomly assigned to three interaction groups, the author found a curvilinear relationship between level of need and rated group membership. Specifically, the need to be included by others, when low to moderate, enhanced the group process; when the need to be included became too intense, the group process was inhibited.

Vraa (1974) also investigated differences in emotional climate of groups formed on the basis of different levels of the FIRO-B inclusion dimension. Emotional climate of the group was determined by measures of interpersonal interaction, namely, warmth, hostility and flight from warmth and/or hostility. Three groups (high, low, mixed) met for an hour once a week for nine weeks. The results confirmed the hypothesis that emotional climate differed as a result of the level of the need to be included.

D'Augelli (1973) formed groups in which all members were rated previously as performing at either high or low levels of interpersonal skills during a behavioural assessment procedure. After a two-hour leaderless group session, 69 males and 70 females evaluated each others' interpersonal behaviour and their group's cohesiveness. Members of highly skilled groups were seen as more empathic, honest and open, accepting and as discussing more personally meaningful topics than low-skilled groups. Highly skilled groups were also seen as more cohesive.

D'Augelli, Chinsky and Getter (1974) studied 66 college students placed in leaderless, audio-taped sensitivity training groups composed of members rated high or low on interpersonal skills. Groups composed of members high in skills discussed more personal and group-related issues than members low on these skills.

In sum, the research clearly demonstrates that composition based upon the homogeneous/heterogeneous dimension influences the change process in groups. Moreover, the data suggest that heterogeneous composition leads sensitivity group members to a wider range of alternative behaviours and change.

Compatible/incompatible. We move now to a summary of research on the compatible/incompatible dimension of group composition. All the studies in this area use the Schutz (1958) definition and his test (FIRO-B) to measure need compatibility/incompatibility. The compatible/incompatible composition literature on assembly effects will be reviewed first, followed by an examination of the effect of compatible composition on self-actualization.

The impact of group composition in assembly effects has attracted the attention of investigators (Collins and Guetzkow, 1964; Shalinsky, 1969; Schutz, 1958; Winch, 1958). *Assembly effect* is described by Collins and Guetzkow (1964, p. 58) as the product which occurs 'when the group is able to achieve collectively something which could not have been achieved by any member alone or by a combination of individual efforts'.

Shalinsky (1969) predicted that groups of interpersonally compatible members would (1) perform better than groups of incompatible members and (2) would perceive each other as more attractive and cooperative. Group productivity was measured by using task situations such as puzzles and singing marathons in which cabin groups competed against each other. Subjects were 113 nine-and-a-half to twelve-year olds in a large resident camp. A revised form was adapted from FIRO-B so that the children could understand the questions. Twelve groups were formed on the bases of FIRO-B affection scores; six were compatible and six were incompatible. The hypotheses were supported. Compatibility around affection led to a higher level of cooperation and production among members.

Underwood and Krafft (1973) tested whether Schutz's (1958) compatibility theory would be confirmed in a context which emphasized rational, non-personal processes. The authors compared two types of interpersonal compatibility as articulated by Schutz (originator and interchange) to two measures of interpersonal work effectiveness and to a measure of sociometric choice. Only two of twenty major hypotheses were supported. It was concluded that interpersonal compatibility does not have the effect in the work context that it does in the interpersonal learning context.

However, Reddy and Byrnes (1972) examined the effects of compatible and incompatible group composition on the problem-solving speed and accuracy of middle managers who were in a work-management conference. Groups which were compatible on the interpersonal dimensions of control and affection completed a model-building task more rapidly than the more incompatible group. While this study contradicts other findings (Underwood and Krafft, 1973), it is possible that, since the managers were at a conference and not at their usual work setting, the major focus was interpersonal relations and not 'real work'.

Reddy (1972) studied 72 participants in six sensitivity training groups in order to examine the relationships between changes in *self-actualization* as measured by the Personal Orientation Inventory (POI) (Shostrom, 1963) and participants' measured compatibility (FIRO-B). He found that members in both intensive (10 days) and non-intensive ($2\frac{1}{2}$ hours, 10 weeks) groups increased their scores on dimensions of self-actualization based upon their affectional compatibility style. That is, the greatest gains were made by group members whose affectional compatibility style, whether high or low, *opposed* the groups' norms.

Smith and Linton (1974) composed one-week sensitivity training groups according to members' scores on FIRO-B. Ten groups were formed: incompatible control, compatible affection (3 groups); incompatible affection, compatible control (3 groups); and incompatible control, incompatible affection (4 groups). Changes in self-actualization (POI) were found in all conditions. However, the effect of a particular composition enhanced certain changes and depressed others on these measures of self-actualization.

As with the homogeneous/heterogeneous studies, the compatible/incompatible research demonstrates the influence of this type of composition upon learning. Moreover, the data indicate that when groups are composed to be incompatible, dissonance and confrontation result in a higher gain in personal learning. Two studies further support this contention of the importance of confrontation to learning.

Jacobson and Smith (1972) studied 40 subjects who had completed the FIRO-B Scale before, immediately after, and two months following their participation in a weekend encounter group. Twenty control subjects completed the measure but did not attend the group. The analysis of the data showed significant changes on a number of dimensions. The most noteworthy of the findings was that subjects preferring low rates of social interchange showed greater change following their experience than did initially high participators. The author concluded that the behaviour of subjects preferring low rates of interchange was more discrepant from encounter group norms. These subjects were more frequently confronted, which in turn led to the exploration of alternative behaviours and subsequent change.

Andrews (1973) tested the hypothesis that growth in human relations training is furthered by working through challenging personal relationships, that is, those relationships in which the members hold expectations that are not fulfilled by the other's behaviour. The interaction then becomes problematic. Andrews measured the interpersonal expectations and behaviour styles of 56 group members with Leary's Interpersonal Checklist, and individual growth by a 'critical incidents' questionnaire. Dyads which were high-challenge relationships showed greater individual growth than did low-challenge dyads. Groups that contained many high-challenging pairings showed the highest level of change.

The research presented on composition, both homogeneous/heterogeneous and compatible/incompatible, clearly demonstrates the impact of this dimension on learning, climate and outcome in sensitivity training. What has been most striking to this author are the findings that heterogeneity and incompatibility lead to dissonance, confrontation and consequently a higher level of learning. Thus far, however, a theoretical model of change based on incompatibility or heterogeneity has not been articulated.

In this section a composition model of change will be described. Specifically, it will be based on one aspect of composition which the author feels to be most important, namely, interpersonal affection compatibility as formulated by Schutz (1958).

The early Harrison–Lubin (1965) model is essentially correct regarding personal change in small groups, change fostered by the participant's personal style being confronted and challenged by some and supported and confirmed by others. The fundamentals of the model as we have seen are strongly supported by research. The Harrison–Lubin model is based upon homogeneous and heterogeneous differences. However, the research data seem to give stronger support to compatible/incompatible interpersonal needs, the most basic of which is affection.

Two studies are of key importance here. Reddy (1972) placed 40 participants into four sensitivity training groups according to their premeasured interchange compatibility for affection as measured by the FIRO-B. Two groups (A and B) each had ten participants. Within each group five members had high need for affection scores (compatible) and five members had low need for affection scores (compatible). The compatible subgroups were incompatible with each other. A second two groups (C and D) were each composed of ten members who had moderate combined affection scores. Trainers were assigned according to how closely their own scores approximated the group affection norm. The laboratory was a five-day, residential undertaking.

Reddy hypothesized that groups (A and B) whose members were partially incompatible and partially compatible on affection would make greater positive gains in self-actualization than groups (C and D) composed of persons compatible in affection. Self-actualization was measured by the Personal Orientation Inventory (POI). The hypothesis was strongly supported. The author concluded that groups A and B engaged both in confrontation (because of their incompatibility) and support (because of their compatibility). This led to greater change. Members of interpersonally compatible groups (C and D) were neither stimulated nor conflicted enough to seek alternative behaviours.

In a second study, Smith (1974) also showed that quite different processes occurred when climates were confronting, supportive or both confronting and supportive. He used group composition as an operational expression of Kelman's (1958) social influence modes. Smith hypothesized that compliance in groups would be highest where the composition was maximally confronting; identification where composition was supportive; and internalization where both confrontation and support were present. The hypotheses were tested in 16 one-day sensitivity training groups. Each group consisted of three men, three women and a male trainer. Group composition was manipulated on the basis of FIRO-B affection and control scores. All three hypotheses were supported. That is, the differences in behaviour found in groups of different compositions were consistent with the differences predicted by Kelman's theory.

A compatibility composition change model

We have seen that the unique member composition of a sensitivity training group will often affect the dynamics, climate and learning of participants. What is lacking is a theoretical model, focusing on group composition, which systematically predicts participant behaviour *over time* in a sensitivity training group. The model I will present deals with one type of group composition—interpersonal affection compatibility.

I will show that into the unique setting of the sensitivity training group the participant brings a set of expectations for change which are reinforced by the 'culture' of this kind of group. The participants' attempts to cope with the ambiguity and the resultant stress leads to moderate (manageable) regression. Individual interpersonal patterns of dealing with affection are manifested as the participant attempts to reduce stress by multiple pairings. The patterns are intensified by group norms developing around affection. Whether the participant learns and changes is contingent upon the interpersonal affect composition of the group. If multiple pairings are possible which are both confronting and supportive then the probability for growth is enhanced. If they are not available then growth is unlikely. Figure 1 shows this change sequence as the participant moves through a sensitivity training experience. The following pages will expand on each of the variables.

Expectations

Participants join T-groups because they wish and expect intimacy, learning, skills, magic, resolution of conflicts and a host of other outcomes. Whatever the specific personal goal, each implies a desire for change, a wish or need for altering some unwanted condition. Goldstein (1962) has documented the impact of set and expectations on change in psychotherapy. He concluded that, '... material clearly pointed to expectations as a major determiner of human behavior', and 'that patient's prognostic expectancies are related to the degree of improvement which actually takes place in the patient' (p. 111). Sensitivity training is not different in this regard. Participants who are primed for change are usually willing to enter into a contract, explicit or implicit, to

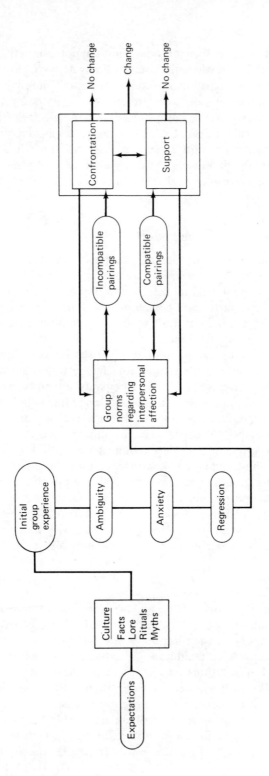

Figure 1. The change process through group composition

bring about change. Indeed, some of the self-reports of learning and change in sensitivity training can probably be attributed directly to the expectation and not to what occurred in the experience. Central to the present model is the assumption that most participants enter into a culture with some sort of expectation for change or self-exploration. This set is, in fact, a precondition to susceptibility to change.

Ambiguity and anxiety

The trainer in the traditional sensitivity training group, after a brief opening statement, essentially tells members that they are responsible for their own learning. The trainer then temporarily withdraws, creating a void in leadership, agenda and structure. The typical effect is anxiety on the members. The effects of ambiguity in a variety of settings is quite clear: anxiety is increased by ambiguity. These effects have been observed in a group setting (Smith, 1957), in psychological experiments (Dittes and Zemach, 1964), and in clinical interviews (Dibner, 1958). However, Rabbie (1963) and Dittes and Zemach (1964), found that subjects exposed to ambiguity and thus increased anxiety also showed an increase in affiliative tendencies although not with those who were responsible for the increased threat or anxiety. Finally, Kanfer and Martson (1961, 1962) found that when ambiguity was decreased, anxiety decreased and subjects in a verbal conditioning task learned faster and a higher level of transfer was obtained.

I believe that ten or fifteen years ago the ambiguity of the T-group was much more likely to cause high anxiety than it does today. Participants today are far more informed and sophisticated regarding sensitivity training groups. They 'move in' quickly to deal with leadership issues. This may reflect a current societal norm of disbelief in leaders; however, regardless of the reasons, the leadership void is readily filled by the membership. As members respond to fill the void of leadership, structure and agenda, behaviours and interpersonal styles of communication are manifested. Norms are created around which interpersonal behaviour and communication styles are acceptable. These norms are specific to and determined by the interpersonal composition of the group.

Trainer role

Before considering the development of norms, a digression to discuss the role of the trainer is necessary.

In recent years, the role of the trainer in sensitivity training has become less clearly defined that it was a decade ago, and, I believe less central to the learning of the participants. While the trainer is important as an anchor and stability to group members, his most important function is as a catalyst for their growth. The trainer is most easily identified because of his unique role, other aspects of group life, particularly norms, have been found to be equally influential on participant outcome (Lieberman, 1972).

Investigations of trainer role imply, explicitly or implicitly, the influence of group norms, probably derived from the unique interpersonal composition of the group, on the impact of the trainer. We cannot effectively look at trainer/ member relations outside of the context of interpersonal group norms. For example, Lundgren (1974b) found that participants responded to both trainer and group to the extent that their own interpersonal needs for control and affection were similar to those of the trainer.

In the present model the trainer is a member of the group with power and influence in a large part contingent upon his own affection needs and their compatibility or incompatibility with other member's needs. As we will see when norms and pairings are discussed, the trainer, like other group members, contributes to the development of interpersonal norms and he engages in pairings with other members.

Norms and pairings

The group interpersonal communication norms which emerge as members seek to reduce their anxiety are contingent upon the interpersonal composition of the group. As we have seen in the literature, learning in sensitivity training groups is in part determined by the confrontation of and deviation from those norms. Participants with a set of expectations enter into a culture that encourages, indeed expects, self-exploration and change. The usual societal supports are temporarily suspended; ambiguity occurs and anxiety results. In this climate regression to finding basic modes of behaviour which will reduce the anxiety are manifested around affection. For Freud, the libidinal impulses surrounding intimacy and affectional feelings are the most significant determiners of the individual's relations to the world. In order to reduce the anxiety, each participant attempts to define and control the interpersonal affection situation by his verbal and non-verbal communication. Overt and covert pairings occur between participants, within the group proper, and outside during breaks and free time. That is, in an attempt to deal with the situation, group members systematically approach each other. Indeed, what at times appears to be 'group phenomena' is in reality the behaviour of participants working out pairings. Over the entire course of a sensitivity training laboratory, each participant makes some implicit or overt attempt at pairing with every other participant. Multiple pairings are formed, broken and reformed.

Clark and Culbert (1965) have shown the importance of pair interactions on learning, as has Rioch (1970) in her description of Bion's work. This author agrees with Schutz (1958) that affection is primarily a dyadic relation. It occurs only between pairs of people at any one time. Relationships and interactions around affection which are comfortable and familiar confirm interpersonal patterns of self-image. They may be gratifying but they do not produce change. Conversely, relationships and interactions around affection which are unfamiliar and uncomfortable, disconfirm interpersonal patterns and self-image. They are anxiety arousing but a first step toward change (Lewin, 1951; Schein and Bennis, 1965).

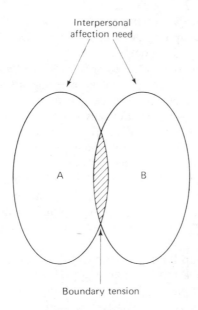

Figure 2. Pairing

What occurs in this support/confrontation model? When participant A seeks to reduce his anxiety by pairing with participant B, they encounter each other's affection boundary. The boundary derives from each person's interpersonal need around affection. The two boundaries create a potential tension point, as seen in Figure 2.

When affection needs are compatible, minimal tension occurs. When affection needs are incompatible, considerable tension is generated with A and B each seeking to control the affection situation by their communication. Interpersonal patterns, styles and behaviours are disconfirmed. New patterns and alternatives are considered, at least to reduce the boundary tension. But learning is not crystallized until the participant is able to gain some perspective and try out new communication patterns or behaviour in another dyadic relationship complementary to his own, that is, where the boundary tension is minimal and the climate supportive. The participant is reaffirmed. But why become involved in a sensitivity training group? Why not seek out multiple dyads in the real world? Actually, given the right circumstances, interpersonal learning would occur and to some degree probably does in day-to-day contacts. The difficulty is that on the 'outside' participants do not have a set to self-explore; they avoid potentially positive tension situations, and are not in cultures which encourage change. Indeed the culture of the outside private and public sector fosters resistance to change. Many natural encounters are brief, business-like or defensive in nature and are not open to exploration.

The amount of tension generated at dyadic affection boundaries is additive and circular. As Figure 1 shows, group norms lead to and affect pairings. The dyadic situations in turn are additive and lead to the formation and/or inten-sification of specific group norms around affection. Subgroup boundaries are formed not unlike dyadic boundaries.

If the group is composed of members with compatible affection needs, there will be minimal tension. If, for example, eight members of a sensitivity training group are compatible, and two incompatible, the eight will have multiple pairings with each other but only two possible with the incompatible members. The group affection norm will be confirming and supportive for eight members and confronting and non-supportive for two members. The probability is that minimal learning will take place, particularly among the eight compatible members. Group boundary tension may be too high for the two remaining members, particularly with little or no support for reaffirmation.

Figure 3 shows what I believe to be the optimal composition for maximal interpersonal learning. Group size is arbitrary; the important factor is the balance.

Members of subgroup I are compatible with each other as are members of subgroup II. But members of subgroup I are affect incompatible with members of subgroup II. Multiple confrontation pairings occur between subgroup pairs as do supportive pairings within subgroups. Moreover, two competing interpersonal affect norms emerge in the group. The intergroup boundary tension is high, but the struggle to reduce it leads to learning.

To recapitulate, when conditions of affection compatibility and incompa-tibility are optimal, leading to balanced pairings of confrontation and support, learning will occur. Conditions of affection compatibility alone or mixed affection incompatibility will at best lead to learning by a few and probably accounts for many encounter group participants 'feeling great' after a group experience but showing minimal learning as determined by objective measures.

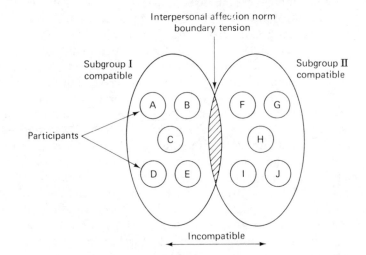

Figure 3. Optimal group composition

Implications

What implications can be drawn from this model? Certainly the group setting itself presents the most obvious. By screening participants and measuring their interpersonal needs, members can be placed into groupings which will maximize their learnings. Confrontation pairings and support pairings may develop naturally or they can be stimulated as part of the laboratory design. The latter case might be particularly appropriate in brief non-residential sensitivity training groups where time does not permit natural emergence of multiple pairings. Similarly, time spent in compatible subgroups will permit norms to develop more rapidly and intensify the boundary tensions between incompatible subgroups.

Lecturettes, discussions and experience focused on specific compatible and incompatible interpersonal needs might encourage participants to develop skills in recognizing and coping with pairings which will enhance their learnings.

There are some indications that learning takes place in groups but is not experienced by the participants until they are in back-home settings. For example, Reddy (1973) completed a one year follow-up of sensitivity training group participants and found a 'sleeper effect'. That is, members who had shown high levels of anxiety and minimal changes on a measure of self-actualization (POI) during a laboratory, recorded increased learnings a year later. Had these participants engaged in too intense confrontation during the experience and received support only when they returned home?

The interaction of composition and trainer/member relations demands research, as do the interactive conditions of feedback, risk, time, anxiety and pathology. An equally important research question is what are the optimal *levels* and *combinations* of compatibility for the generation of growth-inducing confrontation and support? The present chapter also implies that different developmental phases evolve in experiential groups contingent upon the interpersonal composition. That is, sensitivity training groups seem to evolve through quite different phases depending on the interpersonal composition of the members. When a group is high affection, it will have a more intense affection focus in stages or throughout and minimal counterdependent or confrontation periods. Conversely, if the interpersonal norms encourage confrontation, quite different developmental stages will evolve.

What of the role of the trainer? Designing sensitivity training groups around an optimal compatibility/incompatibility model necessitates a re-examination of trainer role. Effective trainer intervention in the context of the present model is an open question and one in need of investigation.

I have focused on sensitivity training groups in this paper, but the model has implications for organizational work groups and teams. Considerable time and money is spent on sending managers to 'stranger' sensitivity training laboratories with little or no guarantee of learning or transfer of training. It might be more appropriate to help ongoing work teams examine their interpersonal compatibility/incompatibility composition, and experiment with the most effective work pairings and group composition.

The composition model presented in this chapter is a working model, and one to be tested, altered and retested. It is in an early stage of systematic development as is the area of composition itself. It is hoped that the model invites challenge and criticism, and offers researchable hypotheses.

All theory is transitory. A specific theory or model is useful only for a particular time in the culture from which it is derived. The culture of sensitivity training is fluid and dynamic. It is itself affected by research, testing and theorizing. As knowledge is gained, expectations and assumptions change, as does the culture. As we theorize, conduct research, and apply knowledge about group composition, it too evolves; participants become more sophisticated, and the influence of composition is changed from what it was for 'naive' members.

References

Andrews, J. D. W. (1973) 'Interpersonal challenge: A source of growth in laboratory training.' *Journal of Applied Behavioral Science*, **9**, 4, 514–533.

Bednar, R. L. and G. F. Lawlis (1971) 'Empirical research in group psychotherapy.' In A. E. Bergin and S. L. Garfield (Eds.), *Handbook of psychotherapy and behavior change: An empirical analysis*. New York: Wiley.

Bolman, L. (1971) 'Some effects of trainers on their t-groups.' *Journal of Applied Behavioral Science*, **7**, 309–325.

Bradford, L. P., J. R. Gibb and K. D. Benne (Eds.) (1964) *T-group theory and the laboratory method*, New York: Wiley.

Clark, J. V., and S. A. Culbert (1965) 'Mutually therapeutic perception and self-awareness in a t-group.' *Journal of Applied Behavioral Science*, **1**, 180–194.

Collins, B. E. and H. Guetzkow (1964) *A social psychology of group processes for decision-making*. New York: Wiley.

Cooper, C. L. (1969) 'The influence of the trainer on participant change in t-groups.' *Human Relations*, **22**, 6, 515–530.

Cooper, C. L. and D. Bowles (1973) 'Physical encounter and self-disclosure.' *Psychological Reports*, **33**, 451–454.

Cooper, C. L. and I. L. Mangham (Eds.) (1971) *T-groups: A survey of research*. London: Wiley–Interscience.

D'Augelli, A. R. (1973) 'Group composition using interpersonal skills: An analogue study on the effects of members' interpersonal skills on peer ratings and group cohesiveness.' *Journal of Counseling Psychology*, **20**, 6, 531–534.

D'Augelli, A. R., J. M. Chinsky and H. Getter (1974) 'The effect of group composition on sensitivity training.' *Small Group Behavior*, **5**, 1, 56–64.

Dibner, A. S. (1958) 'Ambiguity and anxiety.' *Journal of Abnormal and Social Psychology*, **56**, 165–174.

Dittes, J. E. and M. Zemach (1964) 'The effect of cognitive ambiguity on anxiety and affilitative preference.' Paper presented at the American Psychological Association, Los Angeles, 1964.

Furst, W. (1951) 'Homogeneous vs. heterogeneous groups.' *International Journal of Group Psychotherapy*, **1**, 120–123.

Gibb, J. R. (1971) 'The effects of human relations training.' In A. E. Bergin and S. L. Garfield (Eds.), *Handbook of psychotherapy and behavior change: An empirical analysis*. New York: Wiley.

Gibbard, G. S. and J. J. Hartman (1973) 'Relationship patterns in self-analytic groups: A clinical and empirical study.' *Behavioral Science*, **18**, 335–353.

Goldstein, A. P. (1962) *Therapist–patient expectancies in psychotherapy*. New York: Pergamon Press.

Gross, R. L. (1959) 'Therapy group composition: Personal–interpersonal variables.' Unpublished doctoral dissertation, University of Utah.

Harrison, R. (1965a) 'Personal style, group composition, and learning.' *Journal of Applied Behavioral Science*, **1**, Part II, 294–301.

Harrison, R. (1965b) 'Group composition models for laboratory design.' *Journal of Applied Behavioral Science*, **1**, 409–432.

Harrison, R. and B. Lubin (1965) 'Personal style, group composition, and learning.' *Journal of Applied Behavioral Science*, **1**, Part I, 286–294.

Jacobs, M., A. Jacobs, G. Feldman and N. Cavior (1971) 'Feedback II—The "credibility gap": Delivery of positive and negative and emotional and behavioral feedback in groups.' *Journal of Consulting and Clinical Psychology*, **41**, 2, 215–223.

Jacobs, M., A. Jacobs, M. Gatz and T. Schaible (1973) 'Credibility and desirability of positive and negative structured feedback in groups.' *Journal of Consulting and Clinical Psychology*, **40**, 2, 244–252.

Jacobson, E. A. and S. J. Smith (1972) 'Effect of weekend encounter group experience upon interpersonal orientations.' *Journal of Consulting and Clinical Psychology*, **38**, 3, 403–410.

Kanfer, F. H. and A. R. Marston (1961) 'Verbal conditioning, ambiguity and psychotherapy. *Psychological Reports*, **9**, 461–475.

Kanfer, F. H. and A. R. Marston (1962) 'The effect of task-relevant information on verbal conditioning.' *Journal of Psychology*, **53**, 29–36.

Kelman, H. C. (1958) 'Compliance, identification and internalization.' *Journal of Conflict Resolution*, **2**, 51–60.

Lewin, K. (1951) '*Field theory in social science*.' New York: Harper.

Lieberman, M. A. (1958) 'The influence of group composition on changes in affective approach'. In D. Stock and H. A. Thelen (Eds.), *Emotional dynamics and group culture*. Washington, D. C.: National Training Laboratories, 131–139.

Lieberman, M. A. (1972) 'Behavior and impact of leaders.' In L. N. Solomon and B. Berzon (Eds.), *New perspectives on encounter groups*. San Francisco: Jossey-Bass, 135–170.

Lieberman, M. A., I. D. Yalom and M. B. Miles (1973) *Encounter groups: First facts.* New York: Basic Books.

Lundgren, D. C. (1974a) 'Member attitudes toward the leaders and interpersonal attraction in short-term training groups.' *Group Process*, in press.

Lundgren, D. C. (1974b) 'Interpersonal needs and member attitudes toward trainer and group.' *Small Group Behavior*, in press.

Lundgren, D. C. (1971) 'Trainer style and patterns of group development.' *Journal of Applied Behavioral Science*, **7**, 689–709.

Peters, D. R. (1973) 'Identification and personal learning in t-group.' *Human Relations*, **10**, 33–35.

Pollack, H. B. (1971) 'Change in homogeneous and heterogeneous sensitivity training groups.' *Journal of Consulting and Clinical Psychology*, **37**, 60–66.

Powdermaker, F. and J. Frank (1953) *Group psychotherapy*. Cambridge, Massachusetts: Harvard University Press.

Powers, J. R. (1965) 'Trainer orientation and group composition in laboratory training.' Unpublished doctoral dissertation, Case Institute of Technology.

Rabbie, J. M. (1963) 'Differential preference for companionship under threat.' *Journal of Abnormal and Social Psychology*, **67**, 643–648.

Reddy, W. B. (1972) 'Interpersonal compatibility and self-actualization in sensitivity training.' *Journal of Applied Behavioral Science*, **8**, 237–240.

Reddy, W. B. (1972) 'On affection, group composition, and self-actualization in sensitivity training.' *Journal of Consulting and Clinical Psychology*, **38**, 2, 211–214.

Reddy, W. B. (1973) 'The impact of sensitivity training on self-actualization: A one-year follow-up.' *Small Group Behavior*, **4**, 407–413.

Reddy, W. B. and A. Byrnes (1972) 'The effects of interpersonal group composition on the problem solving behavior of middle managers.' *Journal of Applied Psychology*, **56**, 516–517.

Rioch, M. J. (1970) 'The work of Wilfred Bion on groups.' *Psychiatry*, **33**, 1, 56–66.

Schein, E. H. and W. G. Bennis (1965) *Personal and Organizational Change Through Group Methods: The Laboratory Approach*. New York: Wiley.

Schutz, W. C. (1958) *FIRO-B: A Three Dimensional Theory of Interpersonal Behavior*. New York: Holt, Rinehart and Winston.

Shalinsky, W. (1969) 'Group composition as a factor in assembly effects.' *Human Relations*, **22**, 457–464.

Shaw, M. E. (1971) *Group Dynamics: The Psychology of Small Group Behavior*. New York: McGraw-Hill.

Shostrom, E. L. (1963) *The Personal Orientation Inventory*. San Diego: Educational and Industrial Testing Service.

Smith, E. E. (1957) 'The effects of clear and unclear role expectations on group productivity and defensiveness.' *Journal of Abnormal and Social Psychology*, **55**, 213–217.

Smith, P. B. (1974) 'Group composition as a determinant of Kelman's social influence modes.' *European Journal of Social Psychology*, in press.

Smith, P. B. and M. J. Linton (1974) 'Group composition and changes in self-actualization in t-groups.' Unpublished manuscript.

Stock, D. and H. Thelen (1958) *Emotional Dynamics and Group Culture*. National Training Laboratories.

Underwood, W. J. and L. J. Krafft (1973) 'Interpersonal compatibility and managerial work effectiveness: A test of the fundamental interpersonal relations orientation theory.' *Journal of Applied Psychology*, **58**, 1, 89–94.

Vraa, C. W. (1971) 'Influence of need for inclusion on group participation.' *Psychological Reports*, **28**, 271–274.

Vraa, C. W. (1974) 'Emotional climate as a function of group composition.' *Small Group Behavior*, **5**, 1, 105–120.

Winch, R. F. (1958) *Mate Selection: A Study of Complementary Needs*. New York: Harper and Row.

Yalom, I. D. (1970) *The Theory and Practice of Group Psychotherapy*. New York: Basic Books.

Chapter 9

The Leader and the Experiential Group

Martin Lakin
Philip R. Costanzo

Duke University

Introduction

The experiential group in its educational and therapeutic forms develops here-and-now interactions among members as the raw materials for change and therapy purposes. Whether aimed at corrective remediation or at enhancement of reasonably effective functioning, it is based upon the assumption that the group itself is the main vehicle of change, support or improvement. The function of the leader is to facilitate the group's operation. The actions of the leader can be directing or non-directing; he can structure a great deal or leave the process mostly ambiguous; he can 'come across' as dynamic, dominant or even charismatic, or he can be relatively passive and intentionally share the leadership function with participants.

When we use the term 'structure', it is important to qualify it at the outset. It is possible to structure groups in a variety of ways, but none is entirely structureless. Structuring is possible as to specifics. That is, a leader may intervene in a prescriptive way with instruction or ideas about behaviours. On the other hand, structuring may be restricted to a minimum, that is to say, to indication of boundaries and limits. In such cases the leader must indicate in a general way the idea of relative tolerances of intensity and physical contact. Obviously different though these structuring strategies may appear, they are not immediately manifested in experiential groups. They merge with other elements of leadership style to form a composite so that the outlines of differences are not immediately apparent. Our purpose is to expose these stylistic characteristics to scrutiny. After all, it is reasonable to assume that such differences in leader style will have consequences for participants in so far as they affect them.

This chapter will probe the role and actions of leaders for the sources of leaders' styles and to examine their effects upon members. It considers problems of leadership in experiential groups in the light of their avowed therapeutic and educational purposes. The former include such goals as greater emotional expressiveness, interpersonal effectiveness and sensitivity; the latter consist of increases in understanding of personal, interactional and group dynamics. Because of the overlapping functions of therapist and educator, and particularly because of the intense emotionality almost routinely evoked in them, leadership in experiential groups involves various kinds of skills and demands.

The theory of experiential groups is based on a central assumption: in unprogrammed group interactions where a shared expectation of personal and interpersonal learning exists, personal disclosures and interpersonal reactions generated by those disclosures will repeatedly recur and stimulate progressively deeper inner experiencing. The dynamics of group interaction may be counted on to promote identification with the group through sharing of experiences with fellow members. The dynamcis of the group may also be counted on to intensify the emotionality of self-disclosure. Thus, 'feedback' based on self-disclosure to one another should be especially impactful. It is a cardinal assumption of the theory that the feedback will be honest and responsible, assuming the group has developed appropriately. If successful, the results of the process should be a greater sense of community, an increased ability to share emotionally with others and improved insights into one's interpersonal style and its effects upon others.

It is because of their multiple goals that experiential groups have been thought to require a blend of didactic and therapeutic skills. A review of the developments in such groups over the past quarter century should provide some understanding of what leadership in them has been and what it is becoming.

The 'mixed-motive' therapeutic *and* educational group is largely a post-World-War-II phenomenon. Therapeutic groups and therapeutic discussion groups had been known and described since the early part of the century.* However, enormous rehabilitation needs for recently discharged soldiers in the U.S.A. and in Britain stimulated the use of groups as rehabilitative aids. The shortage of available professionally trained manpower made the obvious economies of multi-person treatment format a highly desirable alternative to relatively expensive dyadic therapies.

Closely following the revolutionary expansion in the employment of therapeutic groups was the emergence of the experiential group. Its serendipitous 'discovery' has been recounted elsewhere (Benne, 1964). In brief, an unscheduled 'post-mortem' between researchers and participants led to the regular use of here-and-now reflections by participants on interactions in all their emotional aspects. Thus begun experiential group learning. Through its subsequent development in National Training Laboratories at Bethel, Maine, where it was first called Human Relations Training, this type of 'training' spread throughout the country and beyond under many different rubrics.

Experiential groups have become a feature of the social landscape. Although occasionally employed as 'heroic' measures to achieve integration in school systems, confront law enforcement officers with irate citizens who felt oppressed

---

*The 'Symposium' of the ancient Greeks and Socrates' dialogues were mixed motive relationships involving general educational and frankly therapeutic elements; thus, in a sense experiential groups are no departure from an historic chain of social association for learning and mutual betterment.

by them, or to work through difficult intra-staff relationships in organizational systems, they are mainly offered to volunteer applicants who perceive them as opportunities for self-development or for therapy. Because they are so widely available, under so many varieties of sponsorship, and conducted at such diverse levels of sophistication, it has become increasingly complicated to categorize them. In fact the overlap between educational and therapeutic purposes frustrates both intentions because of the problem of spelling out appropriate selection criteria or specifying what constitutes adequate preparation for their leaders.

Revisionists of its original theoretical underpinnings—a blend of neo-Freudian psychoanalysis, experiential group dynamics and democratically based pragmatism—have spawned their own splinter versions of the educational and the therapeutic purposes of the groups. Some have suggested changes in basic procedures—i.e., the introduction of leader-structured activities which would serve to facilitate their version of group purposes—while others have virtually abandoned the group-as-primary-vehicle in favour of a more individual-centred approach.

Experiential groups characteristically develop an intense emotional ambience, whether confrontational or supportive, as the group develops over time. The emotional intensity generated is usually seen as a *sine qua non* of group success. The emotionality of these groups is in fact rejuvenative and recreational. They permit regressive trends and encourage a certain venture-someness and sense of excitement. The consequent tendencies to disinhibit one another combine to create an atmosphere of fellowship and camaraderie reminiscent of a summer camp.

Most groups are usually minimally structured by their designated leaders (variously called 'facilitators', 'trainers' or simply 'leaders') and involve between 8–15 participants, although this as well as the degrees and kinds of structuring vary to some extent depending upon sponsorship and upon whether the intention is primarily educational or therapeutic. There are no 'pure types' so that considerable overlap exists among all experiential groups.

To list experiential group titles as they currently appear is to give only very general information regarding commonalities or differences among them. In this sense Human Relations Laboratories, sensitivity training ('T'-groups) and Organizational Development ('O.D.') groups share a programmatic aim of interpersonal and intra-organizational problem diagnosis and problem solving. On a learning-therapy continuum the weighting in them is toward learning goals—although therapeutic change is by no means devalued. However, as a general rule, these groups disavow an explicitly therapeutic intention, and they are not as concerned with achieving 'personal growth' for its own sake as for instrumental aims of becoming more productive, more effective or more helpful in a job role or in one's primary relationships.

By contrast, the 'Human Potential Movement' may be said to have grown from among a different ideological wing in the experiential group movement. For instance, encounter groups emerged in the mid-1960s touted as 'therapy for normals' through the evocation of increasing levels of emotional expressiveness and intimate self-disclosures. In fact, the recent history of the term 'encounter' itself reflects the vicissitudes of the experiential group movement. The term has increasingly become applied to any form of relatively unstructured group psychological experience from body awareness to explicit therapeutic groups. In view of the incorporation by 'encounter' of so many types of experiential groups, it seems clear that there has been a drift toward the explicitly therapeutic goals of personal change and away from other learning aims over the past decade.

Positive and negative evaluations of experiential groups are, at this time, based upon a polyglot assortment of methods of assessment and are rooted in contrasting assumptions regarding their social utility. Critics claim that they achieve only superficial, transitory gains if any; moreover, they view post-group good feelings as merely reflections of the emotionality of the group atmosphere, i.e. as essentially revivalistic. Consequently, they consider these group experiences as scientifically suspect because of their quasi-religious nature. Despite this understandable wariness by researchers, the positive effects routinely reported by the overwhelming majority of participants are deserving of continuing scrutiny. Among these effects are positive self-concept changes, greater interpersonal awarness and accompanying willingness to listen to others as well as satisfactions in emotional sharing. Whether these positive effects are long lasting or simply reflect a hyperenthusiasm in the immediate afterglow of the group remains in doubt. The most recent study of outcomes by Lieberman, Yalom and Miles (1973) indicates success proportions quite similar to those of psychotherapy-outcome studies; one-third claiming sustained positive change, one-third unchanged and an equivalent portion either dropping out or claiming a negative experience. In some cases (in proportions varying from 7–14% depending upon the *type* of *leadership*) an adverse reaction was serious enough to warrant listing the participant as a 'casualty'. These latter findings in particular have gained much notoriety among mental-health specialists and lend a sense of urgency to the considerations of experiential group leadership.

Despite the concerns over unwanted negative effects, the majority of participants come away as 'satisfied customers' and continue to send their friends with enthusiasm. Thus, from a retrospective view over 25 years or so, experiential groups appear to have secured a firm foothold in this society. They remain generally popular therapeutic and educational experiences even in the face of frequent criticisms. Their adherents maintain with constantly increasing confidence that they are in fact an effective admixture of potent educational and therapeutic processes, responsive to deeply felt needs in a time of enormous social change and dislocation.

A mini-theory of the workings of experiential groups

We take the position that experiential groups are therapeutically useful as vehicles for effective learning in direct relationship to their resemblance to real-life interactions. This will sound strange to the reader who has some knowledge of the uniqueness of such groups, of their 'contrivedness' in terms of the disavowal of agendas and of the customary rules of procedure. Nevertheless, these are means for facilitating a rapid transition to the heart of the matter — the elicitations and dramatization of the problematic aspects of ordinary interpersonal interaction. Our position may be contrasted with one which holds that experiential groups are valuable contrasts with daily life, a relief and a release from the humdrum. Exciting they may be (and should be!), and they are seemingly at great variance with daily encounters. But their value lies in the evocation of just those universal, ordinary aspects of relationship. Thus, while our mini-theory tells about the special workings of experiential groups, the reader may consider how similar factors determine the qualities of the various real-life groups to which he belongs.

Experiential group processes should be understood in terms of both the group *and* individual personality and are facilitated by designated leaders. To the group that provides acceptance and fulfilment for personal needs, members give loyalty. As members they, in turn, provide the group with its unique spirit. A group viewed as a developing social system progresses, stabilizes stagnates or disintegrates with changes in member involvement and interest. Where membership is valued, a cohesive group 'aura' is created. The cohesiveness is valued for its own sake in terms of the good feelings generated, but it also makes possible effective group actions.

Paradoxically, group membership threatens one's autonomy at the same time that it seems to offer security of a kind. The wish to be warmly nurtured and supported is offset by the fantasy of being overwhelmed and stifled. In ordinary life one can discern a similar ambivalence in the individual's relationship to his family or some other social unit. Most persons experience real deprivation when excluded from groups they want to be part of. On the other hand, many people also *defend* against being enveloped by a group, especially when they fear they might be subject to its controls and denied the expressions of their own individualities.

One way of avoiding absorption is through personal recognition for talents or skills. This involves evaluation whether overt or covert, as is most frequently the case in the 'real world'. During the group experience, member evaluation of one another becomes increasingly explicit. (This is so despite disclaimers of a 'non-judgemental' atmosphere. Evaluation is, as a matter of fact, most explicit in the process termed 'feedback'.) The impelling factors are two: an almost irresistible tendency to engage in social comparison (comparing oneself with everyone else), and a tendency to assess the effects each member has on every other member. A member can be valued by his group for a variety of reasons. One may be outstanding for his communicating abilities; another may be respected for his insights; a third appreciated for stimulating others or for getting things started just when people seem to need active direction. Credit accrues especially to those who practise effective altruism, i.e. who are able to extend help to others at the right time and without sign of immediate personal payoff. Generally there is an effort to have evaluations be of behaviour effects rather than of motivations, of how one's actions made another feel rather than *why* one did what he did (although motivational speculations are almost compulsive and can therefore not be disallowed).

The transaction between member and group involves group acceptance in exchange for member commitment, intimacy in exchange for personal disclosure, and a role in the group for each member. As a member of fact, some participants are so anxious to feel a sense of belonging that they complain at the very onset, 'I don't feel as though I'm really a part of this group.' Such individuals are usually expressing a lack of understanding of how, in fact, one becomes an effective part of the social organization through helping to build it. Such a seemingly simple learning may be an important one for their participation in other groups.

The conditions for membership in the groups are more or less the same for all members. They are as follows: (1) to contribute to the shaping and coherence of the group, (2) to invest in it emotionally, (3) to help move it toward a goal, (4) to help establish its rules and to obey them, (5) to take on specific roles in the group, (6) to strive for deeper levels of intimacy and (7) to give help to other participants. Groups may be distinguished by the conditions which are most salient for them, i.e., those which are most emphasized. A group which is high on conditions 2 and 6 would demand relatively high emotionality. Collaboration and cooperation would be most important for the group which stresses conditions 1, 3 and 7.

The experiential training group requires the exercise of reflection as well as emotional commitment. With *only* intellectual comprehension the process becomes sterile. Emotions and intellect are both needed for a balanced and meaningful experience. Group effects interact with individual needs. How these effects are experienced in a specific group is partly the result of the mix of the personalities in that group and partly due to the influence of its leader. The core processes themselves, however, occur regardless of the quality of members or leader. Let us consider some of these core processes and see how they might interact with personal responses. The general point should be made that these core processes take place in all types of experiential groups that permit the development of group processes. The reader should therefore keep in mind that the facilitation of these processes by the leader will influence the successes of his group.

A. *Achieving and maintaining cohesiveness*

Group cohesiveness is the collective expression of personal belongingness. It leads to deeper association and concern about one's fellow members. Demonstrably, group cohesion (1) binds members emotionally to the common task as well as to one another; (2) assures greater stability of the group even in the face of frustrating circumstances; (3) develops a shared frame of reference which allows for more tolerance for diverse aims of group members.

A negative attitude toward one's group reduces one's participation in the group task, but valued membership in that group leads to a greater commitment to its values and to the tasks the group undertakes. When membership is highly valued, the productivity of the group may be expected to rise. In experiential groups, the wish to be accepted is especially strong and participants are anxious to assure themselves that all members have in fact been 'accepted', i.e. the group's 'success' is measured in terms of cohesion. Concern over the degree of success is epitomized in the question, 'How successful are we in having become a group?'. The potency of this concern is evidenced in the fact that one can even censure one's fellow members by complaining, 'We haven't become a "real" group.'

B. *Behaving in conformity with group norms*

All experiential groups encourage emotional expressiveness, warmth, openness and the like. In fact, such attributes as these become standards by which to judge the progress the group makes. They may even become 'norms' which compel conformist behaviour by participants. The real point is that norms exist in any group; the real problem is to make them understandable in their influence upon the participants. It is less important and even misleading to declare norms for the group—'We will be open'—than to follow the creation, vicissitudes and effects of norms on members. How various kinds of norms come to be important for the group and their relative compellingness for individuals is the important learning issue here.

C. *Consensual validation of personal perceptions*

Another group effect is a press toward agreement. Members continually compare interpretations of events in order to establish meanings of events for themselves. Tracing the consensus processes that develop among the members of the group is in itself an absorbing learning process for attenders. 'How did we come to agree on our feelings about Fran?' is one form of the question. 'Why do we all react the same way to Adam?' is another. 'Feedback' is often given as a type of consensual reaction summary. To discover how this consensus is achieved, and with what consequences for each participant, is the learning objective. Ideally, each participant should be able to see himself in the consensus and evaluate the part he plays in arriving at it. This self-conscious view of group consensus process offsets the tendency for consensus to become merely another mechanism for increasing or enforcing conformity.

D. *The expression of emotional immediacy*

Any experiential group generates emotional expressiveness in participants. Hostile or affectionate feelings are evoked with fewer inhibitions in them than in most other interpersonal situations. There are, however, factors which discourage emotional 'binges' such as the media often portray. Concern for one's standing in the group influences one to monitor personal outpourings. The rapid spread of emotionality among the members of the group *is* helpful in freeing up a participant who is constricted in his expressing of feelings and it is readily apparent that in such cases the unblocking of 'frozen' feelings is a desirable development. This does not mean, however, that any display of emotionality is necessarily helpful, so that there are constraints upon emotionality just as there are facilitating elements for its expression.

E. *Group perception of problem relationships*

In what sense is it appropriate to talk about the group as a problem-solving experience? Experiential groups deal supportively with problems of human relationships and investigate the mutual perceptions which determine their problematic status. For instance, to Phil's query, 'How am I perceived?' Simone tells him, 'You come on too strong' or 'Your pompousness turns us off'. Through general discussion of how his behaviour affects his relationships with others, he is stimulated to try alternate ways of relating that could be more effective. The assumption is that problematic interpersonal behaviours are most effectively looked at from fresh vantage points provided by the views of other group members. While 'many heads' do not necessarily come up with solutions to problems, they provide alternative perspectives on them.

F. *Dominance alignments*

In experiential groups, leadership and influence positions rarely remain static. This is because any member can legitimately try exercising power and influence. His efforts are at best ambivalently received because the other participants are also impelled to try to assume *their* habitual positions of power. With the help of the leader, experiential groups try to develop flexibility in power allocation or 'ownership'. Thus a number of persons, regardless of 'real life' position, simultaneously experiment in the roles of decision-makers or influencers, or are treated as objects of influence. This contrasts with fixed self-perceptions as 'boss' or power victim. Even the 'naturally' dominant member must, after all, garner support from others if he is to continue to exercise leadership. The group thus provides a multiple perspective on power and influence transactions.

G. *Role differentiation*

A group stagnates where there is no diversity of functions and especially where members feel stuck in undersirable and unproductive roles. In experiential groups, the functions of initiating, clarifying, harmonizing, etc., are easily recognizable. Other roles emerge, depending on the people in the group and its purpose. This availability of roles does not mean, however, that role interchange is easily or effortlessly achieved. As in the uses of power, participants gravitate to accustomed roles, such as 'the blocker', the 'group clown' or the group 'foul-up', perhaps to provide some elements of constancy and predictability. This tendency is not productive of learning and change. Thus, from the point of view of the participant who gets stuck in them the aim must be to enable him to experiment with different ways of being in the group. In the absence of such experimentation, stereotypic role stabilizes without constructive change.

H. *Movement towards intimate disclosure*

Objective 'change' indices following training routinely demonstrate increases in feelings of intimacy. Whether these represent only a temporary emotional state precipitated by the experience or something more enduring we cannot say at this point. Nevertheless, in expressiveness forms of experiential groups especially, members are enjoined to push toward greater intimacy on the assumption that it will have considerable 'carry-over' beyond the life of the group.

The interaction between group effects and personal responses is singular for each participant. The same group experience may have rewarding and punishing consequences for two different members. For example, a person with great needs for belongingness may experience the Cohesiveness of his group (group Effect 'A') with a positive response of relieved belongingness while another may have a negative feeling of being hemmed in. With respect to Effect 'B', Conformity, one participant could respond by becomingg more aware of the need to be accountable to his fellows; whereas another simply brings his behaviour into line with everyone else's by uncritical acceptance of group standards. With respect to Effect 'C', Consensus, although its achievement feels satisfying, there is the risk that it may come about at the cost of denying real differences in order to achieve it. What is the range of possible responses to the group effect of 'Emotional Immediacy' (Effect 'D')? On the positive side, one is likely to feel freed up emotionally. On the negative side, one could be coerced to express group evoked emotions. Effect 'E' (Group Perception of Problems) may facilitate one's thinking about one's interactional problems and it stimulates different perspectives. On the other hand, pressured sharing of problems arouses defensiveness.

With respect to Dominance Alignments (Effect 'F'), the important thing is to endeavour that no one remain permanently at either extreme, i.e. feeling either constantly manipulated at one end or able to dominate the group at the other. Group Effect 'G' (Role Differentiation) stimulates the individual to try himself out in hitherto unaccustomed ways. The negative side is a tendency of the group to stereotype the individual or to 'pigeon-hole' him into a category in order to reduce the cognitive complexity of the group situation in one's mind. In regard to group Effect 'H' (Movement toward Intimate Disclosure), a desirable result is intimacy, when based on meaningful feedback. On the other hand, there is risk to self-esteem unavoidably associated with self-disclosure and the evaluative reactions from group-mates.

The group experience is theoretically self-regulating in the sense that belongingness needs and wishes impel members to share intimate experiences and feelings without excessive pressures. In practice, this 'self-regulation' is not completely reliable, and the leader may find it necessary to channel interactions to some extent—for example, away from excessive preoccupation with a personal historical narrative to here-and-now data in the group or to intervene where he perceives that a member is being confronted beyond his capacity to constructively absorb what is being offered.

As we suggested earlier, the self-definitions of leaders differ depending upon the kind of group and its sponsorship. Views of the leader function also vary with views of the group goals and with levels of sophistication. Needless to say, leaders also vary enormously in their grasp of personality and group dynamics. Whatever their understandings, some characteristically encourage confrontation whereas others invariably promote support. Sometimes both tendencies are happily combined in a particular leader who is able to tailor confrontation and support in accord with the demands of specific interactions. Whereas there are leaders who focus primarily on inner individual experiences and foster only those group processes which intensify them, there are also the leaders who point out group process *rather* than individual experiences. Again, one is fortunate if his group is being conducted by a leader who can integrate these elements productively.

What does the experiential group leader do? The generally accepted view of the leader is one who acts to stimulate and channel interactions when necessary but also to prevent excesses, most definitely to protect vulnerable individuals when the need arises. Earlier on we suggested that the role requires the integration of different kinds of skills; how are they integrated? How are they related to those ordinarily considered as leader-like attributes? Is formal training in one of the recognized mental health or social science disciplines necessary? If so, to what extent and with what degrees as a standard?

Probably, everyone would agree that the experiential group leader is not a task-leader in the sense of managing a process which yields a product. Yet, in a sense the results of his efforts are discernible 'products' of insight, expressiveness or feelings of community. The leader's management of the process which lead to such 'products' is in this sense no different from that of leaders who have a task function. Again, most observers would agree that the leader is not a psychotherapist in the ordinarily understood sense of having to provide a 'corrective emotional experience' for persons who see themselves as patients in need of treatment. Yet, the leader does diagnose his group members, assessing possible vulnerabilities as a precaution against breakdowns or other avoidable damage. Clearly he does value therapy-like gains even in the non-therapy-oriented group. Further, it cannot be asserted that participants perceive themselves as *not* needing a corrective emotional experience even if they don't define themselves as patients. Such is the indeterminate relationship between education and therapy in the views of many contemporary participants. The sensitivities of a therapist are in any case especially needed to monitor communication of interpersonal messages when these are ambivalent or hostile.

We argue that although the leader is neither foreman nor therapist, he perforce combines functions associated with both roles. In order to accomplish the group goals he is both permissive and directive. The leader lets happen what will happen but also probes to see what *can* happen; i.e. he is sensitive to the interactive possibilities of the occasion and tries to help them be realized when they can illustrate a particular or a universal problem in relating, in communication or in group action.

This multi-faceted and complex nature of the leader function and the ambiguous context of the group is bound to generate a stressful relationship between the leader and the members. Even the beginnings of the group generate a kind of 'credibility gap' because members naturally and firmly 'know' that the leader 'knows' precisely the outcomes which will occur and even the processes by which these outcomes will develop. Not surprisingly, there is routinely developed a fairly intense, if sometimes hidden, resentment against a leader who appears unwilling to share his knowledge with 'the customers'. This then is the initial paradox which brings in its wake a continuing frustration and generates suspicion and anger. This paradox is also paradigmatic for the leader function in the experiential group. The ostensible leader who does not tell one how to follow is the reality. Such actions and attitudes thwart naturally dependent tendencies. Dependency frustrated does not lead to dependency eliminated, but rather to resentment. Happily, from the learning and therapy points of view, this posture of the leader yields almost immediate gains because the frustration of these dependent needs impels interactions aimed at 'bypassing' the obstacle of seemingly equivocal and reluctant authority. This means that members are accelerated in the business of getting to know and cope with one another for gratification of the same needs or in working out mutual solutions to the shared dilemma of 'what to do', since the leader will apparently not do it for them.

The leader's seeming reluctance to gratify dependent demands for structure and guidance is in some ways equivalent to the dynamic equivocation of the psychotherapist vis-a-vis the gratification of patients' fantasies and wishes for approval and support. The therapist cannot really gratify such wishes either without sacrificing the potency of patient incentive to become increasingly self-reliant. There are, of course, leaders who do structure processes and initiate activities themselves rather than leaving these to the members, just as there are therapists who instruct, advise and model emotional disclosures for their patients. It is our view that these leaders do in great measure give up the group-as-vehicle model for learning and therapy. The participants are after all constantly on the lookout for clues as to what their leader will do. The leader's moves in the inception phase of the group are decisive for whether the group takes on responsibility for self-direction or whether members decide to be 'passive', waiting for pushes and pulls from the leader. (It is curious that a corresponding consensual strategy is so frequently reached covertly by participants. Often there is quickly reached common agreement on how to 'play' the leader—but with little open discussion. We don't know precisely how this occurs.)

The leader's frustration of initial dependency wishes is not an arbitrary, but an integral component in building the group's confidence in its potential to be self-regulating. We believe it is important, for instance, to establish that members have the capability of moving on their own. This statement, however, raises certain questions: Doesn't the leader structure participant expectancies in the final analysis? Further, doesn't the group actually unfold in accord with the leader's view of group processes, so that one may wonder, is there really freedom of choice about direction in experiential groups? Do not well advertised and reinforced expectancies of self-disclosure foreclose other choices in such groups?

The fact is that a leader's refusal to structure a group's beginnings beyond a general orientation and the laying down of elemental ground rules about time, confidentiality and—in certain cases—the limits of physical contact, is a decisive element in the group's development. It poses a challenge to which the members must react by immediately generating ways of being with each other for themselves. We have noted that there are experiential group leaders who prefer to structure the disclosure dimension of the group from the beginning; some even initiate the process by their self-disclosures. Why does the leader do this? It is usually justified as an acceleration of self-disclosures by members, which should eventuate in greater intimacy for all. In addition to the sacrifice of the groups-as-vehicle, the problem is that leader disclosure must inevitably become a standard whereby all subsequent disclosures are measured. Nobody could wish for a disclosure process in which people outdo one another to impress their leaders about the relative depths or sincerity of their revelations. Inescapably, disclosures by the leader, no matter what their value as illustration, risk becoming a standard which could undermine the validity of the growing group norm of peer disclosure, and the primary importance of peer disclosure.

Perhaps it will be useful to emphasize the point that the group is called into existence by a leader, but it is not for his benefit. This obvious point seems to get lost in the advocacy of automatic self-disclosure and emotional ventilation by leaders. In so far as he initiates the emergence of processes such as member self-disclosure, and thus inhibits the development of a more organic (member regulated) pattern of disclosure, he reduces the group to a forum for his own brand of 'interactive health'.

A related point is that whenever the leader 'discloses', he becomes a part of the inner emotionality of his group—assuming his disclosures are sincerely intended. By this fact, he must become to some extent non-objective for the period of the intense emotional contact. We would not insist that a leader abstain totally from personal disclosures, but that he recognize its relative utilities and costs in terms of his effectiveness and his group's capacity to absorb and work with his feelings as well as their own.

We suggested above that permissive and directing elements are intermixed in the leader's functions. In what sense does the leader 'conduct' the group, and in what ways does the leader 'let' the group happen? It is not an easy matter to determine the relative proportions of 'let' and 'push'. In our post-session discussions we have often pondered the issue of how much we influenced interactions during a particular session, and questioned to what extent changes in content or shifts in process were due to our interventions. It was obvious to us that our interventions were often influential in focusing or in shifting focus. But had they been 'good' ones, 'good' meaning facilitative of personal growth, deeper understanding, or increased skills in relating? While we make no claims to unchallengeable criteria, these seem to us to be reasonable. When one assesses one's group and the motives for participation, one ought to be able to come up with similarly reasonable criteria which relate to a group's goals. Our group members are most frequently clinical psychologists-in-training. They take part in our groups to learn about their interpersonal styles and their modes of interacting with others so as to be 'aware' of their future impacts on the clients whom they will serve as counsellors and therapists. The aforestated criteria have obvious relevance to such a future. It seems to us that leaders should be able to assess their intervention effectiveness in a parallel way in relation to the groups they conduct.

Some recent surveys of experiential groups (Lieberman *et al.*, 1973; Schaffer and Galinsky, 1974) described what they called 'typical group leader behavior' for certain types of groups. Among these groups Schaffer and Galinsky included a social work group, a psychoanalytic therapy group, a group dynamic therapy group, psychodrama, behaviour therapy, the Tavistock approach, T-groups, Encounter group and something called Theme-centred interaction method. Lieberman and his colleagues studied Encounter groups, tape recording guided 'leaderless' groups, and Sensitivity Training groups. The former authors describe a series of 'prototypical' leader techniques for each type of group. The latter emphasizes the charismatic aspect of encounter leaders (and the attendant problematic aspects of such leadership style).

In our view, the leadership style and its functions outlined in Galinsky and Schaffer's chapter, 'T-groups and the laboratory method', is the general model for all experiential groups. The manipulation of members is minimal in this approach by comparison with the other approaches. Efforts up to the present to classify group leader behaviour have been rather technique-oriented. That is, they identify a particular exercise or stimulus to feeling—such as starting a group 'hug' as if it were a philosophy of leadership. This is understandable if one wishes to emphasize how leaders try to concretize ideas of how their theories should work or, alternatively, one wants to point out egregious errors that result in 'casualties'. It seems to us, however, that such approaches fall short of helping the reader appreciate the range of strategy choices which a leader faces. It is his strategy choices which have important consequences for his members, more than his 'style', theory of change, or even his 'Theory of Man'— although, obviously, there are strong relationships among these factors.

The strategic choices that leaders make reflect in a natural way leader ideology and values. In a fundamental sense—in the sense that actions speak louder than words—the leader's choices reveal his goals for the group. Not only do they show how he prefers to work with people in the group context; they also reveal what he enjoys doing. Perhaps these choices could be treated as the basis for a critical-incident focused empirical review of group processes.

Structuring

The experiential group is popularly spoken of as 'unstructured'; that is, it is widely assumed to have no structure at all. Obviously there *is* structure. The popular assumption is misleading but it *is* popular. Groups do vary in degrees and kinds of structuring, but all are begun with an orientation which reflects the anticipations of leaders, and the kinds of activities that are permitted. The ambiguity we mentioned earlier is helpful and necessary to the growth of self direction for members. For example, most leaders would hold that the experience of being forced to flounder results in a productive anxiety of tension which is fuel for action when creatively exploited to catapult participants into relating and structuring themselves. By this we mean it energizes participants. However, they are also leaders who begin by providing extensive explanations and by trying to develop anticipations in ways that will minimize this same anxiety. They see it as inhibiting and as a damper on growth rather than its facilitator. Those who structure a good deal, even to the extent of producing themes or topics, operate on the assumption that the anxiety of floundering is not at all useful and that the group should be steered to 'working' at relationships through directed exercises or even modelled disclosures and feedback.

The leader who prefers not to structure beyond a rudimentary orientation believes that there is value to members finding their own way—that his guidance is best used consultatively—that he should stimulate the group but not actively direct it. To the degree that he believes the element of tension is useful in promoting interpersonal exploration and interperson relating, he will minimize structuring. If he believes that the tension from ambiguity merely provokes inhibiting anxiety, he will forecast what is likely to occur and even try to govern its development. A workable balance between these two positions is one which use 'floundering' contingently and is prepared to structure when the former approach yields an emotional dead-end.

Orienting one's self in a strange group, trying to cope with one's reactions to strangers, and finding satisfactory ways to relate to them is a very different experience than being guided by an authority, however benign, into relationships with others. From our point of view of the learning and therapy potential of experiential groups, the problem of the latter alternative is that the assumption of responsibility for activity choice by *authority* reduces needs for members to make their own choices.

Strategy choice has implications for what ensues in the group. Suppose that leaders begin by initiating contact exercises, e.g. touching, looking into one another's eyes or 'trust falls'. The provision of such exercises creates an expectation that the major or the dramatic innovations in the experiences are the leader's responsibility. Thus, the creation of such an anticipation signals the group how much it may depend upon the leader to develop an activity instead of having to create one themselves. What are alternative modes of leading? The leader's presence, his availability, the security of knowing that interventions *will* come if the process bogs down or when a member needs help are different modes of leading from reinforcing the notion that the leader assumes responsibility for producing affect-laden interactions.

In a certain sense, the high-structure leader is behaving in the way that leaders traditionally behave—he sets goals and indicates the paths to reach them. There is reassurance in such authority. It is, after all, authoritative. Clearly, however, the participant's autonomy is not likely to be thereby increased. On the other hand, the leader who hopes to use the tensions of ambiguity and floundering productively has to make sure that they do not become so intense as to impair members' functioning. Of course there is also the danger that they could become a standard to which there develops group adaptation. As an example, even a prolonged unbroken silence the first session could become normative: i.e. succeeding sessions would have prolonged silences, and this would then become so routinized that it ceases to be disturbing (or productive!) as members adapt to the repeated pattern. The stabilization or institutionalization of any pattern dulls members rather than stimulates them to learn new things about themselves and others.

On trusting the group

It is axiomatic that as mutual trust grows in a group, so does greater cohesion. In the ideal instance, this greater togetherness in turn stimulates corresponding intimate feelings, more self-disclosure, greater mutual support and ultimately reinforces the mutual trust. This is why the development of trust is such a crucial issue in experiential groups and why periodic testing for its presence takes on the character of a group imperative. It must be any leader's aim to encourage the growth of mutual trust in his group. On the other hand, experienced leaders also know that fantasy plays a powerful role (whether fearful or wishful) when it comes to trusting in a group. Some desperately want to believe that the group is trustworthy even in the absence of facts that would validate this belief. Frightened members don't even want to try finding out whether it is a trustworthy group or not. These represent extremes, but everyday human relating is also determined by wishes and fears about trusting and distrusting.

The issue of trust–non-trust is one of the more dramatic aspects of the experiential group. It is no less so for the learning group than for the therapeutic group. In both types of groups, disclosing interactions determine that the levels of mutual trust develop over the whole duration of the group experience.

Trust and revelation are interlinked; the one begets the other and, in the same way, the absence of the one precludes the development of the other. Because it so conditions the quality of self-disclosure (and because it is also so genuinely troublesome in everyone's life), trusting is accorded a rather special place in experiential group development.

The leader knows that trust—and even the illusion of trust—is a powerful incentive to committing oneself to the group and to subsequent self-disclosure. On the other hand, the difference between trustworthiness and the illusion of trustworthiness is not trivial, as everyone knows. If the group is to be authentic, how can trust be assumed and not tested? Mutual assurance of trusting is no substitute for personal validation of the other's trustworthiness in life or in the experiential group. If the idea of trust is allowed to prevail as an article of faith ('We shall trust each other fully!'), or if the contrary assertion becomes the group basic assumption ('We cannot possibly trust one another here!'), participants have learned nothing from an otherwise basic human dilemma in which they are ineluctably involved. How can a leader's interventions help the member ascertain for himself another's trustworthiness or his group's trustingness. The approach we suggest queries all assumptions regarding the interactions, with the questions 'How do you know? What's your basis in the facts of this group's life and in your own interactions here for either assumption?'. The inhibitions against openly putting the question to one's self, 'Under what conditions do I dare risk disclosing myself?' or 'What if I risk disclosing my inner feelings to this group? What will happen?' are very strong ones. Our strategy requires that the leader try to reduce these inhibitions and himself periodically restate the query. If leaders allow assumptions rather than demonstrated behaviours to determine conclusions about group behaviour, they have thrown in the 'didactic sponge' in favour of allowing purely intuitive experiencing to determine learning.

Another element in the leader's strategy choices concerning trust is based upon the dynamics of group-shared emotionality. He knows that after buildups of emotional solidarity, group attacks upon minority opinion or action are fuelled by collective conviction of the majority's 'rightness' and the deviate's 'wrongness'. In such cases the leader's query to the group about its own actions will likely elicit intense resentment from his members.

The reader must wonder why is it that when the leader asks a question about the processes involving shared assumptions, for example trust or non-trust, the group reacts so negatively. Why do members get so angry when the leader asks on what basis they are so sure that trust exists, or how the members 'know' that they trust one another? The answer seems to be that shared assumptions of this kind constitute a kind of collective and collusive defensive posture. Bion (1959) first pointed out the defensive utility of such shared (he called them 'basic') assumptions. They are defensive because they preclude examination and thus, as it were, by 'fiat', assure the members of mutual non-agression; they stand for the idea, 'We have *nothing* which separates us. We are totally together!'. To be sure, Bion pointed out a seemingly opposed assumption 'fight–flight' where members shared the assumption that they had only hostility between them. The defensive function is that whether presumably locked in embrace or in conflict, there is no chance of getting caught off guard since the entire aggregate emotionally defines itself by these global shared categories of feeling—as if the worst contingency is to be (as we all indeed *are* most of the time) ambivalent and mixed in our reactions and feelings.

Nobody likes to be stopped in his tracks and challenged, 'Why are you doing what you are doing?'. Especially is this true of a group in active swing. Why? Because one is jolted into awareness of one's participation in the group collusion. Because one's participation has been largely impulsive, one is ashamed as if one were a small child being 'caught in the act'. Suppose, by way of illustration, that the group is aggressively probing one of its members in such manner that the leader concludes that the group is being overly zealous. He decides quickly, having observed the movements in the process, that the effects are likely to be damaging; that the group's own motives are really punitive rather than helpful. The question, 'Why are you doing this to him (her)?', is bound to be resented no matter how it is put because it throws a spotlight on the group's action. Curiously, it is no less resented by the 'victim'. We do not really understand why. We speculate that it may be the implication that he cannot defend himself. Alternatively, one could speculate that a 'sado-masochistic' interaction becomes so invested by the parties involved that the 'outsider' is resented, when the effect is to arrest the processes at the intuitive level and scrutinize them in full awareness.

Leader self-disclosure, pro and con

One of the most compelling elements of any experiential group is its self-conscious equalitarianism. It means that help is expected from everyone, mainly in the form of support but also in terms of forthright feedback. By the same token, so is the disclosure of intimate personal details—particularly in the form of inner feelings and reactions, etc. The self-disclosure aspect of the group is clearly one of the most mutually binding aspects of the group. Everybody knows that if I tell you something very personal about me and you tell me something equally personal about you, it creates a special fellowship that only sharers of confidences can achieve.

To be sure, this can become trite as a kind of adult 'show and tell' with no more enduring significance than the term implies. On the other hand, it can pressage a revolutionary shift in individuals toward a more open approach to others with the mutual facilitating consequences of being more open to them.

It is argued that self-disclosure by leaders models the action for members (Culbert, 1967; Jourard, 1971). The argument continues that self-disclosure by leaders also makes leaders more 'human'—'like us'—and thus eases inter-member communication on an emotional level. On the other hand, as we suggested earlier, leader 'sharing' of his own inner life and history pre-empts the group whenever it occurs. *His* disclosures are more likely to become stable reference points for the members because of the special nature of his relationship to the group. This is not simply another member telling intimate details; it is symbolic authority. As such the leader who tells about *his* inner feelings and experiences evokes reactions that are different in kind and in degree from those elicited by member–member disclosures. The reader will rightly call to mind the parallel in therapy. Transference considerations, i.e. the automatic tendency to view the authority in the light of other authorities from one's past makes every act of the leader potentially 'significant' beyond his intent and exaggerates its prescriptive value in the eyes of his patients.

Is the equalitarian ideal of experiential groups baseless in terms of these considerations and qualifications of leader behaviour? There are ways in which this ideal gains concrete expressions but not via leader 'show and tell'. We would agree that the leader should in fact be disclosing in role; the point of such disclosures is to explain why he does what he does. He is truthful about the reasons for his interventions and the criteria for his strategies—in so far as he can know them himself. This is candid, authentic and, above all, relevant, for it is directly functional for the group to know. At the same time, it doesn't arouse misleading expectations of equally shared intimacy between the leader and his group. The expectation is in any case at least partially transference-based. That is, it reflects the wishful fantasy, the semi-hidden wish to bypass problems with authority instead of openly grappling with them. There can be a strong case made for self-disclosure by the leader when and if he needs to 'get something off his chest' or feels it useful to disclose his personal insight related to the group's present but rooted in his past. We have no objections to feeling disclosures under such circumstances provided the leader bears in mind their potential for influencing the course of group events. Our caveat is intended against an uncritical acceptance of a standard of self-disclosure for leaders.

Earlier on we indicated the outlines of the general problem of leader self-disclosure. Now we have put the problem in the general context of the shared responsibilities of leader and member and the relationship to authority which must arise as an issue in experiential groups. Let us review our points. The leader is in an unavoidably sensitive position in so far as his interventions carry a great deal of insight and influence, no matter how intended. This includes disclosures as well as queries and interpretations. As an authority, he elicits the kind of ambivalent attitudes which makes it difficult for his comments to be viewed objectively. For his part, disclosure—if sincere—must place him in the same inner tumult as members. This means a lessening, however temporary, of objectivity. It means, moreover, a change in status of teacher, guide or healer, which may be useful or damaging. It is for the leader to make an intelligent assessment of these contingencies prior to the event. While one would not wish to restrain the leader to the point of emotional impotence, *he* must be mindful of his assigned task and how his disclosures affect that task.

Group members as the emotionally corrective vehicle

It has again been pointed out in the last section that the experiential group, in its emphasis upon mutual help and self-help values, places high value on equalitarianism. This value has been institutionalized in the therapeutic group. When one stops to think about it, it is an impressive exception to growing professionalism in our society that non-professional persons are deemed able to help one another by producing new insights or in giving mutual support. As important as the equalitarian ideal is in therapeutic groups, it is more explicit in other types of experiential groups, most particularly in the learning group. In the former there is the recourse to the therapist as healer—'in case', perhaps even as dispenser of drugs when needed—with all the emotional dependency implied by such a relationship to the authority–specialist. In the learning groups, on the other hand, the teacher–healer model is less salient, and his functions are to a greater degree interchangeable with those of other members. This means that members are to become skilled in facilitating some of the important processes themselves.

The group experience is the primary vehicle for the therapeutic effect as well as the basic datum from which new learning is generated. The level of exchange in the group and the reactions of peers, communicated to one another, constitute a kind of practice in using the learnings being gleaned from the group experience. As the process develops, one hopes that the leader changes correspondingly from primary interpreter of events to one of facilitator of events among other facilitators as the work of interpretation becomes increasingly the shared responsibility of all the members.

As the group moves beyond its inception phase, the leader must consider how he wants to be perceived. One choice is to remain the 'model', the chief initiator of interactions designed to probe deeper into feelings and reactions (one form could be, as we noted, the first to be a 'self-discloser'. We have already indicated the problems this choice would create for the group.) A second is to act as a resource in-case-of-need. This choice means that the leader intervenes only where the group needs his help in getting out of a non-productive rut or to prevent avoidable pain without redeeming value to an individual. A third is to act as a goad to stimulate the group to continue interactions that falter because of exaggerated fears of the consequences of confrontation.

If the work of helping is to become the group members' and the vehicle of learning should be the group's dynamics, why should the leader intervene in the ways we have indicated? Cannot the group be 'trusted' to work in its own way toward the learning and change goals we have elucidated? The answer is that the dynamics of the group are sometimes both too intense and too opaque for the involved member to fully and accurately perceive all that is going on. Although the group processes are indeed the vehicle of learning and change, aid in steering that vehicle is required on occasion. Management of the process by the leader lends a measure of stability to the process and an increment of security to the otherwise sometimes bewildered participant.

The more effective member behaviour, the less active the leader

It follows from what we have said that we view desirable leadership activity in the experiential group as flexible and sensitive guidance and consultation expended only where necessary and self-restricting in the interests of group self-direction. Our rule of thumb is that for any group of relatively competent persons, that leadership is best which initiates least. As it happens, groups vary sufficiently in composition to warrant tailoring this general policy to fit each case. In general, the relations among group members are shaped by the intelligence of group members, and they are subject as well to the characteristic activity levels represented among the individual members. No blueprint for leader activity can take into account all the possible variations. As examples, a group of eager-to-participate college students will be a far less difficult group to activate than a fearful or ambivalent status-conscious group of teachers. An intergroup experience involving blacks and whites has built in launching pads for interactions different from 'stranger' groups of individuals. The relative defensiveness of members makes a difference. Members who are more 'at home' with their feelings will move more rapidly to intensely emotional levels than will reserved persons. It is our point that notwithstanding habitual levels of activity, shared expectancies of whether one will be guided or one will have to find one's own way will *also* affect the process of the group. It is these expectations which are reinforced or diminished by leaders.

To the degree that group members govern their own processes, if they feel success, they will experience a sense of mastery and gain confidence in their growing interpersonal skills. Conversely, to the degree that the leader instructs, pushes or manoeuvres the group, even though members may feel personally satisfied, the experience is a creation shaped by his efforts. Even when subjective satisfaction is greater in the leader-dominated group, the net value, from the point of view of learning self-governance and achieving personal growth, must be diminished.

As a matter of fact, satisfaction *per se* does not appear to be a reliable guide to the important learning values of these groups. Certainly it is unrelated to the degree of autonomous self-directedness developed by the group. In a way this is puzzling to one who makes the assumption that self-mastery and independence are accompanied by positive emotions. But on deeper thought, there is no reason why this should necessarily be so. Independence in real life is invariably an ambivalent, indeed often a painful process, and it *is* gratifying to be taken care of by authority. It may well be that chrismatic leadership of experiential groups gratifies general dependency longings and thereby is *far* more satisfying than a guidance which does not relieve, but intensifies the demands of self-reliance and adulthood.

How does the leader relate to differences in the *competencies* of members? It is true in experiential groups as elsewhere that competent persons learn more quickly and learn more. They grasp more readily the relationships among members, and they can perceive the dynamics in the group with less effort.

When we consider interpersonal competence, we are not concerned with intelligence *per se* but rather with the intelligent uses of one's social self. This means empathic responsiveness and sensitivities to another's feelings. In this sense, competence in the experiential group must be contrasted with the conventional meaning of defensiveness. Defensiveness is sometimes thought of as a state of dysfunctional obtuseness, of not perceiving what one does not want to perceive about one's self and the less palatable aspects of one's relations with others. Intelligence is not clearly distinguished from the issue of competence although intelligence can be as readily employed to bolster defensiveness as it can serve the interests of candid self-appraisal. Helping the less competent members to follow and absorb value from the group interaction process means to try to reduce the barriers of defensiveness by reassurance, where feasible, to explain in ways that can be acceptable, and to prevent unfruitful pressure from being exerted while defensive barriers are being raised.

The general principle of 'the less need for guidance, the better' having been stated, it is for each leader to assess the needs of the individuals in his group in determining the guidance he will provide. We have communicated our impression that many leaders over-structure and over-interpret, and thus reinforce the members' dependent desires for more and more structuring and guidance. We argue that this only exacerbates the problems of ever-present dependent tendencies by feeding an illusion that they will ultimately be gratified directly. Thus, inadvertently these leaders strengthen and perpetuate the longings for leader charisma and 'miracle-making' instead of the hard work the participant himself must do.

Intervention strategies: how to stimulate groups

Because the leader's position puts him slightly outside the cross-currents of person–person interactions he has the advantage of greater objectivity. We do not claim that he is necessarily more correct in his assessment of the group because of his position. Nevertheless, if he can be objective, and if he can use his experience of having observed many groups, he can stimulate effective movement by his commentary. Sharing his experiential framework with his members in asking well timed questions and in highlighting repeated patterns, he spotlights important learning points for the group. Because one learns by experience in these groups, the leader cannot, without vitiating its impactfulness, teach anything very meaningful about the experience prior to its occurrence. For this reason effective didactic efforts are almost always retrospective. The query—'What's going on now?'—really evokes reconsideration of what *has* been happening *before*. The general question always comprehends particular issues involving personal roles, attitudes, feelings, etc. in which members' personal reactions are involved. That is to say, the question may be general, centring, let us say, on group process or on the parts played by individuals in a specific process. It is detailed in terms of personal likes, dislikes, selective attention, eruptions of feeling, etc. Thus, as a rule, the leader's question elicits responses regarding the global group process *and* the individual–interpersonal reactions that constituted it or are reactive to it.

We have mentioned that the leader makes strategic choices in his 'modelling' of 'desirable' behaviours. It is likely that the leader's forthrightness, humanistic concern and his courage in being willing to tackle difficult issues will be considered by his members as standards for themselves. The same goes for his combativeness, supportiveness and so on. There is nothing inherently wrong with this fact. What is wrong is expecting that members will be able to imitate him. The leader should not see himself as modelling any sort of an 'ideal type' of member. We do not see the evolution of experiential groups as breeding grounds for 'confronters', 'supporters' or 'emoters' as a useful social function. The leader should not set out to *exemplify* such behaviours. Leader interventions are most authentic when they try to clarify factors in interaction, not when they purposefully develop or intensify feelings. The modelling of behaviour that is most effective, role consistent and of enduring value, from our point of view, stresses the 'second look', the reflection on interactions and emphasizes the willingness and patience necessary to consider interactive behaviour and its consequences.

In this connection, we may be rightly considered to emphasize a cognitive element. We see no value in fostering the illusion that impulses are trustworthy. (This does not contradict our position that participants should generally be in closer touch with their feelings. In experiential groups a cognitive–affective balance is important. In an explicitly therapeutic group this balance is also desirable but secondary to the repairative needs of the clientele.) The modelling of 'reconsideration' and 'reflection' is not intended to reinforce obsessiveness, but rather to encourage exploring the meanings and the consequences of feelings and actions based on them. The leader makes it explicit that he is modelling group inquiry, and that members should be themselves asking the questions that he asks of them. The query, 'What's going on in the group now?' should be treated as a common obligation of all the members. A challenge by the leader intends to provoke 'risk-taking' responses. Naturally challenges should be earliest used with those most likely to respond affirmatively to them. For example, the member who criticizes the process as being too slow or too 'boring' is urged to try to change it by 'doing something' about it. The emotions generated by this sort of challenge are typically mixed. There is resentment and the complainant feels at first 'put down' by this confrontation by the leader. If, however, the challenge is made in good faith (and good humour!) one or another participant is likely to take it up sooner or later and try to do something about the course of events in the group rather than just gripe about them. Success in changing the course is then more likely to occur.

The role of the leader in body-awareness techniques

The rationale for this added feature may be briefly recapitulated: Western industrialized society with its attendant processes of urbanization and high mobility and consequent 'anomie' produces people who are alienated from one another, even from their own bodies. Bodily tensions reflect the 'uptightness' experienced by many people. The person who would be freed up emotionally to interact gratifyingly with his fellows must first be disinhibited from bodily tensions. It is up to the leader to initiate activities designed to accomplish this disinhibition. Since the encounter approach aims toward fuller emotional expressiveness this idea of bodily disinhibition is readily accommodated.

The Encounter tradition draws directly from the body-awareness therapies of Wilhelm Reich (1949), Alexander Lowen (1967) and Gestalt awareness taught by Fritz Perls (1951). The guiding assumption of all three points of view is that body sensations and emotional feelings are mutually contingent. In these therapies either the leader explicitly guides the patient through specific body exercises or reacts with interpretative queries to postures, small movements, glances, etc. There are many forms of exercises or movements—far too many to detail here (several handbooks of such exercises are now available). Many are aimed at amplifying conflict feelings or dramatizing combative relations. Thus a struggle for dominance or mastery may be acted out through stylized forms of fighting, e.g. 'Indian wrestling'. For example, fears and ambivalence about being included or excluded are dramatized by a member's efforts to break into a circle of comembers. They 'create' a 'barrier' by linking arms in order to intensify the emotionality of the event so as to give the 'joiner' a feel for the necessary struggle involved and the inner victory of becoming included (thus reinforcing the satisfaction of making it as one of the group!). Falling backward into the (hopefully!) open and receptive arms of coparticipants is an exercise to represent practice in gaining confidence in and relying on others. Similarly a 'trust-walk' (being led about while blindfolded and thus utterly dependent upon one's guides) is used to train a capacity for vesting trust in others.

Such 'exercises'—some with words, most without, are intended (aside from their entertainment value) to produce learning and therapeutic change. All are intended to disinhibit the 'uptight', heighten awareness of one's feelings or to train one in emotional expression.

The increasing uses of non-verbal body-awareness techniques in experiential groups raise some fundamental questions. For one thing their use adds a number of relatively unknown qualities to the group experience. A good deal more is known about verbal than about non-verbal interactions. For another thing, the introduction of body-awareness training into experiential groups must adversely affect the principle of self-direction in experiential groups. One might also question the emotional freedom which is engineered through standardized emotional experiences. But our main focus in this chapter is on the leader function. How can any leader avoid becoming a 'social' director when body-awareness activities are routinely introduced in experiential groups? In point of fact the uses of body-awareness exercises require that participants be even more than customarily dependent upon the guidance of the leader.

The associated likelihood of increasing manifestations of leader charisma seems to us to pose a major problem in that it contradicts the ostensible aims of most experiential groups. In the areas of body-awareness training specifically and non-verbal techniques, more generally, the gaps of expertise between member and leader and lack of member competence virtually ensures the development of 'master–disciple' rather than equalitarian relationships.

Another problem in, the use of body-awareness exercises in experiential groups is one we have alluded to previously, i.e., the dangers in the 'standardization' of emotional experience. This, it seems to us runs counter to the idea of individual self-regulation and self-responsibility. We believe it is a leader's function to reinforce the uniqueness of individual emotional experience and to prevent the experiential group becoming a vehicle for evocation of standardized emotional states, clearly a perversion of the experiential group idea.

We reiterate a point made earlier. The effectiveness of experiential groups for learning and therapeutic change is probably vitiated by the degree to which the groups take on an exotic ambience. It may be that body awareness, valuable in its own right, and experiential groups concerned with interpersonal relationships are simply non-related activities and are each best served in separate contexts.

The problem of professional-trained–paid leadership

The use of professional paid leadership instead of volunteer leaders has been challenged from time to time. A critical view of the professional is a natural consequence of the point of view which emphasizes the group *qua* group as the psycho-active therapeutic change and learning agent. If members are real helpers for one another, so the argument goes, the professional leader is at best an expensive luxury and perhaps even a hindrance to self-help development. From time to time in recent years some psychologists have put searching question regarding the automatic positive assumptions about professionalism, even in the therapist role (Mowrer, 1964). Specifically, Mowrer argued that a collusive conspiracy between paid therapist and paying client too readily absolved the latter of guilt in the absence of appropriate expiation. He also emphasized the moral equivocalness inherent in the strong influence position of therapists *vis-a-vis* their clients.

The problem is even more acute in experiential groups where learning albeit at the levels of expressiveness and emotional reactions is more apt to be the aim than correction or repair. Ideological aspects are more salient in experiential groups than in explicitly therapeutic ones. The leader's views of the 'good life', his ideas of desirable behaviour, and his opinions about appropriate levels of candour and emotionality all play some part in the way he perceives his function. Obviously, his special role carries with it a certain potency for influence. The current criticism of 'paid' group leaders is probably less rooted in fears of mishandling or incompetence than in anxieties about the influences of therapists' ideological–political–social values on group members' behaviour.

But one could argue in a more general way; if what impels change is the group itself, why give up its direction to a paid professional?

This argument has been most salient in political action groups which employ an experiential group format. Examples are various women's rights groups and drug-abuse groups. They are also naturally concerned about outsiders' influence on their movements. When these movements do employ professional leadership such as in 'consciousness-raising' groups, the leaders are usually themselves products of the movements and subscribe to their basic political–social tenets. It is noteworthy that activist organizations reveal a common antagonism to professional intermediaries. It is a related fact that they are also, in general, committed to shared rather than specialized leadership for many political action and social functions.

Another argument against professional leadership of experiential groups is that it has been so variable in demonstrated competence and in standards of practice. Some very experienced professionals proved to be so reckless as to induce psychological distress in 7–10% of Encounter group participants (Lieberman *et al.*, 1973). On the other hand, realistic assessment compels us to recognize that it is in the nature of groups to develop hierarchies of influence and power. No group's ideology obviates the group dynamics of competition for influence. Regardless of purpose or doctrinal commonalities, members complete with one another. Since there *will* emerge leadership in groups in any event, the question is whether one can provide a kind of leadership which is truly professional, i.e., from which one gets responsible performance for those groups needing or wanting it.

Let us consider some reasons for providing a leader. The leader should provide security against injury to any group member. Our experience suggests that active involvement in the group makes it difficult for members to be conscious of all that goes on at a given point in time. Learning to keep it all in mind is in fact one of the goals of the group. The fact is that members are bound to be uncertain about their own perceptions of the group's social reality. We have already mentioned one way members initially deal with this troubling ambiguity. They move rapidly to institutionalize 'trust' or 'distrust'.

A tradition has emerged over the past three decades that an experiential group is basically supportive. Moreover this support is presumed to be both spontaneous and generous. There is actually little evidence for this idea of the group supportive impulse. It is true that groups tread cautiously when there *is* a sense of problematic relating. However, efforts to involve each other are notoriously clumsy. The aggregate is a poor distinguisher between persons who *are* able to pace themselves or those best left to their own tempos as contrasted to those who require nudging. Depending upon group composition, groups may act sensitively or like the proverbial 'bulls in china shops' when they inquire as to why one person is silent and why another talks endlessly. Once a member is involved in exploration of 'style' reactions with the group, his group may have difficulty knowing how to work with him, how far to go and when 'enough is enough'.

The good leader is able to monitor the stress that members can tolerate from his vantage point of professional detachment. From the same position he assesses whether a particular communication is progressing usefully. He bears in mind those diagnostic criteria which help him estimate whether the member is able to assimilate the reactions he receives in a constructive way.

The group should have as broad a basis as possible for relating to each member. Few persons respond well to a challenge to 'start talking'. Many are justifiably wary of the seductive invitation. 'I'd really like to get to know you'. Such 'come on's' prove too often to be ruses for putting one 'on the spot'. The leader encourages maximal participation but keeps the group from too much pushing of a person beyond the level of participation he is willing to try.

Earlier on we discussed the question of leader disclosure. It is clear that although leaders model frankness and authenticity, if they begin to use the group to resolve their own personal problems, the group experience will be overly influenced, if not overwhelmed by their problems. Where leader self-disclosure is a prominent feature of experiential groups, the assumption is that it provides an example of 'openness'. As we indicated, such 'standardized' 'self-disclosure' becomes increasingly less authentic as it is repeated. Leaders should indeed model frankness but his frankness should be role-related, rooted in leader tasks. Concretely, this means that the leader be as candid as possible about reasons for his interventions in the group, not about details of his personal life.

How may the leader help the group establish a degree of candour that is functional in relationships? Every relationship has forms of mutual accommodation, and some mutually reassuring forms are non-candid, i.e. 'polite' exchanges, friendly overtures, etc. The experiential group also starts out with communication of this type. But it is the aim of the experiential group to try for a much higher level of candour because of the positive relationship between candour, self-investigation and growth. In our experience, a group seeks a tolerable rather than an optimal level of candour. Increasing levels come about only over time and on the basis of 'test' interactions. They do not result without pain; however, responsible leaders try to see to it that the pain should not be gratuitous; i.e. that the learning should be worth the discomfort.

If a member details his private fantasies beyond norms adopted by the group as a whole, is this evidence of increasing (and desirable) candour? It could be evidence of deepening authenticity, but it could also represent merely self-indulgent exhibitionism. It is in sorting out the levels, meanings and the veracities of meta-communication that members most need help from their leader. It is in sorting out the meta-messages, i.e. 'What do I want to say to them (him) (her) about me?', 'What are they saying about us, about me?', 'How do I react to what he says?' that leaders can be most helpful. If members perceive such 'meta-messages' on their own, so much the better; if not, the leader's help enables them to recognize and more readily interpret them.

How should the leader deal with 'passive' individuals, i.e. those who 'lay back' or who seem to want something to 'happen' to them but through no effort of their own. In the ideal circumstance the group is sufficiently self-regulating so that passive members are energized by more active ones. But few groups are ideal in composition. The consequence is that the leader joins in the stimulation of passive members at least to see whether and how much can be done. The ever-present risk is in doing too much, 'taking over' and doing for the individual member what all the members should be trying to do for one another.

Co-leadership and its effects on the experiential group

Co-leadership precludes the kind of closeness and identification between a group and its leader that solo leadership generates. Co-leaders are perceived as competitors (which in some sense they are), and they constitute a brake upon transference developments in experiential groups. Consequently, if one's view is that important developments in the experiential group are propelled by transference reactions—say, for example, the evocation of compulsively critical attitudes to authority—this point is a disadvantage for joint leadership. Finally, dependency expressions are attenuated in the same manner as are transference reactions. When the image of authority is itself divided, dependent strivings are not as likely to be vested in the leaders.

Having listed a number of drawbacks, why do we nevertheless suggest that co-leadership is a useful leadership form in experiential groups? One reason is that the experiential group which is co-led presents more opportunities to focus on relations to authority. One has more frequent opportunities to experience and reflect on reactions to two leaders who do in fact evoke different reactions. The possibilities of 'objectifying' leader images are obviously greater where there are in fact alternative leadership positions. As for the leaders themselves, they may disagree with each other on occasion. Multiple points of view are a realistic reflection of the real society where there are competing rather than monolithic views. (Leaders who agree not to disagree, who thus present a prearranged unanimity, actually present a poor situation for learning.)

There is yet another valuable factor in co-leadership, especially for learning groups where the aim is to explore as fully as possible the various facets of relationships with authorities. The complimentarity of the leader function permits the two leaders to be differentially emotionally engaged *in* the group process *with* the group members. It thus becomes possible for the group to gain insights into its relationships to the one with the aid of the other and vice versa. (This point incidentally indirectly affirms the difficulty participants and leader have in attaining a mutually objective view of one another; but this is also a great part of that irritating ambiguity which impels so much of the learning process in the first place!) These considerations make co-leadership especially important as a leader-training technique and for the experience of students of group processes.

Balancing the group and the person

The productiveness of any group is dependent upon some optimal balance between cooperative and competitive interactions within it. The leader is concerned to facilitate the dialectic process between harmony and competition to make sure it does not miscarry into excessive supportive attitudes on the one hand or extremes of competitiveness on the other.

A patient in a therapeutic group is understandably indifferent to group dynamics. However, the group process is the psycho-active ingredient in group therapy just as it is in other types of experiential group. They all potentiate the merging of communitarian and individualistic impulses. Managing the most useful balance of these factors is the leader's hardest task. It is not difficult to focus on the dyadic or person–group relations. Indeed, members often take on one after another on individual feedback without establishing a group 'data base' for the feedback they give one another. In fact, those members who try to have the group review its basis for feedback find that their initiatives are likely to be rejected. It requires the leader's intervention to initiate such a review. This frequently results in an oscillation between group and person focus. If the members get stuck over-long in global issues of procedures and structure, the leader suggests exploring the parts played by individuals in creating the particular structure. If the focus lingers too long in individuals, the leader queries the group process. His strategy is thus aimed at correcting a one-sided concentration on group or person.

It takes independence and some courage to 'insist' that members consider behaviour when they angrily object. As we indicated above, members bridle at the question, 'What is going on in the group at this moment, and what led up to it?'. They would rather continue giving feedback, a far more gratifying aspect of experiential groups. The leader has the often unpleasant obligation to keep the group on the move whenever it gets too 'comfortable' or perseverates in an unproductive pattern of interaction.

Qualifications of leaders

We have seen that the primary mediator of interactions in any type of experiential group is the leader, be he experienced or novice, wise or foolish. This fact would seem to demand a high quality of professional preparation. The clarification of theoretical issues and the evaluation of group forms may take years, but we can begin at once to insist on better standards of practice and preparation. Exotic and attention-catching practices are partly a response to popular pressures, and thus, more than anything else, opportunistic gestures to the marketplace. Since rigorous standards of practice have not yet been sufficiently well established and because there is a relatively laissez-faire attitude toward qualification, many essentially unqualified persons now conduct group experiences. Practising a helping role in an experiential group awakens in many people the desire to continue in a helping role beyond the group's termination; in some it arouses the aspiration to take on the leader role as a permanent one. Enthusiasm for the helping role is a natural consequence of learning to listen better to others, experiencing empathy oneself and having the satisfaction of giving support effectively. Participants are naturally attracted to the leader function that embodies such experiences. A talented participant should be encouraged to seek higher levels of preparation, but he must be dissuaded from assuming a function for which he is inadequately prepared, no matter how much native skill he may have. For the leader's training we suggest what we believe to be desirable.

A. *Leader-investigators*

In the category of leader-investigators we include persons who approach experiential group practice from fields broadly designated as education, health or social sciences. Ordinarily they are specialists in such disciplines as psychology, psychiatry or intergroup relations, and hold advanced degrees. They should be able to contribute conceptually or through research to our knowledge about processes and interactions, and they should participate in the preparation of group leaders.

B. *Leaders*

Leaders should have a background in personality theory, psychopathology and group dynamics, including extensive supervised practice, centred in any of a variety of disciplines and fields. Although there could be exceptions, they should in general hold the equivalent of a master's degree. If they lack adequate background in the areas specified, they should be required to take relevant courses. These individuals may practise in many settings.

Before a person in either category functions as a leader, he should have a three-year sequence of practical experiences in something like the following order:

(1) Participate as a member in at least two groups conducted at the highest possible level.

(2) Observe group meetings and meet after sessions with their leaders to discuss the interactions of members and other processes. This should be done with at least five groups.

(3) Co-lead five groups with experienced leaders.

(4) Lead five groups as sole leader but be consulted in postgroup sessions for the purpose of monitoring his functioning in the leader role.

(5) Have psychotherapy or some equivalent individual experiential self-study. (A group experience, in this sense, is not the equivalent.)

(6) Be evaluated by experienced, well-qualified leaders, who focus on his general fitness of character, background and preparation and review with care evaluations and recommendations that others make about him.

(7) Keep his functions as a leader refreshed by local seminars, periodic supervision and emphasis on the ethics of the leader function.

234

Following such guidelines as these does not resolve all the problems that confront the experiential group movement, but they reduce poor practices and provide some direction for aspiring group leaders. They also reassure the public that standards and checks do indeed exist.

Summary

This chapter has discussed the mix of qualities and functions that emerges as the leadership role in experiential groups. It is certain that the rapid change we see in current group forms will stimulate many types of group leadership in the future. To the extent that the principles of experiential group processes remain constant, however, the issues we have raised are bound to continue to occupy the attention of practitioners, consumers and researchers. If experiential groups have come to be an enduring part of the social scene, so have the questions regarding competent leadership skills and good leadership practices.

References

Benne, K. D. (1964) 'History of the T-group in the laboratory setting.' In L. P. Bradford, J. R. Gibb, and K. D. Benne (Eds.), *T-Group Theory and Laboratory*. New York: John Wiley and Sons, 80–135.

Bion, W. R. (1959) *Experiences in Groups*. New York: Basic Books.

Culbert, S. A. (1967) 'The interpersonal process of self disclosure: It takes two to see one.' *In Explorations in Applied Behavioral Science*. Vol. 3. New York: Renaissance Editors.

Jourard, S. M. (1971) *The Transparent Self: Self Disclosure and Well Being*. Princeton: Van Nostrand.

Lieberman, M. A., I. D. Yalom and M. B. Miles (1973) *Encounter groups: First facts*. New York: Basic Books.

Lowen, A. (1967) *Betrayal of the Body*. New York: Macmillan.

Mowrer, O. H. (1964) *The New Group Therapy*. Princeton: Van Nostrand.

Perls, F. S., R. F. Hefferline and P. Goodman (1951) *Gestalt Therapy*. New York: Julian Press.

Reich, W. (1949) *Character analysis*. New York: Argone Institute Press.

Schaffer, J. B. P. and M. D. Galinsky (1974) *Models of Group Therapy and Sensitivity Training*. Englewood Cliffs, N. J.: Prentice-Hall.

Chapter 10

Winners, Losers and the Search for Equality in Groups

Richard D. Mann

University of Michigan

There is something which happens in the early stages of many new groups which I and my fellow group members find confusing and even disappointing. The group starts out with a presumption of equality, and before long it has become a jousting tourney, an elimination match. This fellow over here seems to have become the one who awards more or less points to each comment. These nice people over here look like they may never venture forth again. The person who has now left his/her chair (as it were) and is expansively pacing back and forth in the centre of the group looks suddenly unstoppable—the early winner. Scapegoats are set up, and then knocked off. The early losers emerge, creating or having created for them the appropriate images of timidity, naiveté or chronic discouragement about their fate in groups.

It isn't really happening, of course. It only seems that way to me and to some others. What's so disappointing is how familiar it all seems, and it wasn't supposed to work out this way. This was supposed to be a new group, a new start. We were going to do it all right, and yet here we are with victors and vanquished. Is this something we can understand better and do something about? Could a decent theory about winning and losing have an impact on those developments? Could a theory, once internalized, prevent, slow down, or even reverse the drift toward win–lose relationships in groups?

The history of my experience with 'theory' is complicated, and even if it serves only to clarify the stance from which I would attempt to build a theory, perhaps that is reason enough to say a few words about what a theory, for me, is and is not. I do keep looking around for ideas which will relieve some of the confusion I experience in a new group. And I do (occasionally) feel the urge to share a clarifying thought or two. But these exchanges of clarity and insight, if they proceed via the path of theory at all, seem to demonstrate primarily my hunger for useful metaphor, my pleasure at experiencing new connections and my eagerness to do better than before. The game of metaphor adds so much to life: it rescues us from frozen perspectives, it provides us with gifts to give. But what does it have to do with theory?

One way in which theories differ is whether the operative metaphor reduces humankind to an inanimate state. The brain is a *tabula rasa*, a switchboard, a computer. Human interaction involves feedback loops or is sort of like the collision of steel spheres of differing mass and velocity. Some people seem delighted when the operative metaphors convey the rigour of the natural sciences, where the formulations have such seemingly desirable traits as operational clarity, parsimony and testability. But my problem is that when I am actually in a group, trying to grasp what in the world is happening, these are about the last metaphors to enter my head. So I am not tempted to seek out or to formulate metaphors of the 'People are sort of like things' variety.

Another way in which theories differ is whether they are cast in the predictive or fateful mode. For example, 'People (rats) (earthworms?) seek the shortest path between two points (ABC < ADC).' I am as able as the next person to test out this sort of theory. Yes, I do seek the shortest path. More when I'm in a hurry; less when path ADC leads by the waterfall; even less when I'm trying to avoid the mob scene on path ABC. Of course the formulator of the theory knows this too, and all that is meant is 'other things being equal' or 'in the absence of other factors'. But that's the whole issue really, and the predictive mode is, at best, merely a summary statement that accounts for all the times people are in a hurry, don't have time for a waterfall and don't care if there's a mob on the path. If the predictive mode would always have us mumbling to ourselves that there may be other factors, and if there always *are* lots of other factors, then maybe it would be easier on us all if we just said, 'Look, this is one way it can all work out, and here's the best sense I can make of it.'

To be a bit more specific, I don't take Bion (1959) to be saying that his theory would be disproved if a group failed to elevate him to the status of priest or magician. It's just that when they do, they do. Bion's theory, if it is proper to call it a theory, turns out to be a metaphor of great complexity and power. It evokes some of the most primitive, ubiquitous and condensed group phenomena in our culture: the family, the army, the church, dark mysteries and the hope for a messiah. To read Bion is to replace one's boredom and impatience in a newly developing group with an almost unbearable sense of the high drama lurking behind the apparent surface of events. Or so it was for me a dozen years ago. If that is theory, then despite its imprecise, untestable features theory can serve as the conveyor belt for useful meanings and metaphors. Theory can call our attention to the possible, loosen our fixed imagery, stir the depths of our own not yet conscious associations, and that, I would argue, is a worthy addition to the lives of people in groups.

Some theory is designed mainly to support and further the effort to change something. Freud was not rooting for men to kill their fathers, marry their mothers and then blind themselves after they discovered what had happened. He was trying to capture the recurrent, painful dramas of at least some of his male patients. The theory was not a prediction; it was an adjunct to the pressing business of trying to help people grasp their own histories and reshape their not too distant future. The Oedipus theory was Freud's response to a particular sampling of human pain and disability; it was an offering, a metaphor. Freud's mode of sharing insight calls to mind Leonard Cohen's gentle lines: 'I've been where you're hanging, I think I can see how you're pinned.' Human beings are constantly passing around explanations of why something isn't going quite right: 'Maybe it's something you ate'; 'Maybe it has to do with your child-hood'; and so forth and so on.

We seek explanations. Sometimes it's just idle curiosity which drives us. Sometimes it's the distress of people we are personally (and/or professionally) bound to care about. And then there are the times when we seek to alleviate our own pain. I seek to understand certain facets of human interaction because they are the recurrent themes of my life, my subculture and my time. I wasn't the only victim, but I can still hear those charming fifteen-year-olds plotting to sacrifice me to the moon god. I wasn't the only one laughing at the plight of my classmate with the hare-lip and the awkward speech. But these and thousands more vignettes are the root cause of my current preoccupation with why groups get so entwined in patterns of winning and losing. From the dormitory of long ago to the classroom of today, from my own pain to the distress of those I now 'teach' about group processes, the recurrent themes which absorb my interest lead me to try to understand, and to change, how groups often turn out.

I seek in each new group, and in my ruminations about all the old ones, a system of ideas, explanations and meanings because if we don't understand why these things keep happening, then they will probably happen over and over again. My need for a useful theory is bound up with the following questions: What does it mean that so many group members experience a painful kind of losing, while others experience a painful kind of winning, and still others find that the whole win–lose modality blocks their involvement in the group and offers them an either/or in which neither winning nor losing holds much appeal? Can I, as a professional or simply as the one with experience and concern in this area, understand how I contribute to this winning and losing, and can I alleviate the distress which such win–lose scenes cause in me and in others? And, then too, must these contributions to change remain intuitive, particular and unsystematic, or can I through writing and talking share the insight which prompts the intervention, thereby connecting with people I've never met and causing them to add their insights to a collaborative effort at understanding and change?

We need to be somewhat clear about which kinds of groups are likely to spawn the kinds of win/lose development I wish to describe and understand. The groups to which I will refer most specifically are groups where: (1) the people didn't know each other beforehand, (2) there is something in the initial contract which permits the group to talk about or try to work out difficulties, (3) there is relatively little which absolutely must be done by a certain deadline, no urgent or prescribed task. These stipulations fit some new roommate situations, some staff relations, some social groups, and the usual sort of self-analytic group found in group therapy, T-groups and the classroom groups

I have worked in for twenty-two years. Much of the fluidity of these groups is absent, or even devalued, when the group has a long past to preserve or when it is assumed that there is no time for feelings and nothing to be gained by draining energy away from the concrete task at hand.

It's not that stable or formally organized groups know little of the pain of winning and the pain of losing. It's more that the pain appears to be unalterable, or else any expression of that pain is rejected as a distraction, as cry-babying and soft, or as demanding that the group pay attention to what is obviously a personal problem best kept to oneself.

The kind of classroom group where I have learned the most has already received a good deal of attention in the group literature. Slater (1966), Mills (1964), Bales (1970), Dunphy (1968), Gibbard (1969), Hartman (1969), Ringwald (1974), Winter (1974), and Mann (1967) have all either taught or been students (or both) in the kind of 'group course' (at Harvard, Michigan, Brandeis and Wesleyan) to which I refer. Tempting as it is to think one has been a participant in Everygroup, I recognize that much of what I have learned has the stamp of these particular groups. Since I intend to keep on working in this setting, I can willingly suspend my recurrent wish to glimpse the universal in favour of a little clarity about my own work and preferred setting. But anyone not familiar with these sorts of groups needs to know some of their particularities, the better to sense what probably would not happen under rather different circumstances.

The students, mostly undergraduates, who are drawn to these courses may know only the course title, usually some variant of Analysis of Interpersonal Behaviour. More often they are warned in preregistration material not to expect lectures on the topic but to expect, instead, to learn about group processes by participating in and observing the development of their own group. Some course descriptions cover the other flank as well, alerting the prospective student that this group is not a reasonable setting in which to pursue his or her desire for psychotherapy. This latter warning has its constricting consequences, but it seems to survive, perhaps as a gesture of appeasement to the clinicians who fear a proliferation of wild or amateurish bungling within their 'territory'. Many students arrive at the urging of their friends. The course is often deemed 'unique', 'pretty heavy' and 'a real experience', and throughout the underground rumour network there are some messages which are congruent with the intentions of the instructors: that participation in the group might be a useful way to learn about group process and interpersonal relations. In most settings the student must apply, and the odds of getting in are usually only one in two or three. But upon arriving in the group room for the first time most participants seem to have only the vaguest of ideas about what will happen, what is supposed to happen, and how it all will work out for them as individuals.

What does happen? What theory or theories might we construct which will both describe and explain the way these groups develop? Can we be more explicit about exactly what we mean by winning and losing?

Since any description of the phenomenon of winning and losing is simultaneously a sketch of the contours of the theory being advanced, I need to pause just briefly before presenting the first of three theory-descriptions. The first might be called a peer group psychodrama theory, and it approaches the phenomena of winning and losing as derived or derivable from the nature of peer-relations. The first theory adopts the stance common to much of the psychoanalytic literature, most of the work on small groups observed through a one-way glass, and most of the work on school children. As with the whole array of patients, groups and classrooms studied from roughly this stance, the focus is on what we can learn about the objects of our scrutiny: the members of the group who are viewed as responsible for the phenomena of winning and losing. The focus of this theory, as with Freud's case studies or Slater's work in *Microcosm*, is on the motives and prior history of the people whose behaviour is fascinating but as yet poorly understood. The leader, or the analyst in other such studies, is more symbol than substance, more the recipient of distorted, transference-like projections than a full participant. The questions which guide this first theory are relatively constant: What is it that makes a group of relative strangers create an interpersonal scene so full of winning and losing? How does it get started? How does it evolve? How does it all end?

Without further preamble, then, we can examine the peer-group theory of winning and losing. The drama begins as with any new, unformed relationship. All the group members in the first moments seem pretty much on balance but somewhat tentative in their self-assertions, unsure of whether this or that other person will turn out to be an ally or not. In the first session or two of a new group there is often a sense that the conversation is a kind of collective monologue. People want to get into the conversation, but it's clear that each new speaker has just barely heard the speaker who went before. Scene one is filled with the process of sizing up the other strangers. The evolving relationships are still quite blurred and indistinct. And in contrast to most of the scenes which will follow it is a time when the primary expectation is of equality of gain for all, a hope (if not a firm belief) that everyone will or can get what he/ she wants. Still suppressed or unrediscovered is the nub of future scenes: that the satisfaction of one may come at the expense of the dissatisfaction of another, that there may well be winners and losers.

Where does the idea of winners and losers come from? How does it intrude into the new relationship? Obviously this idea is part of the baggage each group member brings along from previous groups, from families, from school days. For some group members the idea that there will be winners and losers is so strong that they simply can't stand the suspense. They may precipitate the show-down through self-assertion and challenge, through self-deprication, or simply by noting some flagrant example of early differentiation—but certainly one factor in the emergence of a win–lose situation is that this is the outcome many expect and thus create. There's no monopoly on who sets out to create this scene. Sometimes it takes the form of a first-strike assault: letting it be known that one has had lots of experience in groups like this, letting it be known that one usually wins, or needing to point out how dumb, nervous or inept somebody has been in the group. Sometimes it takes the form of self-directed ridicule: 'Don't mind me. I'm just a silly, incompetent person. I usually lose.' Like the kid who makes a joke out of coming in last in the race, the self-announced loser adds to the common awareness that before long there may be a whole lot of winning and losing going on.

The possible precursors of what may eventually become a more general pattern of organized conflict emerge very early. The first sharp retort, the first collision can seem terribly important, followed as it often is by a collective gasp and then an awkward silence. A clear, unambiguous disagreement, especially if there is some element of put-down in it, can become the big event of an early session. People are going around and just saying a few words about themselves. One young woman says she's planning to be a police officer. The tension-level rises perceptibly, and suddenly the tentative questionning which others had received is replaced by expressions of disbelief and opposition. The pressure mounts and then drops conspicuously as peace-makers rush in to help the group move on to the next person. But the seeds are sown. In the next session or two during a lull in the conversation someone returns to the topic so avoided before: 'Say, I was thinking, did you really say you were going to be a cop?' 'Yeah, I did. I was wondering if anyone was going to really react to that.' And the way is clear for a real collision. The opportunity presents itself for quite a few people to unload on cops, on why you can't work within the system, on racism and so on.

We would miss the whole point of this scene if we only focused on overt behaviour. Of even greater importance in the long run is the gradual sharpening of impressions, the gradual accumulation of evaluative assessments still very much unspoken and even unconscious. As the early data begin to accumulate, it is clear that that guy over there is strikingly attractive, that that other girl is probably a whole lot smarter than everyone in the group, and so on. As the conversation progresses, the sizing up process begins to stabilize. For each group member there may be those who seem to have more and those who seem to have less of whatever matters to that person. Feelings of respect, awe, jealousy and resentment are, if not fully formed, at least beginning to emerge from the early interactions. On the basis of still very minimal cues, and with a strong push from those confusions of present and past which are sometimes called transference relationships, feelings of equality and mutuality begin to tilt over to one side or the other. The sense that one will maybe, or surely, emerge a winner or a loser relative to him, her, her, him and so on gradually intrudes on the consciousness of many if not all group members.

Those first few encounters in which it seems that the whole accumulated tension of the new group gets focused on one remark or on one person say a great deal to the group members. They say: 'Watch out.' Watch out that you don't get clobbered. But they also say watch out that you don't get into the lynch mob which almost seemed to get organized. And they say, more diffusely, watch out that you don't get in over your head. Better be careful. Confusion, a numb blankness, disorientation—these states of mind seem more likely to follow the first encounters than any clear antagonisms.

The explosion of doubts, scornful appraisals, confused impressions, attractions and repulsions of surprising intensity—these are the stuff of the early moments of the new relationship forming in the new group. To put this in context, it must be added that we have ignored the vast number of more benign and usual reactions. We have not chronicled the less intense reactions: 'People here seem nice.' 'I'm going to like this group and everyone in it.' 'I'm O.K.' To emphasize the more intense and the more disquieting feelings is not to deny the validity of the bland or calm reactions of some group members. We are, after all, trying to understand the evolution of only one of many outcomes in new groups: the win–lose relationship.

To return to this pursuit, then, we are at a critical juncture. The accumulating impressions and doubts are creating pressure for a more momentous step than simply the process of sizing up others. For the moment at least, the new group begins to raise questions which are more global and which extend into the past and onto the future.

It is at this point in the evolving drama that the first tentative impressions and implicit comparisons are drawn, like bubbles in a whirlpool, into a more centralized and seemingly coherent pattern. The centre of the pattern varies infinitely but we can certainly distinguish between one, the depressive pattern of self-deprecation and impending defeat and, another, the manic or euphoric pattern of the success, the winner. This crucial juncture in which some relationships, or all, are seen as taking on a larger meaning is precisely the moment of altered time perspective. Into the emerging pattern are added memories and conclusions drawn from past relationships. And added in as well are predictions, fantasies of how things will probably go in this or that new relationship.

The reason why this emerging pattern is so much more than simply a cognitive accumulation of cues and 'feed-back' in the actual situation is that each person walks into any new group with a unique set of memories, long-harboured wishes and the nucleus of a self-concept which weighs heavily on the meanings given to each new event. Given the ambiguity of the new situation and the tension which this ambiguity can create, it is not surprising that the human mind creates and recreates the two simplified patterns we sometimes label depressive and manic or, more simply, disheartened and euphoric.

Depression takes many forms. A resigned and empty dread of what is to come is but the starkest of its many forms. In the new group, one often learns from group members' later retrospection that the first few sessions were filled with portents of humiliation. But a more moderate and widespread expression of the depressive pattern involves what might be called the loss of nerve. It happens so subtlely and so quickly that it seems to defy careful analysis. I refer here to a form of interpersonal flinch. Credentials are compared, willingnesses to express aggression are matched, or the nerve to press in and assert one's commitment to closeness is at issue, and suddenly one participant veers off. The arm-wrestling is terminated by what seems almost like resignation and deliberate collapse. The retreat is on. What for an army is called a sudden drop in morale is paralleled for an individual by a precipitous drop in self-confidence. If only momentarily, the ghosts of failures past fuse with the spectres of humiliations future, and the present appears to be of a piece with the depressive pattern which each group member already knows well.

For others the data come up looking very different indeed. Out of the swirling ambiguity of the early group some people find evidence for feeling that almost by magic or without opposition or effort there seem to be no real competitors, no one in the group as strong or as 'cool' or as intelligent or whatever forms the basis of 'success' for each person. The emerging pattern seemingly gathers in more and more confirming evidence: semi-deliberate challenges to the self-assurance of this or that other are met with confused retreat or anxious deference, surrender. The pattern's 'validity' seems enhanced. One can do no wrong. One struts up and down, daring anyone to match wits or strength—no takers. Conversations built more around tender and mutual expressions of uncertainty can be disrupted by statements of utter self-confidence or by recounting past glories. The 'others', seemingly intimidated (awed?), fade back. The strong survive. Or so it seems. Eyes are averted, their owners not daring to contend with such heavy competition. Giggles and forced smiles express the deference of more and more of the others. Fantasies of having become the *ubermensch*, the queen bee, the prima donna and/or the heavy abound in the manic construction of reality. It is one way to make sense out of the data generated by developing group relations.

We need to appreciate some of the reasons why some people are alarmed at the evidence or prospect of victory. The prospects facing the person singled out as the leader include a rise in resentment, jealously and a string of efforts to cut the person down to size. Small wonder that nominations for informal leader, especially early in the group, are turned away with denials and protestations. There is an unsteady boundary between being seen as leader and being seen as domineering, power-hungry, etc. or between being seen as attractive and being seen as narcissistic and demanding of attention or enthralment. Better, people seem to say, to lay low until one's centrality or attraction for others can be established without great risk of being attacked for one's success. Thus the early moments of group formation are filled with that perplexing oscillation back and forth, up and down, as group members try to find a safe, middle range of status within which to operate.

To recapitulate the major events of this scene, we have moved from the ambiguities of the new relationships to a stage where depressive constructions of reality, on the one hand, and manic constructions of reality, on the other, are tempting, threatening or merely absorbing various group members. At one extreme, we find the group member who feels that a past history of defeat and a chronically anticipated future of more of the same have simply converged on a particular present, and it all makes familiar if discouraging sense. At the other extreme, we find the group member whose fates seem to have ordained a degree of power, attention or affection which is exhilarating to consider. Somewhere to the centre of each extreme are those who do experience moments or intimations of these two constructions of reality, who are unnerved by these moments, and who struggle to preserve both an external and an internal sense of balance. And probably near the very centre of this continuum we would find persons who for one reason or another are very little affected by issues of winning and losing. Some bring with them a complex and available personal history which prevents the ups and downs of the new group from having any massive effect on their sense of well-being. Some bring with them a capacity to bear the ambiguities of the new situation, and they are not driven to figure it all out, one way or the other. And still others, one might guess, are so terribly self-absorbed or so engrossed in some aspect of the task that their awareness of others in the group is slow to develop.

Given the variety of responses to the new situation, what next? Where do these developments lead? Before looking at the more complex outcome we have called the win–lose relationship, we must consider a highly likely next step for those at either the defeated or the euphoric end of the continuum. This next step is withdrawal, silence or absence. For some the option is pursued indefinitely. They become 'silent members' or they drop from sight for brief or extended periods. Why? The answer for those whose apperception of the evolving reality is suffused with depression and impending defeat is not difficult to guess. They retreat to try and figure out what went wrong. They retreat in a mood of somewhat forced indifference, rejecting those who seem about to reject them. They retreat in some sense simply because they don't have the energy to plunge into the maelstrom one more time. Whether pained or indifferent, unhappy or aloof, those who withdraw because they feel that the group holds out few chances for satisfaction are acting in a way most of us can readily understand. More perplexing are those who withdraw after a period of considerable centrality, support and evident satisfaction. Why the sudden and unexpected absences or periods of unreachable silence?

Two quite different ways of viewing the withdrawal of the early winner suggest themselves. For some, the withdrawal is an integral part of the manic construction of reality which has already taken hold. For others, the withdrawal is designed to dampen down and control the mania. A good example of the first sort, the manic withdrawal, is found in those instances where the group members, sensing their power to menace and intimidate others, leave deliberately, thinking all the while that surely the group will fall apart, be a boring waste of time, or come to realize their need for their absent central person. Their withdrawal is thus a continuation of the grandiosity and deprecation of others which was already the basis of the manic construction of reality. When the group member returns, the individual's mania may if anything be heightened and the group subjected to insulting questions designed to prove that without their dramatic, heroic star things really were quite dull indeed. These provocative and manipulative withdrawals lead directly on to the further evolution of the win–lose relationship. The second sort of withdrawal, one which is a move to control and dispel the growing mania, is more nearly the complement to the depressed retreat.

Why would someone pull away from a group just when everything was going so well? The boundary between a warm feeling of being appreciated, liked, admired and the mania which drives people to flight is a really crucial boundary in the intrapsychic map we are all constantly making and revising. There is a shifting threshold beyond which rewards are not experienced as rewards at all and instead serve only to intensify the mania, to produce greed, painful addiction and a sense of being insatiable. When the thing sought only makes things worse but the seeking continues unabated, total withdrawal and avoidance come to seem like the only sensible course. Sometimes in the midst of abstinence or self-isolation this strategy may not seem so brilliant, but when the cycle of seeking and success leads not to satisfaction but to mania, then the door to flight is thrown open. A time apart, a chance to catch your breath, even a time to put into perspective the success which has become so upsetting—the allure of flight is really not all that incomprehensible.

Where does the evolving group go from here? Some, but not all, of the group members have moved either in the direction of depression or in the direction of mania. Some of these have found this drift quite unpleasant and for various reasons have opted for withdrawal, either through absence or through the adaptation of numb but dogged endurance. But still others remain engaged, and our task now is to trace out some of the consequences of both the depression and the mania which they are feeling. What next?

The next event of unique and lasting importance for any developing group is the creation of one, two or more crystallized roles which serve to express, intensify, and at the same time bind in the accumulating moods of discouragement and euphoria. A terribly important transition point has been passed when group members move from the private experiences of depression and/or mania to an interpersonal drama in which one or more persons come to symbolize the group's consciousness of how far the win–lose relationship has evolved. Just as the depressive or the manic construction of private, individual reality served to crystallize the ambiguity of early experience, so too the emergence of stock characters, scapegoats, labels and the like serves to crystallize the ambiguity of individual differences.

The people who feel they are losing begin to search for the person and the role which seem to be organically related to their feelings of losing out. They start looking for one or more winners. Meanwhile, the people who feel they are winning start to search for one or more losers. And this process is accompanied by some of the most intricate and intensely ambivalent feelings known to groups. Those who are losing, who feel their future in the group sliding more and more into conformity with their worst initial fears, conspire to locate the proto-winner who is at once the object of their envy, admiration, bitter rage and deference. They may, in part, seek out the proto-winner in order to make concrete their sense of having already lost, but, as we shall see, the complexity of the individual and collective motives is simply dazzling. So too, the location of one or more proto-losers is a collective act which can be fuelled by the most diverse underlying intentions.

Let's start with the search for the winner. Perhaps 'the winner' is the wrong way to label the role we seek to define. Perhaps on paper it is too difficult to convey how sarcastically this word is meant, how loaded with resentment this search can be. But other phrases seem too awkward. The search for the winner must be understood as simultaneously a search and an accusation. For the more deferent and unconflictedly self-abnegating, it is a search for those admirable people who evidently can manage the stress and the confusion of the new group and emerge as helpful, self-confident or whatever. For the more depressed and resentful, the search is also an accusation that the winners have set themselves up to dominate or intimidate others, that to win *is* to create losers. The accusation conjures up a winner whose motives include the need to dominate and the need to create anxiety and unhappiness and whose faults include conceit, insensitivity and indifference to the havoc created in the feelings of others. The search for winners becomes a search for villains.

The creation of a search party, as it were, sets in motion a highly unstable coalition. Those who seek a leader because having a leader might relieve the unmanageable pressure to contribute to the general good find themselves in cahoots with those who are angry at all the ego-tripping, smug people who have dominated the group thus far. This coalition is a reflection of the mixed feelings harboured by the individual participants, but in these temporary coalitions there is a temporary parcelling out of individual ambivalences. For the time being people are willing to play out only a part of their complex inner reality, allowing others to carry the messages they choose not to emphasize.

At the very same time as the search for winners is getting under way the search for losers begins. Just as evidence accumulates that some people are dominating the group, so too some in the group begin to notice the silent people, the anxious people, the immature people, the submissive people and so on. Some of those who call attention to people already squeezed out of the discussions do so with expressions of distress and in the name of concern. They want to help. Others call attention to the same evidence but they are less sympathetic. They express anger that some people just sit quietly by while the vocal group members struggle with the stresses of group life. Or they may express scorn at the petulant, demanding quality of those who talk only of their anxiety and unhappiness. They express impatience and irritation. From the ranks of those who want to help and the ranks of those who are increasingly irritated a second search party is formed, a second unstable, unlikely coalition is created.

The motivational basis of this search for losers is likely to be exceedingly complex. On the one hand, some instigate or join the search for the loser because the very existence of the loser provides an explanation for their own increasing dominance. If all around are filled with self-doubts and inhibitions, then quite naturally some will have to talk more than their share or take the leadership role. The explanation for winning can be found in the widespread need which others have to lose. On the other hand, the proto-winners are part of the other drama, the search for winners, and, at least at times, it does seem that the need to be found, to be found out, is part of the unfolding scenario.

The function of being found out as winner, just as for the loser, is that others can play a role in punishing or controlling the very performance one seems not to be able to control oneself. In the case of the 'winners', the plaguing self-doubt is that, intermixed with all the motives which propel one toward the head and centre of a group, there just may be the very sadistic or destructive motives which the search party has asserted. Who knows? How can anyone with total assurance plead innocent to the charges of narcissism, cruelty and insensitivity which, it is claimed, are the means used to gain centrality?

The ways in which both winners and losers relate the two search party games are strikingly similar. Both search but also wish to be sought. Both hide but wish to be found. The search party is resented but welcomed as a source of external control, needed to bolster shaky inner controls. Winners and losers, wavering between accusations that others are culpable, and painful insights into their own complicity, play the double role. And when caught, when found out, they often wiggle free, and the game is on again. Yes, yes, they say, our timidity is a problem or our arrogance, and then all that is gone, and no, no, the problem is elsewhere, in others, in the setting, the cast of assembled players.

There are occasions when the very acts of searching out and locating 'winners' and 'losers' lead to a clear alteration of the relationships. The winner may come to see the legitimacy in the losers' complaints; the losers may come to find strength in their discovery that others were feeling intimidated. By what-ever means, the insights which derive from the search may have a calming, depolarizing effect on the group. In addition, participation in the search opens up new options: winners can express sympathetic concern toward the silent or anxious group members, thus modifying the impression given earlier of utter insensitivity, while the losers can express righteous indignation at the central members and in that very process undo some of their self-presentation of terrorized ineffectualness. All sorts of insights, modifications of role, and new patterns of interaction may occur, but there are other possibilities as well. We need to turn now to the less malleable individuals and relationships. We need to follow down the further evolution of the win–lose relationship because the search party games can lead also to an intensification of the win–lose patterns already developed. How does this happen?

Two developments lie ahead for those relationships which have become ensnared in the win–lose impasse. One involves a contest over the purpose, implicit ground-rules and morality of the developing relationships; the second flows from the first and raises the question of eliminating or totally isolating persons unwilling and/or unable to abide by the group's purpose, rules and morality. As these two developments would suggest, it can get pretty intense and pretty nasty. Let's take a closer look at how this all works.

My impression is that the first serious effort to raise collective consciousness regarding the underlying goals and morality of the evolving relationships tends to be initiated by those who feel they are losing. The sense that things aren't going quite right, that others are getting more than their fair share of the air-time or the respect and affection of the group, leads not only to a search for the would-be winner. It leads as well to an effort to distinguish between improper and proper goals, between rules which benefit only a few and rules which benefit the majority, and between narcissism and mutual responsibility as the basis of interpersonal relations. The winner is not only sought out; the effort expands naturally into an exposure of the illegitimate, destructive and selfish elements of the winner's whole manner. Although the ways in which the loser can accuse the winner of leading the group astray are innumerable, I wish to focus for purposes of clarity on one accusation which seams to recur with great frequency.

The winners stand accused not only of winning but of creating an ugly game: competition for power. They stand accused of sexualizing the scene, thereby creating a chasm between the chosen and the rejected. The attack on the so-called winners thus broadens to become an attack on the very goals and ethics which appear to underly their pre-eminence. It is but a short step from locating the emergent leaders and stars of a group to the posing of a choice, a strategic decision: Is the group content to operate with goals and rules which permit (or encourage) an unequal distribution of the satisfactions of group life? The fact that some talk a lot and some hardly at all or the fact that some are consulted for approval more than others can suddenly seem like conclusive proof that some members prefer hierarchies, prefer groups with inner circles and ruling elites.

If some people are determined to make others unhappy in order to achieve their own gratification, if some people are callous enough to turn the group into a dog-eat-dog power struggle, then mustn't they be opposed? Must not the group come to its senses, formulate a different set of goals and rules, and control/eliminate the would-be winners? So go the rhetorical questions of those who mostly feel they are losing. The new vision emerges from the criticism of the old. If the old way thrived on narcissism and ego-tripping, the new way will encourage sensitivity and concern for others. If the old way involved a constant series of horn-locking contests for dominance, the new way will eschew domination and 'leadership' in favour of equality.

There are two ways to pursue the egalitarian vision, and it is crucial to be able to tell them apart. One tends to arise early in the group's history, in reaction against the early domination of the many by the few. This might be called the levelling approach to equality or the no-win approach. It seeks to create equality of satisfaction (or at least of possibility) by restricting the satisfaction of the few who have already attained some degree of centrality and by seeking somehow to 'redistribute' their assets. In contrast to this no-win policy a quite different approach to equality builds on some of the real insights of the first approach but incorporates as well an awareness that restriction often leads to a shared poverty which leaves everyone behind rather than ahead. The second approach to equality I would call the dialectic approach because it draws on the reality of both winning and losing, seeks to curb some of the ugly consequences of narcissism without pretending to outlaw it and seeks to engage, not restrict, the creative energies of all. I break away from the sequential, narrative history to distinguish between these two approaches only because my implicit criticism of much that happens in the name of equality should not be taken as an attack on the goal of equality. We will return to the more dialectic approach to equality and try to understand how and why it differs from the dynamic now under consideration, the no-win approach.

Accompanying the value issue in the evolution of the win–lose relationship is the emergence of a new coalition of losers, which tends to be led by a newly emergent role specialist, the spokesman, and which is organized around a new set of group goals. Forging a new set of group goals in this case is part of a larger development, the strengthening of the losers' position by the invocation of a presumably shared morality. With the introduction of this morality the fluid struggle for dominance, attention, affection, respect or any other desired reward is transformed. Those who 'succeed' may find that their success serves as ample evidence of their violation of the as yet only vaguely specified goal of equality.

The new coalition of losers, near-losers, and the spokesman for the losers combines to oppose the winners, those who appear to derive their satisfaction at the expense of the others now allied against such selfishness and insensitivity. The scene is not hard to imagine. 'There you go again' is the repeated charge, expressing the growing awareness of the many ways certain people have of shutting others off, of speaking without affirming the previous speaker's existence, of focusing everything on their own agenda, etc. At best, this new coalition can have dramatic and positive effects simply by heightening the 'winners'' awareness of their own behaviour and by heightening everyone's awareness of how these behaviours affect others. We will return to these positive effects. For now we may return to the less pleasant consequences of the losers' coalition.

There are times when the mounting attack upon winners and upon winning itself looks like it's going to turn into a rout. A large segment of the group, buttressed by widely shared values on equality and sensitivity and led by a spokesman for both persons and values, seems like an overwhelming force. The early winners come under enormous pressure and their response is not always very helpful. To the demand that they talk less, they sometimes respond by talking not at all. They sulk, absent themselves, or appear utterly indifferent to the proceedings. To the demand that they show more sensitivity to others they sometimes react by making it clear that only petulant weaklings would place such a high value on sensitivity that the group could only become stiflingly polite and cautious. To the demand that they 'share' their power, charisma, *manna*, or whatever, they react by abandonning the group at one moment and defiantly persisting in their old ways at the next. Still and all, the odds would seem to be against the would-be winners. It might seem that all that remains is for the objects of this pressure either to leave or to humble themselves and to try and reform. Except for one utterly crucial fact of group life: ambivalence.

Presumably the ambivalence of those who are losing toward those who are winning has been there all along, but nothing intensifies it so acutely as the scene in which the winner is 'cut down to size'. Gradually at times, with lightning speed at others, the scene can shift. The central persons are attacked for 'setting themselves up', they react by withdrawing, and suddenly the ambivalence of the attackers comes to the fore. Or maybe it surfaces only after a long boring stretch in which many come to realize how much they needed and enjoyed the performance of at least some of the early central figures. 'Come back', they now say, 'we didn't really mind your dominating everything. Maybe it'll be better the next time around.'

The clearest form for the expression and resolution of the ambivalence people feel toward the central members of the group often is provided by the growing struggle between one or more winners and 'the spokesman'. It is this conflict which crystallizes the win–lose impasse. As the clearest voice of protest against the domination and insensitivity of some early winners, the spokesman earns the gratitude of many who up to that point had wondered if they were utterly alone in their annoyed or depressed reactions to the early winners. As the clearest voice formulating the values and norms violated by the early winners, the spokesman earns the gratitude of those who could not be sure whether their anger at the early winners was legitimate or merely the product of pettiness and jealousy. 'No, not at all', says the spokesman, 'our opposition to this callous domination and spotlight-grabbing is an expression of a higher value than the narcissism and power-hungry style of these would-be leaders.' The spokesman confronts the early winners not in his/her own name but in the name of interpersonal morality, not in his/her own defence but in defence of the depressed, over-awed, and intimidated members of the group. 'Well', the spokesman seems to say, 'I of course could handle you would-be leaders. You don't bother *me*, but there are those among us who *are* upset at your behaviour.'

It would be incorrect to imply that all morality lies in the hands of the spokesman. The winners have their moralism and when pressed they present whatever parts of their self-defence they can get organized. Sometimes the central value seems to be freedom. People should do their thing, free from the constraints of excessive concern for the consequences. Excessive self-consciousness is a key negative value. Spontaneity, openness, expressiveness—these are the familiar touchstones of the morality which is set against the values enunciated by the spokesman. Better, they say, to encourage all to speak up at will than to squash some by insisting that they speak less. Better, they say, that everyone sense and give expression to their own power and sexuality than that some be hidden away, Cinderella-like, lest their beauty seem to negate that of others.

One state of affairs which is crucial to the development of the win–lose impasse is that at least some group members are torn in their loyalties and attractions. Given their early reality of sensing that others are stronger, better informed, quicker, more self-assured, etc., there is reason for some division in their loyalties. On the one side there are the spokesmen who verbalize their distress and lead the opposition to the early winners. On the other side there are those very people whose troublesome centrality is not altogether a negative thing. The ranks of the early winners often include persons who start things off, keep things going, provide a continual challenge and excitement to the group. The obvious negative effects of their centrality, the distress and silence which follow in their wake, are counterbalanced by the negative effects of being protected, spoken for and championed by the spokesman. And if the would-be winners do make the group overly competitive and unruly, perhaps the spokesmen sometimes bring about a group which is overly considerate, self-conscious and dull.

The list of counterbalancing positives and negatives could be extended, but the main point here is that many persons are caught in an unpleasant dilemma. There are times when neither the early winners nor the spokesmen who emerge to challenge them are able to provide people with a satisfactory set of options. The result is a fluid, shifting pattern of coalitions which threatens to immobilize the group. Whenever some would-be winner takes off on a solo trip, dominating the discussion, announcing his/her views on things in a particularly insensitive way, the coalition of the spokesman and the spoken for emerges, and the would-be winner is cut down to size. But as the implicit morality of this counterattack takes hold on the group and the attack generalizes to everyone who seems to talk more than their share or to be excessively cool and self-confident or whatever, then the coalition tends to break down. The spokesman can become increasingly isolated, his/her complaints about insensitivity and authoritarianism less and less supported by others. Suddenly, as the coalitions are rearranged, the early winners are back in the limelight. Their jokes are funny again, their counterattacks against the spokesman strike responsive chords. Those who were distressed before suddenly peek around the contours of their spokesman to reestablish contact with their 'oppressor'. Charisma is back in style. Hostile barbs are in again, tippytoe sensitivity is out.

And then, just as quickly, the whole scene can shift again. One early loser suddenly gets upset, hurt by a thoughtless remark or angry at the reversion to the group's earlier state of being pushed around by a few. 'Right, right', the cry goes up, 'Who the hell do these bullies think they are!' Back come the spokesmen, back come the strictures against domination, aggression, seductiveness or whatever seems to threaten the precarious sense of safety and balance so many find essential.

The result is an unstable, shifting impasse: the win–lose impasse. Each shift seems, at worst, to debilitate the group still further. Each switch from being enthralled with the charismatic leaders to being grateful to the sensitive spokeman, and each switch back the other way, leaves the group more hopeless that any stable and satisfying group will ever emerge from so much struggling.

It is clearer in retrospect than while it is going on that the unfolding win–lose drama can be seen as a play in two acts. In the first act the winning and the losing are relatively uncoordinated. Two people can be losing because they are so anxious they never can get a word in edgewise, while at the same time a win–lose dyad is evolving over whose position on the Vietnam war is more coherent, and assorted others are feeling ugly, cool, out of place, eloquent, etc., etc. In the first act some terribly intense and portentious encounters may take place. The feelings engendered may be resolved, and the win–lose pattern dispelled forever within that dyad, or they may linger and become part of the emotional material from which the second act is created. The second act involves larger segments of the group. Its theme is how the tension of the first act, with its dyadic or isolated winning and losing, can lead to collective actions: the search party, the emergence of the spokesman, the development of conflicting moralities, the shifting alliances and the win–lose impasse which drains the energies of a group.

The win–lose drama need not be performed in two acts. There is nothing inevitable about any sequence we are recording in this schematic portrait of group life. In some new or unstructured groups the various dyadic encounters need not fall into the win–lose groove, or they may do so only to be resolved and the distress drained away. And once the drama has become a group-wide encounter, complete with roles and norms, it need not terminate at the dreary win–lose impasse. How then are these impasses resolved? What might happen in act three which would break up the log-jam of act two? How does a group get out of such a mess?

No one answer will account for the various ways in which the win–lose impasse is surmounted, but we might as well start with the simplest answer. As absurdly simple as it may sound, it is not uncommon for the win–lose relationship to just dissolve, to fade away, to evaporate. Like the child who returns in daylight to the scene of some dusky terror, only to find that the phantasms of evening were commonplace objects utterly without menace, it often happens that first impressions yield to newer perceptions with quite other implications. In the development of the win–lose dyad, that first tilting imbalance wherein one person suddenly experiences the other as stronger, more attractive, more together is so often built on misperceptions and incorrect guesses that new data serves, as the morning sun, to dispel the worst of one's fears. The very person who yesterday had seemed so smugly confident of his capacity to handle the new situation seems today to have his share of self-doubt, and, almost without any conscious adjustment, the win–lose drama loses its grip upon the actors involved. When the very person who seemed so seductively reserved and so indifferent to other women suddenly adds to the gestalt clear evidence of inner distress and a history of shyness, the gestalt falls apart. The earliest win–lose impasses are so often based on wild extrapolations from the barest evidence that it is no wonder how effective the accumulation of more and more data turns out to be in exploding win–lose perceptions.

It would be foolish to overlook how each group member is constantly shading and counterbalancing the impression he/she thinks is being created. One member follows up a speech which verges on bragging with a subsequent speech emphasizing his/her 'other side', while people who have revealed too much insecurity or weakness too soon may rush in with their 'strong suits'. People pick up from the responses to their offerings thus far crucial evidence about whether they have come off looking too strong, too weak, too insensitive, too solicitous, etc. And as they move to present a balanced picture of themselves the imbalanced perceptions which are the basis of the win–lose dyad are sometimes altered enough to make locking in on the win–lose drama very unlikely.

At the same time as both members of the win–lose dyad come to adjust their self-presentation, they may also be engaged in catching themselves as they are just about to make their own familiar, defensive distortion of reality. Not only does more data accumulate from the other side; one can also recognize in one's early perceptions, based on minimal data, one's tired old ways of making sense out of new, ambiguous and threatening situations. Some people can jolt themselves out of the emerging win–lose scene simply by recognizing how quickly they had superimposed on the realities swirling around them their habitual first perceptions of others. Just as tourists in a strange land constantly think they see persons who are still back home, so too the first inclination in a strange group is to think one is once again among a known cast of characters. To catch oneself doing this is a big step toward dispelling the perceptions which make one feel uncomfortably inferior or uncomfortably superior.

If data and more data, even insight and more insight were enough to dispel all the win–lose dyads, there would be no second act, no group-wide drama. And there need not be a second act. Any group can come together, begin to create a set of win–lose dyads, then resolve all or nearly all of them, and move on to some other drama altogether. But what if they cannot? What are the elements of group life which lead toward a more satisfactory resolution of the win–lose drama than the one in which no one really ever wins?

The first answer to this question might be that we have only discussed the negative consequences of the group-wide win–lose drama. Some of the events which we asserted lead to a further impasse do not in fact always lead that way. Let's look first at the search parties and the isolation of winners and losers, then at the loser–spokesman coalition and the creation of rival moralities, and finally at the shifting coalitions which develop as the group struggles to resolve the win–lose drama.

Two search parties set out, one to isolate and control the oppressive winners and the other to operate on the losers who drag the group down with their petulant complaining, and these search parties can sometimes set in motion the very changes which will in time end the win–lose drama. In the process of searching out the winner those who felt they were losing find other sources of support than the enthralling but frustrating hero. The spell is broken when instead of always courting the favour of some seductive, powerful figure, and always enduring the slim rewards (or abuse) in silence, the vast bulk of the group discovers others who are more rewarding, less self-absorbed, and easier to relate to. Then too, the sudden jolt to the 'winner's' self-esteem, the sudden realization that maybe he/she hadn't really been all that sensitive, hadn't really given the others a chance to work on their own agendas, these insights can turn people around. Some will sulk, counterattack, rigidify under pressure and so on, but some will change. That mania-producing illusion that one can do no wrong, cannot overtalk and cannot fail to charm can be dispelled by the search party and the hostile confrontation set up with the would-be winners. People can climb down off their high horse, and as they do they contribute to the resolution of the win–lose impasse.

One of the major demands made by those who feel themselves to be losing is that the would-be winners should show their frailties more, be more 'human' in their mix of strengths and weaknesses. Sometimes their attack is an utter fiasco, with the object of the attack railing against the Lilliputian attackers who take strength and give nothing of value in return. Sometimes the call for greater expression of weakness is rejected as a pathetic effort to glorify defeat and resignation. But sometimes the call is effective. In fact, it is often with an enormous sense of relief that the so-called winner begins to reveal his feet of clay, the person behind the facade. Mere mortals have throughout mythology and scripture succeeded in rescuing gods who are frozen in postures of isolation and perfection. So too, as the ambivalence of the search party is made clear, as the mixed motives and goals of the attack become evident, then everyone can begin to depolarize the situation.

With different means, but a rather similar goal, the second search party, the one trying to locate losers, may also play its part in resolving the win–lose impasse. Ugly as they can get at times, the various efforts to isolate, confront, and change the losers are not always hopeless. Faced with the losers' complaints that some people grab all the attention, that some people are insensitive and unkind, that some people are arrogant know-it-all's, the search party has a terribly difficult assignment. The first impulse, especially for those who are being accused of such monstrous crimes, is to fight back, to turn the tables—in short, to turn the loser into the scapegoat. But the process need not always go this way. The impatience and irritation of those who now reject the loser's complaints may carry a second message beyond the obvious one of rejection. This second message says that there are limits to how totally anyone can collapse into depression and defeat before they will be met with disbelief. This message says, in effect, that the complainers are suspected of exaggerating their distress and of exploiting their bruises to create sympathy. It is in this mood that the loser is told to stop underrating or understating his/her own strengths. That the loser would deny his/her strengths is clearly as major a cause of the win–lose impasse as that the winner would deny his/her weaknesses.

Strange as it may sound, it may be just as important that the messages of the search parties be resisted as that they be accepted. The message of either search party is all too often an insult, either through misperception or malevolence, and for the winner or the loser to accept the charges uncritically would hardly seem to lead toward resolution of the win–lose impasse. To be sure, one search party is convinced that the early winner, while appearing smug and insensitive, really is human and weak inside. But the limits of their insight are soon reached. To be sure, the other search party is convinced that the loser's anxiety and relentless complaints are signs of a chronic, pitiable weakness which still could be covered up somehow. But how many-layered a person is, how full of contradictions! It follows then that any lasting resolution which may flow from the encounter of the seekers and the sought depends not only, or even primarily, upon having the search party convince the winner or loser of some key insight. Rather, it will flow from a mutual process of learning, insight, altered perceptions, altered self-presentation, apologies, humour, trial and error, and so on.

The process of accommodating to the complex realities of 'winners' and 'losers' takes place on many levels. The moralism of the winner, the heroic stand for openness and freedom, may survive, but only as part of a new synthesis which incorporates as well the spokesman's value on sensitivity to differences and the vision of equality of satisfaction for these different individuals. Equality of satisfaction? Or guaranteed minimum satisfaction? Uniformity of reward or an intricate system of rewards designed so as to match the unique needs and definitions of satisfaction of each group member? The synthesis of the 'winners' and the 'losers' takes different forms, but it seems to revolve around the question: How can everyone win, or if that's not possible then how can the number of winners be maximized, while at the same time raising the floor level of pain and distress below which no one will dip for long, if at all? The emergent synthesis necessitates a compromise between attending to each individual's special sources of satisfaction and competence on the one hand and the relief of depression and hopelessness on the other.

It may well be impossible in any group to prevent those down-drafts of discouragement which start off the whole win–lose cycle, nor can one imagine how to thwart all those manic, insensitive flights which so easily upset any group equilibrium. Thus, tempting as it may be to imagine a group where people never feel they are losing and where people never bolster their own self-esteem at the expense of others, such a phantasy does not correspond to reality as I know it. But when these down-drafts and solo flights do happen, then comes the crucial test. Does the group move to resolve the feelings that have been stirred up or does it turn away from an unpleasant reality only to have that reality absorb more and more of the group's energy in another rendition of the win–lose drama?

The end of a drama may be prolonged, with a few still insisting on reassembling the search parties, or it may be abrupt. It may be that the collective absorption with winners and losers suddenly seems as foolish as it once seemed compelling. The very terms, winners and losers, are of course nothing but metaphors, and any metaphors can seem as delightfully apt one minute as they seem clumsy and misleading at the next. As the metaphors lose their hold, people can return to the more stable realities. With whatever terms they are labelled, what remains are individuals with shifting or relatively stable levels of self-esteem, depression and euphoria. What remains is the growing appreciation of just how complex any individual is. What remains, and is more widely understood, is a diversity of individual styles and satisfactions which defies any easy categorization, including the metaphoric one of winners and losers.

The peer-group theory of winning and losing, even in as stylized and partial a form as just presented, makes a fairly coherent story. It isolates one of the most universal contradictions between people: the natural animosity which develops between those who get ahead and those who fall behind. It touches on persistent issues in personal and interpersonal development: issues of self-esteem, depression, anxiety, euphoria, morality, ambivalence and so on. But does it do the job? Does it put one in a place from which to reverse the trend toward a totally locked impasse? Does it exhaust the array of causes of winning and losing, or does it leave untouched major sources of the dynamics of winning and losing?

How about taking a hard look at that (thus far) almost invisible figure in the evolving drama: the leader, facilitator, therapist, trainer, teacher or whatever he/she is called. How does the leader influence the evolution of the group, especially the evolution of those patterns we have examined under the rubric of winning and losing?

What do we really know about leaders? The literature is slanted toward the understanding of group process in peer-group terms. We don't learn much about the motives or the unhelpful and unique contributions of Bion, Slater. Mills or, in my own studies, the anonymous professionals labelled Dr A, Dr B, Dr C and Dr D. I may have known five or six hundred group members, but I really know only one group leader: me. And although it raises the familiar issues of personal discretion and defensiveness, I can't see any way to move on to a second theory about winning and losing without making it, at least to some extent, a personal theory concerning my effect on these very developments.

I never feel more alone and vulnerable than I do the first few days of a group. And I never risk being thought stupid, cruel, ineffective, disappointing, irrelevant, to name only a few of the possibilities, as much as I do when I first enter the group discussion. In the terms of this discussion I certainly do lose a lot, but then I win a lot, too. But on what terms do I win? I share with most other humans an aversion to winning for the wrong reasons, which for me as leader is how it seems when the basis of that outcome is deference, fear, false assumptions concerning my omniscience, efforts to forestall my devastating depth interpretations and so on. The problem is how not to lose and how not to win for the wrong reasons, and beyond these pressing, early problems there is in me, as in most group members, a strong need to search for a way out of the whole win–lose modality. I greatly prefer the kind of individuated equality reached in most of the groups I have been in to the subtle but powerful hierarchy which is there from the first moments on. However, much as I profess to reject it, I do see myself as reproducing and exploiting the very inequalities which I sense are in fact a major contribution to the dynamics of winning and losing. Other topics and examples come to mind, but I would propose to explore this matter in one area: the way in which I respond to hostility. Although it will not be complete, this review may lead to the beginnings of a leader theory of the origins of winning and losing in groups.

Let's consider for a moment the entire range of hostile, rebellious or complaining remarks directed to the group's formal leader. Some are mocking, suggesting that the group should wake up and see just how patheticly rigid and defensive the leader really is. Some are accusing: well-aimed barbs which confront the double-standards, the manipulation, the retentiveness or the favouritism of the leader. And some are outright challenges to the power and privilege of the formal role of the leader. The list is a long one. There are the simple (or apparently simple) acts of substantive disagreement or differences of opinion. There are expressions of personal anxiety which not so incidentally portray the leader as merely the latest in a string of malevolent, sadistic teachers. What does the leader's response (or non-response) to these remarks have to do with the evolution of winners and losers?

The leader can respond as he or she would to any friend or important person: with concern that the relationship is in such trouble that hostile feelings are beginning to surface. Or the leader's response can lead down the familiar paths of counterhostility and humiliation. Most of these responses are fully available to anyone in the group, but a few tend to fall in the special province of the leader, at least early on in the group's development. The leader as target has special relevance to a set of questions which torture everyone who expresses or witnesses hostility: 'Is this hostility justified?' 'Is it legitimate to express such feelings?' 'Is the hostility being expressed merely an acting out of old (neurotic?) angers? Is it taking advantage of the professional forebearance of the leader to say such things—picking on the person one knows cannot retaliate without cracking the facade of benign acceptance?' 'Is it based on reality?' 'Will one be punished for this expression of feeling?'

In the context, then, of fairly widespread apprehension over how these questions will be answered, the leader's response tends to influence, one way or the other, the evolution of the group. I can think quickly of five quite different responses, and obviously this doesn't exhaust the possibilities. But we might consider what happens when the leader expresses delight, shows concern, fails to respond at all, patronizes or counterattacks.

I can be clearer about all this if I can speak for a moment as the leader in question, drawing on my own experience and thus avoiding the implication that I am describing all groups and all leaders. For example, I cannot think back to the summer group of 1961, to the hero of group I given the pseudonym of Harry, without seeing now, as I really did see then, how delighted I was with Harry's defiant, virtuoso performance. I didn't dare to be very explicit about all this when I wrote up the results of our research on this group. Countertransference, as one was encouraged to label it in those days, was so shameful, so unprofessional. But I know now that at least some leaders love to swap stories about outrageous heroes whose hostility was so breathtaking, so endearing that they can't help laughing about it even as they describe the horrible things these people said and did. It's not very different from the parents who live out their desires to defy unjust authority by finding their troublesome children utterly charming, a source of pleasure, even if some of the rebellion lands on them. One problem, though, is that for the heroic rebel all this delight can become a trap. The manic, desperate quality of someone who is constantly set up for this limited role (*cf. Cool Hand Luke* or McMurphy in *One Flew Over the Cuckoo's Nest*) is one decidedly negative feature of this whole dynamic. In reasonably small doses, however, the leader's delighted response sets up all kinds of possible developments. It's obvious that the hero and the leader have something special going on between them. The leader's bored, half-frozen expression disappears whenever the hero jabs at some poor soul who only wants the leader to be the nice, kind leader of his or her dependent dreams, and the leader's pleasure in being directly confronted as the bogus authority is equally visible. Issues of jealously, favouritism and mistrust of the leader all flow from such events.

How differently things seem to develop when my reaction to hostility is one of concern. Sometimes I already know a few people in the group, or have some basis for taking them seriously as people. Among the rest there are, of course, some whom I include very quickly among those whose anger or irritation I take/as a bad sign for me, for what I am doing and how I am relating to this new situation. Hopefully everyone is in such a place for me by the end of the group, but my ancient snobberies do always reappear in some form or other. I can't see everyone right away. But those I do see matter, and their hostility remakes my personal agenda in a flash. For the most part, the consequences of concern are positive. We want concern, I suspect, but we can't always believe it's there. And I would be foolish to imply that my concern and my eagerness to work things out are well expressed at all times. I'm usually feeling other, more off-putting things at the same time, and besides, even if I were feeling little else I am still far too inhibited and awkward to find just the right words at just the right moment. But when it works, it works, and it is precisely the rising level of concern and human contact which forestalls the hostility and makes it more resolvable when it does develop.

The one response to hostility which is most clearly in the province of the professional is silence. In ordinary conversations it very seldom happens that an attack leads to the kind of mid-air suspension which a leader's non-response can produce. Groups are often immensely creative in their effort to figure out what's happening and why. Perhaps the leader, unbeknownst to anyone in the group, has become a Buddhist monk; perhaps he has *petit mal* seizures; perhaps he's dead. It's hard to get consensus over any of these constructions, and the effort to explain the leader's silence tends to flow in the direction of classical psychoanalytic technique. That seems to be it: the leader, just like the analyst, doesn't have to respond at all. To some the message in the silence is benign: 'Yes, is there more? Any other associations?'. To some it is merely a replay of the parent–child scene: the child calls the parent 'an old doodie-poop-butt' and the parent pretends not to have heard. But in a group it is hard to avoid several implications of non-response. The leader is usually seen as creating (preferring?) an asymmetrical, quasi-therapeutic relationship. The member who expressed the hostility in the first place usually feels humiliated in front of everyone else, and the onlookers are torn between their sympathy for their fellow group members and their fear of the elusive, cool, situation-controlling leader. People vary all over the map, but the potency of silence is well established for all.

There is no unequivocal answer to the question of whether silence, non-directive mirroring or any other professionally stylized response to hostility is a useful or good thing for the group. People may start trying it out on each other and usually reveal thereby that they experienced it as a brilliant way to turn one's inner fear and rage into a disorienting counter-coup. It looks sadistic in the hands of neophytes, so it probably looked sadistic to them when the leader did it. But that isn't the whole story. To the extent that we are aware that our hostility is sometimes overdetermined, and to the extent that we regret how partial an expression of our ambivalence emerges in our hostile moments, we are ready for even the bizarreness of silence and the disjunctive, professional response. At some level or other, we do, upon occasion, thank those who know we're a little out of control and need another chance to say more accurately what we really mean. Silence, if seen as benignly intended, provides just that needed chance.

From the leader's point of view, as well, there is no unequivocal answer to the question of whether silence is a useful or a good thing. I can recall a few times when I was terribly glad I waited long enough for the whole story to come out, instead of blurting out a snappy rejoinder to someone's first probing action. There were times when just listening some more was the most useful way to express my concern and my eagerness to get at what had gone wrong. But there's silence and there's silence, and I confess that more often than not this paricular professional style has turned out to be an unhelpful exercise of control. To stay silent when my attacker pauses for a response can be tanta-mount to saying: 'Look, this is entirely your problem. Your anger is a symptom of something deeper in you which I will wait patiently for you to discover.' An even more intense form of the silent-treatment says, in effect: 'Your charges against me are so ridiculous that I won't even bother to answer them.'

Support and sympathy for a person whose anger meets with non-response is often forthcoming, but perhaps more often the attacker loses status, as does any defeated challenger. To humiliate the challenger is to cast oneself, as leader, into a role which some admire, some despise and most people fear. The role of the distant, composed and covertly cruel leader arouses so much mistrust that, if there is not much besides that role being enacted, only the intensely counterphobic will hurl themselves against it.

The fourth possibility on any list of my reactions to hostility is to patronize the attacker. For the leader to verbalize the feared and unspoken message of the silent-treatment is certainly one form of patronizing, but there are others. The basic message is that the attacker is immature and/or irrational in his or her anger, but that's all right. We were all children once upon a time, and it would be too much to expect everyone to be mature in a group like this. The attacker is evidently being allowed to be judged by a different set of rules, rules usually reserved for people who can't be expected to manage the stress of normal, adult life.

In one of the National Training Laboratory groups studied by O'Day (1974) the hostility of some group members was accepted for a while and then rejected, hard. For members to still be upset at the leader for seeming to control everything in the group, when that anger was supposed to have subsided in the early phase of the group, was unacceptable to the leader. It's as if the leader had an idea that early rebellion was to be expected..It's a phase that groups go through, but then this is all supposed to change. Everyone is supposed to realize that their anger was based on a misreading of the actual leader in the actual situation: 'See, I'm just a resource, not a bully or a manipulator', the leader seems to say. People who patronize have a problem: they lose patience. To tolerate anger, on the grounds that it's good to get it out of your system, works poorly if the anger doesn't go away. If it reappears and there's no more patience left, then there's trouble in maintaining one's composure.

One message sent by the patronizing teacher, parent or group leader is that anyone getting out of line will be offered temporary status as a laggard or a child, but even this offer can be withdrawn at the pleasure (or displeasure) of the one who defines adequate progress and maturity. As a leader my tolerant smile can be but one fact of my total response. I can call for help. I can give others in the group a look of slightly confused, slightly irritated exasperation which quite directly invites others to help me set this attacker straight. Sure enough, help is often forthcoming. I can sit back and watch while my defenders point out that the attacker is distorting, exaggerating, overreacting and generally disrupting the group. 'Did anyone *else* see what Pete is saying he saw in my last remarks?', I can ask, all innocent and eager to know the truth. But no one supports Pete in his perceptions. Surprise, surprise. Pete turns out to be all alone. Why? Well, maybe he *is* all alone, but maybe no one wants to be on the receiving end of my patronizing counterploy. That this is in fact the reality is sometimes clearly established, much later, when people refer back to the day Pete 'got into that hopeless tangle', and it turns out that I was being roundly condemned behind all those impassive faces. It turns out that I had been 'rotten', 'mean', 'unsympathetic', etc., but no one dared to say so. And those judgements usually coincide with the way I had seen myself that day, much to my own chagrin at discovering how often I still use all the old, dirty tricks of authority.

There are endless variations on the general theme of how hostility can be met with a patronizing response. And patronizing someone doesn't always make them even madder. Sometimes it causes headaches, stomach cramps or an intense desire to be somewhere else. Still other times it works. Rightly or wrongly, the attacker accepts the offer to regress a little, and the topic becomes 'How did I ever come to misperceive or overreact so badly?'. To the extent that the attacker wrongly accepts the offer, the next moments are filled with what often is later recognized as 'garbage', which is a rather apt description of what sometimes emerges when one tries to 'account for' the anger without ever returning to the attack. But it isn't always garbage, and in the slightly regressive space made possible by the leader's response to hostility what happens is often a real breakthrough into awareness of the transference, the inverted longing for attention or respect, the play for rebel status or whatever. Life would be much simpler if we could just decide that the responses which are sometimes ugly and unhelpful are always so, but even patronizing seems to be useful at times.

Sometimes anger is met with anger, accusation with counteraccusation. What then? As with any category of other behaviour, it all depends. It depends partly on how it is taken, and that in turn depends partly on how it is meant. Some counteranger is meant as an invitation to an intense, whole relationship in which such feelings are unavoidable. Sometimes the ensuing dialogue is sexualized, flirtatious, even while the onlookers fear that someone will be demolished. But other times the effort to destroy really does predominate, and the scorn and deliberate effort to wound are apparent to all. In the more everyday sorts of exchanges, a jab here, a hint of menace there, the group cannot fail to notice that the leader is sometimes thrown off balance. The more moderate the response, the more varied the impact of the leader's hostility. Some are pleased that the leader has become a human being; some can't see the hostility for what it is; and others are disappointed or apprehensive or hurt. Clearly this would-be category, counterhostility, is too heterogeneous in its meanings and consequences to be more than a temporary storage bin, the contents of which still need careful scrutiny.

For better or for worse, I have never found much guidance in the general proposition that any and all expressions of hostility are good for the group. As a group leader, as in all of my life, I struggle to discover whether hate can, in Melanie Klein's (1957) phrase, be mitigated by love. Not covered over and suppressed by love, just bound loosely to it, coexistent with it. The alternative, a sort of schizoid oblivion to the consequences of anger for me or for anyone else, may intensify the drama, but the long-run effects of such a stance are seldom what I have in mind. I think we can tell, or learn better to tell, the difference between cruelty, momentary rage, ambivalence, resentments accumulating in a larger context of affection, and so forth. It is the cruel version of hostility which troubles me. I can't think of any time when my cruelty has led to any development other than justifiable mistrust and/or hatred in return. The reality of life in groups is that it's terribly difficult to separate the drive to dismiss or to devastate one person from the meaning which that overt hostility might have for one's friends or allies. Horrifying as it may seem to most witnesses, there always seem to be a few who are delighted to find in the leader someone who will turn an ordinary conflict into a holy war. The dehumanization of the enemy, an essential part of such wars, is a process which tends to be irreversible, usually because the victim becomes and remains inaccessible, for good reason. Who needs cruelty?

Somewhere midway through this process of discussing how a leader, or how I as leader, might respond to hostility I realized I had omitted the one response which originally I most identified with the leader role: the interpretive, analytic exploration of the meaning of that hostility for my attacker. The reason for that omission is clear. Such a category has exploded, and its fragments are in each of the responses I have discussed. My delight, my concern, my basically patronizing attitude or my anger can all find expression through my implied or expressed interpretation. To merely search for and announce my best guess as to why this person is on the attack seemed to me at one time to be all that could possibly be asked of me in such a situation. In retrospect, I conclude that some of the interpretations were amazingly accurate, but all of them were even more amazingly incomplete.

I find rereading the transcript of an old group to be a painful process. There is some solace in recalling how strange the leader role was to me and how much I was oriented to my internal image of the mysterious, unflappable and brilliant analyst/leader. There is some solace in discovering that the group gradually weaned me from my stylized affection of the professional. But the transcript is scattered with interpretations which are basically teasing, partisan, cute, smug and unhelpful. The implications of my response to various group developments included the message that from my Olympian heights the gyrations of the group followed familiar paths or phases. My comments tended to undercut the level of the conversation and create for the group the humiliating option of (a) carrying on in spite of the new awareness that topic x was really a shadow play reflecting theme y or of (b) shifting levels and trying to discuss theme y even though it had been given only the faintest, haziest of explications. The group could choose between ignoring, or pretending to ignore, the interpretation (but surely there would be more) or shifting to the awkward process of puzzling out, attacking or defending, or demanding an elaboration of my elliptical, obscure intervention.

I exaggerate, of course. I'm leaving out the other qualities or comments without which I doubt we would have made it through the thirty-two group meetings. But even if what I say is only part of the truth, the implications of that part for an understanding of winning and losing are important. The entire structure of the group and especially the role of the leader make it so that some will win, some will lose, some will find both alternatives of winning and losing unattractive, and some will set out, successfully, to alter the structure of the group and redefine the leader's role.

Who would one expect to win under these conditions? Who would one expect to lose? And who to win or seem to be winning but suddenly start to lose? Is there any correspondence between the leader's way of reacting to different people and their fate in the early sessions of the group? I would say there is quite a bit of correspondence, and while it won't unravel the mystery unaided by additional perspectives there is enough substance to this line of thinking to call it the leader theory of winning and losing. The leader theory would have it that one important determinant of the evolving pattern of winning and losing is found in the behaviour, in the feelings and perceptions, and in the goals of the leader. This theory would have us look closely at what the leader sees as a good group, what the leader feels about various members and how each member's efforts to relate to the leader are received.

One kind of early winner is the hero. If the leader expects and hopes for a group in which people will be expressive or spontaneous enough to break the conventional rules of polite conversation, the emergence of the hero is good news for the leader. If the leader feels even slightly uncomfortable in the role of high priest/evaluator/formal authority, then the hero's mocking assaults on this pompous and ridiculous figure do more to rescue the leader than enrage him or her. If the leader had ever felt like challenging teachers or had ever felt scornful of those who adopted a more dependent, loyal stance toward authority, then the hero, despite some tendency to 'go too far', will still receive the leader's covert encouragement. It doesn't take long for most people to sense that there's something going on between the leader and the hero. The fusion of rebellion and the prospect of a friendship, the sexualizing of their angry exchanges, and the nervy efforts to break down the role and status of the leader are all there to be seen. The major crisis between the leader and the hero tends to come when, having perceived all this, the group tries to trap the hero into very role he or she least wants: the teacher's pet, the cunning lieutenant, the favourite child. Sometimes the trap works and the hero withdraws, unable to move into the kind of egalitarian, mutually respectful relationship which was wanted in the first place.

The hero or heroes are not the only winners. There always are a few and then a few more people to whom the leader responds with the same liking and attentiveness which characterize the reactions of many if not all of the rest of the group. In Bennis and Shepard's (1956) analysis of group development these are the independents. In Slater's (1966) writings on groups these are the members, usually females, who can transcend the either–or's of 'Are you rebellious or docile?' and 'Shall we focus on the leader or on each other?'. They are the people whose anger at the leader tends to pull the response of concern. Their attacks do not cause the leader to express delight, but neither are they received with silence, patronizing interpretation or counterhostility. And it is they who can, usually with the help of the hero, break what Slater calls the thralldom which binds the group to its leader.

Then there are the early winners who quickly and dramatically become the early losers. The leader theory would have us look very closely at how the leader responds to certain of the early attacks (and early approaches) by these group members. The trail starts with the fact that many of the most teasing and humiliating interpretations are directed toward these people in the group. What is it that pulls from the leader neither delight nor concern, but instead pulls either silence or a deliberate effort to undercut and look clinically at the hostility being expressed? Several clues: something about the attack seems petulant, guilt inducing; there is little affection and quite a bit of blaming conveyed by the attack; and, sometimes, the attack is just too accurate in portraying the leader's faults. These attacks, if not blunted quickly, would lead most people to view the leader as the major and permanent obstacle for the group, and the successful revolt would have the leader with no future but that of the scorned and rejected former leader. Those who launch these attacks come in from the blind side. They seem to reject the very *raison d'etre* of the leader in the group, or so it seems to the leader. And from the leader's panicky counterattack we can infer how much he or she felt that the future integrity of the leader's role was at stake.

The interpretation which is mostly an effort to expose the false pretender is a desperate gamble. Part of the explanation for this gamble lies in the leader's (not necessarily warranted) conviction that certain directions or elements are crucial to the group's future development. To this conviction is appended a fear that the group can and will get off the track if certain other tendencies are allowed to grow, like an unchecked cancer. Bion's (1959) set of basic assumptions constitute one of the many possible listings of how the group can wander off course. The group can flee from its task; it can collapse into stagnant dependency; it can consume itself with preparations for a war which will never come; it can dream blissfully of the fruitfulness of a group without stress. And so forth. Only when the group is committed to what Bion calls work does the leader find fulfilment in his or her work, in being the leader of a group trying to face reality, understand it and develop new modes of relating. That's part of the explanation, sometimes a large part. But it also is true that the leader is fully as capable as anyone else of veering off from the goal of work, getting lost in 'basic assumptions', and usually there's someone in the group perceptive enough to name what the leader is up to. The leader gets caught. The most common basic assumption to pull the leader away from work might be what Bion calls the dependency group: the leader really *does* want to have his or her every word listened to and kept in mind, and not questioned. Sometimes that happens. But the leader gets caught being sadistic, goofing off, falling for mystic reveries about the group's capacity to be the new seed for a new form of social organization, to name but a few of the possibilities. And the leader resists having these (largely unconscious) motives exposed just as the group members resist the leader's efforts to undercut their performance in the group.

There's no need to choose between the two explanations for the leader's actions. Most commonly, the person who arouses strong counterhostility or rejection in the leader manages both to strike at some weak spot in the leader's self-image *and* to seem to the leader to be pulling the group in completely the wrong direction. One place to look for evidence of the latter dynamic is in the staff meeting of group leaders. Leaders sometimes get together to exchange their exaspirations, and they can usually count on sympathy and a matching story which validates their impatience. 'So then he said . . . And I interpreted . . . And then the group . . .' Leaders sometimes try to reassure themselves and each other that the person who wanted to know exactly how to proceed, or the person who wanted to turn the group into a debating society, or the person who kept on being angry really is beyond the pale. They imitate the tone of voice of their attackers; they make them look preposterous. They give them belittling nicknames: the puppy dog, the stud, the eager beaver, etc. It's not unlike the teacher's lounge in a blackboard jungle or the residents' retreat adjacent to the emergency ward.

I'm not saying that these staff interactions are inevitable, and I'm certainly not saying they are excusable. But they happen. Students pull away and exchange their feelings toward the teacher; teachers pull away and exchange the perceptions which they could neither express nor control. All I am saying is some of the counterhostility or rejection which emerges in the form of patronizing interpretations is revealed in a more blatant and venomous form when professionals get together in staff quarters to talk things over. It would be a rare (and wonderful) staff which helps professionals understand their own part in producing the behaviour which angers or amuses them so. Instead of the jovial, superficial support which professionals sometimes provide each other, it is certainly possible for the staff meeting to be the place where leaders look at why certain attacks or certain forms of non-compliance with the ephemeral group norms provoke in this particular leader so much anger and defensiveness.

To return to the question of winning and losing, it seems reasonable to imagine that some losers are early, would-be winners who are simply knocked off by the leader. Why the leader would do this we have already touched upon, but how can this effort by the leader to diminish the influence of some members be so effective? What is the leader saying which has (at times) the effect of demoting certain group members? Certainly one of the most potent, but veiled, messages is something like this: 'I know you invested a lot of hope and a lot of money in this new group. I've said in various ways that it's your group, and it is. But from my years and years of experience I have learned that the group doesn't go well if you get stuck in a rut or veer too far off course.' In other words, the group discovers that it will be notified when it employs its freedom to go in the wrong direction. One simple explanation of how the leader can bring about the rejection of some early winners lies in the group's lack of confidence that they can defy the leader's hints and still have 'a good group'.

Even if the group fails to foresee any dire consequences from following the lead of a particular early winner, the group may still allow the formal leader one or two pre-emptory challenges. We have all been in classrooms or organizations in which the authority took what seemed to be an inexplicable aversion to one of our peers. The result, at times, is that this person becomes a pariah, at least while the authority is around. Outside the group, people may come up to their peer and express their sympathy and their confusion about why the teacher or boss is so negative, but inside the group the pariah remains isolated.

If some of the transformations of winners into losers can be traced to the leader, so also can the creation of losers. Just as most prayer groups need a sinner or most Alcoholics Anonymous groups need a backslider, the early moments of some self-analytic groups seem to cry out for something or someone to be analysed. It need not be, but it does happen that one or more group members establish themselves as unusually tense, withdrawn or mistrustful. In one encounter group recorded on film a woman began her self-presentation by wondering what it might mean that people could come to care a great deal about pets. Drawn out a bit more by the co-leader's questioning, she revealed that she herself felt closer to her cat than to her husband, whereupon the co-leader said: 'Isn't that pathetic?'. The ensuing conversation revealed a deep sadness in this woman, but I was left with some doubt about how far she would ever be able to move out of her early status. She had become the early loser. The film, as edited, was not clear about her fate, but I was left unclear about what she got from the encounter beyond a good cry and a little sympathy. The attention and respect of the co-leaders were clearly elsewhere by the end of the group.

It wouldn't take much to read Bion, Slater, Rogers or other group leaders' descriptions of typical group processes in this light and derive fairly accurate portraits of who will win and who will lose in their groups. In fact, the winners in one sort of group might well be losers in another. Some leaders seem to thrive on appreciation, some on direct challenge and others insist on preserving their oracular isolation.

Perhaps every leader tends to create a mythic, as-if situation by signalling the kinds of member performance which do or don't correspond to the way things should work out in a good group. Perhaps it's even more complicated, in that the leader may signal both the goal and the route to the goal, such that some members are told that they are rushing things too fast or short-circuiting what the leader imagines to be the proper sequential phasing of group development. It is the leader typically who blocks some sort of performance or other because 'the group isn't ready for it'. It is the leader who worries about one member's performance scaring, offending or turning off some or all of the other members. Not that others don't worry about the general good, but it is the leader whose worries are taken most seriously. Sometimes.

It turns out that the list of reasons why a leader would intervene to create winners and losers bespeaks a jumble of motivations: professional responsibility for the group (or its wobbliest members), personal affection or personal animus, countertransference, the impulse to retaliate, the leader as stage director cueing actors at the right moment, the leader as scientist unconsciously trying to make the group fit the theory or the prediction, etc., etc. It doesn't matter to me whether every leader has his or her own set of reasons. What matters is that we see our groups as the result of all our motives, all our perceptions, and not merely the result of our best intentions, our approach and our selective recollection of our cleverest interventions. We can't explain the disasters or near-disasters if, in true 'blaming the victim' style, we talk only about the members' motives and weaknesses. And we can't fully explain the times when things go well if we ignore those of our comments or gestures which were helpful but don't fit into our conception of our 'style'. From this perspective much of the literature, and I include my own work especially, turns out to be a complex mixture of the theory we need and a promotion campaign (which we probably don't need) for our chosen approach and for the network of colleagues who share our approach.

Two would-be theories, the peer group theory and the leader theory of winning and losing: How do they fit together? What do they leave out? It seems to me that these two theories support and extend each other. For example, it seems quite likely that some of the mystery about where all the depression and mania come from is reduced by thinking for a moment about the impact of the leader. The leader who appears to be bored, who appears to be comparing the group with previous groups, or who appears to see the track the group keeps getting away from is a source of both anxiety and depression. How much of the early self-assertion, often at the expense of some fellow group member, is rooted in the desire to make the leader sit up and take notice? Could one predict the first, fateful disaster in a group, in which someone is jumped on for being insensitive, reactionary, or behaviourist simply by knowing whether the group saw the leader as being big on sensitivity, politically radical or way into psychoanalysis? I suspect so.

The peer group theory leans very heavily on the way the self-esteem of individual group members can drop, setting up a pattern of losing, or can rise, defensively, into the strutting, euphoric performance of the early winner. It leans heavily on the developmental history of these individuals. On the other hand, the leader theory suggests that the more proximate cause of these unpleasant changes in self-esteem is found in the leader's impatience, disguised judgements, attractions, personal history and so forth. The peer group theory seems to suggest that a group unfolds along the lines laid down in the individual personalities of the participants.

I am reminded of the days when Golding's *Lord of the Flies* (1955) was taken to be an allegory for groups such as the ones we are looking at here. Ralph, the besieged liberal, was locked in a struggle with Jack, the bad boy, the bully. The peer group theory of this island adventure couldn't handle the key events at the start and the finish of the book, the events of the boys' being dumped on the island, 'for their own good', and their eventual rescue. Their terror, their rage and the gradual discrediting of adult forms all make more sense when one takes account of the peer group's relation to a most baffling and disappointing set of authorities. Instead of being a parable about the prospects for democracy or for mob rule, the book can be seen as a parable of the prospects for any group which feels betrayed by an inaccessible authority and left to express their anger toward the only targets at hand. So too the development of the win–lose relationship can be seen as one huge experimenter effect, a saga of how the inaccessibility of the frustrating, and at times cruel, authority sets in motion a repetition of the hazing and the unhappiness of earlier days.

Is there any way out of all this? Two ways to answer 'Yes' to this question come to mind. One stays very much within the confines of the leader theory and the other opens up the possibility of a third theory. If we stay within the leader theory, it follows that one way out proceeds via the path of far greater self-awareness and self-control on the part of the leader. In their effort to construct the perfect blank screen the psychoanalysts work exceptionally hard to understand the sources of their own countertransference, the better to remove themselves from the set of disturbing factors blocking the patient's progress. The leader can try to become aware of and to transcend his or her own hang-ups. Or leaders can be selected partially on the basis of their relative lack of malice, moralism or whatever. The would-be perfect master has a lot of work to do internally, as most of them make very clear. So does the would-be group leader.

The weaknesses of any theory treating events as complex as the evolving win–lose relationships are most apparent if we ask what the theory ignores. Rather than continue to elaborate upon the anxieties, the manipulations or the various entanglements of the members and leaders of these groups, we could try to look for the blind spots built into this way of viewing groups. To name but a few, no mention has been made, yet, of (1) whether these phenomena have been stable over the past ten or twenty years, (2) how the groups reflect, if they do, the changing cultural and political milieu in which they are set, (3) whether the members and leaders tend to be drawn from any particular segment of humanity and (4) whether the goals or values of the participants seem to be crystallizing around some still unspecified, emergent vision of what life in groups might become.

First, a few historical notes: in the past twenty years the forms of winning and losing have changed appreciably. The rise of the hero as a key figure in the developing group was a phenomenon of the late 1950s and early 1960s. Throughout much of the fifties classroom groups of this sort struggled hard with the shock of finding not the usual kind of authority but, instead, a 'non-directive' or interpretive (psychoanalytic) leader. One central concern was how to carry on in the face of the leader's surprising behaviour, and the early answers amounted to an effort to encourage one or at most a few people to emerge as leaders, to fill the vacuum and thereby to recapitulate the expected order of things. These developments were accompanied by highly symbolic and seemingly irrational bursts of rebellion, the killing and eating of the primal father, as Slater (1966) saw it in *Microcosm*. But they were also sustained by the kind of normative development, the creation of a new culture, described by both Mills (1964) and Slater.

It was not until the early or mid-sixties that the heroic challenge to any and all authority became a fairly regular part of group development The sometimes manic and insensitive, sometimes depressed and repentant hero presented a direct challenge to the unspoken assumption of earlier groups, the assumption that some authority and some norms were needed to preserve the safety and the security of group members. The heroes, often with the collusion of the delighted leaders, became a central focus of the win–lose drama. And it is the unfolding of this drama which this essay has examined, primarily. But then things began to change again. By the mid- to late sixties the leader's way of carrying on was neither as frustrating nor as unexpected as before. The leader's style was more easily recognized as congruent with the anti-authoritarian urges rising throughout the student culture in which the group was embedded.

If I had to peg the next significant change to any event in the larger, and especially the student, culture, I would peg it to the rise of the women's movement. Coming as it did out of the brief but intense history of the civil rights and anti-war struggles, the women's movement challenged the overriding *machismo* of the heroic style, in and out of the groups. The message was complex, combining an accusation that men excluded women from any dominant or street-fighting roles with a scornful rejection of the whole heroic facade. The fate of any male who initiated the rebellious, seductive and insensitive performance of the hero tended, increasingly, to be an unhappy one. In our earlier, empirical study of self-analytic groups all of the heroes were males. To the extent that anything remains which might be called the heroic performance, I would suspect that our observational analysis would isolate more females than males in such a role and, as Winter's (1974) data reveal, more blacks than whites.

I am not saying that the groups are no longer arenas for the win–lose drama. But how one wins has changed. It is far less possible for a group member to cut down or to put down other group members, to score points by deriding the naiveté or vulnerability of others. New words and phrases have entered the culture: ego tripping, *macho* and 'heavy' (here referring to the 'political heavy' who is quick to denounce and condemn). More and more, as the sixties wore on, group members came to act as if there were a dual menace to be confronted: (1) the bogus, punitive authority and (2) the peer who, on the one hand confronts that authority but, on the other hand, makes his or her fellow group members feel just as small, intimidated and vulnerable as they had felt in front of the old, discredited authority. The early winner, up to the mid-sixties, was accused of saying and doing things which shouldn't be said and done to authorities. The issue was dependency and loyalty *vs* rebellion. But as the notion of rebellion against authority seemed to gain in general acceptance, the issue shifted and the early winner was accused of 'laying trips on people' and of turning them into early losers if they didn't agree with everything the early winner said. Echoes of post-revolutionary China: commandism and ultra-leftism became dangers of major concern only after the old feudal powers *and* the new entrenched bureaucrats had been confronted and largely defeated.

These historical changes suggest to me that a third theory of winning and losing could be constructed, a theory which looks hard at the larger culture. If the groups we study are, at least to some extent, transient microcosms of the larger society, we don't need to see them as harking back only to the primal, patricidal and totemic family/tribe. We can just as plausibly look to the contemporaneous society for the themes which agitate the groups. And here we must face a few facts concerning the group members.

How much does it matter that most of the people I have known in groups are young adults, North Americans, born of and raised by the winners of their parents' generation? How much does it matter that this particular generation of parents had an increasingly difficult time, in the 1960s especially, defending the culture they were trying to pass along to their offspring? *Fortune* magazine told us that 'going into business' suddenly failed to appeal to the young. The civil rights movement told us that white supremacy was, for some, a rejected birthright. The anti-war movement and the rise of student activism told us that college students were trying to put considerable distance between themselves and what their elders saw as the disagreeable necessities of empire and privilege. And within this new generation of proto-elite there developed a very complex, but nonetheless startling, set of attitudes about winning, losing and equality.

The idea of equality, even the first disjoined formulation of the idea of equality, reverberated throughout the culture. The path was never clear, or if clear, unthinkable. Rather, the search for winners, or oppressors as they were more often called, led in many directions. Who was blocking free speech on campus? Who owned the newspapers that distorted the nature and numbers of the demonstrations and strikes? How about tracking? How about competition, especially when the winners keep being the products of the real 'operation headstart': the suburban school system? Why so few women in the tenured ranks, why so few blacks? The trail led in every direction, or so it seemed.

The very idea of winning became suspect. The comforting thought that, after all, competition toughened the mind and served to locate the very best was never quite as sacrosanct after examining all the stacked decks, biased tests and the latest tuition hike. And the direct translation of these thoughts into the process of group interaction was that win–lose outcomes were just plain wrong. It was wrong for the leader to have such power to intimidate, via grades, and it was wrong for group members to intimidate, via bullying, cozy collusions with the leader, *macho* trickery or whatever. The groups slowly became places where both achieved and ascribed power were scrutinized for their roots. Efforts to recapitulate the familiar distribution of winners and losers were rejected as unwanted carry-overs from 'the old culture'. Failure to block these outcomes became an important source of people's discouragement and frustration with the group.

The political analysis of inequality and the vision of the politically egalitarian society are not the only ways to deal with winning and losing. In fact, I can think of three rather different reasons why the political effort to confront inequality gave way, in the early seventies, to alternative approaches. First, the current winners of the larger society didn't like the way things were going. Some students were killed, many were jailed and suspended, and even more were treated with unexpected antagonism by their parents, professors and presidents. They had gone too far, and the message was perfectly clear: 'You have made your point. You are jeopardizing your career. Some of you bums are really going to get hurt'. The political drive for equality was repressed, flattered and coopted, and it lost energy partly because continued activity seemed to be only a noble, but futile, effort. The trade-off of visible risk for potential gain seemed less worthwhile. The second reason why the political approach to equality subsided is realted to the first. In a toughening fight the pressure mounts to separate the really tough from those who are just going along for the ride. So, paradoxically, one way station on the quest for equality seemed to involve a new class system: heavies, vanguards, people who 'have got it together' on one side, liberals, 'wimps' and sell-outs on the other. The stratification of those who are political into winners and losers becomes, for some, a mockery of the sought-after goal of equality, and they simply drop out or turn to other paths. Finally, those who turn away from politics and from the consequences of using power to fight power find that other paths have been there all along. It turned out that equality has been and could still be thought of as the natural outcome of a religious or spiritual quest. Just as political people led the search party in opposition to the oppressive winners, those on the spiritual trip, in any of its many forms, seemed to be opposed to the idea of winning.

The search for equality goes on, and to the political path has been added a path based on a sometimes ancient and sometimes newly conceived commitment to people, one by one. Pulling together old religious forms, the pleasures of community and the explosive insights of altered states of consciousness, the search for equality has become less risky but no less intense. The question remains: Are some (or all) forms of winning and losing contrary to what is fair and good, contrary to the ultimate purpose of human life, or contrary to the path of greatest satisfaction or fulfilment for all people? The old religious forms which rationalize poverty and reassure the rich are not seen as terribly relevant to this search. But what is growing is a dazzling array of efforts to grasp the unity, the preciousness or the essential equality of all mankind. Perhaps the largest share of this new cultural development has nothing explicitly religious about it. Paths leading through intimacy and sensuality, paths leading through psychedelic drugs and cosmic consciousness, and paths leading through appreciation of human potential and growth are all likely to converge on the idea of equality, and with this comes an intolerance of the win–lose paradigm.

To say that a group is or can at times seem like a microcosm is only to indicate the general form of the operative metaphor one wishes to employ. One can go on to find points of resemblance between the group and any number of classical, recent or contemporaneous arrangements. One can emphasize how faithfully, or how pathetically, the groups recapitulate the structures and affects of earlier times. Or one can see in the groups reflections of the current struggle to find new ways around old impasses. I see the evolution of the group in terms of how winners and losers are created, or how winning and losing are viewed, as reflecting quite faithfully the competing visions concerning equality which are or were active at the time of the group's coming together. If, in this limited sense, the group is a microcosm, how then might the leader's style or perspective influence the evolution of the group?

It seems to me that a leader's capacity to contribute positively to the group's pursuit of equality can be viewed along political and/or spiritual lines. If, in political terms, the group is struggling with the leader–member power differential or the overlearned patterns of male–female relations, then the question is whether the leader can understand what is happening and be useful in search for a stable, satisfying outcome. To the extent that I have set myself up within the group as the ever-elusive, interpretive leader, I have thwarted this political press for equality. To the extent that the leaders connect themselves with alien and alienating forms of data-collection and data feedback, they run the risk of becoming the unbudgable bureaucratic expert. The leader as technocrat may have rejected some forms of power and domination, but not all. To the extent that the leaders in the Tavistock tradition see their elevated status as given and all efforts to alter this as interesting material for analysis, they enervate at least some of the forces leading toward genuine equality. Any effort to deny or suppress the feelings stirred up by the unnecessary trappings of authority tends to block the development of a bottom-up, group-based system of respect and leadership.

If, in spiritual or 'human' terms, the group is grappling with the idea of equality, then the very idea of domination becomes an anathema. One core element of the spiritual belief system is that each person is on his or her own trip, alone and unique. The fragility of that trip, its instability in the face of other people's assertions that the true meaning is already known, is one of its most discouraging features. We are easily thrown off the track by well-meaning helpers. It is in this light that I see the new techniques and styles of group leadership. Rogers (1970), Schutz (1967), Perls (1951) and many others seem particularly able to respect and to facilitate the solo trip. They know how to work with a person. They are guides, at best, and their impact on the search for equality can be very positive. To the extent that all group members come to be seen as many-layered, as seekers and as utterly one-of-a-kind, then they can create together a culture in which blocking another person's trip would be a negative thing to do. The basis for mutual facilitation is strengthened by the depth and complexity of the emergent group understanding of what it means to be human.

No approach to equality seems to be all-inclusive, and the tensions encountered while attempting to merge the political with the spiritual approaches are many. The undoubted charisma of some leaders seems to produce, at times, not equality among all, but only equality among the paying customers. Awe can develop at the expense of inner conviction and self-realization. The leader, under these conditions, may be seen more as the cause than the occasion for the stirrings of new growth, and the long-run consequences of any such confusion tend toward addiction rather than sustained growth. The political path has its vanguard, the spiritual path its true believers and its elect. But more fundamental than any excesses or miscarriages of the approach, there are times when each approach displays a genuine irritation with the preoccupations of the other. The belief that by straightening out power relations, or each person's relation to the means of production, human beings will enter a new era may seem hopelessly superficial to someone engrossed in yoga or some other form of spiritual development. Conversely, the belief that 'we are all just individuals' sometimes blocks inquiry into how one person's winning is related to another person's losing, to the great benefit of the country, class, race or sex which is in the more powerful position. A subculture, such as the subculture of college students, which is easily discouraged about the prospects for political equality can find the spiritual approach to equality nicely changes the focus to each person's private search.

I am not arguing that the political and the spiritual approaches are incompatible, just that in their present form in our present culture they often lead in quite different directions. My own need for a theory about winning and losing boils down to a need for a theory which will integrate the insights, urgencies and ethics of both approaches, and of more besides. I feel that neither the peer group theory nor the leader theory are supplanted by these notions of how the group connects with the struggles going on in the larger society. The need for integration operates at all these junctures: how to keep track of the individual life histories and personal need systems, how to understand the evolution of peer groups, how to remain alert to the leader's impact on all this, without falling into the trap of seeing the group as cut off from the events of the day and the changing cultural priorities. Each perspective can serve as a corrective to each other. Each can help the leader and the group members define where the group is, has been and could, with considerable effort, manage to go.

References

Bales, R. F. (1970) *Personality and Interpersonal Behavior*. New York: Holt.

Bennis, W. G. and H. A. Shepard (1956) 'A theory of group development.' *Human Relations*, **9**, 415–437.

Bion, W. R. (1959) *Experiences in Groups*. New York: Basic Books.

Dunphy, D. C. (1968) 'Phases, roles, and myths in self-analytic groups.' *Journal of Applied Behavioral Science*, **4**, 195–226.

Gibbard, G. S. (1969) 'The study of relationship patterns in self-analytic groups.' Unpublished doctoral dissertation, University of Michigan.

Golding, W. (1955) *Lord of the Flies*. New York: Putman.

Hartman, J. J. (1969) 'The role of ego state distress in the development of self-analytic groups.' Unpublished doctoral dissertation, University of Michigan.

Klein, M. (1957) *Envy and Gratitude*. New York: Basic Books.

Mann, R. D. with G. S. Gibbard and J. J. Hartman (1967) *Interpersonal Styles and Group Development*. New York: Wiley.

Mills, T. M. (1964) *Group Transformation: An Analysis of a Learning Group*. Englewood Cliffs, N. J.: Prentice-Hall.

O'Day, R. (1974) 'The T-group trainer: A case study of conflict in the exercise of authority.' In G. S. Gibbard *et al.* (Eds.), *Analysis of Groups*. San Francisco: Jossey-Bass, 387–410.

Perls, F., R. Hefferline and P. Goodman (1951) *Gestalt Therapy*. New York: Julian.

Ringwald, J. W. (1974) 'An investigation of group reaction to central figures.' In G. S. Gibbard *et al.* (Eds.), *Analysis of Groups*. San-Francisco: Jossey-Bass, 220–246.

Rogers, C. (1970) *Carl Rogers on Encounter Groups*. New York: Harper.

Schutz, W. C. (1967) *Joy: Expanding Human Awareness*. New York: Grove Press.

Slater, P. E. (1966) *Microcosm: Structural, Psychological, and Religious Evolution in Groups*. New York: Wiley.

Winter, S. K. (1974) 'Interracial dynamics in self-analytic groups.' In G. S. Gibbard *et al.* (Eds.), *Analysis of Groups*. San Francisco: Jossey-Bass.

Index

276

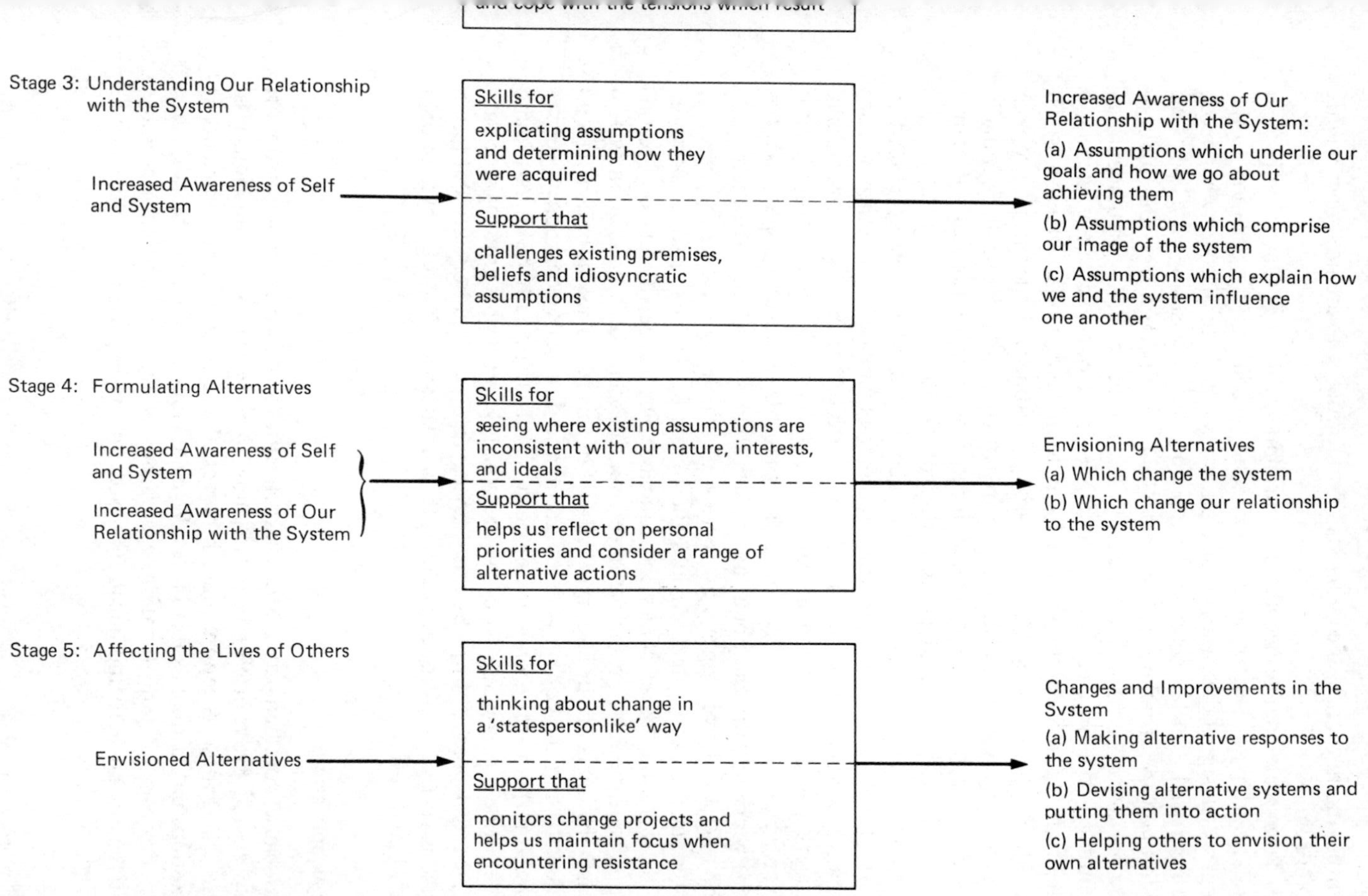

Stage 3: Understanding Our Relationship with the System

Increased Awareness of Self and System

Skills for

explicating assumptions and determining how they were acquired

Support that

challenges existing premises, beliefs and idiosyncratic assumptions

Increased Awareness of Our Relationship with the System:

(a) Assumptions which underlie our goals and how we go about achieving them

(b) Assumptions which comprise our image of the system

(c) Assumptions which explain how we and the system influence one another

Stage 4: Formulating Alternatives

Increased Awareness of Self and System

Increased Awareness of Our Relationship with the System

Skills for

seeing where existing assumptions are inconsistent with our nature, interests, and ideals

Support that

helps us reflect on personal priorities and consider a range of alternative actions

Envisioning Alternatives

(a) Which change the system

(b) Which change our relationship to the system

Stage 5: Affecting the Lives of Others

Envisioned Alternatives

Skills for

thinking about change in a 'statespersonlike' way

Support that

monitors change projects and helps us maintain focus when encountering resistance

Changes and Improvements in the System

(a) Making alternative responses to the system

(b) Devising alternative systems and putting them into action

(c) Helping others to envision their own alternatives

and cope with the tensions which result

Figure 1. Consciousness-raising model for social and organization change

zations giving in to meet the demands of minorities who are no longer willing to compromise.

But large-scale change begins with our simplest feelings that something in our relationship with the system is 'off'. Only when we pay attention to the feelings which signal that something is off, can we hope to discover what needs to be improved. But knowing what is off does not necessarily tell us what we need to know to formulate an alternative that actually improves our situation. Oftentimes what we think is off is merely a symptom of an as yet unidentified ill. Until we develop greater understanding about ourselves, the system and our relationship to the system we are likely to make illusionary changes which remove us further from seeing what is wrong. Dealing with the surface problem makes it less likely that we will come to grips with the fundamental ill. Eventually we need a structure or a model that insures our progress is real. Of course relying on a single model can put us in the worst kind of trap.

The consciousness-raising model I'm about to describe was developed to help people who work in large organizations to formulate and put into practice alternatives which better fit their needs and interests than current organizational practices.* However, subsequent experiences with consciousness-raising groups in a variety of settings have convinced me that this model also applies to inter-actions we have with just about any social system or social institution.

The model has five stages, an overview of which is portrayed in Figure 1. The outputs of each stage provides the inputs for the next, so it is impor-tant to carry out these stages in sequence. The model directs our recon-sideration of the relationship we have with the social or organization system which is the focus of our inquiry. One part of this reconsideration depends on our indentifying and coping with unnatural and destructive components of the system. Another part depends on our viewing and coping with the immature and self-defeating components of our own personality. A support group is necessary or we can get bogged down by our preoccupation with either part and fail to take constructive steps towards putting our relationship with the system on a higher plane of inquiry.

The support group

Some brief comments about the characteristics and formation of the support group should prove useful in envisioning the five stages of consciousness-raising that follow. Keep in mind, however, that I intend these comments as suggestions rather than as fixed rules. When it comes to consciousness-raising, each person is different, therefore each group is different, and all procedures must remain open to modification based on the experiences of the people involved.

---

*The theory from which this model derived, as well as the model itself, is described in a book I wrote on its application to large organizations: *The Organization Trap and How to Get Out of It.* New York: Basic Books, 1974.